Human
MOTIVATION

Human
MOTIVATION

Metaphors,
Theories,
and Research

Bernard
WEINER

SAGE Publications
International Educational and Professional Publisher
Newbury Park   London   New Delhi

For information address:

SAGE Publications, Inc.
2455 Teller Road
Thousand Oaks, California 91320
E-mail: order@sagepub.com

SAGE Publications Ltd.
6 Bonhill Street
London EC2A 4PU
United Kingdom

SAGE Publications India Pvt. Ltd.
M-32 Market
Greater Kailash I
New Delhi 110 048 India

Printed in the United States of America

Library of Congress Cataloging-in-Publication Data

Weiner, Bernard, 1935-
    Human motivation : metaphors, theories, and research / Bernard
Weiner. — 2nd ed.
        p.   cm.
    Includes bibliographical references and index.
    ISBN 0-8039-4658-9 (hardcover) — ISBN 0-7619-0491-3 (paperback)
    1. Motivation (Psychology)   I. Title.
BF503.W45   1992
153.8—dc20   91-42869

96 97 98 99 00 01 10 9 8 7 6 5 4 3

Sage Production Editor: Astrid Virding

Contents

xi-17

19-58

111-151

153-167

168-200
220

Preface

This is my third textbook on motivation, the first being *Theories of Motivation* (1972), and the second *Human Motivation* (1980). Hence I fortunately have been able to contribute motivational texts in three different decades and, like a marathon runner who has accomplished his long-term goal, I feel proud, tired, and committed never again to repeat this rewarding masochism.

I honestly did not anticipate writing another motivational text, but I found I was becoming increasingly dissatisfied when using *Human Motivation* in my course. First of all, the material on attribution theory, my personal field of study, was badly dated, resulting in some embarrassment at focusing on an early period of its development. Second, my prior book included material that now seems irrelevant, in that it did not produce any lasting empirical or theoretical contribution. Third, emotion had been badly neglected in the prior text; writing a new book provided me an opportunity to give emotion some of its rightful credit in the understanding of motivation. And finally, the idea of organizing this field around two major metaphorical themes gave me increased understanding and insight about the history and study of motivation. I wanted to impart this information to others and use this as an organizing theme in the course that I teach.

There are a number of other features that I consider positive that have been incorporated into this book. I have included 12 experiments for students to complete (I guarantee that all will "work"), each of which captures a key prediction of the theory or idea under consideration. Second, a box at the beginning of each chapter provides a brief biography of the theorist being discussed. Third, the material has been organized in what is, I hope, a pleasing symmetry; the contents present an unfolding story, with plot and characters. After an introduction to metaphors and their usefulness, I offer a historical context for the machine metaphor in motivation, followed by the theories (Freudian, Hullian, Gestalt) guided by this metaphor. An epilogue summarizing the contributions that the machine metaphor has made to the understanding of motivation comes next. There is then a transitional section revealing why the metaphor was abandoned, followed by a historical context for the next (Godlike) metaphor. Again, this precedes the pertinent theories (expectancy-value and attribution) and an epilogue. Continuing this flow, there is another transitional section revealing why the rationality aspect of the Godlike metaphor is being questioned, followed by a presentation of the growing "judge" metaphor. Finally, a concluding chapter examines various phenomena from different theoretical perspectives, compares the theories that have been reviewed, and provides suggestions for future theoretical development.

Throughout the book, I have endeavored to give the "big picture" rather than small experiments; to highlight the positive contributions of each approach, rather than being too critical; and to portray the field of motivation as an evolving scientific enterprise searching for general laws of behavior, rather than as a static topic focusing on the specific. Readers should come away with the sense of the difficulty of the field, the progress that has been made, the competence of the scientists trying to understand human behavior, and the fun and value of this work.

This book, like the previous two, is aimed toward upper-division psychology majors and graduate students. I supplement the book in my undergraduate course with original excerpts from Freud, Spence, Miller, Heider, and others, thus maintaining the historical focus while providing firsthand commerce with the shapers of the field. I have ignored the physiology of motivation, for it is not possible to capture all aspects of motivation under one cover while presenting a coherent story. I have provided some examples of applications of the theoretical principles to personal functioning, but that has not been my focus. It is, however, a good avenue to pursue with thought questions and student essays.

I want to thank my many students over the years, particularly Sandra Graham and the "attribution elders," for contributing to my thinking; various agencies for grant support; the University of California, Los Angeles, for fostering an environment where both research and teaching are possible; and Amy Hofstein and Chris Williams for their help with this manuscript.

BERNARD WEINER

Introduction and Overview

Poetry is more philosophical and a higher thing than history,
for poetry tends to express the universal, history the particular.

ARISTOTLE

The concept of motivation appears in many fields of psychology. We read, for example, about the need to be motivated in order to *learn*, the innate motivation of the child to master the environment in order to *develop*, the motivated selectivity in the processing of environmental stimuli in order to *perceive*, the motivation to improve in order to benefit from *clinical intervention*, and so on. Hence motivation lies at the heart, the very center, of psychology.

Definition of Motivational Psychology

The most encompassing definition of the subject matter of the field of motivation is *why human and subhuman organisms think and behave as they do.* Various motivational psychologists have phrased this somewhat differently:

[We may] define the study of motivation broadly as a *search for determinants (all determinants) of human and animal activity.* (Young, 1961, p. 24)

Questions about motivation, then, are questions about the *causes of specific actions.* Why does this organism, this person or rat or chimpanzee, do this particular thing we see it do? The study of motivation is the search for principles that will help us understand *why people and animals initiate, choose, or persist in, specific actions in specific circumstances.* (Mook, 1987, p. 4)

1

[Motivation has to do with why] behavior gets started, is energized, is sustained, is directed, is stopped and what kind of subjective reaction is present in the organism when all this is going on. (Jones, 1955, p. vii)

CLIPE

Motivational psychologists therefore observe and measure what the individual is doing, or *choice* behavior; how long it takes before the individual initiates that activity when given the opportunity, or the *latency* of behavior; how hard the individual is working at that activity, or the *intensity* of behavior; what length of time the individual will remain at that activity, or the *persistence* of behavior; and what the individual is feeling before, during, or after the behavioral episode, or *emotional* reactions.

As the reader progresses through this book, he or she will note that varying aspects of these definitions and observations have attracted theorists and researchers at different periods of time. For example, the earlier motivational psychologists were especially concerned with activation, or what initiates behavior, whereas contemporary theorists are more interested in choice, or what activities an organism undertakes. Further, early researchers focused on observable actions, whereas current concerns include judgments and emotional feelings. However, the motivational question has remained *why*—that is, not *how* one learns or *how* one perceives, but rather *why* one acts.   Why, not how

It is evident that the search for motivational answers is not limited to motivational psychologists—all of us, as participants in everyday life, attempt to reach "why" conclusions to explain the behavior of others as well as our own actions. For example, when a child (or an adult) does not eat his or her food, we ask why: Is it lack of hunger or dislike of the food? If a student fails an exam, the teacher considers why: Does the student lack the capacity? Did the student not study enough? Were the questions too hard or unfair? And if our cat or dog seems listless, we ask why: Is it sick? Bored? Lonely? To function adaptively, we continuously consider why questions and, if possible, come up with answers. Because we all function as motivational psychologists, the professional faces the difficult task of providing a "better" answer than that given by the layperson. This also distinguishes the field of motivation from other process areas in psychology, such as learning and perception, for knowledge about these processes usually is unavailable to the layperson.

Characteristics of a "Good" Motivational Explanation

What is meant by a "better" answer to a motivational question than the layperson can provide? It may be that the explanation is more accurate; that is, it improves predictions of the future as well as predictions about other concurrent reactions. For example, if a teacher attributes the failure of a student to lack of ability, then that teacher is likely to expect the pupil to fail in the future, and perhaps to feel embarrassed or ashamed. On the other hand, if the motivational psychologist believes that the "why failure" answer is lack of effort, then he or she might anticipate success for the student if circumstances can be changed so that the student is more engaged in learning, and might also surmise that the student is experiencing some guilt or sorrow. Accuracy of prediction is one indicator of the "correctness" of the motivational diagnosis.

It should be anticipated that the answer of the trained motivational psychologist will be "better" than that of the layperson. The naive observer often simplistically places the answer to a why question within the acting person; for example, reluctance to accept a date is interpreted as due to "shyness" or "introversion," acting in a bossy manner is ascribed to "aggressiveness" or "dominance," and so on (Jones & Nisbett, 1972; Ross & Nisbett, 1991). In sum, the why answer is a trait, a stable characteristic of the person that unfortunately often merely defines or describes the behavior to be explained (e.g., the definition of an introvert is one who prefers to be alone, and choosing to be alone is explained by the trait of introversion). However, there typically are many determinants of an action, interacting in intricate ways. Some of these determinants are located within the person, others are in the environment; some of the determinants within the person are traits, others may be states, moods, and emotions; some determinants are conscious thoughts, and others are unconscious attitudes; and so on. This complexity too often is ignored in everyday analyses.

But there is another characteristic of a "better" explanation that is of particular importance in the present context, and this property guides the organization and contents of this book. Namely, a "good" explanation is one that may be applied in different situations to interpret specific actions. That is, a scientific explanation includes general principles that transcend the specific instance. For example, when a layperson explains why an individual is drinking water, he or she may say that the person is thirsty. When the layperson accounts for why another individual is eating, he or she may infer that the person is hungry. The motivational psychologist, in contrast, attempts to use the same construct(s) to interpret both instances. It could be postulated, for example, that behavior is directly related to the amount of deprivation (whether water or food), the level of arousal (whether the source of arousal is the absence of water or food), and so on. Thus the same concept explains disparate particular cases. Further, the analysis shifts from concrete instances to abstract issues, such as the presence of any need. One of the goals of a science is the development of general explanatory principles.

Now further assume that a person is observed to improve at a skill-related task after some practice. For example, with experience, typing goes faster, a ball is thrown into a basket a greater percentage of the time, and so on. The layperson explains the improvement as due to learning, or skill acquisition, which is related to the number of practice attempts. We all know that "practice makes perfect." This interpretation is totally removed from the motivational question of why an individual is drinking or eating. The motivational psychologist, however, attempts to comprise these very disparate observations within the same theoretical network or explanatory system. Perhaps it is postulated that behavior is determined by the amount of deprivation and the number of rewarded experiences. Thus a very parsimonious explanation for an array of phenotypically divergent behaviors is supplied, and one might be able to predict not only how long a person will play basketball, but also the percentage of successful shots.

The task of the motivational psychologist is to account for or explain as broad a swath of behavior as possible with as few constructs as possible. This is not a conscious goal of the layperson, who generally is satisfied with ad hoc explanations of behavior; that is, a why answer is provided with a particular end or purpose in mind, without reference to wider applications. Conversely, the goal of motivational psychology is to develop a language, an explanatory system, a conceptual representation, or what is more commonly termed a *theory*, that is applicable across many domains of behavior and explains why behavior is initiated, sustained, directed, and so forth. This is how the reader should think about the problem of motivation (see Atkinson, 1964). It is assumed here that motivational laws of breadth and generality can be discovered.

Problem- Versus Theory-Focused Textbooks

Now, what has this to do with the organization and the contents of this book? Textbook writers often face the choice of analyzing their scientific fields with a problem- or a theory-focused orientation. Each approach has advantages and disadvantages. For example, one might write a motivation book including chapters on problems or topics—achievement, affiliation, aggression, anxiety, authoritarianism, to name just some motivational concerns at the start of the alphabet. In the chapter on aggression, it would be revealed that aggression is influenced by a multiplicity of factors, such as environmental temperature (aggression is augmented in hot weather), social class (more aggression is found among the lower classes), unconscious forces (Freud contends that there is unconscious family rivalry), and so forth. But it is unlikely that this analysis will be theoretically satisfying, as determinants with little conceptual coherence are merely listed and cataloged. Furthermore, the behaviors discussed in other chapters, after it is decided what motivational issues in the remainder of the alphabet to leave in or eliminate, will have different motivational determinants. Hence the chapter on altruism could include a discussion of diffusion of responsibility (personal tendencies to help decrease if other potential helpers are present), feelings of empathy and sympathy (which promote aid giving), and so on. But the insights that can be provided by encompassing theoretical frameworks will be missing; there is likely to be prediction without scientific understanding, and making sense without making deep discoveries that link aggression to altruism and to other aspects of the dynamics of motivation.

An alternate approach when writing a motivation book, which is more consistent with scientific goals, is to have a theory focus. Some of the theories, but surely not all, will address issues related to aggression and/or altruism. These topics therefore would be examined within an overarching theoretical framework so that, for example, in a chapter considering Freud's theory of motivation, aggression could be related to wit, or to slips of the tongue, or even to love. In this way, the topic of aggression is parsimoniously addressed and unexpected insights might be communicated.

The danger of this strategy, however, is that the many determinants of behavior that fall outside the range of psychoanalytic theory or, for that matter, outside the conceptual reach of other general theories of motivation would be ignored. It is unlikely that the discussion of aggression or altruism within a chapter on Freud or any of the remaining theories of motivation would consider weather conditions or diffusion of responsibility, even though these factors affect hostile and altruistic behaviors, respectively.

Furthermore, theories come and go in psychology relatively quickly and seemingly capriciously. Thus, although the present book contains a chapter examining Hullian drive theory, this theory is neither current nor contemporary. Hence a theory book often appears to be "dated" because it discusses theories that already have been discarded (also see Mook, 1987).

In defense of a theory-focused book, it can be contended that science consists of the slow building of conceptual systems, with each new theorist seeing a little further because he or she is standing on the shoulders of prior contributors. To understand current knowledge, the scientist as well as the student must be able to trace the course of development of the science. Often some surprising and unknown connections to earlier theories are made that even contemporary researchers do not realize. For example, research in motivation is now examining self-consistency notions—the idea that a person wants to engage in actions and accepts information that is consistent with his or her self-concept (e.g., Swann, 1987). This hypothesis can be traced back to Gestalt psychologists and their analysis of perceptual units, as well as to their acceptance of concepts regarding forces in physical fields, as will be shown in this book. Hence examining a "dated" theory, such as the Gestalt theory of motivation, is not a vice, particularly if the building blocks laid down by that theory are highlighted. That approach is taken here, and the challenge I must face as writer is to ensure that "dated" is not equated with "irrelevant" or "worthless." At the same time, it is not possible to follow a theory format without ignoring many pertinent topics in the field of motivation that do not readily fit within a larger conceptual framework. It does sadden me to exclude important issues within this text.

The Nature of Being

The decision to describe or portray the field of motivation within a theory framework forces one immediately to confront metaphysical issues—basic philosophies and a priori judgments about the nature of the person that are not subject to empirical verification or disconfirmation. All motivational theories have as their starting points first principles or philosophies about what it "means" to be an animate agent versus an inanimate object, and human as opposed to subhuman. These metaphysical beliefs, which greatly affect the study of motivation, have changed markedly over time and differ among theories. Two central figures influencing such key motivational presumptions and dogmas were René Descartes and Charles Darwin.

Pre-Darwinian Thought

Just as asking about why organisms think and act as they do is not limited to motivational psychologists, it also is not confined to this point in time. Throughout history, there is evidence that individuals sought to know the causes of behavior (see Bolles, 1967; Cofer & Appley, 1964). Simple observations well before Darwin surely revealed that the reasons for the behavior of humans and subhumans must be differentiated from the causes of motion of inanimate objects. Among these differences, only humans and subhumans seem capable of self-induced motion, whereas inanimate objects *appear* to be motionless until acted upon by some external force.

More central to the concerns of motivational psychology was a distinction between the determinants of subhuman versus human action. This differentiation is intimately connected with what has been called the "mind-body" problem in philosophy.

Mind and Body

Metaphysical systems addressing the nature of the universe postulate either one or two basic elements or factors. Those specifying one element are referred to as *monistic* systems; those presuming two elements are referred to as *dualistic* systems. The elements in both monistic and dualistic systems are called mind and/or body, or spirit and/or matter, or soul and/or material. The mind is conceived as subjective, nonmaterial, and known only by the possessing individual, whereas the body is considered physical, material, and objectively observable. The mind-body distinction is consistent with the self-observation that when the body is inert, as during sleep, there is mental activity such as dreaming. Thus the spirit or soul inhabits the body yet is independent of that body. Further, it typically is

René Descartes
(The Bettman Archive)

Charles Darwin
(The Bettman Archive)

accepted that the mind, which is the location or seat of the intellect and rationality, is superior to the body.

Prior to Darwin, monistic systems consisting of only body or physical elements were used to explain the behavior of subhumans, whereas dualistic systems including both the mind and the body were called upon to explain the behavior of humans. To understand the contrast between the perceived causes of subhuman and human behavior, one also must be aware of some of the social and cultural influences on psychological thinking.

Conceptions of Humans

The general metaphysical beliefs about humans prior to Darwin, and continuing after his writings, were that they were created by God and that they were created in the image of God. Humans were considered uniquely rational and had souls, properties bestowed by God. The rational soul partakes in what is defined as immortality. The rationality of humans was presumed to give rise to the use of tools, the development of language and symbolic capacities, the ability to anticipate ends, and so forth.

Further, humans also were believed to have bodies that were the source of desires and the origin of physical forces exerting internal pressure on the organism. The belief in a mind-body coexistence, or what is known as *Cartesian dualism*, is summarized by Ryle (1949) as follows:

> The [coexistence] doctrine, which hails chiefly from Descartes [1596-1650], is something like this. With the doubtful exceptions of idiots and infants in arms, every human being has both a body and a mind. His body and his mind are ordinarily harnessed together, but after the death of the body his mind may continue to exist and function.
>
> Human bodies are in space and are subject to the mechanical laws which govern all other bodies in space. Bodily processes and states can be inspected by

external observers. So a man's bodily life is as much a public affair as are the lives of animals and reptiles and even as the careers of trees, crystals, and planets.

But minds are not in space, nor are their operations subject to mechanical laws. The workings of one mind are not witnessable by other observers; its career is private. Only I can take direct cognizance of the states and processes of my own mind. A person therefore lives through two collateral histories, one consisting of what happens in and to his body, the other consisting of what happens in and to his mind. The first is public, the second private. The events in the first history are events in the physical world, those in the second are events in the mental world. . . . [The] problem of how a person's mind and body influence one another is notoriously charged with theoretical difficulties. (pp. 11-12)

Given this dualistic position, there are a number of possible positions regarding "how a person's mind and body influence one another." One viewpoint is that they in fact do not influence one another, but are completely independent. This process is depicted as follows:

$$\text{mind (thought):} \quad A \ldots\ldots B \ldots\ldots C$$
$$\text{body (action):} \quad A' \ldots\ldots B' \ldots\ldots C'$$

The body and mind processes, however, may be related. For example, perhaps sexual forces originating in the body lead one to think about sexual behavior, to experience a sexual "intention" toward another, and to approach that other. However, given this model, the thoughts and intentions do not affect the action, which is entirely determined by bodily processes, such as automatic reflexes or fixed instincts. The thoughts or actions of the mind are then considered epiphenomena (*epi* indicates "upon").

In contrast with this position of independence are beliefs accepting interaction. One such view is that the mind intervenes between bodily desires and the motions of the body; this may be depicted as follows:

$$\text{body (desires):} \quad A \ldots\ldots B \ldots\ldots C$$
$$\text{mind (thought):} \quad A' \ldots\ldots B' \ldots\ldots C'$$
$$\text{body (action):} \quad A'' \ldots\ldots B'' \ldots\ldots C''$$

This was the viewpoint expressed and accepted by the Church that was dominant prior to (and again, after) Darwin. That is, physical forces originating in the body could be controlled by the soul—there could be mind over matter, or spirituality over materialism. Hence individuals were held responsible for their actions and were guided or governed by the rules of the Church. Behaviors therefore could be judged as "good" or "bad" and were subject to punishment. Korman (1974), quoting from Thilly (1957), summarizes this argument:

Man has sensuous desires, and rational desire, or will. He is not absolutely determined in this desire and actions by sense impressions, as is the brute, but possesses a faculty of self-determination, whereby he is able to act or not to act. . . .

> The will is determined . . . by a rational purpose. This, however, is not compulsion; compulsion exists where a being is inevitably determined by an external cause. Man is free because he is rational, because he is not driven to action by an external cause without his consent, and because he can choose between the means of realizing good. (pp. 232-233)

This account of the body's movements is derived from the older Aristotelian image of a machine with organs that responds to the command of the soul, as the foot soldier obeys the general.

Conceptions of Subhumans

In contrast to the dualistic explanation of human behavior, the actions of subhumans were interpreted with a monistic system. Actions were believed to be determined entirely by mechanical forces or pressures initiated either internal to the organism (e.g., hunger) or external to it (e.g., a painful stimulus). The actions were considered to be reflexes or instincts. As noted by Bolles (1967), "If an animal was without food, its physiology would be disturbed in such a way that it would eat; it was compelled to eat by its physical structure" (p. 25). Hence there was no intervention of the mind or will, as in the interpretation of human behavior.

This explanation was consistent with the extant culture. The dilemma created for the motivational thinker was that, if subhumans had minds, then they also must have souls, inasmuch as the mind was the location of the soul. This clearly was antithetical to religious doctrine. Further, if subhumans had will, then their actions would be subject to the restrictions of the Church. This was not possible—subhumans could not be held accountable for their actions. Hence animals were considered to be automata, or machines. Given the absence of rational souls, they could not develop language or symbolic capacities, they did not anticipate ends, they were not able to have self-initiated recall, and so forth. Machines also are devoid of emotion, so that, as Descartes (1649/1911) noted, animals "eat without pleasure and cry without pain." Descartes compared the ingenious mechanical *homunculi*, or automata, constructed by seventeenth-century craftsmen with the living subhuman machines produced by nature.

The Darwinian Revolution

What has been evident in the prior discussion is that Christian theology had a considerable impact and influence on the development of Western science. The Christian doctrine and its implications were in part called into question in the work of Darwin.

Surely it was observed prior to Darwin that humans and subhumans engage in the many of the same activities—eating, sleeping, reproduction, and so on. For humans, as just discussed, these behaviors were presumed to be governed by rationality, whereas they were determined in subhumans; for humans, these actions could be judged as "good" or "evil," but not in subhumans. However, as discussed by Mook (1987):

> The developing conception of animals as machines posed a problem for nineteenth-century biologists. The machines worked! Most species of animals, it appeared, were remarkably well suited to the habitats in which they lived. If behaving animals are bundles of reflexes as Descartes supposed, how is it that they have just the reflexes necessary to perform their full-time jobs of finding food, avoiding becoming food, finding mates, and caring for the young? (pp. 34-35)

Darwin (1859/1936) supplied the answer to this dilemma. He presented carefully accumulated evidence that those "most fit" in their environments survive, whereas others who are less fit do not. *Fitness* meant that the anatomical structure of the organism increased its chances of satisfying basic needs, including reproductive success. For example, tall giraffes were better able to reach food in times of scarcity when height was an advantage in securing food. Thus those giraffes with the longest necks survived, and this trait was inherited, in turn, by their offspring. Darwin did not discover evolution, but he did provide the mechanism with the principle of survival of the fittest.

Darwin also proposed that there was a mental continuity, a mental evolution, between humans and subhumans so that they were presumed to differ in degree, or quantitatively, but not in kind, or qualitatively. More than two decades prior to the publication of his book *The Origin of Species*, Darwin wrote in his notebooks:

> Man in his arrogance thinks himself a great work, worthy of the interposition of a deity. More humble and I believe true to consider him created from animals.

Humans, therefore, were not considered to be unique inasmuch as phylogeny was continuous rather than dichotomous.

It has been said that this revolution in thinking humanized animals and brutalized humans. This so-called brutalization is part of a long tradition that Copernicus started by snatching the earth from the center of the universe, and later continued with Freud's postulation of the unconscious and with the making of computers that were smarter than their makers.

The documentation of a human-subhuman continuity had great implications for the explanation of motivated behavior. Given this continuity, it was not defensible to have a monistic conception to explain animal behavior and a dualistic system to account for human behavior. Rather, human behavior, like the behavior of other animals, must to some extent be determined by reflexes and instincts; that is, behavior was determined directly by physical forces and was preprogrammed or built into the organism on the basis of evolutionary principles. Indeed, William James

(1890) said that humans had more instincts than any other animal. One could therefore propose a monistic system to explain the behavior of all organisms, and this gave rise to a conception of persons as machines. This position clearly took the study of psychology out of religion and philosophy and made it a part of biology. Psychologists then could study the structure and the function of the human machine. It will be seen that this conception of humans greatly influenced the early, dominant motivational theories formulated by Sigmund Freud and Clark Hull. It also was a great impetus to the experimental study of motivation.

On the other hand, given that animals are like humans, they also must possess intelligence and rationality. Thus the behavior of all organisms also might be explained with a dualistic system including the mind and the body, although the mind must be equated with thinking and divested of its association with the soul. The belief that both subhuman behavior and human behavior are guided by thoughts also was a tremendous influence on the study of motivation and guides contemporary theories.

In sum, what Darwin accomplished for motivational psychologists was to provide altered ways of thinking about the nature of being. This produced a foundation for the study of motivation.

Metaphors and the Nature of Being

One need not (and, I believe, should not) take literally, or with exact meaning, the proposal by Descartes and others before him that subhumans are machines and humans are Godlike. In a similar manner, one need not and should not presume that Darwin's continuity postulate literally means that both subhumans and humans are machines as well as Godlike. Rather, these correspondences can be thought of as metaphors (from the Greek, *meta* = trans, and *pherein* = to carry; hence *metaphor* = to transfer or, more specifically, to transfer meaning).

It will be contended in this book that the basic or core metaphors of human motivation involve thinking of the person as a machine or as a totally rational and knowledgeable being (Godlike). Hence Cartesian dualism and the contributions of Darwin, which provided these metaphors, are key historical antecedents for the growth of the scientific study of motivation. Further, the major theories of motivation were guided implicitly or explicitly by the two core metaphors stating that humans are machines and/or Godlike. It is therefore important to examine the definition and the properties of metaphors before turning to an overview of the theories in this book and their metaphorical roots.

Definition and Properties of Metaphors

There is disagreement among linguists and philosophers concerning the definition of the term *metaphor*. In addition, many complex issues that need not here concern the reader, and that I do not well understand myself, remain to be resolved (see Leary, 1990; Ortony, 1979). I therefore will only briefly and without pretension convey the general meaning and function of metaphors.

Typical metaphors include such expressions as "He is a shark" or "She is a rock." Such metaphors involve comparisons that have conflicting characteristics. On the one hand, the metaphors given as examples imply that the persons and the comparison objects are similar in some respects. Yet these statements are deliberate fabrications, so that, if taken literally, they appear to assert something that is known not to be—after all, a person literally is neither a shark nor a rock. A tension thereby is created in that objects known to be dissimilar are declared to be similar.

But what function does this fulfill? What is the purpose of using a metaphor? It is generally agreed that a metaphor provides a new way of seeing the world. A metaphor restructures perceptions or creates a perceptual shift so that an object is "framed" differently, producing a new mental construction.

The general process that makes metaphors "work" is that the primary subjects of the metaphors (the "he" and "she" in my examples) have projected upon them a set of "associated implications" derived from their comparison objects. These implications are based on the preexistent knowledge of the metaphor maker. In our example, this relates to knowledge about sharks and rocks. Hence one knows that sharks are aggressive, cunning, persistent, strong, deadly, and so forth. A metaphor, which typically involves a visual image, then "structures less concrete and inherently vague concepts in terms of more concrete concepts" (Lakoff & Johnson, 1980, p. 112).

Hence the subject of the metaphor is now thought of differently; a similarity has been created that bridges the known to the unknown. The new perception or construal depends on which subset of factors of the comparison object are focused upon or are salient. We do not, for example, now think that the subject of the metaphor has a tail, or many sharp teeth, for behavioral rather than physical characteristics of the comparison object are more salient and appropriate. And, once created, the metaphor itself acts as a schema or filter or lens, so that myopia is generated. In the case of the shark metaphor, for instance, one may tend to notice acts of the person that have been aggressive, rather than acts of kindness that do not fit within the new construction.

Metaphors function at all levels of understanding and discourse, from everyday interaction to the development of scientific theories. Indeed, it has been contended that new scientific theories require the availability of new metaphors. At the level of scientific theorizing, metaphors often function as heuristic devices, pointing out relations that previously were unnoticed or did not actually exist prior to the introduction of the metaphor. For example, one of Freud's metaphors for behavior was to depict the ego as the driver of a horse-pulled chariot, with three horses pulling in different directions that represent the demands of the id, the ideals of the superego, and the restrictions imposed by reality. The image of three horses straining in opposing directions and a driver attempting to steer a straight course vividly conveys Freud's view of the person as beset by conflict and compromise. It creates a novel view of the dynamics of human behavior, permitting us to see ourselves in a new light or framework. This metaphor makes salient certain observations regarding the human condition that are far different from those evoked by a metaphor such as "Life is just a bowl of cherries."

Metaphors and the Study of Human Motivation

As stated previously, the metaphors provided by Descartes and Darwin were key historical antecedents to the growth of the scientific study of motivation. Recall that two metaphors were introduced—the person is a machine (derived from the monistic understanding of subhumans), and the person is Godlike (derived from the dualistic understanding of humans). What, then, are the "associated implications" of these metaphors? We are not led to think that persons are plugged into sockets, that persons are made of metal, or that persons created the world. Rather, a different set of associations are called forth that shed light on human motivation, which is the unknown that we are attempting to understand.

What, then, are the characteristics of machines that may be said to be shared by human beings? We first of all think of machines as functioning automatically, with automatons as one type of machine. Their more detailed characteristics are as follows:

(1) The behaviors of machines are involuntary, or without volition, and hence are reflexlike.
(2) The behaviors of machines are performed without conscious awareness.
(3) The reactions of machines are necessary or predetermined to a set of circumstances or activating stimuli.
(4) The actions of machines are fixed and routine.
(5) Machines are made up of parts (they have structure).
(6) The whole machine is a unit of mutually interacting parts.
(7) Machines transmit forces and energy. The forces may be in balance or equilibrium, where no tendency to change is present, or out of balance, with a tendency toward change.

(8) Machines are designed for desired ends; they have specific functions.

It is evident, then, that casting the person as a machine provides a striking image that alerts one to new characteristics regarding human motivation.

The portrayal of the person as Godlike does not lend itself as readily to a set of associated implications as does the machine comparison, for the image of God is itself vague and unknown. Among the properties that make metaphors "work" are that they are concrete and vivid (compare, for example, calling a person sneaky with calling that person a snake). However, the following characteristics are usually associated with God:

(1) all-knowing (all-wise)
(2) final judge; all-just
(3) noncorporeal
(4) all-loving and merciful
(5) all-powerful

These attributes surely bring to mind a different conception of the person from that produced by the machine metaphor. It is these two visions—the person as a machine and the person as Godlike—that shaped motivational thought and supply the overriding framework for the organization of motivational theories that are presented in this book.

Overview of the Book

The two dominant metaphorical themes in motivation—humans as machines and humans as Godlike—generated and subsume a number of different specific theories that are reviewed in this book. The machine metaphor is represented in the biological conceptions proposed by Freud (psychoanalytic theory), Lorenz and Tinbergen (ethology), and Wilson (sociobiology) that are presented in Chapter 2. The machine metaphor also plays a dominant role in drive theory as formulated by Hull and in extension of drive principles to the study of cognitive dissonance (Festinger), reviewed in Chapter 3. Finally, the Gestalt theory of motivation, which gave rise to Lewinian field theory and to Heider's conception of balance, is based on notions about physical forces and is presented in Chapter 4. It will be seen that although each of these theories was guided by the machine metaphor, different associated implications influence each conception.

Following this, theories derived from the metaphor of the person as Godlike are presented. These include the expectancy-value formulations of Lewin, Atkinson, and Rotter, which depict the person as a completely rational, knowledgeable decision maker, presented in Chapter 5. Chapter 6 then reviews attribution theory as developed by Heider and Kelley; this theory is guided by the construal of the person as a scientist. Then, in Chapter 7, which is based in good part on my own work, I show that attribution theory also embraces the Godlike metaphor that the person is the "final judge." Again, therefore, distinct associated implications direct disparate theories and research. Finally, the book concludes with a review chapter that compares and contrasts the theories and considers some psychological problems and issues from the divergent perspectives of the theories that have been reviewed. In addition, postulates for the formulation of a motivational theory are offered.

Throughout this book, I anchor the theories of motivation within the larger historical framework and evolution of this field. Further, I examine the empirical focus of the theories and the certainty or replicability of the evidence; that is, the theories are judged with respect to their "crucial" predictions. The reader also has an opportunity to evaluate some of these theoretical predictions by completing the experiments presented throughout the book that are derived from the conceptual frameworks in the chapters.

It will be evident that, for the most part, the theories reviewed here are "incommensurable." That is, they have no common basis of comparison— no specific prediction on which they can be compared so that one theory is pronounced to be "better" than another. That is because the theories, guided as they are by disparate metaphors, are concerned with different aspects of motivation, or different parts of the elephant. If, for example, one refers to a person as a "shark" while another thinks of this person as a "rock," then diverse observations will be used to support these construals. Finding that the individual is aggressive at sports and calm during stress supports one theory or the other, but is inconsistent with neither. This same state characterizes the field of motivation and the relative evaluation of theories.

However, motivational theories are commensurable with respect to their guiding assumptions and foundations. Among the distinguishing features of the conceptions that permit relative comparisons are the following:

(1) guidance by the mechanistic or the Godlike metaphor
(2) empirical focus and empirical range
(3) acceptance of genetics and evolution versus learning and culture as determinants of behavior
(4) historical versus ahistorical (at this moment in time) analyses
(5) inclusion or exclusion of a mathematical representation or model of motivation
(6) acceptance or rejection or ignoring of homeostasis as a basic motivational mechanism
(7) acceptance of hedonism versus mastery (understanding) as the basic spring of action

These points will be made clearer and elaborated throughout the book.

The theories presented in this book, then, are not comparable in terms of empirical predictions regarding the same phenomena, but they can be compared on other dimensions, such as their assumptions and characteristics. Does this therefore mean that the theories cannot be evaluated and "rank ordered" in terms of acceptability? The answer to this is both yes and no. Clearly, the more accurate and replicable the unique predictions, the greater the theoretical breadth (range of predictions), and the clearer the concepts and specified interrelationships between the terms of the theory, the more satisfactory it is.

However, at the outset I must make clear my position concerning the status of motivational theories. At this time, they are not able to make exact or "point" predictions as is true in the natural sciences. Rather, at best, they can predict differences between groups of people or between situations. For example, achievement theory does not predict how long someone classified as high in achievement needs will persist when attempting to solve a task. Rather, it predicts that individuals high in achievement needs will persist longer than persons considered to be low in achievement needs. Along these lines, the theory predicts that among those high in achievement needs, persistence will be greater when the task initially is perceived to be of intermediate difficulty than when the task initially is believed to be very difficult or very easy. Such hypothesis-testing procedures that merely contrast two conditions have been questioned (see Meehl, 1990), but at present we must be modest and accept this state of affairs.

Hence, rather than accepting or rejecting theories, in this book the questions raised are concerned more with issues such as the following:

(1) How do the theories deal with the motivational questions of choice, intensity, and persistence of behavior?
(2) What concepts have been utilized within each theory?
(3) What theoretical networks have proven to be useful in the understanding of some phenomena?
(4) What foundations have the theories laid for others to build upon?

My assumption is that writing a theoretical book in motivation is not merely adding to environmental pollution. Rather, it is my hope that this book will show that ingenious attempts have been made to deal with exceedingly difficult problems. I think it can be said that the conceptual approaches have been good tries, not that they have been correct or near correct. I hope that the book is realistic, yet not apologetic.

SUMMARY

Motivation is the study of the determinants of thought and action—it addresses *why* behavior is initiated, persists, and stops, as well as what choices are made. In attempting to develop a scientific explanation that examines these questions, researchers have formulated general theories that are guided by metaphors of what a person "is." These theories provide constructs that enable the theorists to transcend explanations of only specific instances; instead, they offer languages and general interpretations that are applicable across a variety of observations and situations.

The roots of the motivational theories that have been developed can be traced back to the seminal contributions of Descartes and Darwin, for these giants provided new metaphors for—or ways of thinking about—human motivation, shedding light on the unknown by making comparisons to that which is known. Descartes suggested that subhumans are machines, and Darwin documented that, therefore, humans also are machines. Furthermore, both fostered the notion that humans are Godlike—that is, they have minds and engage in rational thinking and the judging of others. Darwin further presumed that rationality was characteristic of subhumans as well.

These two metaphors spawned two types of motivational theories—those accepting some aspect of the machine comparison (psychoanalytic, ethological, sociobiological, drive, and Gestalt theories) and those guided by the Godlike comparison (expectancy-value and attribution theories). These theories, along with their historical contexts and empirical supports, are reviewed in this book.

THE MACHINE METAPHOR IN MOTIVATION

Man is a marvelously constructed machine.

LEONARDO DA VINCI

The Historical Context

The psychological bible states that in the beginning there was Wundt. In 1879, Wilhelm Wundt started what is controversially called the first experimental laboratory in psychology (this is arguable because some historians believe that William James established the initial laboratory). Wundt championed structuralism, or the science of the contents of the mind. His goal was to obtain a systematic description and explanation of consciousness. This goal was to be accomplished by using the method of introspection to study pure sensations. Individuals were asked to analyze their sensations and perceptions into the smallest possible components, thus discovering the elements or atoms of sensation.

The work of Wundt was brought to the United States and continued by Edward Titchener at Cornell University. Titchener made some basic changes in Wundt's methodology, arguing that not every person is a qualified introspectionist. He stressed that training was needed for an individual to be able to attend to the basic elements or dimensions included within a stimulus.

However, structuralism, or the science of consciousness, was short-lived in the United States. Boring (1950) vividly conveys this when describing Titchener's role in American psychology:

> Titchener was important in the history of American psychology because he staunchly represented the older conservative tradition against overwhelming numbers. West of the Atlantic in psychology there was "America" and there was Titchener. Names often stand out in history because their owners have opposed something older; movements of thought are always movements away from other thought. However, in Titchener's case the situation was reversed. He has stood out in bold relief because everyone near him moved away from him. If all movement is relative, then Titchener moved—backwards with respect to his advancing frame of reference. (p. 419)

The reason that Titchener was moving "backwards with respect to his advancing frame of reference" is that the dominant movement at this post-Darwinian time was toward the metaphor of persons as machines. The structuralists were opposed by three different movements in psychology, all of which in part embraced a machine metaphor and were in opposition to the focus on consciousness manifested by Wundt and Titchener.

One conflicting position was represented by psychoanalytic theory, as proposed by Freud and elaborated by his followers. The psychoanalysts argued that persons are not aware of their own motivations. Thus guided introspection, or free association, was substituted in place of the pure introspective method that had been advocated by the structuralists. Furthermore, the psychoanalysts presented a conception of the person that was entirely different from that of the structuralists, as illustrated in the chariot metaphor introduced earlier. In addition, the psychoanalytic conception stressed instinctive behavior, or behavior not mediated by consciousness, and energy systems that are associated with mechanical forces. Psychoanalytic theory as formulated by Freud and other biological conceptions advanced by ethologists and sociobiologists are presented next, in Chapter 2.

A second movement antithetical to structuralism was functionalism, and subsequently behaviorism, in the United States. The functionalists, led by John Dewey, revolted against the static, descriptive approach of the structuralists. They stressed the adaptive nature of behavior, as had Darwin, and maintained that one must ask about the causes of events. Functionalists were determined to foster a psychology that included the concepts of purpose, cause, and capacity. The functionalists accepted introspection, but only as one method of psychological investigation. They also believed in the study of the behavior or movement of organisms. Hence the functionalists represent the transition between structuralism and behaviorism.

TABLE I.1 Overview of Part I: Machine metaphors

Theory	Theorist	Chapter
Psychoanalytic	Freud	2
Ethological	Lorenz; Tinbergen	2
Sociobiological	Wilson	2
Drive	Hull; Spence; Festinger	3
Gestalt: Field	Lewin	4
Gestalt: Balance	Heider	4

Behaviorism received its formal impetus from John Watson in 1913, although its historical antecedents include a long history of associationism, a belief in the analytic approach to science, and the desire to produce an objective study of human behavior. All these antecedents are consistent with thinking of the person as a body, or as material rather than spiritual.

Watson, the chief apostle of behaviorism, argued that introspection is not an adequate methodology of science because the data are not reliable; two investigators cannot agree on the same facts. The apparent fruitlessness of this approach was dramatically revealed by the introspective analysis of the color green. While Titchener maintained that "you can see that green is neither yellowish nor bluish," Holt asserted, "On the contrary, it is obvious that green is that yellow-blue which is exactly as blue as it is yellow" (reported in Osgood, 1953, p. 647). Watson therefore discarded the study of consciousness, turning instead to the study of the movement of organisms.

Subsequently, drive theory as formulated by Hull grew from the thinking of Watson and other learning theorists. Hull asserted that drive or energy is needed to propel the organism, and that the direction of behavior is automatically determined by prior stimulus-response pairings. The machine-guided metaphor formulated by Hull and other theorists, including Festinger, is reviewed in Chapter 3.

Finally, a third group opposing the structuralists were the Gestaltists, directed by Wertheimer, Koffka, and Köhler. The Gestaltists convincingly argued that the search for and analysis of basic elements in a sensation did not constitute the proper method for psychologists. Rather, they contended that one must study the whole and the relations between the parts of the whole. For example, one does not understand the motion perceived in a movie marquee caused by the near simultaneous onset of lights by analyzing each of the individual lights. Rather, the perception of motion is determined by the relations of neighboring lights.

It will be seen that Gestalt theory influenced the conceptions of Kurt Lewin (field theory) and Fritz Heider (balance theory) presented in Chapter 4. Both these approaches are based on machine-derivative concepts such as energy, tension, and equilibrium.

An overview of Part I of this book is shown in Table I.1. The chapters in this part document that each of the antagonists to structuralism adopted somewhat different "associated implications" of the machine metaphor, which was inconsistent with the science proposed by Wundt and Titchener. Hence different aspects of human motivation are addressed in Chapters 2 through 4.

Psychoanalytic, Ethological, and Sociobiological Theories:

Mechanism in Biology

In this chapter, three mechanistic approaches to motivation are examined: psychoanalytic theory, ethology, and sociobiology. These three conceptual analyses have much in common: All are grounded in biological functioning; all impose evolutionary principles to explain motivated behavior, and thus were influenced by Darwin; and all employ explanations of some behaviors that have generated a great deal of excitement, controversy, and criticism. However, the three approaches also differ quite fundamentally in their scientific goals.

The historical perspectives I have assumed in examining these theories vary. Psychoanalytic theory and ethology were developed much earlier than sociobiology, which is a relatively recent addition to science. Hence between the initial formulations of these theories and present-day thought there has been a great deal of reformulation and recanting. In this context, however, I examine the early psychoanalytic theory proposed by Freud and the initial ethological theories of Konrad Lorenz and Nikolaas Tinbergen. Hence I focus on the original perspectives in these fields. This is because these early formulations most clearly highlight the influence of mechanistic thinking, and they provide the historical perspective that I wish to emphasize in this book. It also is true, however, that subsequent contributions to these fields have done relatively little to advance our understanding of human motivation. Sociobiology, on the other hand, has yet to undergo major shifts in its motivational foundation, so that I am more accurate or current in the portrayal of that approach.

Freud's Psychoanalytic Theory of Motivation

Freud's psychoanalytic theory offers the most general and well-known conception of motivation. However, his embrace of the machine metaphor often is not sufficiently recognized or understood, in part because this

SIGMUND FREUD

Sigmund Freud was born in Frieberg, Moravia, on May 6, 1856, and died in London on September 23, 1939. The vast majority of his life was spent in Vienna; he left that city only when the Nazis invaded Austria in 1938. Freud started his scientific career as a neurologist and quickly established a reputation for his neurological research and medical investigations. He conducted this work despite grave financial difficulties that even forced a temporary postponement of his marriage.

During 1885 Freud traveled to Paris to study hypnosis and the alleviation of hysteria with Jean Charcot. However, he found hypnosis an unsatisfactory method and began to use a treatment technique developed by Joseph Breuer, in which patients were cured by talking about their symptoms. In 1895, Freud and Breuer published *Studies in Hysteria*, which contained Freud's first ideas about the unconscious.

The self-report and introspective data that Freud collected led him to concentrate increasingly on sexual conflicts as the cause of hysteria. Thereafter, Freud and Breuer parted ways, and Freud worked alone to develop startling and original ideas about psychosexual development, the Oedipus complex, dreams, the unconscious, and a wealth of other psychological processes and phenomena.

Freud surrounded himself with a group of disciples, including Jung from Switzerland and Adler from Austria, but often his interpersonal relationships were stormy and friendships aborted. His fascinating life included his own psychoanalysis, years of addiction to cocaine, cancer of the jaw, and an invitation to Clark University in 1909 that paved the way for his acceptance after a long period of ostracism by other scientists.

There are a number of reasons Freud was not accepted by the scientific community. He did not communicate with other scientists, having virtually no academic correspondence. Furthermore, he did not present carefully accumulated evidence to support his ideas, and he gathered his "data" in a mysterious and secret atmosphere that was closed to all but his patients. Finally, Freud came from a relatively obscure Jewish family at a time of religious discrimination. Thus his theory initially met with a very negative reception from other scientists. For a fuller discussion of Freud's life and his difficulties in gaining acceptance, see Jones (1953-1957) and Shakow and Rapaport (1964).

(Photograph provided by the Bettman Archive)

---

formulation was vague and inconsistent, of interest or relevance to few clinical psychologists, and did not give rise to a body of empirical data that documented the value of this metaphysical point of view.

In this chapter, I present those aspects of Freudian theory that most directly bear upon his construal of the person as a machine. There are, of course, many other facets of Freudian thought, including his model of the mind and unconscious processes, stages of development, analysis of neurosis, and so forth. These central aspects of Freud's theory are ignored here, although they do have relevance to motivational issues. In addition, Freud was guided not only by a machine metaphor; his writings make use of many other metaphorical views of the person to shed light upon the difficult topics with which he was concerned. One such metaphor—the bedeviled person as a rider in a chariot driven by three horses pulling in different directions—was introduced in Chapter 1. Another oft-cited metaphor from Freudian theory is his view of mental structures and processes, which he illuminated with a spatial metaphor that included thoughts passing from one "room" (the unconscious) to another "room" (the conscious), through a door separating these chambers that was guarded by a "censor." Thus, although I concentrate here on the mechanical roots of Freudian motivational theory, it was also the case that Freud was concerned with mental processes (although not only rational thinking, as would be derived given a Godlike metaphor). As noted in Chapter 1, disparate and even antagonistic metaphors may exist side by side, each making a unique contribution to the understanding of motivated behavior. Freud (1926/1936) certainly acknowledged this, writing: "In psychology we can only describe things by the help of analogies. There is nothing peculiar to this; it is the case elsewhere as well. But we have constantly to keep changing these analogies, for none of them lasts us long enough" (p. 195).

Finally, I take the liberty here of not including aspects of Freudian theory that did not contribute to the accumulation of knowledge or to the building of a science of motivation (e.g., the "death instinct" and arguments regarding the number of instincts), or concepts that are of less importance in the field of motivation than in other areas of study (e.g., the superego). In addition, I do impose my own interpretation of Freudian theory to render it more understandable and internally consistent.

Background Influences

When searching for the background or antecedent factors that affected Freud's thinking regarding mechanism, three come to mind: the observations to which he was exposed, his training in medicine and biology, and the general *Zeitgeist* provided by the physical sciences.

The Data or Observations of Freud

There are reciprocal influences among observations, experimental data, and theory development. Certainly the phenomena to which one is exposed influence the type of theory that one formulates. Freud observed neurotic clients, such as the famous Anna O, who experienced uncontrollable gagging at the sight of a glass of water. In addition, early in his career Freud became acquainted with and used hypnosis as a clinical tool. In one experimental demonstration conducted by Bernheim, a French physician with whom Freud studied, a woman was given a posthypnotic suggestion that, after waking, she should walk to the corner of the room and open an umbrella. Upon awakening, and after the experimenter-designated time had elapsed, she did exactly that. When questioned about the reason for her behavior, she said that she wanted to see if the umbrella was hers.

On the basis of his observations of phobic and fixated patients and his witnessing of the potency of hypnosis, Freud was sensitized to account for behaviors that were preemptory and unconscious. *Preemptory behavior* may be defined as actions that seem to be mandatory; such behavior does not have a "take it or leave it" quality and may be experienced as beyond one's will. Further, the person is not necessarily aware of the origin or reason for his or her action (see Rapaport, 1959, 1960). In Chapter 1, it was revealed that among the "associated implications" of machines are that functions are performed without awareness on the part of the machine and without the intervention of a "will" that might establish control over the action.

In addition, once a theory is formulated, that theory, along with its guiding metaphor, serves as a lens or filter, sensitizing the holder of the theory to particular aspects of the environment and causing "biased" interpretations of behaviors. Thus once Freud adopted the notion of a person acting without willpower and awareness, he noted other aspects of human behavior, including slips of the tongue and dreams, as examples to support his theoretical ideas. That is, slips and dreams, like neurotic symptoms and posthypnotically suggested acts, were believed to be imposed without control of the person and without awareness of their psychological significance. Freud's theory, like all other conceptions, thus had both *top-down* and *bottom-up* qualities, to use terms from cognitive psychology: Observations influenced theory development (schemata), and theory then influenced subsequent observations and interpretations.

Medical Training

The importance of Freud's medical training to his theoretical position was implicit in the prior discussion because this brought him into contact with neurotic patients, and the failure of medical science to deal with this disorder initially led him to the use of hypnosis. But other aspects of his medical training also are essential to his embracing a machine metaphor. As a medical doctor, Freud was trained to focus on the structure of the body—its parts and their functions. As noted in Chapter 1, machines have structures and functions, with the parts interrelated so that they operate as a unit. Furthermore, as a trained neurologist, Freud observed a hierarchical ordering of neural structures. Just as the onset of some neural firings can inhibit other neural firings, it will be revealed that Freud postulated that the "higher" structure of the person (the so-called ego) can inhibit the strivings of the "lower" structure (the so-called id). This hierarchy is captured by the chariot metaphor, in which the superior driver must keep in line the opposing pulls of the horses. The possibility of the blocking of impulses is a central aspect of Freudian theory.

Advances in the Physical Sciences

As part of his medical training, Freud was exposed to the newest conceptions in the physical sciences. His teacher in medical school, Ernst Brücke, stated that "no other forces than common physical-chemical ones are active within the organism" (quoted in Boring, 1950, p. 708). Freud was additionally aware of the views of Hermann von Helmholtz, who believed that physical and chemical explanations could be found for physiological events. Helmholtz articulated a universal law of the conservation of energy. He conceived of all the forces of nature as but the myriad forms of a single, universal energy, what he called "the ground work of all our thoughts and acts." Scientists in various disciplines were captured by these ideas, which then influenced advances in many fields.

Others also fostered the idea of the body as a motor—a machine for transforming energy into work—no different from a steam engine. That is, the human body is but an exemplar of a universal process in which energy is converted into work. An animal's body therefore does not differ from the steam engine except in the purpose for and the manner in which the force is employed. Freud advanced this position further and made similar assumptions regarding psychological events (although it must be remembered here that I am presenting the early visions of Freud; he later was to retract this position).

Freud came under this influence even prior to his psychoanalytic discoveries. Cofer and Appley (1964) include the following personal correspondence from psychoanalyst Robert Holt regarding this point:

> The concept of energy was a pre-occupation of Freud's from the very beginning of his scientific work, considerably ante-dating any psychoanalytic model. When Freud was a student, energy was so much the rage, as stylish a concept as information is today, or perhaps even more so. The brilliant discoveries that the apparently different forms of physical energy (heat, light, mechanical, etc.) were interchangeable and interconvertible was a profoundly exciting one, and it seemed to suggest that the work done by biological organisms, in all of the many different ways they used energy, could be looked on as a further instance of these transformations. (p. 596)

In sum, Freud's exposure to neuroses and hypnosis, his training in medicine, and the general tenor of the times all predisposed him to the acceptance of the machine as a metaphor for human behavior.

The Mechanical Concepts

Now let us turn to Freud's view of human motivation. Guided by the ideas of Brücke and Helmholtz, Freud contended that all psychological work, whether thinking or actually engaging in actions, requires the use of energy. The adoption of an energy notion is consistent with the intuition that there is a force in nature that makes things "go." Three energy-related concepts are especially pertinent to Freud's explanation of human behavior: conservation of energy, entropy, and a distinction between kinetic and potential energy.

Freud conceived of humans as closed energy systems, with each individual endowed with a given amount of energy that remains constant over time. This idea was in part derived from the principle of conservation of energy proposed by Helmholtz in 1847, which states that energy is neither created nor destroyed. That is, nature as a whole possesses a store of energy that cannot be added to or subtracted from.

Entropy, another concept from the study of mechanics, is the amount of energy that is not available for doing work. The optimism of energy conservation was offset in the 1850s and 1860s by the revelation that there was an inevitable dissipation of force so that only a fraction of the total existing energy is available for work or conversion. Freud, guided by these ideas, contended that some energy is kinetic, or bound. Such bound energy is referred to as *cathected*. A cathexis (from the Greek *kathexo*, meaning "to occupy") involves an attachment to some object that is desired but has not been attained. The attachment, or cathexis, does not mean that energy literally leaves the person. Rather, there is a feeling of longing for the object and there are repeated thoughts, images, and fantasies about him or her. A cathexis may be only temporary, for if the desired goal is attained, then there is a freeing of this energy. As a result, the bound energy is transformed into free (potential) energy that is now available for use in other functions. If all one's desires are fulfilled, then all energy is free. Hence energy distribution is related to happiness.

To review, consider how Freud might analyze a situation in which a loved one goes away for a period of time. Because that person is no longer available as a need satisfier, he or she becomes an object of cathexis. Energy is now bound and the unsatisfied individual might fantasize about being with the loved one, daydream about reunion, and so forth. The binding of energy is unpleasant, indicating that needs have not been fulfilled. In addition, the energy is not available for other activities. The individual therefore might experience a lack of interest in other friends and hobbies, might have a short attention span, and may even take to his or her bed. When the longed-for person returns, the individual's needs are again fulfilled, the cathected energy is freed to do other work, and the person experiences a state of pleasure.

Homeostasis and Hedonism

Two major psychological concepts are implicitly involved in the prior analysis: homeostasis and hedonism. *Homeostasis* refers to the tendency toward the maintenance of a relatively stable internal environment. It is assumed by Freud and many other biologically oriented theorists that there is a propensity for the organism to remain in a state of internal equilibrium. If, for example, the organism is too hot, then sweating automatically occurs; if too cold, then there is reflexive shivering. In these examples, there is an automatic action, without mental causation or intervention, that brings the organism back into a state of equilibrium. At a more molar behavioral level, if an organism is hungry, then food-related activities are initiated to again bring about equilibrium. The underlying assumption of this analysis is that a detected discrepancy between an ideal and an actual need state initiates activity to reduce the need.

Hedonism is a utilitarian doctrine associated with the philosopher Jeremy Bentham (1779/1948). The hedonistic creed asserts that pleasure and happiness are the chief goals in life. If homeostasis is the governing principle of behavior, then pleasure is the result or the by-product of being in a state of equilibrium, where all one's goals are gratified.

Freud championed the doctrine of hedonism and the principle of homeostasis. For him, the satisfied individual is not in pursuit of any stimulation, for activity indicates dissatisfaction. On the contrary, nirvana is the absence of tension or need and is accompanied by quiescence. One logical extension of this position is Freud's postulation of a "death instinct" or "death wish," for in death there are no unsatisfied desires. This is also similar to the alleged wish to "return to the womb," where all needs are fulfilled and one is completely under the care of a benevolent other.

The Instincts

A number of concepts essential to Freud's theory of motivation have now been introduced, including homeostasis and hedonism, free energy and bound energy, a closed energy system, and cathexis. But we have yet to examine one of Freud's main concepts—the instincts.

Instincts correspond to bodily needs. They are represented mentally as wishes and desires. Thus Freud contended that an instinct is a "measure of demand made upon the mind for work." Instincts therefore are represented as drives, and most Freudian scholars believe that translators were in error in using the word *instinct* rather than *drive* when interpreting Freud's writings. We might therefore think of an instinct as a force or drive within the person that activates behavior. It is a source of tension, created by internal stimulation or excitation. Thus Freud regarded an instinct as an internal pressure "from which there is no flight."

The instincts include the drive to preserve the self and the species; they involve sexual and aggressive urges. These forces are assumed to be cyclical and can be satisfied in diverse ways.

To elaborate on the definition of instincts further, Freud thought of them as appetitive sources of behavior. They are appetitive because they are directed toward objects, and they are sources of behavior because the instincts instigate activity.

There are four basic properties of instinctive forces. First, they have pressure or strength. This corresponds to the impetus of the need, and is determined by factors such as the length of the time the need has existed. Second, instincts have aim. This aim, implied in the earlier discussion, is their removal, for this brings about equilibrium and is pleasurable. Regarding the tendency to discharge any increase in internal excitation, Freud and his colleague Breuer (1892/1959) wrote:

> The nervous system endeavors to keep constant something in its functional condition that may be described as the "sum of excitation." It seeks to establish this necessary precondition of health by dealing with every sensible increase of excitation . . . by discharging it by an appropriate motor reaction. (p. 30)

Later, Freud (1900/1938) went on to say that psychological functioning

> is regulated by the effort to avoid the accumulation of excitation, and as far as possible maintain itself free from excitation . . . the accumulation of excitation . . . is felt as pain, and sets the apparatus in operation in order to bring about again a state of gratification, in which the diminution of excitation is perceived as pleasure. (p. 533)

In addition to pressure and aim, instincts have objects or goals through which they are satisfied. These objects may vary and be changed. Finally, instincts have sources, which are the bodily processes mentioned earlier. The four characteristics of instincts are illustrated in Figure 2.1.

In sum, to review the entire conceptual system as presented thus far, individuals are endowed with a fixed amount of energy at birth. Energy is needed for all psychological activity. The prime demand on the energy system is to satisfy the instinctual needs or drives. These arise cyclically and are dealt with by the organism because they create tension and generate disequilibrium. The psychic apparatus seeks to reestablish equilibrium and therefore initiates actions to satisfy needs. This is pleasurable and brings the organism back into balance, thereby freeing the bound or cathected energy so that it is available for other psychological work.

Psychological Structures

Thus far, the dynamics of behavior or the function of activity has been the focus of this discussion. But a machine, in addition to having a function, also has a structure. A machine is made up of parts, and these parts operate together as a unit to accomplish the machine's goals. Freud did consider the parts or structure of the person. There is a particular reason or problem that compelled Freud to be concerned with psychological structure, namely, that immediately acting to satisfy the instinctual drives may be

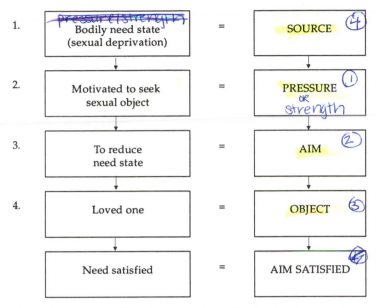

Figure 2.1. Freud's four characteristics of instinctive forces and how they relate to behavior.

harmful. Hence, in addition to the dynamics of behavior, some structures, some erected barriers, must be brought into the system.

Three quite well-known hypothetical structures were identified by Freud: the id, the ego, and the superego. In this context, I examine only his descriptions of the first two, and not at the level of detail that typically is exhibited in personality and abnormal psychology textbooks. Further, these structures are considered only in relation to the dynamic principles of motivation that already have been introduced.

The Id

The id was conceived by Freud to be the first system within the person. It is most intimately related to the biological inheritance of sexual and aggressive drives. The individual is unaware of the existence of many of these inborn drive states. Hence the contents of the id are primarily unconscious, or beyond the immediate awareness of the person.

The id is the seat of the instinctual drives, or the source of psychological tension. It operates according to the "pleasure principle," or the doctrine of hedonism. Immediate pleasure is sought, and this is accomplished through homeostatic processes and tension reduction.

Id functioning is characterized by "primary process" thinking. This mode of thought is perhaps best known to us through our personal dream experiences. Primary process thought is illogical and timeless; it does not distinguish reality from unreality. In primary process thought, for example, hallucinations are not distinguished from actual occurrences. Thus internal mental acts, like actions, can fulfill wishes. The infant, according to Freud, can imagine that it is ingesting milk to reduce tension. In a similar manner, extensions of this theory suggest that we might dream about great accomplishments to fulfill some of our achievement desires. One of the surprising strengths of this machine metaphor is that there is flexibility in responsiveness, or in the objects and therefore the behaviors that satisfy the instinctual demands. Plasticity is not one of the usual "associated implications" of a machine.

The Ego

It is evident that for survival, organisms must learn to differentiate between, for example, milk and the idea or image of milk. There must be a match between the mental image and the object in the real world for some of the need systems to be fulfilled; that is, fantasy must be distinguished from reality. The id, inasmuch as it follows the rules of primary process thinking, is unable to make this differentiation. In addition, at times immediate goal gratification will lead to more pain than pleasure, as in the case of a sexual or aggressive action that later is punished by society.

Because the id seeks immediate satisfaction, gratification is not delayed when it is realistically self-serving to do so. Thus, to meet the problems of discrimination and the necessity of delay, a new structure is created out of the id that can come to terms with the objective world. This structure is the ego. (Critics of classical psychoanalytic theory have pointed out that since the id cannot "know" or "recognize" the distinction between fantasy and reality, it is illogical that it would create a structure to deal with this issue.)

Those who develop ego structures are better able to survive, inasmuch as such structures come about because lower-level functioning by itself is unsatisfactory and results in harm to the self. Thus ego functioning lies at the very heart of psychotherapeutic procedures.

The ego is governed by the "reality principle" rather than by the pleasure principle. But this does not mean that hedonism is given up. Rather, as intimated already, the ego serves the id in its pursuit of pleasure and tension reduction by taking into account the demands of reality. The ego follows the rules of "secondary process" thought. This is adult thinking, characterized (usually) by logic, time orientation, and a distinction between reality and unreality. The ego also has the tools of memory and attention, and the control of motor activity. Thus its existence provides a means or mechanism for delay of gratification, long-term planning, and the like.

The postulation and functioning of an ego are not readily compatible with the metaphor characterizing a person as a machine. Certainly higher-order thought and self-regulatory processes are not linked with the image of a machine; nor are psychological barriers that prevent goal attainment because of anticipated harm. As previously reported, the machine meta-

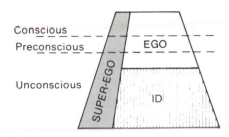

Figure 2.2. The relationship of the personality structures to the levels of awareness.

phor is consistent with only some aspects of Freudian thinking, and Freud called on many metaphors in attempting to explain human behavior. Ego functioning is introduced here because one cannot explain Freudian theory without it.

The contents of the ego are primarily conscious (see the geographic or spatial metaphor in Figure 2.2). However, the person is not aware of all aspects of ego functioning. The ego includes the mechanisms of defense, such as repression, which protect the person from psychic pain. These defenses generally are not part of conscious experience. Furthermore, most prior experience is preconscious, that is, not in consciousness but readily available to us from memory storage.

The Relation Between the Id and the Ego

As indicated earlier, Freud was greatly influenced by his training in neurology, where he observed a hierarchical ordering of neural structures. The ego, he said, can inhibit the strivings of the id. Freud conceived the ego to be the executive agency or "highest" structure of the person, responsible for final behavioral decisions. In this capacity, as the rider in the chariot, it must satisfy the constant demands of the id while being bound by the constraints of reality. This conception is consistent with the notion that a machine has separate parts, but the parts act in unison as an integrated structure with shared aims or purposes.

Formal Motivational Models

With this background in mind, we are now in a position to examine more closely Freud's formal models of behavior. Recall that all behavior is instigated by instinctual (id) wishes. These wishes are represented in the mind as demands made on the body, and they instigate actions that reduce the instinctual urges. Further, a wish is conceptualized as cathected or bound energy; this energy is freed when the desired goal is attained.

One empirical or observational base of this theory is the restlessness that is displayed by hungry infants, and their subsequent quiescence when the breast or bottle is reached:

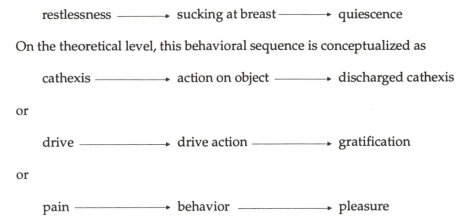

restlessness ⟶ sucking at breast ⟶ quiescence

On the theoretical level, this behavioral sequence is conceptualized as

cathexis ⟶ action on object ⟶ discharged cathexis

or

drive ⟶ drive action ⟶ gratification

or

pain ⟶ behavior ⟶ pleasure

The observational and theoretical analyses depicted above pertain to what is known as Freud's "primary model of action" and are based on the pleasure-pain, or hedonic, principle. This motivational model accounts for behavior without considering thought processes; that is, it represents "actions motivated by basic drives without the intervention of psychic structures" (Rapaport, 1959, p. 71). It is therefore a "reflex arc" model, or a model of a driven machine with input-output or antecedent-consequent relations. It best captures the machine metaphor that guided part of Freud's analysis.

Freud posited three other simple models of motivated behavior in addition to the primary model of action. These stray in varying degrees from the machine metaphor because of the role given to thought processes and/or ego structures. One of these models is called the "primary model of thought." Thoughts, like overt behaviors, are initiated by instinctual desires or wishes. However, in this case, the object that will satisfy the wish is absent or for some other reason unavailable. The individual can then attain gratification by remembering past experiences with the satisfying object and hallucinating that such experiences again are occurring:

cathexis ⟶ absence of drive object ⟶ hallucinatory idea

A hallucinatory idea is an example of primary process thinking. As previously discussed, primary processes do not distinguish reality from unreality. Thus internal mental processes may serve as a means of gratification. All thoughts governed by primary processes, such as dreams, are therefore wish fulfillments, and all cognitive processes are derived from basic needs. This means that ultimately all thoughts, no matter how apparently remote from sexual and aggressive urges, serve to satisfy these desires.

Freud's primary models of thought and action coordinate drives, or instinctual wishes, with immediate expression. There are no intervening processes (ego functions) that aid the organism in its adaptation to the environment. However, Freud noted that at times immediate gratification may result in more pain than pleasure. Therefore, the ego intervenes between the driving instinctual stimuli and the behavior, imposing delays and altering the direction of behavior. This is possible within the theory because the ego, as the "higher" structure, has the power to prevent immediate gratification. This is accomplished by establishing a "countercathexis." The countercathexis, or force opposing goal satisfaction, takes the form of a psychological defense, or a defense mechanism. The defense might be, for example, repression, which banishes the threatening wish from consciousness so that the wish is not directly acted upon by the individual. The existence of this conflict between an id cathexis and a countercathexis established by the ego is the heart of Freud's motivational theory that is less tied to machine comparisons. Freud viewed the person as in a state of continuous conflict between personal desires and the demands of society, which creates barriers. Such conflict, according to Freud, provides the foundation for the development of neurosis.

These principles are captured within Freud's "secondary models of thought and action," which include delay mechanisms:

cathexis $\longrightarrow$ delay of gratification $\longrightarrow$ detour activity $\longrightarrow$ gratification

cathexis $\longrightarrow$ drive object absent $\longrightarrow$ delay, with thoughts given to anticipation and plans for reaching the goal objective

The four motivational models proposed by Freud are outlined in Table 2.1. The difference between the primary and secondary models is that only in the secondary models does the ego intervene between the onset of the wish and expression. These models therefore represent situations of cathexis/countercathexis conflict. The differentiating feature between the action and thought models, as the label indicates, is that action models deal with overt behavior, whereas thought models consider mental events or cognitions directed toward attainment of the goal. As Table 2.1 shows, the primary model of action is most closely linked with a machine metaphor, although all the models assume the necessity of energy to drive behavior.

Further Integration of Models of Motivation and Energy Constructs

Let us now consider a specific example to help clarify Freud's views of motivation as well as to review some of the complex material presented in the prior pages. Assume that an individual has 40 units of energy. (Freud did not discuss this in detail, but it can be presumed that the amount of energy one has remains constant throughout life and that persons vary in their supply of energy.) The individual is completely satisfied, with no unfulfilled needs or wishes. Because of the cyclical nature of the instincts,

TABLE 2.1 Freud's Models of Motivation

	Action	Thought
Primary	id—activity—satisfaction	id—object absent—hallucination—satisfaction
	"reflex arc" machine metaphor	fantasy behavior as a wish fulfillment
Secondary	id—ego—delay behavior—satisfaction	id—ego—plans—satisfaction
	ego prevents immediate expression	cognitions aid goal attainment

however, after a certain period of time aggressive or sexual urges make demands on the individual for satisfaction.

Let us assume that there exists an object in the external environment that can satisfy this individual's urges. The appropriate external object then becomes "cathected." If the cathected object binds 5 units of energy, reflecting the strength or the intensity of the need, then 35 units of energy remain unbound and free for the individual's use. The subsequent attainment of the goal object by means of reflex action or other overt behavior (as specified in the primary action model) dissipates the cathexis so that again there are 40 units of free energy available; the individual is thus returned to a satisfied state.

It may be, however, that attainment of the desired object will result in greater overall pain than pleasure. If this is the case, then the ego establishes a countercathexis that prevents immediate goal attainment (we now shift from a machine metaphor, inasmuch as both thoughts and self-regulation barriers have entered the conception). The countercathexis takes the form of a defense, such as repression or denial, that inhibits the undesirable wish from entering consciousness. As with any psychic reaction, the countercathexis requires energy to maintain itself. Let us assume that the countercathexis binds 5 units of energy so that it is equal in force but opposite in direction to the cathexis. Now the individual is in a state of conflict (cathexis versus countercathexis), with 10 of his or her 40 units of energy bound and unavailable for use. This leaves less energy available to the individual for action upon other goals and for plans and thoughts.

If the ego is doing an effective job, then alternative goals are selected, plans are made, and so on to aid the id in its goal of reducing the internal need state. Attaining partial satisfaction via a substitute goal object or a modulated response, which represents the secondary model of action, will release some of the cathected and countercathected energy. But if the ego is "weak," then a potential for neurotic-type behavior is established, for an inadequate method of coping with stress and fulfilling wishes is likely to be selected. An inappropriate method, for example, could be the development of a neurotic symptom such as an arm paralysis. This symptom might gain attention and affection from a loved one or even serve as a miniature aggressive response. But in the long run, symptom formation is an ineffective and inadequate means of tension reduction.

This example highlights some of the basic principles and assumptions of Freud's theory of the dynamics of behavior:

(1) The subject matter of the psychoanalytic approach to motivation is thought and behavior, both of normal and pathological individuals.

(2) The foundation for the explanation of overt and covert action is a belief in psychological determinism.

(3) Hedonism and homeostasis are the governing principles of motivation.

(4) All behavior is ultimately drive determined, with the crucial determinants of behavior unknown by the actor (unconscious).

(5) All behavior disposes of psychological energy and is regulated by it.

(6) The functions of the ego, which fall beyond the range of convenience of the machine metaphor, are to prevent immediate goal gratification, to inhibit action, and to control the id.

(7) Behavior is determined by many factors, including dynamic forces originating in the id and structural barriers created by the ego.

Testing the Theory

In Chapter 1, I indicated that each theory would be evaluated in relation to the significant and crucial research that was generated to test the conception. Freudian theory, however, must be exempted from this scrutiny. The theory is too broad and too imprecisely stated for one to seek for experimental verification through exact predictions. A vast number of investigations have been dedicated to demonstrating the validity of some of Freud's ideas. For example, today no one doubts that motivations and thoughts may be unconscious; that repression, denial, and other defense mechanisms are operative; that sexual and aggressive urges have motivational significance; and so forth. These propositions have been established empirically. However, this research activity has not typically been formally linked with Freud's theory of motivation, or with his conception of the person as an energy-regulated machine.

Many of the basic ideas incorporated within Freud's machine metaphor—the person is a closed energy system, object cathexis leaves less energy available for other functions, goal attainment frees energy, and so on—are not amenable to psychological test. Rather, they are basic assumptions, axioms, and postulates that guide or sensitize observers to particular phenomena.

Freud was trained as a medical scientist and was well acquainted with the scientific method, so his neglect of experimental testing cannot be attributed to inability or ignorance. Rather, in his functioning as a psychoanalyst he believed that his methods paralleled those of other experimentalists. He would set forth a hypothesis, collect relevant data by observation of his therapeutic patients, and then alter his ideas to fit the new data. Therapeutic sessions were the "microscope" that enabled Freud to uncover the pertinent evidence. Freud believed that proper tests of his theory could be conducted only during psychoanalytic treatment; no other validation was needed. His method therefore might be described as primarily dialectic; that is, he arrived at "truth" through a critical and logical examination of the arguments and issues.

Freud was unimpressed by the demonstrative or experimental laboratory procedures used by psychologists in their search to understand the dynamics of behavior. When American experimental psychologist Saul Rosenzweig apparently demonstrated the existence of repression in a laboratory study, Freud wrote to him:

> I have examined your experimental studies for the verification of the psychoanalytic assertions with interest. I cannot put much value on these confirmations because the wealth of reliable observations on which these assertions rest make them independent of experimental verification. Still, it [experimental verification] can do no harm. (Figure 2.3)

The Experimental Study of Catharsis

There are some research topics that bear centrally upon Freud's conceptions of motivation and his use of energy concepts, although they do exist apart from or independent of general Freudian theory. For example, recall that Freud's primary model of thinking proposed that hallucinations, like real events, may serve as goal satisfiers. That is, fantasy activity can reduce drives and therefore free cathected energy. There is a rather vast literature pertinent to this issue that can be used in this context to illustrate some of the difficulties faced in the testing of Freudian theory.

There has been a long-standing belief that fantasy activity can have substitute value or can serve to satisfy unfulfilled needs. Aristotle, for example, stated that one function of witnessing tragedy in the theater is that the observer is "purged of passions." This has been labeled a catharsis of emotions. The research most resembling this Aristotelian conception is derived from Freudian thinking and examines the general hypothesis that observing motivational expressions of others or engaging in fantasy goal activity reduces one's own motivation. Stated more concretely, the "catharsis hypothesis" leads to the predictions that watching one's hero hit a home run reduces achievement strivings, that one's sexual desires are reduced by one's reading or viewing erotic material, and that watching a powerful leader reduces one's desire for power. Providing proof for these hypotheses would support the Freudian primary model of thought (although other ways to test this conception certainly are possible).

The experimental study of catharsis has been virtually restricted to the area of aggression. The specific hypothesis examined is that fantasy

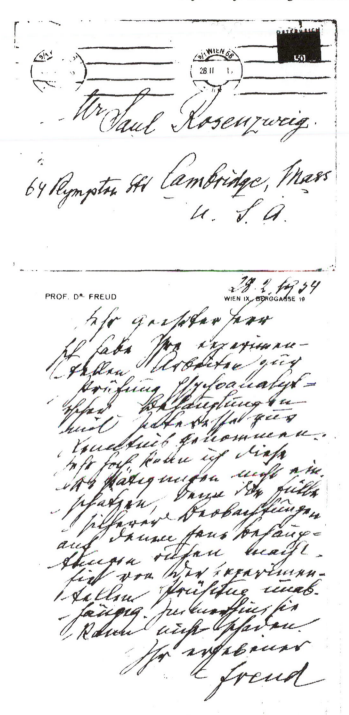

Figure 2.3. Freud's letter to Rosenzweig. (From Sigmund Freud Copyrights Ltd., London.)

undertaking or observation of an aggressive act reduces the viewer's aggressive tendencies. This has been the subject of much testing because an important current debate concerns the possible effects on children's behavior of viewing aggressive television programming. Parents fear that their children will become more aggressive because of exposure to fantasy aggressions. On the other hand, the notion of catharsis and Freud's primary thought model suggest that violent television programming might reduce personal aggressive tendencies.

Unfortunately, the question of whether viewing aggression increases or decreases aggressive tendencies and hostile expression is exceedingly difficult to answer. One reason for this difficulty is that the observation of violence can have contrasting effects upon a variety of psychological processes and mechanisms (Feshbach, 1964). For example, new aggressive strategies or instrumental behaviors might be learned from viewing television violence. The hijacking of airplanes did not emerge as a widespread threat until this form of kidnapping was portrayed in a television program, thus planting a new idea in the minds of potential aggressors. Viewing also can lead to imitation, and thus increased expressed violence. Hence the depiction of violence on television might be teaching aggressive behaviors. At the same time, avoidance tendencies generated by fear and guilt may be reduced when one witnesses successful violations of social rules. And finally, perhaps there also is a catharsis, or a decrease in persisting tension and object cathexis that accompanies the viewing of violence. But because so many processes and structures may be affected by the same event, it is difficult to provide a definitive test of the catharsis notion and Freud's primary model of thinking.

But what about the experimental evidence? If one compares the amount of empirical support in laboratory research for augmentation versus reduction of aggressive behavior following some fantasy expression or observation, there is clearly much more support for the hypothesis that exposure to aggressive fantasy behavior increases aggression. In one type of experimental paradigm not tied to television viewing, subjects are induced to act angrily. If anger feelings are "relieved" by such cathartic expressions, then these subjects should act less angrily and report feeling less anger following these actions. However, the typical finding is that subjects' anger in fact increases (see, for example, Kaplan, 1975; Mallick & McCandless, 1966; also see review in Tavris, 1984).

One might feel that such experimental laboratory studies are too far removed from the phenomena of interest to Freud, and that naturalistic field studies of actual viewing of fantasy material would provide a better test of Freud's hypothesis. However, the results of naturalistic field studies also are mixed. The primary method of such field research is correlational. These studies have found that the frequency with which aggressive television programs are viewed is positively (rather than negatively) correlated with the degree of aggressive behavior. However, in this research it is difficult to determine the direction of cause and effect. Do aggressive children prefer and select aggressive programs to view, or does the viewing of aggressive programs cause viewers to become aggressive?

There is other research that attempts to specify more carefully those conditions under which fantasy aggression might reduce aggressive tendencies. These studies suggest that for aggression reduction to occur, the individual must be angry at the time of any direct expression, and that the reduction is stronger when the fantasy aggression is expressed directly against the initial target of aggression (see, for example, Konecni, 1975; Manning & Taylor, 1975). However, others question any effects of fantasy and argue that only direct, overt expressions of aggression are cathartic (Hokanson & Burgess, 1962).

In sum, examining this one area of research that directly bears upon hypotheses derived from Freudian theory reveals that the conclusions are inconclusive. Psychological life is too complex to reach any definitive statement. Given the kinds of hypotheses derived from Freudian theory, this finding is not inaccurate as a general description of research conclusions—there are no clear experimental demonstrations that unambiguously can be considered support for (or against) Freud's broad motivational thinking (as opposed to, for example, unambiguous demonstrations of unconscious processes or specific defenses). Philosophers have contended that if a theory is not subject to disconfirmation, then it has not met the criteria to be considered a theory. This criticism must be acknowledged when we attempt to evaluate Freud's conception of motivation.

Rather than ending on this negative note, however, it must be recognized that the main contribution of this theory does not lie in the confirmation of hypotheses. Rather, the theoretical networks proposed by Freud have been heuristic; new knowledge has been generated. In addition, subsequent theories were importantly influenced and guided by Freudian thinking. It is this generative aspect of Freud's psychoanalytic theory of motivation that has been most important and should not be forgotten.

Ethology and Mechanism

The foregoing discussion of Freud documented his usage of a machine metaphor in the understanding of human behavior. He reasoned that some behaviors were

(1) volitionally uncontrollable
(2) not determined by thoughts
(3) propelled by energy and the distribution of energy
(4) directed toward specific end states
(5) guided by the structure of the organism

All these are "associated implications" of a machine. (However, for the sakes of both accuracy and completion, it must be recalled that Freud also used other metaphors and championed the role of both conscious and unconscious thoughts and emotions in influencing motivated action.)

There is another aspect of Freudian thinking that was not emphasized in the prior analysis but is important here as the reader's attention is turned to ethology and then to sociobiology: Freud's training in medicine and his knowledge of Darwin resulted in his strong theoretical grounding and belief in biology and evolution. In accordance with biological assumptions, Freud assumed behavior to be in part determined by inborn givens, such as the amount of energy with which one is born; reflexes, including sucking at the breast in times of need; fixed sequential stages of personality development; and basic sexual and aggressive urges that "demand" satisfaction. These urges, when labeled as instinctive (recall that in the prior discussion they were called *drives*), particularly place Freud within a biological tradition, where there has been an acceptance of the role of instincts as motivators of action.

Definition and Characteristics of Instincts

There are two basic meanings of the term *instinct*, and they are often confused (Valle, 1975). On the one hand, *instinct* or, more appropriately, *instinctive behavior* refers to an unlearned, fixed, stereotyped pattern of activity. Such behavior is displayed by all members of a species when in a given environment, assuming that the members within the species are of like sex and at the same level of development. Responses of birds to particular mating calls, the web spinning of spiders, and the hoarding of food by squirrels are examples of such unlearned patterns of responses. These behaviors primarily are caused by genetically transmitted physiological states and functions: They are akin to the built-in behaviors that are exhibited by plants, such as a tropism toward light. Instinctive behaviors frequently are not single responses, but action sequences that follow a predetermined and predictable course (e.g., nest building and hoarding).

A sequence of preprogrammed behaviors that are inflexible once set in motion clearly is consistent with a machine metaphor of motivation. Perhaps the "irrationality" of the animate machine is best exhibited in sequences in which the ultimate goal of the behavior cannot be accomplished, yet the "instrumental" activity sequence continues. For example, birds may continue to engage in particular movements to return an egg to a nest even after the egg has been removed by an experimenter during the process. The behavioral sequence, once started, must run its course; the feedback that the responses are no longer instrumental to the attributed goal does not deter the activity. (This thoughtlessness also influences the behavior of my cat; I get him to leave the house by loudly adding food to an already filled dish outside his cat door in which he has no apparent culinary interest at the time.)

The stereotyped response definition of instinct has played a relatively minor role in the motivational analysis of human behavior, for the importance of learning and response variability in all but the simplest reflexes is evident at the human level.

2. The word *instinct* is also used to refer to a specific motivational tendency that is inferred from overt behavior. Instincts in this sense are potentialities for action that are considered unlearned "wants," "urges," or "internal commands" that are built into the structure of the organism. They are imperatives that "must" find expression, although they do not have to be recognized or labeled by the organism. Whereas the ends or goals of the instincts are presumed to be fixed, the means of expression can be quite diverse. For example, Freud suggested that aggressive instincts can be satisfied through war, antisocial behavior, or self-destructive acts. Because an urge can be gratified in a variety of manners, some believe the reality of instinctive desires to be antithetical to a mechanical model of humans that equates humans and machines. Indeed, the instincts are thought to document the purposiveness and flexibility of behavior. However, early ethologists (as well as other scientific groups) conceptualized these urges as internal, instigating forces linked with energy systems. Hence their analysis is quite compatible with considering the person a machine.

Some version of the "instinct as urge" doctrine was adopted not only by Freud, but by many other prominent psychologists as well during the early 1900s. Perhaps the most elaborate instinct theory was proposed by McDougall (1923), who postulated that instincts or propensities propel the organism toward certain end states. McDougall believed each instinct to have a cognitive, affective, and conative component. For example, he thought that the instinct of escape caused animals to attend to aversive stimuli, exhibit the emotion of fear, and initiate avoidance behavior or flight. McDougall believed that all behavior has an instinctive origin—behaviors are driven by motivating energies that push one toward certain goals.

The instinct doctrine reached its peak during this period. Psychologists employed the term as both a descriptive and an explanatory concept to account for the behavior of animals and humans. Osgood (1953) wrote:

> Holt (1931) has summarized this nonsense neatly . . . [asserting] "if he walks alone, it is the 'anti-social instinct' which activates him; if he goes with his fellows, it is the 'herd instinct' . . . if he twiddles his thumbs, it is the 'thumb-twiddling instinct'; if he does not twiddle his thumbs, it is the 'thumb-not-twiddling instinct.' " Thus, everything is explained with the facility of magic—word magic. (p. 428)

At the beginning of the 1920s, the enthusiasm for the instinct doctrine began to wane, and an anti-instinct revolt ensued. Dunlap (1919) and Kuo

(1924) published articles questioning the existence of instincts; they argued that instinct is not a necessary concept in psychology. Bernard (1924), a sociologist and anthropologist, noted that more than 2,500 instincts had been postulated. He called attention to the great variability in the patterns of behavior across cultures and asked how inborn, fixed characteristics could explain the great diversity in observed behavior. (For a more complete discussion of the decline of the instinct doctrine, see Beach, 1955.)

Thus the concept of instinct was dying in the 1920s. However, it was to reemerge about two decades later in the conceptions of ethologists and others interested in animal behavior.

Instincts in Ethological Theory

The term *ethologist* initially was reserved for zoologists interested in the biological aspects of behavior—that is, behavior's "value to the organism, its evolutionary history, and its causation in terms of stimulus, hormonal, and neurological events" (Valle, 1975, p. 10). Ethologists are interested in the adaptive significance of behavior, and they have concentrated their attention on unlearned behaviors that often seem relatively stereotyped.

A few beliefs have played central roles in ethologists' analyses. Of particular importance is the concept of a *fixed action pattern*. Fixed action patterns are highly stereotyped responses that are assumed to be genetically programmed reactions that occur given the presence of a particular "sign" stimulus. The most cited of these behaviors in the ethological literature is the attack response of a stickleback fish toward the color red. Sticklebacks have this color on their bellies, so that an attack chases away other competing sticklebacks, resulting in a spreading of the species and increased likelihood of survival and reproduction.

Lorenz and Tinbergen, the central early figures in the field of ethology and subsequently the first Nobel laureates in psychological studies, used a "lock and key" metaphor when explaining the relation between fixed action patterns and the sign stimulus. Only one key fits, and that key fits only one particular lock, so that, for example, attack takes place only given the color red, and this color does not engage other responses.

It has been stated that in the presence of a particular stimulus, a programmed pattern of activity will be initiated. However, Tinbergen and Lorenz contended that when the responses do occur, they are not so much elicited by the stimulus event as much as they are *released* by them. Tinbergen (1951) states:

> Ongoing impulses are blocked as long as the innate releasing mechanism, or IRM [which is presumed to inhibit the occurrence of the fixed action pattern], is not stimulated. When the adequate sign stimuli impinge upon the reflex-like IRM, the block is removed. (p. 124)

Nobel Prize-winning ethologist Konrad Lorenz at his research center in Seewiesen, Germany. (Photo by Hermann Kacher.) (UPI/The Bettman Archive)

Nikolaas Tinbergen (UPI/The Bettman Archive)

Thus, given this conception, it is not merely that a sign stimulus instigates a response; rather, there is a response or a behavior (the instinctive urge) that is "pushing" or "striving" to be released, but its display or expression is being blocked. The sign stimulus then removes this block and frees or releases the behavior.

This seemingly unparsimonious explanation is then elaborated with the inclusion of energy concepts. For Lorenz (Tinbergen had a somewhat different conception), each fixed action pattern pushing for release, or each internal urge, is accompanied by or motivated by its own action-specific energy. Lorenz described the working of this energy within a hydraulic metaphor. He postulated that the energy for each instinct "accumulated" in a "reservoir" given the absence of a releaser, and was discharged when the releasing stimulus appeared. Thus the greater the time since the last display of the instinctive behavior, the greater the amount of accumulated energy in the reservoir.

This hydraulic metaphor gave rise to some specific predictions regarding the variability of the conditions under which a fixed action pattern would be displayed. According to Lorenz (1952):

All these behavior patterns respond more rapidly if they have not been released for some time. The threshold value of releasing stimuli decreases during quiescence. Moreover, an instinctive movement that is not "used" over a long period literally becomes a "motive." . . . All these phenomena—spontaneity, lowering of threshold, discharge at inadequate objects, periodic-rhythmical occurrence . . . —suggest a process of accumulation. "Something" is accumulated (generated) rhythmically and continually, and used up by the consummation of an instinctive act. . . .

Instinctive behavior thus consists of at least three components. First, appetitive behavior motivated by internal accumulation of readiness for a specific action. Second, activation of an IRM, which disinhibits the innate reaction. Third, discharge of the "consummatory act," which is the purpose of the behavior. (pp. 289-290)

This conception has been summarized somewhat differently by Hinde (1960):

> Lorenz's "reaction specific energy" [can be thought of as] a liquid in a reservoir. [It] is supposed that the reservoir can discharge through a spring-loaded valve at the bottom. The valve is opened in part by the hydrostatic pressure in the reservoir, and in part by . . . the external stimulus. As the reservoir discharges, the hydrostatic pressure . . . decreases, and thus a great weight is necessary to open the valve again. (p. 200)

Pertinent Research

Two types of observations have been especially called upon to support this hydraulic conception of instinctive behavior. These relate to what have been called "vacuum behavior" and "displacement activity."

Support for Hydraulic Models

(1) Vacuum Behavior

Ethologists have demonstrated that the probability of the appearance of some responses increases as a function of the time since the response was previously made. The increasing response readiness is most dramatically displayed in vacuum behavior, or behavior patterns that appear when the sign stimulus is not identifiable. For example, if a captive starling is raised in a cage, at times the bird may engage in complex sequences of hunting, killing, and even "eating" prey, even though there is no prey in the cage. In a similar manner, caged female birds have been observed to take hold of some of their own feathers and go through the motions of building a nest. Thus the greater the accumulation of energy, the lower the threshold for a stimulus to release the IRM, until the point where no identifiable stimulus need be present to instigate the action. This theoretical analysis therefore can account for the variation in the probability of occurrence of an action as a function of the recent history of the organism. Note that it is the separation of the behavior from the normal releaser that provides the crucial evidence suggesting the existence of internal urges. In a similar manner, the unavailability of gratifying objects provided Freud with evidence from which he inferred some of the dynamic principles of behavior.

old record player repeating

Aggression as Internal Agitation and Catharsis

Aggressive instincts have been postulated by Lorenz and Tinbergen to correspond to a state of internal agitation. As already revealed, this internal urge persists as long as an appropriate stimulus or object of attack is absent.

Nonexpression of the instinct then results in an accumulation of action-specific aggressive energy. This conception, then, is close to Freud's notion of aggression as a biologically rooted instinct or drive that constantly (cyclically) seeks an outlet.

To reduce human aggression, Lorenz argued, we need to have activities that "drain off" aggressive energy. Otherwise this aggression-specific urge will grow stronger and will be expressed in the presence of a very weak eliciting force. That is, when aggression is not expressed, its threshold for evocation constantly increases.

How can this energy be drained? Lorenz (1966) suggested that sporting activity could be one outlet: "The main function of sport today lies in the cathartic discharge of aggressive urges" (p. 217). It should be noted again that Lorenz's expectations are consistent with Freud's views regarding the potential cathartic value of the reduction of instinctive urges through alternate goal attainments. This view also is closely related to the layperson's metaphor of anger, the affect linked with aggression, as internal pressure within a container, as exemplified in such expressions as "He is filled with anger," "Get the anger out of your system," and "She could not contain her anger" (Lakoff, 1987, p. 383).

Displacement Activity

Another interesting observation that is pertinent to the idea of an instinctive urge is labeled *displacement activity*. Displacement activity occurs when two incompatible response tendencies are simultaneously aroused. For example, a bird might be faced with a rival who elicits both attack and flight. In this situation, behaviors may be displayed that appear to be irrelevant to the situation, such as grooming. At times the activity differs from normal grooming behavior in that it seems hurried and is discontinued before it is completed, but on other occasions the behavior is indistinguishable from normal grooming. Certain species of fish, such as the already-mentioned stickleback, also exhibit such out-of-context displacement activity. When one stickleback is at the boundary between its own territory and that of another stickleback, where both attack and escape behaviors are elicited, inappropriate nest-building behavior often is displayed (Tinbergen & van Iersel, 1947).

While the conception including the accumulation of energy can readily account for vacuum behavior, it is less appropriate for explaining displacement activity. Tinbergen (1952) therefore suggested that action-specific energy is arranged in a hierarchical, interdependent organization such that specific energy can motivate a number of different responses. Thus, during a conflict, the thwarting of the prepotent responses is presumed to activate other behaviors because the undischarged energy "spills over" into those systems.

Criticism of Ethological Energy Models

The energy models proposed by Lorenz and Tinbergen in the early stages of the development of ethology did not meet with widespread acceptance (see Hinde, 1960; Lehrman, 1953). The main criticism has been that the so-called accumulated energy is nowhere to be found. Inasmuch as ethologists have operated at the molecular level of analysis, with detailed analyses of the hormonal and physiological substrates that influence action, this criticism is especially embarrassing.

There have been other interpretations of displacement activity and vacuum behavior that do not invoke the notion of accumulated energy (see Zeigler, 1964). It has been suggested that displacement activity emerges because the dominant habits or responses are not being made, thus allowing the next most dominant response or habit in the organism's hierarchy to be expressed. There is some empirical evidence supporting this "response repertoire" explanation that will be prevalent in the following chapter. Specifically, it has been found that the type of grooming behavior displayed during a conflict can be varied by altering the stimulus situation, so that when water is placed on a bird's feathers just prior to the conflict, preening is the displaced activity, whereas placing sticky material on the bird's bill generates bill-wiping behavior during conflict (Rowell, 1961).

In another argument that also makes use of principles from learning theory, it has been suggested that vacuum behavior is a result of "stimulus generalization" in which stimuli related to the sign stimulus acquire the capacity to elicit the response when it has not been expressed. (However, this explanation does not deal with the essential issue of why lack of responding increases stimulus generalization.)

Ethologists have been sensitive to criticisms of these earlier theoretical positions and now confine their work primarily to a search for the mechanisms that control action. There has been less defense of the concept of instinct as an internal urge or energy system, and hence less use of machine comparisons and less relevance of their findings to human motivation, as well as to the ideas expressed by Freud. Nonetheless, some puzzles remain, such as vacuum behavior, that are very relevant to human motivation.

Sociobiology

Ethologists have focused their attention on animal behavior and what can be called the *proximal* determinants of behavior—the hormonal conditions of the organism, the sign stimuli in the environment, and the like. These influence action at a given moment in time. More recently, other approaches that bear upon motivational issues have become highly visible within the field of biology. These perspectives consider a longer time frame and are concerned with what can be called the *ultimate* determinants of behavior, that is, the function of the behavior within the larger evolutionary context. One such approach is known as sociobiology, which has been defined as the study of the biological bases of social behavior, or the application of evolutionary theory to the study of social behavior (Wilson, 1975).

Ethologists and sociobiologists often examine different phenomena and disparate issues, but at times interpretations derived from one level of analysis bear upon explanations at the other level. For example, guided by a concern with the survival value of behavior (an ultimate explanation), Power (1975) claimed to have demonstrated that altruism does not exist among mountain bluebirds (here defining *altruism* as helping others not immediately related to oneself, and without personal benefit). He reached this conclusion by first removing one mate of a pair caring for some newborns. He then examined the behavior of the replacing mate. If the newly arrived mate helped care for the offspring, then altruism would have been demonstrated inasmuch as the new partner was unrelated to the nestlings and there was no personal advantage in helping. Observations revealed that the new mates ignored the needy infants, leading Power to reject the hypothesis that these birds are altruistic. He argued that the ultimate determinants of behavior are selfishness and genetic survival; "altruism" is nonexistent.

There is an abundant literature, however, demonstrating that birds usually do not accept young unless they are hormonally prepared. This usually requires the birds' having passed through a sequence of events leading up to hatching and the presence of the newborn (see Beach, 1978). Hence an alternative and more plausible hypothesis advanced by ethologists is that the failure of the new mates to provide care was due to the absence of the appropriate hormonal conditions.

In sum, as stated by Barlow (1989):

> It is a truism that each biological phenomenon can be explained at both the proximate and ultimate levels. . . . Proximate hypotheses are often more immediately falsifiable. Because of their primacy over ultimate mechanisms, they set boundaries for ultimate explanations. . . . Considerable effort can be wasted pursuing the ultimate explanation if there is none. (p. 23)

It is not really possible, however, to select one approach over the other on the basis of empirical evidence. Rather, proximal and ultimate explanations stand side by side, as do contrasting theories based on different metaphors.

When considering the mountain bird example, one might think that a "crucial" experiment (one that decides which theory is "better") could be conducted by, for example, introducing a new mate that had gone through the appropriate hormonal changes. In this case, the ethologists but not Power would predict altruistic helping of the young. However, either side could still introduce alternative explanations in the presence of disconfirming evidence. For example, if altruism was exhibited, then Power might contend that there was no way for the newly introduced bird to "know" that it was not helping its own offspring, which is a behavior not considered "pure" or unselfish altruism. Conversely, if altruism was not exhibited, then the ethologists could contend that the unusual sequence of events, which included changing nests, interrupted the naturally occurring conditions and altered the hormonal substrates that promote helping the young.

Self-Testing Some Hypotheses

Before introducing a few of the basic concepts and hypotheses associated with sociobiology, I would like the readers to complete the questionnaire in Experiment 2.1. In Chapter 1, I mentioned that it would be possible to perform some theoretical tests with data generated by the readers. When constrained to relatively simple paper-and-pencil measures, such tests are not feasible regarding Freudian and ethological approaches to motivation, but sociobiological theory has generated hypotheses that can be explored with self-report judgments. Readers should give their responses before reading further, so that they are not "biased," either positively or negatively, by knowing the "expected" answers, that is, the answers predicted by the theory. Subsequently, these answers should be compared across class members; validity is enhanced for sociobiology if there is consistency among responses in the direction predicted by that theory.

Basic Concepts

According to sociobiologists, all organisms (including humans) are "gene-producing machines" or "survival machines" (Dawkins, 1976), with the basic motivation of perpetuating their own genetic pool. This is accomplished by surviving, reproducing, and aiding in the survival of offspring and others related to oneself if this promotes personal genetic pool continuation. Behavior therefore is entirely selfish. As Dawkins (1976) speculates:

> Our genes have survived, in some cases for millions of years, in a highly competitive world. This entitles us to expect certain qualities in our genes. I shall argue that a predominant quality to be expected in a successful gene is ruthless selfishness. This gene selfishness will usually give rise to selfishness in individual behaviour. (p. 2)

Individuals are generally unaware of this unique source of all motivation. Hence humans are machines with ends or functions, but these are neither subject to volitional change nor known by the acting person. For sociobiologists, other associated implications of the machine metaphor are not central. The behavior itself may be flexible in that anything that

Experiment 2.1

(1) You are on a boat that overturns. It contains your 5-year-old and your 1-year-old children (of the same sex). The boat sinks and you can save only one. Whom do you choose to save? Circle one:

   (5-year-old)   1-year-old

(2) That same boat (you are slow to learn lessons) contains your 40-year-old and 20-year-old children (both of the same sex). Neither can swim. As the boat sinks, whom do you choose to save? Circle one:

   40-year-old   (20-year-old)

(3) Have you (or would you) rather marry someone older or younger than yourself?

   (older)   younger

   By how many years? _at least 2_

(4) Of the following six, which three are most important in the selection of your mate? Circle the answers:

   (a) good financial prospects ♀
   (b) good looks ♂
   (c) a caring and responsible personality ♀
   (d) physical attractiveness ♂
   (e) ambition and industriousness ♀
   (f) an exciting personality ♂ ♀

(5) You and your spouse are the proud parents of a new child. The grandparents are ecstatic. Who do you think will be kinder to the child? Circle one:

   (the mother of the mother)   the mother of the father

(6) Who will mourn more at the death of a child? Circle the answer in each pair:

   (a) father   (mother)
   (b) parents of the father   (parents of the mother)
   (c) younger parents   (older parents)

(7) Which will elicit more grief?

   (a) (death of a son)   death of a daughter
   (b) death of an unhealthy child (death of a healthy child)

"works"—that is, that promotes personal well-being—will be adopted. Hence the exhibited actions are not necessarily mechanical, which is consistent with earlier interpretations of instinctive behavior proposed by Freud and McDougall. In addition, energy concepts are not necessarily invoked, and there is no general concern with integrating structural concepts in the explanation of behavior. Rather, evolution has dictated the ultimate purpose of life—to maintain one's genetic pool. This instinctive urge underlies all activities and is what links the sociobiological analysis of human behavior to a machine metaphor.

Contrast to Darwinian Theory

As already discussed, evolutionary theory as proposed by Darwin was based on the idea of survival of the fittest; that is, those whose structural/ behavioral characteristics gave them an evolutionary advantage were most likely to find food and to reproduce. These properties, in turn, were then passed on to their offspring.

This perspective readily accounted for the evolution of aggression in humans and lower animals, so that Darwinians successfully applied evolutionary theory to some motivational issues. It is well documented that the dominant members of a tribe or species receive more than an equal share of food and account for a disproportionate amount of sexual behavior and reproduction. Hence those who are most aggressive survive and reproduce, resulting in aggressive offspring. Conversely, those who are least aggressive are least likely to survive and have children, resulting in the elimination of genes that might inhibit aggressiveness. Note, then, that aggressive displays can be explained with reference to the proximal determinants of behavior outlined by ethologists (the red belly of the stickleback, hormonal readiness, and so forth), or to the ultimate determinants of behavior specified by evolutionary biologists (aggression aids in the survival of the species, the self, and/or the genetic pool).

But how can Darwinians or evolutionary theorists and sociobiologists account for altruism? Altruistic behavior benefits the survival of others but detracts from personal fitness inasmuch as it entails costs—such as risking one's life, sharing needed resources, and the like—that reduce "fitness" or the likelihood of personal survival. Hence altruistic genes would be anticipated to disappear gradually over evolutionary history. Yet it is evident that, across many species, parents protect their young; there are social colonies such as those of ants or bees in which some members give their lives to protect the colony; and in many groups, members sacrifice themselves to aid others, as when a bird in a flock gives a warning call that attracts attention to itself and causes self-related danger while alerting others to flee. Of course, protecting the young and self-sacrifice are also well known in human societies.

Whereas Darwinians cannot easily incorporate altruism into their evolutionary analyses, sociobiologists have been able to account for these behaviors by contending that survival of the self or species is not the ultimate motivation. Rather, what one is selfish about is the perpetuation of one's total genetic pool, which is the ultimate motivator of action. Consider, for example, the following illustration. A mother enters a burning house to save her children, but loses her life in the process. Let us assume that three children were saved by this heroic deed. Each child carries 50%

Freud = Ethology = sociobiology

of the genes of each parent. For ease of calculation, assume for the moment that each of us has four genes, two from each parent. With the saving of three children, six of the mother's genes (two from each child) are enabled to live. Hence self-sacrifice results in the continuation of six rather than four self-related genes (without taking into account the likelihood that the saved children themselves will reproduce, with each grandchild carrying one gene [25%] from each grandparent). Hence, as Dawkins (1976) notes, "There are special circumstances in which a gene can achieve its own selfish goals best by fostering a limited form of altruism at the level of individual animals" (p. 2).

A rather dazzling and diverse array of behaviors, ranging from altruism and courtship rituals to child abuse and grief, have been apparently amenable to explanation based on the postulate that the organism's ultimate motivation is the continuation of its total genetic pool. Most typically, sociobiologists tend to be especially concerned with reproductive activity—mate selection, sexual practices, and parenting. Of course, extrapolations from subhuman to human behavior often are questionable, as perhaps illustrated in the analysis of the function of sports offered by Lorenz. And, as already indicated, ultimate explanations are difficult to disprove and have questionable scientific status. Nonetheless, predictions derived from sociobiology are eye-catching, and the theory has provided fascinating yet speculative explanations for some mysterious behaviors.

Empirical Evidence

The vast majority of investigations pertinent to sociobiology have involved the study of subhumans. However, even at the human level there are a variety of phenomena that sociobiologists call upon to support their claims. As might be anticipated, all these observations can be interpreted with alternative theories, usually focusing on proximal antecedents. And, as intimated already, some of the observations are very general and the explanations quite speculative and seemingly post hoc (falsely inferring a causal relationship), although other phenomena are more specific, with the analyses clearer and more closely tied to the conception. None of the data cited in support of the sociobiological position is "crucial"; rather, the total picture is compelling. In this sense, it has much in common with Freudian theory.

Altruism

It has been revealed that altruism is expected from an organism only when it is in service of the maintenance of that organism's genetic pool. Hence this is "selfish altruism" (which might be an oxymoron). The first two questions in Experiment 2.1 illustrate one application of this principle. Sociobiologists contend that reproductive concerns are one determinant of altruistic decisions. In reference to Questions 1 and 2 in Experiment 2.1, inasmuch as some children die between the ages of 1 and 5, and 5-year-olds are therefore more likely to reproduce later than are 1-year-olds (since they are less vulnerable to death), it would be most instrumental for the genetic pool to save the older child (with all else being equal). In a similar manner, a 20-year-old is more likely to reproduce than is a 40-year-old (particularly if both are female). In this example, then, the younger offspring should be chosen to be saved. Based on discussions in my own courses, I suspect that virtually all readers answered in the predicted directions. As already indicated, the responses may be amenable to interpretation based on other theories. Nonetheless, it is the case that the predictions are clearly derived from sociobiological tenets.

As discussed in the study of mountain birds, alternative interpretations of helping behavior directed at children that specify the proximal eliciting conditions of an action have been offered to supplement, or replace, the ultimate interpretations of sociobiologists. At times proximate and ultimate analyses can lead to conflicting predictions, as suggested in the discussion of the mountain bird research. Considered together, the two approaches point out some of the complexity and multiple determinants of altruistic decisions. Concerning responses to Question 1, it has been found that facial and bodily configurations that are associated with infants, including large forehead, small nose, small chin, and shortened limbs, particularly generate sympathy and help-giving (compare your reactions to the faces on the left and right sides of Figure 2.4; see Berry & McArthur, 1986). It has even been suggested that this accounts for why we are so fond of penguins. Hence it is possible that when actually confronted with the situation described in Question 1, a person's behavior may differ from his or her abstract judgments, or at least be more conflicted.

Of course, regardless of age, relatives should be helped rather than nonrelatives (blood is thicker than water). This tendency is apparent and at times has been considered destructive, so that on occasion rules or laws have been passed against nepotism (favoritism, in the workplace or elsewhere, based on kinship rather than merit).

It also is evident, however, that humans often come to the aid of nonrelatives. Strangers risk their lives for others who are unknown to them, many sacrifice money and time to help the needy, and so on. These facts are difficult for sociobiologists to explain, given their belief in selfishness. To account for these observations, they suggest that "reciprocal altruism" has evolved, in which help is programmed for nonrelatives because it also may enhance the self (Trivers, 1971). To understand this concept, consider the following example. Assume that an individual is in danger and that, without help, the likelihood of his or her living is .10, while with help that probability increases to .50. For the potential helper, the probability of living without offering help is 1.00, while helping decreases that likelihood to, for example, .90. That is, the help-giver decreases his or her own personal fitness by 10%. Now, given no help, over all occasions 55% of the combined

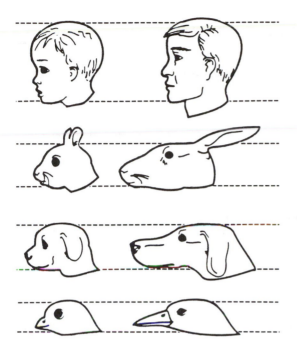

Figure 2.4. Contrasts in infant and mature faces. (From Feshbach & Weiner, 1991, p. 13.)

or total genetic pool for these two individuals will remain (10% + 100%, or an average of 55%). On the other hand, given help, the remaining genetic pool is 50% + 90%, or an average of 70%. If individuals are equally in need, and there is mutual help, then this will be in service of the genetic pool of each. Therefore, individuals with this "reciprocity" gene are more likely to survive.

There are external cues, such as skin color, that help reveal if someone might or might not be related to oneself and thus aid in altruistic decision making. Sociobiologists suggest that racial prejudice may be one manifestation of a bias against nonrelatives.

Mating Behavior and Reproduction

Mating and reproductive behaviors involve the use of strategies that best enable the genetic pool to survive. Less-than-optimal strategies supposedly would have disappeared during the long evolutionary history. Sociobiologists contend that each sex faces unique reproductive problems. For the female, the main predicament is that reproductive capacities are restricted; among humans, 25-30 children approximate the upper biological limit. On the other hand, for males reproductive potential is (almost) limitless. Because of the greater parental investment of the female in each child, she must be careful to select a mate who will aid in child rearing to enhance the likelihood of the survival of the offspring as well as facilitate her survival. The male, on the other hand, must select females who can bear children.

Based on these assumptions, it has been contended that males want to marry younger females because they are more likely to give birth, whereas females prefer to mate with older males because they have a greater amount of resources to aid in rearing the children. A great deal of data gathered across diverse cultures and historical periods have documented that males tend to be 2-3 years older than their mates (Buss & Barnes, 1986). The answers to Question 3 in Experiment 2.1 should confirm this preference. Furthermore, in Question 4, females should select items a, c, and e, which concern resources, caring, and responsibility, whereas males should select items b, d, and f, which relate to sexual preoccupations. Again based on data from my classes, I strongly suspect this is how the majority of readers responded.

Females are said to have one sexual advantage—a woman can be sure any child she bears is hers. Thus, following childbirth, the maternal grandparent, assured of 25% genetic carryover, should be particularly happy (see Question 5 in Experiment 2.1). The male, however, must determine that the female has really borne his child. Sociobiologists point out that courtship rituals, such as extended engagements, allow the male to monopolize the female's time to ascertain that she is not already pregnant and that any future child will be his own. During this period, the female also can observe whether she has selected a reliable and caring male.

Emotions

Sociobiologists have been concerned with both the determinants and the role of emotions in social behavior (Trivers, 1971). Given the importance of reproductive success, strong emotions are anticipated at the loss of kin. It has been argued that the greater the investment in a child, and the more likely that child is to reproduce, the greater the experienced negative emotion (grief). Hence greater grief should be experienced by the mother, the parents of the mother, older parents (who are less able to reproduce again), and the death of a healthy and male child as opposed to the other alternatives presented in Questions 6 and 7 of Experiment 2.1. Such findings have been documented in research that has unobtrusively measured the amount of displayed grief at funerals and then tracked the duration of this grief (Littlefield & Rushton, 1986; see also Crawford, Smith, & Krebs, 1987).

Sociobiologists contend that other emotions have evolved that aid in the maintenance of the social order and prevent deceit. For example, anger from others signals that an individual has committed an unacceptable transgression, and this prevents the transgression from reoccurring. Guilt serves the same function, although it is a self-directed rather than other-directed form of anger. Conversely, both pity and gratitude promote positive reactions and social equity. These concepts will be discussed further in Chapter 7.

Antisocial Behavior

Inasmuch as each individual is presumed to be entirely selfish, antisocial behavior should be engaged in to the extent that it provides the individual with a competitive advantage. Like Freud, sociobiologists see culture as imposing restrictions and barriers that block their instinctual urges.

There are many ways to gain a competitive advantage and to protect oneself from potential harm, including the employment of deceit (e.g., conveying that help will be reciprocated when it will not), "using" others, and so forth. Males particularly are in favorable competitive position over females because of the biology of the birth process. Sociobiologists point out that females are present at the time of birth (although this is not true of all species, such as fish, in which case some gender problems will be reversed). Hence females are placed in what has been called "the cruel bind." If they remain to bring up the offspring, increasing their genetic pool, they become less personally fit because of the demands of child rearing. But females can have relatively few children, so they must be especially concerned with the survival of each child. Males, on the other hand, by not being present at their offspring's birth (they are away, seeking to have more children!), may try to gain advantage by leaving the child rearing to the mother and thereby having the best of all worlds—increasing their genetic pool without personal cost. It is quite evident that many more mothers than fathers are the remaining child rearers in one-parent households; indeed, 95% of single-parent families are headed by women.

Often a child enters a family and is unrelated to either one or both of the parents. This decreases personal fitness without genetic gain for one or both of the caregivers, which is the worst of all worlds. Hence stepparents, for example, may tend to reject the child and forgo personal commitments. The data are quite overwhelming in documenting that the majority of child abuse takes place between adult males and their stepchildren.

Finally, sociobiologists argue that rape is a reproductive strategy used by low-status males to increase their genetic pool while not involving any subsequent child-rearing costs. There is one interesting statistic that can be considered as supporting this viewpoint—the vast majority of rape victims are of childbearing age (rather than, say, older women who may be easier to victimize in terms of ability to resist).

Summary

The conception of a gene-producing survival machine led to the examination of a vast array of phenomena and speculations guided by a view regarding the ultimate determinants of human behavior. Some hypotheses have supporting data, although all the phenomena that have been addressed are likely to raise doubts and concerns about their interpretation. Yet the broad spectrum of observations that have been examined by sociobiologists is a credit to the heuristic value of the theory. As I indicated in Chapter 1, it is not my concern in this volume to decide which theory discussed here is "correct," for none of them is. Rather, the critical questions are whether the conceptions have shed light on some phenomena and whether others can build upon the findings. That is, is there a "payoff" with the use of a survival, gene-producing machine metaphor to explain human action? Given this perspective, sociobiology certainly has proven its value.

GENERAL SUMMARY

In this chapter, three biological approaches to human motivation—Freudian theory, ethology, and sociobiology—have been considered. All view behavior as a product of a long history of evolution, and all are to some extent based upon the metaphor that the person is a machine. The pairing of biology and machine is not coincidence, for if behavior is viewed as a product of evolutionary history, then it will be shaped or determined by past history rather than (in addition to) current consciousness. The biological perspectives conceptualize behavior as inflexible and rigid, without conscious awareness of ends or goals, and/or driven by energy. All three approaches also are very much concerned with the function or the instrumental value of behavior. This is because it is assumed that we live in a world of limited resources, and restrictions are placed by the social and cultural world upon the basic tendencies that are striving for satisfaction. Hence the expression and the inhibition of sexual, aggressive, and/or altruistic tendencies, and the conflicts around these motivations, are of central importance.

Of course, the approaches also differ in some very fundamental ways: in their empirical focus and range, in the constructs they use, in their assumptions about energy, in their acceptance of proximal as opposed to ultimate determinants of behavior, in the importance of subhuman research, in the belief in and use of accepted scientific methodology, and on and on. As will be further documented in the next three chapters, the mere acceptance of a machine metaphor does not greatly restrict the differences between the theories or the phenomena that they attempt to explain.

Drive Theory

It was pointed out in Chapter 2 that mechanism was "in the air" in Freud's Europe. This also was true in the United States in the early 1900s. There was ferment about the general laws of mechanics, the notion that energy can be transformed in myriad manners—ideas that contributed heavily to the Industrial Revolution in America. It was in this atmosphere that Clark Hull, an early robotic engineer, formulated his general theory of motivation and linked it with experimental psychology. The biologically based conceptions of ethology and, much later, sociobiology were not devised to be motivational theories. Rather, they happened to be applicable to motivational issues. It is even arguable that Freud chiefly had as his goal the formulation of a motivational theory. In contrast, Hull not only devised an experimentally based motivational theory, he also had motivation at the center of his thoughts. It is uncertain whether Hull should be credited with the formulation of the first experimentally guided motivational theory—both Kurt Lewin, discussed in the next chapter, and Edward Tolman, also considered in this chapter, were developing their theories about the same time as Hull. But there is no doubt that, in the United States, Hull was the first dominant motivational figure.

There also can be no doubt about Hull's acceptance of the metaphor that the person is a machine. In 1943 he wrote, "The behaving organism [is] a completely self-maintaining robot"; and he later remarked, "It has struck me many times of late that the human organism is one of the most extraordinary machines—and yet a machine" (1962, p. 820).

Freud and Hull: Some Conceptual Comparisons

Freud and Hull had dissimilar backgrounds and training: Contrast the culture of Vienna with a log cabin in Michigan and the study of medicine with mining engineering. In spite of these historical differences, there are many similarities in the two men's conclusions about motivated behavior (see McClelland, 1957). First of all, both Freud and Hull were determinists. That is, they assumed that acts are caused and that the causes can be identified. Second, both believed that physiological and psychological laws

CLARK L. HULL

Clark Hull was born in 1884 in New York, but he was reared on a farm in Michigan and attended a one-room rural school. Early in life he contracted polio, and one of his legs remained permanently paralyzed. Hull was totally dedicated to his work; he completed his fifth book just prior to his death in 1952.

Hull played a dominant role within academic psychology, although he is little known among the lay public. Between 1940 and 1960, more than 30% of the articles published in the two main journals covering the fields of learning and motivation cited his work. Furthermore, in a recent poll psy-chologists voted him the most important contribu-tor to psychology during the period of 1930 to 1950.

Hull had three relatively independent careers in psychology. He first studied aptitude testing and statistical procedures. Then he turned to hypnosis and conducted classic experiments on suggestibil-ity. It is interesting that both Freud and Hull were involved in the study of hypnosis and both moved away from it—Freud because it was not a reliable therapeutic method, and Hull because the tech-nique was opposed by medical authorities and be-cause he believed it nothing more than a form of normal, waking suggestibility. During this period, Hull also was concerned with robots (he majored in engineering as an undergraduate); his postula-tion of a mechanical model of humans may have grown from this interest. But Hull's main contribu-tions to psychology came during the next phase of his work and involved the study of learning and motivation.

Hull spent the major portion of his academic life at Yale University, where he provided the leader-ship for the Institute of Human Relations. This in-stitute embraced people from all fields and, under Hull's influence, gave rise to one of the most fruit-ful periods of collaborative research in the history of the social sciences.

complement one another. In addition, they accepted tension (need) reduc-tion as the basic goal of behavior, with organisms striving to maintain a state of internal equilibrium (homeostasis). They also both believed in the principle of hedonism; that is, behavior is guided by the pleasure-pain principle. And finally, both were greatly influenced by Darwin and searched for the functional significance of actions.

There also are some fundamental disparities in the theoretical systems and the methods employed by these two researchers. Hull did not conceive of the organism as a closed energy system. Rather, he believed that prolong-ing deprivation, or needs originating from multiple sources such as hunger and thirst, increases the total energy available for "work." In addition, as indicated in Chapter 2, Freud did not place much faith in laboratory experiments; his data were free associations drawn from therapy, his personal dreams, or the reported dreams of his patients. On the other hand, Hull's data were generated in carefully controlled experimental studies, primarily of rats running through a maze for a reward of food. Further, Hull was explicitly quantitative in his approach, formulating behavioral postulates from which exact hypotheses could be derived. The majority of his concepts were anchored to operational definitions. For example, he defined hunger in terms of hours of deprivation, indexed habit strength as the number of reinforced responses, and so on. Freud was little concerned with the precision of his concepts and their measurement. Finally, Hull denied that mental processes are determinants of any action. Thus, for example, the idea of "purposive" behavior, or action undertaken "in order to get something," was accounted for entirely by bodily reactions, without appealing to mental capacities and properties such as foresight and anticipation. As previously pointed out, although Freud used many mechanical or physicalistic concepts in his discussion of human behavior, he also believed that thoughts do influence action; for example, the ego can inhibit overt action by invoking a defense such as repression to prevent a wish from entering consciousness. Even instincts were regarded by Freud as "demands made on the mind." Thus Hull was much more mechanistic in his approach to motivation than was Freud.

In this chapter, Hull's theory is presented along with some of its precursors and subsequent elaborations. I will not document the shortcomings of this conception in any detail; criticisms already have been voiced in numerous sources (e.g., Atkinson, 1964; Bolles, 1975; Weiner, 1972, 1980b). Rather, I will portray this theory primarily from the point of view of its adherents, and focus on its mechanistic roots. Various phenomena that have been analyzed from a Hullian framework, including anxiety, conflict, frustration, social facilitation, and cognitive dissonance, will be examined because they are particularly relevant to human motivation.

Mechanistic Learning Theory Prior to Hull

Hullian theory was partly derived from, and is part of the context of, the growth and centrality of learning theory in the United States. This field of study dominated psychology from its initial experimental beginnings until, perhaps, 1955. In the early 1900s, operant or instrumental learning was first systematically examined by Edward Thorndike (1911). Thorndike began his investigations in the basement of William James's home in the mid-1870s. His general procedure was to place an animal, frequently a cat or a chick, in an enclosed box, outside of which food was placed. If the animal made the "correct" response—the one the experimenter had designated as the response that would release it from the box—then it received the food. Thorndike observed that initially the animal engages in relatively random (trial-and-error) behavior until it accidentally emits the response that results in its release. When returned to the box, the animal makes that response sooner and sooner. Ultimately, the correct response becomes the most immediate in the animal's response hierarchy, or repertoire.

To explain this change in response hierarchies, or learning, Thorndike postulated his well-known "law of effect," which states that when a stimulus-response bond is followed by a satisfying state of affairs, the strength of that bond increases. Conversely, when a stimulus-response bond is followed by an annoying state of affairs, the strength of the bond is weakened. This has been called a "hedonism of the past" and is contrasted with Freud's formulation, which is a "hedonism of the future." Thorndike believed that reward or punishment strengthens or weakens the preceding response, while Freud contended that anticipated pleasure or pain determines future responses.

The law of effect has the same consequences on behavior at an individual level as survival principles have on behavior at a species level. Assume, for example, that an animal may run into a light or a dark compartment to seek a reward of food, which always is located in the dark compartment. Over time, the animal will increasingly choose to run toward the dark side; soon, this will be the choice 100% of the time. Now also assume that organisms of a species can search for food during the day or during the night. However, they are more likely to be caught and killed during the day. Over time, those with a genetic disposition for night activity will survive; after many generations, only those with nighttime tendencies will remain and the species therefore will be nocturnal. Thus individual learning recaptures in a short time frame the effects of nature and biology over a long time frame.

Thorndike's conception, like the biological account, is indeed mechanistic. No mention is made of higher mental processes. Rather, the contiguous association of a stimulus and a response, along with the presence of a reinforcer (satisfier), produces a mechanically rigid coupling, or an adhesion; the satisfier provides the "glue" for the stimulus-response association. Hull was greatly influenced by Thorndike and accepted that reinforcement provided the necessary "cement" for the establishment of stimulus-response connections.

Thorndike knew that if an animal was not hungry—that is, was not "motivated"—then it would not engage in the associated action. However, he did not incorporate motivational rules into his behavioral system. This was precisely the problem that engaged Hull.

The Drive Concept

Prior to the advent of Hull, motivational concepts were used to explain a different set of phenomena than those focused on by learning theorists. The behaviors set aside for motivation were grouped under the term *instinct*, the so-called inner urges that were striving for expression. But, as already explained, the instinct doctrine was called into question in the 1920s, primarily because it was capriciously invoked to account for all behavior. In the face of severe criticism, the use of instinct as an explanatory principle began to wane (see Beach, 1955). However, as is so often true in science, the theory or construct did not die—it was replaced. The concept of instinct was replaced by the concept of drive.

The introduction of the drive concept to motivational psychology is attributed to Woodworth (1918), although, as I have indicated, Freud may be considered a "drive" rather than (or in addition to) an instinct theorist. Drive was in many respects a "better" motivational construct than was instinct. First, it provided mechanists with a clear principle of mechanical causation. Second, drives, unlike instincts, promised to be empirically tied to some physiological base. Finally, it was possible to investigate drives in the laboratory. Drive antecedents, such as hours of deprivation, could be manipulated systematically, and their behavioral effects could be observed under controlled conditions.

Early Experimental Investigations
Guided by the Concept of Drive

Various experimental procedures were established in the 1920s to assess the strength and the consequences of deprivation (drive) on behavior. A number of studies, particularly those by Richter (1927), demonstrated that deprivation is related to general level of activity. That is, the greater the level of deprivation, the more active the organism becomes until enervation from lack of food sets in. Of course, if an animal is active when deprived, it is more likely to find the needed goal object. Thus the relationship between deprivation and activity was believed to have survival value. The pervasive influence of Darwin thus again is evident.

In addition, Richter observed cyclical variations in behavior, with a period of relative activity followed by a period of quiescence. In one investigation of the linkage between periods of activity and hunger, Richter allowed rats to eat whenever they desired. Activity level and consumption were measured. It was found that the period of maximum food intake corresponded to the time of maximum activity. Thus it was again concluded that activity is related to specific physiological (tissue) deficits.

| Start Box | Electric Grid | Goal Object |

Figure 3.1. The Columbia Obstruction Box.

A second general experimental procedure for studying drive effects made use of what is known as the Columbia Obstruction Box (see Figure 3.1). In investigations using this apparatus, animals were first deprived of a commodity necessary for survival, such as food or water. Then an incentive relevant to the drive (for example, food for a hungry organism) was placed in the goal chamber. Between the organism and the goal object was an electrical grid. The animal had to cross the grid and receive a shock to obtain the goal.

Investigators making use of the obstruction box varied the strength of the "drive to action," which was considered to be a function of the number of hours of deprivation, and the strength of "resistance," which, in turn, was a function of the magnitude of shock. The general finding was that there is a monotonic relationship between deprivation and the likelihood of crossing to the goal—with greater deprivation the animals were willing to endure higher levels of shock to reach the food. The broad implication of this work was that investigators believed drive could be measured with some precision.

Hull's Conception of Drive

Guided by the empirical evidence reviewed above, Hull (1943) suggested that physiological deficits, or needs, instigate the organism to undertake behaviors that result in the offset of those needs. Drives, therefore, are a motivational characteristic or property of need states. They result from physiological disequilibrium and instigate behaviors that return the organism to a state of equilibrium. In sum, needs generate the energy that is required for survival. Hull (1943) summarized his position as follows:

> Since a need, either actual or potential, usually precedes and accompanies the action of an organism, the need is often said to motivate or drive the associated activity. Because of this motivational characteristic of needs they are regarded as producing primary animal *drives*. . . . The major primary needs . . . include the need for foods of various sorts (hunger), the need for water (thirst), the need for air, the need to avoid tissue injury (pain), the need to maintain an optimal temperature, the need to defecate, the need to micturate, the need for rest (after protracted exertion), the need for sleep (after protracted wakefulness), and the need for activity (after protracted inaction). (pp. 57, 59-60)

Hull's conception of the relationship between need and drive can be illustrated as follows:

antecedent operation ——————→ need ——→ drive (energizer)
(e.g., deprivation, shock)

In adopting this position, Hull also was greatly influenced by Darwin's notion of the survival relevance of action. Just as it is survival relevant to become active when in a state of need, it is debilitating for an organism to search for food if satiated. That is, it is adaptive for behavior to occur if, and only if, a need exists that is not satisfied.

In addition, Hull stated that drive is a *nonspecific* energizer of behavior. All drives pool into one, and this aggregate drive energizes the organism. Hull (1943) contended:

> The drive concept, for example, is proposed as a common denominator of all primary motivations, whether due to food privation, water privation, thermal deviations from the optimum, tissue injury, the action of sex hormones, or other causes. . . . This implies to a certain extent the undifferentiated nature of drive in general contained in Freud's concept. . . . However, it definitely does not presuppose the special dominance of any one drive, such as sex, over the other drives. (pp. 239, 241)

The Integration of Drive and Habit

Recall that according to learning theory as developed by Thorndike, a previously linked response will be repeated when the appropriate stimulus reappears. However, it also was known that when the organism was sated, it often would not exhibit a response to the previously paired stimulus. Hull therefore asserted that the associative or stimulus-response linkages provided the direction, but not the energy, for action. In order for prior associations to be displayed, there must be some unsatisfied need. Furthermore, because drive is a nondirectional energizer of behavior, any extant need would activate whatever associative linkage was most probable of evocation, or highest in the organism's habit structure. Drive, then, does not have to result in overt behavioral activation. If the dominant habit in a fear-inducing situation is to "freeze," then augmentation of drive merely intensifies or energizes the freezing response.

In addition, Hull specified a mathematical relationship between the drive (energy) and habit (direction) determinants of behavior:

$$\text{behavior} = \text{drive} \times \text{habit}$$

In sum, Hull's conception of motivation can be portrayed as follows:

$$\left.\begin{array}{l}\text{drive operation} \text{——— need ——— drive} \\ \qquad\qquad\qquad\qquad\qquad\qquad\quad \times \\ \text{learning operation —— habit ——— direction}\end{array}\right\} = \text{behavior}$$

TABLE 3.1 Additive Relation of Deprivation and Habit Strength

	Deprivation Level	
Habit Strength	1	2
1	2	3
2	3	4

Of course, Hull realized the complexity of behavior and included many other terms in his final theory of motivation, but his best-known statement is simply that behavior = drive × habit.

It is reasonable for the reader to ask, Why should drive multiply habit? Why, for example, isn't the relation between drive and habit additive, so that the principle of motivation is drive + habit? One of the major implications of having these terms multiply is that if either one has a value of zero, then the value of the entire equation is zero. Thus Hull anticipated that if drives were all satisfied, there would be no action. As indicated, Thorndike realized that if an organism is sated, then the prior stimulus-response pairings would not be exhibited in action.

There is a relatively simple visual principle to suggest whether two variables are related multiplicatively or additively. Assume that drive and habit are related in an additive manner. This is depicted in Table 3.1, where drive and habit are both given values of 1 or 2. The numbers in the cells show the total of these values. These totals are then plotted in Figure 3.2. Note that the lines in Figure 3.2 are parallel.

On the other hand, if drive and habit relate multiplicatively, then the values of the cells are changed, as shown in Table 3.2. When these are plotted in Figure 3.3, it can be seen that the lines diverge. Thus parallel lines reveal an additive relation between variables, whereas divergent lines indicate a multiplicative relation.

To ascertain the relations between the variables, psychologists typically manipulate their strengths in an experimental setting (e.g., three versus nine hours of deprivation) and generate graphs similar to those shown in Figures 3.2 and 3.3. Experiment 3.1 allows the reader to do this.

It is now a relatively simple matter to determine if drive (deprivation hours) and incentive (what is being served for dinner) influence behavior.

TABLE 3.2 Multiplicative Relation of Deprivation and Habit Strength

	Deprivation Level	
Habit Strength	1	2
1	1	2
2	2	4

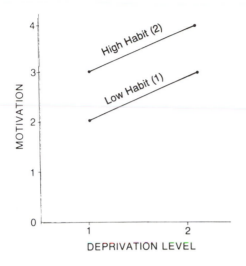

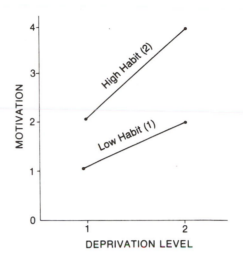

Figure 3.2. Additive relation of deprivation and habit strength.

Figure 3.3. Multiplicative relation of deprivation and habit strength.

Add the values over both incentives for the low (3-hour) drive level, as well as the numbers for both incentives given the high (9-hour) drive level. If the latter is bigger than the former, then it documents that drive augments (reported) behavior. In a similar manner, for both low and high drive, add the numbers associated with spinach, and then with ice cream. If there is a difference, then incentive also influences (reported) motivation. Finally, plot the data and examine the curves to see if they are parallel or diverging. This will reveal in this study whether drive and incentive relate additively or multiplicatively.

Empirical Support for Drive Theory

The statement that behavior = drive × habit generated a vast amount of research. Many empirical studies were undertaken to support one or more of the following assertions:

(1) Drive energizes behavior.
(2) Drive and habit relate multiplicatively.
(3) Drive is a pooled energy source.

A brief review of some of that research will more concretely show the kind of data generated by the Hullian conception. It will be evident that these

Experiment 3.1

Assume that you are a psychologist and want to predict how fast a child will come to dinner when called. You know two facts: how long the child has been without food, and what is being served for dinner. The child has been without food for either 3 or 9 hours, and the food is either spinach or ice cream.

The child can run for food from 0 (not moving at all) to 20 miles per hour. Please indicate how fast the following children will run (we will assume that this actually is the speed of running).

Hunger	Food	Speed (0-20)
3 hours	spinach	_____
9 hours	spinach	_____
3 hours	ice cream	_____
9 hours	ice cream	_____

---

investigations primarily employed lower animals as subjects; it was assumed that the findings would generalize to human motivation as well.

Perhaps the studies most often cited as models of the research generated by drive theory are those of Perin (1942) and Williams (1938). These investigators trained rats to make a simple bar-press response to receive food. The animals learned this response while under 23 hours of food deprivation and received from 5 to 90 reinforced trials. The groups were then subdivided, and extinction (nonrewarded) trials were administered when the animals had been deprived for either 3 or 22 hours. Figure 3.4 shows the results of these experiments. The figure shows that both the number of reinforced trials (learning or habit strength) and the amount of deprivation (drive) influence resistance to extinction. As anticipated, the greater the magnitude of drive during the extinction trials, and the greater the number of reinforced trials during original learning, the stronger the tendency to emit the previously learned response. The curves representing the two deprivation groups also diverge. This reveals that the relation between drive and habit is multiplicative. As just discussed, if the two determinants were related additively, the curves would be parallel rather than divergent. The general pattern of results reported by Perin and Williams has been replicated many times with somewhat different experimental procedures and various dependent variables (see reviews in Bolles, 1975; Brown, 1961).

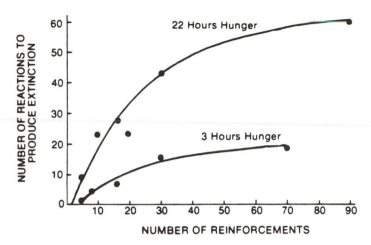

Figure 3.4. Graphic representation showing the combined effects of two levels of drive (hours of deprivation) and habit (number of reinforced trials) on resistance to extinction. (Adapted from Perin, 1942, p. 101.)

Consider now a subtler hypothesis and experiment from research conducted by Newman (1955). This experiment is one demonstration of the power of Hullian motivational theory, in part due to specifying the mathematical relations between the terms in the theory. It is doubtful that such complex predictions often generalize to human motivation, but this does not detract from the sophistication of the conception.

Newman trained rats to run toward a circle for food when under 23½ hours of food deprivation. After training, half of the animals were shifted toward a higher level of deprivation (48 hours), while the rest were shifted downward (12 hours' deprivation). This manipulation created a high- and a low-drive group at the time of testing. In addition, within each of the groups, some of the animals were tested with a circle of the same diameter as the one used in training, while for other animals the diameter was changed. The question raised is, What are the effects of varying deprivation level (drive) and the similarity of the training and testing stimulus (associative or habit strength) on performance level?

Some simple mathematical procedures supply the answer to this question and elucidate Hull's theory. For the group high in drive (D_H), the strength of motivation is represented as

$$\text{motivation} = D_H \times H$$

The strength of motivation for the low-drive (D_L) group is

$$\text{motivation} = D_L \times H$$

Thus the difference in motivation between the two groups is

$$(D_H \times H) - (D_L \times H) \text{ or } H(D_H - D_L)$$

It therefore follows that as H (habit) decreases, the motivational differences between the high- and the low-drive groups also will decrease. Substituting a few numbers will clarify this point. Assume that $D_H = 5$, $D_L = 2$, $H_H = 4$, and $H_L = 1$. Given a high habit strength ($H_H = 4$), the motivations of the drive groups are

$$\text{motivation (high drive)} = 5 \times 4 = 20$$

$$\text{motivation (low drive)} = 2 \times 4 = 8$$

But for the low-habit ($H_L = 1$) condition, the strengths of motivation are

$$\text{motivation (high drive)} \times 5 \times 1 = 5$$

$$\text{motivation (low drive)} = 2 \times 1 = 2$$

Note that the difference in motivation between the high- and low-drive groups ($20 - 8$ versus $5 - 2$) decreases as habit strength decreases from 4 to 1. It follows that, in the experiment by Newman, as the diameter of the training circle increasingly differs between the periods of training and testing (thus decreasing habit strength), the differences in performance between the high- and low-drive groups will decrease. However, in all cases the groups with high deprivation will exhibit greater motivation than the groups low in deprivation if habit strength is equal for both groups.

The data from Newman's study are shown in Figure 3.5. As drive theory predicts, the curves tend to converge as habit or associative strength, which in this situation is a function of the similarity of the training and testing circles, decreases. In sum, Hullian theory is able to make precise predictions that are derived from basic motivational postulates.

Evidence for Drive as a Pooled Energy Source

The conception of drive as a pooled energy source has been tested with a variety of experimental procedures. In one paradigm, attempts are made to demonstrate that responses acquired under one deprivation condition (the "relevant" drive) can be energized by a different biological deficit (the "irrelevant" drive). The prototypical experiment utilizing this methodology was conducted by Webb (1949). Webb trained rats to make a simple instrumental response to attain food while the animals were under 22 hours of food deprivation. The animals then were tested under varying degrees of water deprivation while satiated with food. Table 3.3 shows that resistance to extinction of the response instrumental to the attainment of food

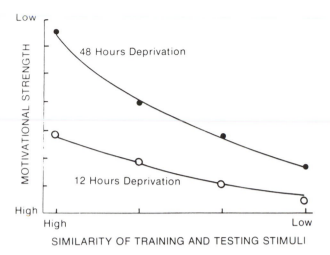

Figure 3.5. Data from Newman (1955) showing the joint effects of hours of deprivation and habit strength on motivation (response latency). Habit strength was varied by manipulating the similarity of the stimuli during the training and testing periods. (Adapted from Spence, 1958a, p. 84.)

is a function of the amount of water deprivation during testing (Groups I-IV), although extinction is slowest when nonreward is introduced under the conditions present during initial learning (Group V). This type of study, however, has been subject to some criticism, for hunger and thirst are not independent. Thirsty rats do not eat as much as rats that are not thirsty. Thus the rats on greater water deprivation also may have been hungrier.

TABLE 3.3 Measures Obtained During Extinction

Group	N	Motivating Condition (Hours of Deprivation) Hunger	Thirst	Mean Number of Responses to Extinction
I	18	0	0	2.8
II	18	0	3	5.2
III	18	0	12	5.1
IV	18	0	22	7.2
V	16	22	0	14.2

Source: Adapted from Webb (1949, p. 10).

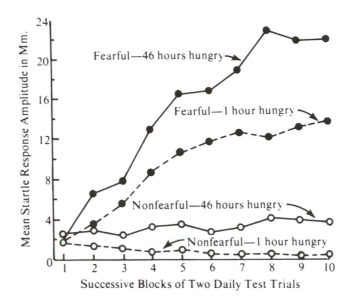

Figure 3.6. Investigation by Meryman (1952) examining startle-response amplitude as a function of fear, no fear, intense hunger, weak hunger, and their combinations.

Another experimental procedure used to demonstrate that drive is an aggregate of various sources of motivation employs fear or shock in conjunction with a deprivation condition. This general procedure is illustrated in an experiment conducted by Meryman (1952). Meryman investigated whether food deprivation would influence the sound-induced startle response, and whether hunger and fear together would produce greater augmentation of startle than either of these motivators acting alone. Some of Meryman's animals learned to fear a stimulus during the training period. Then fearful and nonfearful animals were deprived of food for either an hour or 46 hours. The amplitude of a startle response to a loud noise for the four groups (2 levels of fear × 2 levels of hunger) was tested. The results are presented in Figure 3.6, which shows that the group both fearful and hungry exhibits the greatest amplitude of startle, while the nonhungry, nonfearful group manifests the least intensity of response. This is in accord with the conceptualization of drive as a pooled energy source that multiplies all habits aroused in a stimulus situation.

Secondary (Learned) Drives

It is evident that humans engage in behaviors that are not energized by the absence of food or water or by the presence of a pain-inducing stimulus.

That is, behaviors occur when primary drives are lacking. But given the logic of Hull's conception of motivation, there must exist a drive in these situations that is activating the behavior. Thus Hull and his associates increasingly emphasized the importance of *learned* or secondary drives.

Fear as a Learned Drive

The basic procedure in the investigation of fear as an acquired drive (Miller, 1948; summarized in Miller, 1951; Mowrer, 1960) is straightforward. Rats are placed in a two-compartment shuttle box. One of the compartments is painted white; the other is black (see Figure 3.7). The two compartments are separated by a door. When placed in the white compartment, the animals receive an electric shock. The construction of the apparatus permits escape from the shock by running through the door into the black compartment. Initially the animals make this escape response with a relatively long latency and, when receiving the shock, exhibit signs of fear and pain, such as urination, defecation, and squealing. When the rats are subsequently placed in the white compartment, the escape response rises in their response hierarchy, and the response latency becomes shorter and shorter. After a number of trials, the animals run into the black compartment before actually being shocked. That is, they *avoid* rather than *escape* the shock.

The experimental procedure then is slightly modified. The door between the black and white sides remains closed when the animals attempt to escape. A new response, such as turning a wheel that opens the door, is required for escape. Further, the shock in the white compartment is not turned on. In this situation the animals again initially exhibit signs of fear when they discover that their previous avenue of escape is no longer available. They then engage in what appear to be random activities. But eventually some of the animals discover the response that enables them to escape. Again, over trials, this response is made with a shorter and shorter latency. (Some of the animals in this situation freeze and do not discover the correct response.)

This experiment had tremendous impact on Hull's conception of motivation. Recall that according to Hull a tissue need acts as a drive and goads the organism into activity. Given no deficits, Hull argued, it would be maladaptive for the organism to continue to expend energy. Yet, in the second phase of Miller's experiment, a new response is learned when the shock is off. In that condition, what motivates the organism or energizes the behavior? There is no damage to any body tissue before the onset of shock. Within the framework of Hull's 1943 conception of behavior, it is impossible to explain the activation of avoidance responses.

Hull corrected this deficit in his 1951 book, *Essentials of Behavior*, in which he distinguished between primary and secondary sources of drive: "It is a matter of common observation that situations which are associated

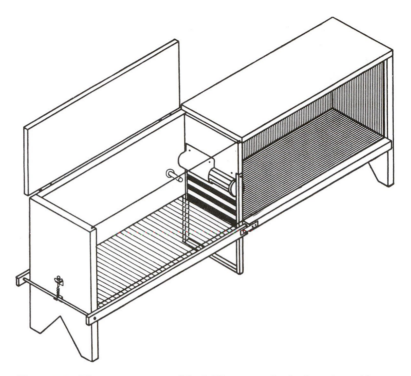

Figure 3.7. The apparatus used by Miller to study the learning of fear. The left compartment is painted white; the right, black. The striped black and white door can be raised so the rat can go from the white into the black compartment, and a shock can be administered through the floor of the white compartment. (From Miller, 1948.)

with drives themselves become . . . drives. . . . Such acquired associative conditions . . . have motivational powers" (pp. 21-22).

In Miller's investigation the cues in the white compartment were contiguously associated with a drive state induced by shock. Therefore, the cues acquired the character of the drive itself. That is, they become secondary drives, or secondary motivators of behavior. Miller and Mowrer labeled this secondary drive fear, or anxiety, which is a learned emotional reaction.

Brown (1961) has contended that many human actions are mediated by learned fear. For example, he states:

> In many instances, if not all, where adult human behavior has been strongly marked by money-seeking responses there appears to be little need for postulating the operation of a learned money-seeking drive. One does not learn to have a drive for money. Instead, one learns to become anxious in the presence of a variety of cues signifying the absence of money. The obtaining of money automatically terminates or drastically alters such cues, and in so doing, produces a decrease in anxiety. (p. 14)

Brown may have emphasized the importance of anxiety in money-seeking behavior because it has proven difficult for stimuli paired with appetitive drives to become secondary drives. This could be because the onset of drives such as hunger and thirst is a relatively slow process. Hull recognized that for something to become a secondary drive, there must be a rapid change in the primary drive state.

An Alteration in the Conception of Action

The investigations of learned fear changed the 1943 Hullian conception of motivation. Sources of drive were no longer limited to tissue deficits. Rather, any internal stimulus could acquire drive properties, if it had sufficient intensity. That is, strong internal stimuli motivate behavior. The conception of drive advocated by Hull in 1951 was

drive operation ⟶ internal stimuli (if intense) ⟶ energize behavior

Incentives

The expansion of Hullian theory to incorporate secondary drives was accompanied by another important conceptual development: the inclusion of the incentive value of the goal, or the properties of the goal object, as a motivator of behavior. The late acknowledgment of the independent role of incentives in motivation was, in part, due to the relatively narrow focus of the early experimental investigators. Researchers employing the Columbia Obstruction Box, for example, rarely manipulated the quantity or the quality of the incentive in the goal box. When they did vary incentives, it was because they believed that the goal object must be appropriate to the drive being manipulated (e.g., food when the animals are hungry, and water when they are thirsty). But subsequent investigators, particularly those under the direction of Edward Tolman, became concerned with the behavioral consequences of a *change* in incentives during the course of learning. These investigations led to the emergence of incentive as a determinant of performance.

Latent Learning

The classic experiment involving an incentive change was conducted by Blodgett (1929). In Blodgett's investigation, three groups of rats were trained in a multiple T-maze to approach a reward of food. One group of animals received food at the goal box on every trial. A second group

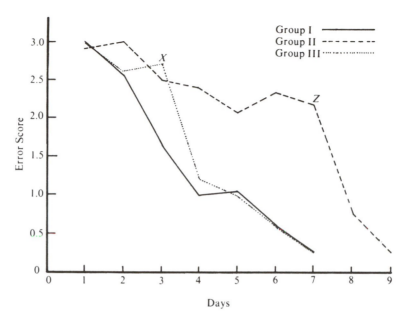

Figure 3.8. The latent learning phenomenon. Group I was given a food reward on every trial. In Group II, the food reward was not introduced until the seventh day (at point Z). In Group III, the food reward was introduced the third day (at point X). Both Group II and Group III show a substantial decrease in errors after the first rewarded trial. (From Blodgett, 1929, p. 120.)

received nothing for two trials, and then food was introduced at the goal box. For a third group of rats, there was no reward for six trials, then food on all subsequent trials. The groups' error scores, which serve as an index of the effectiveness of behavior when running through the maze, are shown in Figure 3.8. It is clear from Figure 3.8 that immediate and disproportionately large drops in errors occur in the performance of the groups first receiving rewards on the third and seventh trials.

An experiment by Crespi (1942) also varied the rate incentive value of the goal. But instead of changing the incentive value from zero to a large amount, Crespi shifted the magnitude of reward during the course of his experiment. One group of animals, after receiving a reward of 256 food pellets, found a reward of only 16 pellets at the goal. On the other hand, a group of rats receiving only 1 pellet was also shifted to the 16-pellet reward. A third group consistently received 16 pellets.

The data from this investigation, shown in Figure 3.9, again reveal abrupt shifts in the performance levels of the groups. The decreased-reward group displayed immediate declines in performance, while the increased-reward group showed marked performance increments. A particularly interesting aspect of the data is that the decreased-reward group responded below the level of the third group, which received consistent rewards. This

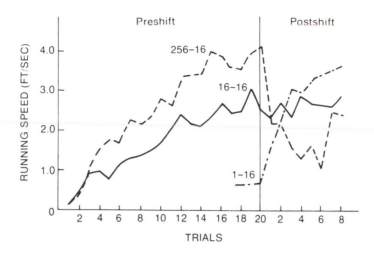

Figure 3.9. Speed of running in a long runway as a function of amount of reinforcement. For the first 19 trials different groups were given 1, 16, or 256 pellets of food (acquisition data for the 1-pellet group are not presented); after trial 20 all subjects were given 16 pellets. (Adapted from Crespi, 1942.)

has been termed the "depression effect," and is now well documented in the literature (see Bolles, 1975). In addition, the increased-reward group responded above the level of the consistent-reward group. This has been termed the "elation effect," but it is not a reliable finding.

The results of the studies reviewed above had important implications for Hull's conception of behavior. In these experiments the changes in the level of performance occurred suddenly and dramatically, soon after the introduction or change of the reward. Therefore, it follows that incentive does not influence habit (or at least not only habit), for habits do not vary abruptly, but grow in incremental fashion with each rewarded trial. In addition, within the Hullian framework as presented thus far, it is impossible to account for the performance decrements exhibited in Crespi's experiment when the reward was shifted downward. Drive level had not changed, and habit strength did not decrease, for the response was still being rewarded. Thus these investigations posed a challenge to Hullian theory.

To account for the data discussed above, Hull (1951) included incentive value as a determinant of performance. His altered conception of behavior specified that motivation is determined by drive, habit, and incentive:

$$\text{motivation} = \text{drive} \times \text{habit} \times \text{incentive}$$

This expansion in Hull's conception enabled the theory to incorporate the results of the research discussed above. Consider, for example, the findings reported by Crespi. Changing the magnitude of the incentive increases or decreases the strength of motivation. This, theoretically, is expected to change the level of exhibited performance.

Contrasting Drive and Incentive

The equation introduced above shows that drive and incentive multiply habit strength or activate learned responses. Indeed, it later was suggested by Spence that incentive and drive be added together, inasmuch as they both energize behavior. Why, then, is there a distinction between drive and incentive as motivators of behavior?

The main difference between these two determinants of action is that drive corresponds to a "push," while incentives "pull" the organism (see Bolles, 1975). The two concepts also are tied to different antecedent conditions. Drive typically is influenced by hours of deprivation, while the incentive value of the goal varies as a function of some property of the goal object, such as its magnitude or taste. Finally, the incentive value of the goal must be learned; the organism is not affected until it "realizes" the value or has knowledge about the goal object. Since incentive value necessitates some learning, the clear distinction between an energizer and a habit that Hull initially maintained had to be discarded when the new conception was introduced.

Incentive, Learning, and Purposive Behavior

The manner in which incentives are learned and function as motivators was clarified by Spence (1956), although in the early 1930s Hull had made similar suggestions. Spence contended that events in the goal box, or the goal responses (R_G), become conditioned to the cues in the goal box. That is, the cues in the goal box come to produce goal responses automatically because of their immediate contiguity with the presentation of the reward. The goal responses include, for example, chewing and salivation. Furthermore, the goal responses produce their own stimulus feedback (S_G). The goal responses and the stimulus feedback that originate in the goal box then generalize to situations that resemble the goal box. Thus if an organism is placed in a straight runway and fed at a goal box, the pattern of responses and stimulus feedback also will be displayed at the start of the runway (see Figure 3.10).

The runway goal responses are labeled by Spence as *fractional anticipatory goal responses*. They are "fractional" because the entire goal response is not emitted (e.g., eating behavior is not possible at the start of the alley because food is not yet available). And they are "anticipatory" because the animals appear to be expecting a reward. They lick their lips, salivate, and make chewing motions (for criticisms of this point, see Bindra, 1969; Bolles,

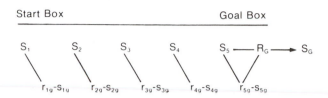

Figure 3.10. Stimulus situation in a straight runway, according to Spence.

1975). Hence one might infer that the animals are acting in a purposive manner and have foresight of the goal when at the start box. However, Hull and Spence would argue that this mentalistic analysis is incorrect. The stimuli and response associations direct the organism, and incentive and drive produce the energy. Thoughts are not needed to account for behavior.

Spence states that the anticipatory goal response $(r_g - s_g)$ is the mechanism that underlies the incentive construct. The goal responses, by producing their own stimulation, increase the total amount of internal stimuli acting on the organism. Miller's studies of fear as a learned drive resulted in the belief that any strong stimulus would act as a drive. Therefore, because incentives generate an increment in the internal stimulus situation, they have drive properties. This conceptual change had great popularity and influence in the study of motivated behavior in the 1950s, and in the early part of the 1960s.

In the preceding pages a very brief overview of drive theory has been presented. Although the theory was not examined in detail, it is evident that it can account for a great deal of the data generated by hungry and thirsty rats running down a straight runway or a T-maze for a reward. In the remaining sections of this chapter, anxiety, conflict and displacement, frustration, social facilitation, and cognitive dissonance are examined from the drive theoretical framework. These are phenomena more clearly related to human motivation.

Anxiety

Anxiety is one of the most frequently used psychological terms, permeating the vocabularies of both professional psychologists and laypersons. A theoretical analysis directly integrating anxiety into drive theory is shown in Figure 3.11, which depicts a conceptual framework for the analysis of aversive events, such as those associated with physical pain. For example, a neutral cue, such as a tone, is presented prior to the onset of an

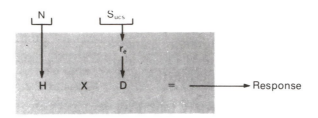

Figure 3.11. Portion of theoretical schema relevant to data for classical conditioning. (Adapted from Spence, 1958b, p. 131.)

aversive stimulus, such as a puff of air to the eye. The investigator is then interested in the likelihood of closure of the eyelid given the presentation of the conditioned tone stimulus.

The symbols outside the box in Figure 3.11 signify linkages with the external world that are manipulable by, or visible to, the experimenter. The terms inside the box are constructs, or intervening variables, that are inferred by the experimenter. It can be seen in this figure that habit strength (H) is determined by the number (N) of prior presentations of the conditioned and unconditioned stimuli (tone and air puff). Drive (D) is determined by the strength of the unconditioned stimulus (S_{ucs}), such as the force of the air puff. In addition, in aversive situations it is assumed that drive is mediated by a persisting, emotional response (r_e). This emotional response is similar to the notion of fear proposed by Miller and Mowrer. That is, the air puff causes the individual to react with a negative emotion, and this affective reaction is presumed to be the mechanism that is responsible for the drive state. Drive and habit, in turn, influence the intensity and the direction of behavior (the eyelid response to the tone), as shown to the right of the box.

One immediate implication of the theory shown in Figure 3.11 is that the reflexive eyelid response to the noxious air puff should vary directly with the manipulated intensity of the stimulus. That is, the greater the aversiveness of the puff, the greater the inferred emotional reaction and magnitude of induced drive. Increased drive augments motivation and the likelihood of the conditioned response (eyelid closure).

Spence (1958a) reports a number of studies demonstrating that the probability of a conditioned eyelid response is a function of the intensity of a puff of air to the eye. Figure 3.12 portrays the results of one such experiment, in which four different intensities of air puff were used. Subjects were given repeated conditioning trials, thus varying habit strength during the course of the experiment. Figure 3.12 reveals that high puff intensity (drive level) and increased trials (habit strength) augment response strength. In addition, the curves representing the various drive

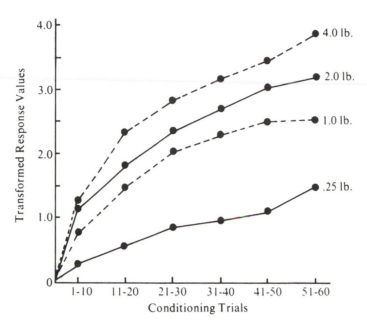

Figure 3.12. Performance during acquisition of eyelid conditioned responses as a function of the intensity of the *UCS* (units in lbs.). (Adapted from Spence, 1958a, p. 78.)

levels diverge over trials, supporting the belief that drive and habit relate multiplicatively.

The Manifest Anxiety Scale

In addition to the strength of the aversive stimulus, scores from an anxiety scale also can be used to infer drive level. Spence and his colleagues reasoned that, given the identical magnitude of an aversive stimulus, some individuals might act as if it were more intense than other individuals. If these highly reactive persons could be identified, then it would be inferred that they are relatively high in drive and, therefore, should exhibit behaviors consistent with this state. Thus anxiety can be operationally defined as a response (an individual difference indicator), rather than exclusively linked with a specified manipulation, such as the strength of an air puff or shock. Note also that the operation of setting two levels of air puff intensity and the operation of setting only one intensity level but identifying two degrees of emotional reactivity (anxiety) are logically equivalent.

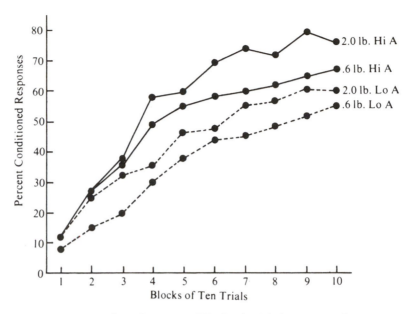

Figure 3.13. Data from Spence and Taylor (1951) showing performance in eyelid conditioning as a function of level of anxiety and intensity of the *UCS*. (Adapted from Spence, 1958b, p. 134.)

To assess the tendency to respond emotionally to an aversive stimulus, Janet Taylor (1953) developed the Manifest Anxiety Scale. The scale consists of 50 keyed items taken from the Minnesota Multiphasic Personality Inventory. These items were agreed upon by four out of five clinicians as being manifestations of high anxiety. Following are two typical items and the anxiety responses:

I cry easily. (true)
I work under a great deal of tension. (true)

Spence and his colleagues have conducted a number of experiments comparing the performance of subjects classified as high or low in anxiety (drive) in eyelid conditioning situations. A representative experimental result obtained by Spence and Taylor (1951) is shown in Figure 3.13. In this investigation, two levels of puff intensity were combined with two levels of emotional reactivity, yielding four different experimental conditions. Examination of Figure 3.13 shows that within each of the levels of puff intensity, subjects high in anxiety (Hi A) exhibited more conditioned eyelid responses than did subjects low in anxiety (Lo A). This adds validity to the contention that the Manifest Anxiety Scale is a measure of drive. In addition, the higher-intensity air puff produces faster conditioning than the lower-intensity puff, as also was found in the research shown in Figure 3.12.

And finally, the divergence of the curves again indicates a multiplicative relationship between drive and habit.

Paired-Associates Learning

Spence and his associates also have applied the drive × habit conception to the learning of simple and complex paired associates. In a paired-associates task, a stimulus, such as a word, is displayed, and the subject must anticipate the response with which it is paired. Spence reasoned that a simple list of paired associates is one in which the correct response is dominant in the person's response hierarchy. That is, the response paired with the stimulus is the most probable response that the individual will give even prior to the learning situation. Spence contended that in this situation an increase in the level of drive will result in faster learning and fewer errors.

The derivation of this hypothesis requires that an increment in drive level increase the absolute difference between the tendencies to emit the correct and incorrect responses to a stimulus. Assume, for example, that a stimulus elicits two responses, one correct (C), the other incorrect (I). Further, assume that the strength of $C = 2$ while the strength of $I = 1$. For a low-drive group ($D = 1$), the difference in the motivation (M) to exhibit the two responses is as follows:

$$D \quad H$$
$$M(C) = 1 \times 2 = 2$$
$$M(I) = 1 \times 1 = 1$$
$$M(C - I) = 2 - 1 = 1$$

However, for a high-drive group ($D = 2$), the difference in the motivational strengths would be represented as follows:

$$D \quad H$$
$$M(C) = 2 \times 2 = 4$$
$$M(I) = 2 \times 1 = 2$$
$$M(C - I) = 4 - 2 = 2$$

Thus the difference between the strengths of motivation between the correct and incorrect responses is greater for persons with high drive. Subjects classified as high in anxiety (drive) therefore are expected to perform better on this simple task than subjects classified as low in anxiety. This analysis is identical to the one in the conditioning experiments, for in those investigations the eyelid reflex also is dominant in the person's hierarchy of responses. Thus the more aversive the puff or the higher the anxiety, the greater the aversive conditioning.

The theoretical analysis of performance on a complex task is more difficult and necessitates the use of concepts not yet introduced. Spence reasoned that a number of competing responses are aroused by the stimuli of a difficult (complex) task. Some of these responses are below the threshold level. *Threshold* here refers to the minimum level of response strength that must be reached before the response can be overtly expressed. The threshold concept, in part, determines the speed of learning on a complex task. Assume a task in which the magnitude of C again is equal to 2. But now assume that there are two competing incorrect responses, $I_1 = 1$ and $I_2 = 2$. Further, assume that the threshold level is 2; that is, 2 units of motivation are necessary for the response to be overtly expressed. For a weak-drive group ($D = 1$) this situation can be represented as follows:

$$D \quad H$$
$$M(C) = 1 \times 2 = 2$$
$$M(I_1) = 1 \times 1 = 1$$
$$M(I_2) = 1 \times 2 = 2$$
$$M(C - I_2) = 2 - 2 = 0$$

Thus the strength of the motivation to give the incorrect response is equal to that of the motivation to give the correct response. I_1 is not included among the competing responses because the strength of motivation to give that response is one unit below the threshold level.

For a strong-drive group ($D = 2$), the situation is conceptualized as follows:

$$D \quad H$$
$$M(C) = 2 \times 2 = 4$$
$$M(I_1) = 2 \times 1 = 2$$
$$M(I_2) = 2 \times 2 = 4$$
$$M[C - (I_1 + I_2)] = 4 - 6 = -2$$

Thus the combined strengths of the incorrect responses exceed that of the correct response by two units, for both I_1 and I_2 are above the threshold level and have some probability of competing with the correct response. Hence, in this situation, the heightening of drive interfered with performance.

An interaction is therefore expected between drive level and performance at easy and complex tasks. Given an easy task, individuals high in drive are expected to perform better than those low in drive. Conversely, given a difficult (complex) task, persons high in drive are expected to perform worse than those in a low-drive group.

Spence and his associates established the experimental conditions they believed necessary to test the above hypotheses (Spence, Farber, & McFann, 1956; Spence, Taylor, & Ketchel, 1956; Taylor & Chapman, 1955). They employed paired-associates tasks and created easy (noncompetitive) and difficult (competitive) lists by varying the degree of preexperimental associations between the stimulus-response pairs in the lists. In the easy list, the stimulus words tend to elicit the responses prior to list learning. Examples include the following:

roving-nomad
tranquil-quiet
pious-devout

Because the response members of the pairs are synonyms of the stimulus members, they are high in the repertoire of response associates to the stimulus words. Heightened drive should therefore increase the differences between the motivation associated with the correct and incorrect responses and facilitate learning.

To create a difficult or competitive list of paired associates, the researchers selected the response members of the pairs from words low in the subject's response hierarchy before the task was started. In addition, incorrect responses that were high in the subject's hierarchy were included among other responses in the list. Examples of pairs used to establish competitive lists include the following:

tranquil-placid
quiet-double
serene-headstrong

The stimulus words in this example are synonyms, and all tend to elicit the response of "placid." Thus two pairings are created in which an incorrect response has a reasonable probability of being elicited.

The actual experiments are straightforward. Subjects scoring in the upper and lower extremes on the Manifest Anxiety Scale form high- and low-drive groups. They then are presented with the stimulus-response pairs, and must correctly anticipate the response members in the list. The results of this research have been in accord with the interaction predicted by drive theory (Spence, 1958b). Thus general laws of behavior based initially on animal research apply to predictions regarding the speed of human learning in a paired-associates task. This is an impressive accomplishment.

Some Reservations

As previously indicated, the purpose of this chapter is the presentation of drive theory from the perspective of its proponents; space has not been given to criticisms or shortcomings. Nonetheless, a word of caution regarding the predictions is warranted, for the ease of the derivations may be more apparent than real (see Weiner, 1972). For example, assume that there exists an easy task in which all the incorrect responses are below threshold for a low-drive group, but, for a high-drive group, some of these responses rise above the threshold. Hence, given this easy task, heightened drive should decrease performance. It is not possible to predict accurately the relative level of performance of high- and low-drive groups without a complete and exact specification of all the potential responses and their numerical strengths as well as an exact statement about the threshold level. Such precision is not possible.

Conflict

Many types of conflict have been identified, but the one most prevalent in human behavior is labeled approach-avoidance conflict. This conflict occurs when both hopes and fears are associated with the same action. For example, we like to buy new clothes, but they are expensive; we want to eat candy bars, but they are fattening; we would like to hit father and be closer to mother, but these actions might be punished.

Observation of approach-avoidance conflicts reveals "ambivalent" behavior. For example, consider a hungry animal in a runway with food at the opposite end and an electrified grid separating it from the food, as in the Columbia Obstruction Box (see Figure 3.1). This illustrates an approach-avoidance conflict, for running down the alleyway will have both beneficial and aversive consequences. In this situation, the animal often approaches the food, turns back from the shock, returns to approach the food, and so on. The behavior oscillates from approach to avoidance, and thus is called ambivalent.

Applying the principles derived from the drive × habit conception of motivation, Miller (1944, 1959) was able to describe and predict behavior in approach-avoidance conflicts. His conflict model is among the most cited works in the study of personality and motivation and well illustrates how mechanistic principles derived from the study of infrahumans can aid in the explanation of complex human behavior. We will see, however, that Miller had to modify certain aspects of drive theory to account for some of his data.

DIAGRAM 3.1 Strength of the Tendency to Approach a Goal in a Runway

	Start Box				Goal
Hunger drive	2	2	2	2	2
Approach habit	1	2	3	4	5
Drive × habit	2	4	6	8	10

Miller's Conflict Model

Miller included six postulates in his analysis of approach-avoidance conflicts. The postulates, and their relations to Hullian theory, are as follows:

Postulate 1: The tendency to approach a goal is stronger the nearer the subject is to it.

Derivation: It is again useful to consider a hungry rat running down a straight runway to receive a food reward. As the animal traverses the runway, drive level, defined operationally as the number of hours of food deprivation, remains relatively constant. That is, hunger does not greatly change as the animal runs toward the food. However, habit strength does vary as a function of distance from the goal, with approach habit increasing as the goal is approached. (This principle from learning theory will not be examined here and must be accepted on faith.) In Diagram 3.1, values are assigned to both drive and habit to illustrate the strength of motivation as the goal box is approached. Drive level is given a constant value of 2, while habit strength varies from 1 to 5. The diagram indicates that approach motivation increases as the animal approaches the goal. Thus it should run faster, pull harder, and so on as the goal box is reached.

Postulate 2: The tendency to avoid a feared stimulus is stronger the nearer the subject is to it.

Derivation: The reasoning is virtually identical to that already given for Postulate 1.

Postulate 3: The strength of the avoidance tendency increases more rapidly with nearness to the goal than does the strength of the approach tendency (see Figure 3.14).

Derivation: This is the key postulate in the conflict model, and follows from principles of drive × habit theory and the conception of fear as an acquired

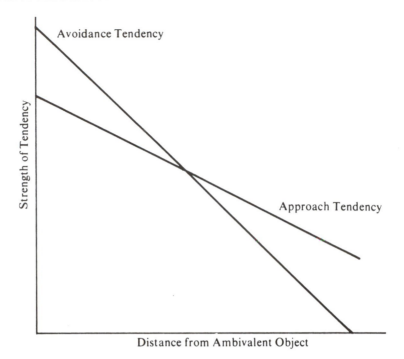

Figure 3.14. Graphic representation of an approach-avoidance conflict situation. The individual has tendencies to approach and withdraw from an object. The point at which the gradients cross indicates the place of maximal conflict.

or learned drive. As already indicated, in an appetitive situation, the level of a drive such as hunger is operationally defined in terms of hours of deprivation. The changes in an animal's appetitive drive during the time it takes to traverse a runway are minimal. On the other hand, in an aversive situation the drive, labeled fear or anxiety, is learned. The degree of fear varies as a function of the similarity between the immediate stimulus situation and the stimuli present at the time the aversive stimulation was received. In a runway it is assumed that the cues in the start box are least similar to the cues in the goal box. Thus if an animal receives shock at the goal, its fear increases as it approaches the goal box. (For example, one exhibits little fear when walking a few feet from the edge of a cliff, but stepping a few paces closer to the edge greatly increases fear.) In addition, the habit strength of avoiding shock also increases as the goal is approached (see Solomon, 1964, for discussion of this point). The avoidance tendency is conceptualized in Diagram 3.2.

When compared with Diagram 3.1, Diagram 3.2 indicates that the avoidance tendency is steeper than the approach tendency (see Figure 3.14). That is, the change in the strength of the tendencies as a function of the distance from the goal, or the slope of the functions, is greater for the

DIAGRAM 3.2 Strength of the Tendency to Avoid a Goal in a Runway

	Start Box				Goal
Fear drive	1	2	3	4	5
Avoidance habit	1	2	3	4	5
Drive × habit	1	4	9	16	25

avoidance than for the approach tendency. This is because both drive and habit vary with distance in the avoidance situation, while, for approach motivation, only habit strength is affected by distance from the goal. This means that when one is a great distance from the goal, the dominant motivation often is that of approach and attraction. But as the goal is approached, feelings of fear may come to dominate overt expression. The potential bride or groom becoming more and more uncertain as the date of the wedding nears, or the little boy running to the water for a toy and then away from the waves, has been observed on many occasions. Figure 3.14 reveals that Miller's theory can account for such oscillation and ambivalence by construing approach and avoidance motivation as differentially influenced by the distance from the goal.

The above analysis suggests that in certain situations the gradient of approach may be steeper than that of avoidance. This should occur when the approach drive is learned and aroused by external stimuli, but the avoidance drive is based upon internal stimuli that do not vary as a function of distance from the goal. For example, if sexual avoidance behavior is influenced by a strong and fixed superego, while sexual approach drives are aroused by cognitions, such as the sight of an attractive partner, then the steepness of the approach and avoidance gradients might be reversed. This should lead to all-or-none behavior. That is, the individual either will totally avoid the goal or, once beyond the point of ambivalence, will go directly to the goal.

Postulate 4: The strength of the tendencies to approach or avoid the goal varies directly with the strength of the drive on which they are based.

Derivation: This follows because the gradients are determined by drive level multiplying habit strength. Hence increasing drive, or habit, increases the strength of the motivational tendencies. This postulate suggests that drive is not nondirective, but selective; only the relevant habit is energized by an increment in drive. If drive multiplies habits both relevant and irrelevant to the specific source of drive, as the drive × habit conception specifies, then as hunger increases, the strength of both the approach and avoidance tendencies will increase. It would then be impossible to conclude that animals approach closer to a goal given increased hours of food depriva-

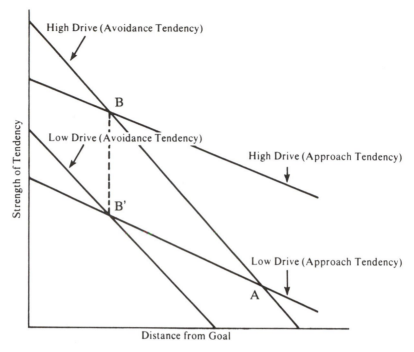

Figure 3.15. Graphic representation of an approach-avoidance conflict situation in which the drive generated by food deprivation also energizes the avoidance habit. The animal does not approach closer to the goal although food deprivation has increased (low-low [B'] versus high-high [B]) intersection.

tion. This is illustrated in Figure 3.15, where it can be seen that both the approach and avoidance tendencies are enhanced by increased food deprivation; there is no change in the distance traversed toward the goal in this particular situation (compare B and B'). However, if only approach behavior is influenced by deprivation level, then the organisms will approach closer to the goal (e.g., from Point A to Point B, if there is a high avoidance tendency). Thus Miller does not accept the totally nondirective conception of drive.

Postulate 5: Below the level of the asymptote of learning, increasing the number of reinforced trials increases the strength of the response tendency that is reinforced.

Derivation: Identical with Postulate 4.

Postulate 6: When two incompatible response tendencies are in conflict, the stronger one will be expressed.

Tests of the Model

Miller, Brown, and others have conducted a number of experiments to test Miller's conflict model. In one of the original investigations, Brown (1948) developed a technique to measure the strength of approach and avoidance tendencies in rats. Each rat was fitted with a harness device that allowed the experimenter to assess how hard it pulled. Animals that had been trained in separate goal boxes either to approach food or to avoid a shock were placed at various distances from the food or shock. As hypothesized, the strength of pull varied directly as a function of distance from the goal. In addition, the distance from the shock compartment influenced the intensity of the pull away from the shock more than the distance from the reward compartment influenced the pull toward the food. This finding has often been replicated.

Miller's Conflict Model and Displacement

Displacement refers to the observation that objects of behavior change although the desire to attain the original goal has not subsided. Freud contended that there are "vicissitudes of the instincts"; in other words, there are a variety of goals that may satisfy an underlying wish. The most frequently cited example of such displacement activity is in the study of aggression. It is often pointed out that the worker in the family cannot express anger at the boss, and therefore comes home to "take it out" on the unsuspecting mate. In one primitive society, displacement activities are institutionalized. Outside every hut is a dog; when the male of the household is angry, he may punish this unfortunate animal. Freud (1915/1934) used a similar but humorous example to illustrate displacement:

> There was a blacksmith in the village who had committed a capital offense. The Court decided that the crime must be punished; but as the blacksmith was the only one in the village and was indispensable, and as on the other hand, there were three tailors living there, one of *them* was hanged instead. (pp. 174-175)

Displacement activity, or the shifting of goal objects, has been incorporated into Miller's conflict model. Consider the employee who is angry at the boss, but does not directly express this hostility. Miller reasoned that the aggressive tendency directed toward the supervisor is inhibited by a stronger avoidance tendency. Thus the person will respond aggressively only to someone similar to the boss (e.g., the person's spouse). Aggression is expressed "farther" from the goal because the change in the stimulus situation reduces the avoidance more than the approach drive. This analysis assumes that the spouse, for example, is similar to the boss along some psychological dimension.

Figure 3.16. Example of the dynamics of displacement.

If the horizontal or X axis in Figure 3.15 is altered so that it represents objects, rather than temporal distance, then displacement behavior can be readily illustrated within Miller's conflict model (see Figure 3.16). Figure 3.16 indicates that there is an approach tendency to aggress against the boss, and an inhibitory motivation that functions to prevent direct hostile expression. The individual in this situation would not aggress against the boss, because at that point avoidance or inhibitory motivation exceeds approach motivation. The aggression theoretically would be expressed at the point of gradient intersection (the neighbor) or the point at which the approach motivation most exceeds the avoidance motivation (the dog). Thus the aggressive behavior is "displaced," that is, directed toward objects that did not provoke the action.

Miller has derived a number of postulates concerning displacement activity from his conflict model. A few of these postulates, along with illustrative examples, are listed here:

(1) When the direct response to the original stimulus is prevented by the absence of that stimulus, displaced responses will occur to other similar stimuli, and the strongest displaced response will occur to the most similar stimulus present. For example, a girl who is prevented from marrying her sweetheart by his death, and who is completely recovered from her grief and other possibly negative factors, will be expected to prefer the suitor who is most similar to him.

(2) When the direct response to the original stimulus is prevented by conflict, the strongest displaced response will occur to stimuli that have an intermediate degree of similarity to the original one. Thus a girl who is prevented from marrying her sweetheart by a violent quarrel would

be expected subsequently to prefer someone not completely similar to, but not completely different from, the sweetheart.

(3) If the relative strength of the inhibitory response is increased, the point of strongest displacement, and hence object choice, will shift in the direction of stimuli that are less similar to the original one eliciting the direct response. In other words, the more unhappy the girl's experience with her previous sweetheart, the less similar should be her choice of a second love object. (Miller, 1959, pp. 218-219)

In sum, it is again evident that principles derived from Hullian drive theory and the study of infrahumans can explain some complex human behaviors and their resolution.

Frustration

Frustration has a diversity of meanings for psychologists. The term may refer to an independent variable, or to experimental manipulation. Often this involves blocking the attainment of a goal, inducing failure, or delivering a personal insult. Performance of a "frustrated" group is then compared with the performance of a "nonfrustrated" or control group to assess the effects of the independent manipulation. Frustration also may have reference to a dependent variable, in which case the investigator measures the amount of frustrated behavior. For example, one might examine whether individuals high in anxiety display more frustrated behavior than persons low in anxiety. Finally, frustration frequently pertains to an intervening variable, or a complex process that is inferred from certain observable responses. For example, on the basis of observed aggressive behavior, one might conclude that an individual is frustrated. Many response indicators of frustration have been observed in laboratory situations. These responses include aggression, enhanced goal striving, fixation, and regression. Drive theory, as might be expected, is best able to explain the instigating or enhancing properties of frustration.

The Brown-Farber Theory of Frustration

Brown and Farber (1951) assumed that frustration results from interference with an ongoing action. The source of the interference may be something that delays response completion, such as a barrier or a competing habit. For example, frustration may be experienced when a flat tire prevents someone from playing in a baseball game, or when a person's competing habits interfere with one another while he or she is batting, thus

TABLE 3.4 Latency of Crying as a Function of Time of Withdrawal of Bottle

Ounces of Milk Taken Before Withdrawal	Latency of Crying (in seconds)
0.5	5.0
2.5	9.9
4.5	11.5

Source: Sears and Sears (1940, p. 298). *Journal of Psychology, 9*, pp. 297-300, 1940. Reprinted with permission of the Helen Dwight Reid Educational Foundation. Published by Heldref Publications, 1319 18th Street, N.W., Washington, D.C. 20036-1802. Copyright 1940.

resulting in the person's failure to get a hit. Brown and Farber postulated that frustration has drive properties and that the drive generated by goal thwarting multiplies all the habits aroused in a particular situation.

In one study guided by this conception, Haner and Brown (1955) hypothesized that the amount of frustration produced following goal interference is a function of the strength of motivation to reach the goal. Thus, for example, the more one wants to get to the baseball game, the greater the frustration that results from a flat tire. Following drive theory, Haner and Brown conceived motivation to be equal to drive × habit. Thus they expected that frustration would be positively related to the magnitude of the drive being prevented and the habit strength of the goal response.

Haner and Brown manipulated habit strength in an experimental investigation by employing a task that required subjects to place marbles in holes. To complete the activity, subjects had to fill 36 holes within a given time. The experimenters interrupted the subjects (children) after they had filled 25%, 50%, 75%, 89%, or 100% of the holes. Guided by the work of Miller and others, Haner and Brown assumed that the closer the person was to the goal, the greater the strength of approach motivation. In this example, the experimenters assumed that "distance" from the goal, defined as the number of marble completions, theoretically corresponds to the strength of the habit to approach the goal.

Interruption was signaled by a buzzer, followed by the marbles falling to the bottom of the apparatus. The subjects could then push a plunger that turned the buzzer off and allowed them to begin the next trial. The measure of the dependent variable in the experiment, or index of frustration, was the pressure the subjects exerted when pushing the plunger.

The results of the study are shown in Figure 3.17. The data reveal that the intensity of the push response is a function of the distance from the goal at the time of thwarting. Thus Haner and Brown's hypothesis is supported. The results apparently demonstrate the nondirective energizing function of a frustration drive.

Well before the Farber-Brown conceptualization, a study relevant to their thinking was conducted by Sears and Sears (1940). These investigators produced frustration in infants by withdrawing the bottle during feeding. They then measured the latency of the crying response. The results of this study are given in Table 3.4. As the table shows, the greater the frustration

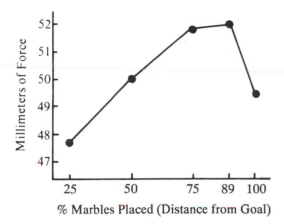

Figure 3.17. The effects of frustration related to five degrees of goal proximity. The dependent variable was the millimeters of force exerted following the interruption of the task. (Adapted from Haner & Brown, 1955, p. 205.)

(the less the hunger satisfaction), the faster was the prepotent crying response. This is in accordance with the belief that frustration has drive properties and energizes habits.

Amsel's Theory of Frustration

The most systematic theoretical analysis of frustration from the drive theoretical perspective is the work of Amsel and his colleagues (Amsel, 1967, 1990; Amsel & Ward, 1954, 1965). These investigators related frustration to nondirective drive and built upon the model of Brown and Farber. Amsel and Roussel (1952) defined frustration as a state resulting from the nonreinforcement of a response that had been consistently reinforced. That is, if an expectancy of reward is established and the response no longer results in a reward, frustration is experienced. The more one expects a reward, the greater the frustration that occurs when the reward is not given. Amsel conceived of frustration as having drive properties. In addition, Amsel postulated that frustration is aversive and that cues similar to those present when frustration is encountered also generate some degree of frustration.

This theory becomes clearer when one considers Spence's analysis of the $r_g - s_g$ mechanism that underlies the incentive value of a goal. Recall that, according to Spence, originally neutral cues elicit the expectation of a reward because these or similar cues appear during the time of reward. In a similar manner, Amsel asserted that originally neutral cues paired with frustration become aversive. And cues similar to those appearing when frustration is experienced also become aversive. Therefore, following the failure to attain an expected reward in a straight-runway situation, the

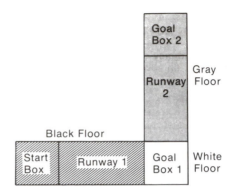

Figure 3.18. Apparatus for the demonstration of the frustration effect used by Amsel and Roussel (1952).

animal experiences frustration throughout the runway. Amsel labeled the frustration experienced before entering the goal chamber "anticipatory frustration." Again guided by Spence, Amsel suggested that frustration responses produce their own pattern of stimulus feedback. The increased internal stimulation accounts for the drive properties of frustration.

A demonstration of the drive properties of nonreward was reported by Amsel and Roussel (1952). These experimenters employed an apparatus in which two runways were joined (see Figure 3.18). The goal box in the first runway served as the starting box for the second runway. During the training period the animals were fed in both the first and second goal boxes; in the testing phase, food was withheld in the first goal box. Amsel and Roussel reported that following nonreward in the first goal box, the vigor of performance in the second runway increased above the previous level. They contended that this performance increment demonstrates the drive effects of frustration. The immediately augmented response strength following nonattainment of an expected reward is termed the "frustration effect."

Additional research isolated some of the determinants of the frustration effect. For example, the energizing effects of frustration increase as a function of the number of rewarded trials (Marzocco, 1951). This logically follows from Amsel's theory, for the greater the number of reinforced trials, the greater the anticipation of the reward, and the greater the amount of experienced frustration when reward does not follow the instrumental response. Amsel also was able to use this theory to account for extinction (the lack of responding when reward is no longer expected) and the partial reinforcement effect (the fact that resistance to extinction is greater given partial rather than continuous reward). However, these phenomena are not intimately related to drive theory per se, and thus will not be examined here (see Amsel, 1990).

Social Facilitation

Some questions of primary interest to social psychologists also have been examined from the perspective of drive theory. Foremost among these is: "What is the effect of the mere presence of other individuals upon the *performance* of the single individual?" (Cottrell, 1972, p. 185). This has been called the study of *social facilitation*, even though it has been demonstrated that other individuals can impede, as well as augment, task performance.

When two or more people act together, the intensity of their individual behavior often increases. Social facilitation among both humans and infrahumans is well documented in the experimental literature. For example, as early as 1897, Triplett observed that bicycle racers seem to ride faster when in direct competition with others. To test this notion, Triplett had riders race alone (against a clock), with a "pacer," or against another rider. As expected, the presence of a second rider resulted in a faster bicycle speed. Social facilitation also has been reported by other investigators examining performance at a variety of activities, particularly simple motor-learning tasks.

Perhaps surprisingly, the bulk of the early research concerning social facilitation was conducted with infrahumans. For example, socially enhanced eating by chicks is a relatively well substantiated phenomenon: Chicks eat more in the presence of other chicks than they do when eating alone. Fish and rats also consume more when in the presence of others. In a similar manner, responses such as running, pecking, and nest building are augmented among a variety of infrahumans given the presence of members of their own species (see reviews by Cottrell, 1972; Zajonc, 1965).

Three distinctive paradigms have been identified in the research on social facilitation. The first is the *audience* paradigm, in which one performs in the presence of passive spectators. Second is a *coaction* paradigm, in which others in the same setting are independently engaged in the identical tasks as the performer. Finally, there is an *interactive* paradigm, in which numerous individuals are working together on a task. To account for social facilitation, researchers have proposed various interpretations that are differentially applicable to the three social paradigms.

The Drive Theory Interpretation

The drive theory explanation of social facilitation, first proposed by Zajonc (1965), contends that the observer or the coacting worker induces an irrelevant drive (see Weiss & Miller, 1971). Inasmuch as the presence of others allegedly increases drive level, it follows that performance increments, or social facilitation, should occur on tasks for which the correct or measured response is dominant in habit strength. The increased drive level multiplies habit strength, augmenting the difference between the likelihood of responding with the dominant versus the subordinate response. Hence performance at simple motor tasks (e.g., eating responses among hungry infrahumans) should be facilitated in social settings. On the other hand, performance at difficult tasks, or during early phases of learning, should be impeded by the presence of others because the incorrect responses dominant in the individual's habit hierarchy are most augmented by the heightened drive. Note that Zajonc's analysis is identical to the one presented earlier in this chapter concerning the relation between level of drive (score on the Manifest Anxiety Scale) and performance on easy and complex paired-associates tasks. A review of the social facilitation literature by Zajonc (1965) revealed a great deal of support for the hypothesized interaction between task difficulty and the presence or absence of others.

Zajonc and others performed a number of experiments that directly tested the drive interpretation of social facilitation (see, e.g., Cottrell, Wack, Sekarak, & Rittle, 1968; Zajonc & Sales, 1966). These experiments all involve "pseudorecognition" perceptual tasks, word associations, or task performance.

Pseudorecognition

In an experiment by Cottrell et al. (1968), nonsense words were first presented at unequal frequencies (1, 2, 5, 10, or 25 repetitions). This created disparate levels of habit strength or response potency. These words were then exposed on a tachistoscope for very brief time intervals, and subjects were instructed to report the words they had seen. However, on crucial "pseudorecognition" trials nothing was exposed. Half the subjects were tested alone; the rest were tested in front of an audience of two other individuals.

The results of this study are depicted in Figure 3.19, which shows that subjects responding in front of an audience were significantly more likely to respond with words of high response strength (frequent exposure) than subjects tested alone, and less likely to respond with words of lower response strength. These findings are in accord with the hypotheses derived from drive theory. A third condition in the study, labeled "mere presence," will be discussed later.

Zajonc (1965) offers an interesting implication of this work:

> If one were to draw one practical suggestion from the review of the social-facilitation effects which are summarized in this article, he would advise the student to study all alone, preferably in an isolated cubicle, and to arrange to take his examinations in the company of many other students, on stage, and in the presence of a large audience. The results of his examination would be beyond his wildest expectations, provided, of course, he had learned his material quite thoroughly. (p. 274)

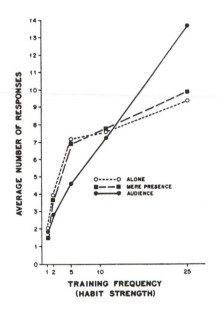

Figure 3.19. Number of responses of different training frequency classes emitted on the pseudorecognition trials. (From Cottrell, Wack, Sekarak, & Rittle, 1968, p. 247.)

Cottrell (1972) then took issue with Zajonc's analysis, while still maintaining belief in a drive theory explanation. According to Cottrell, the drive induced by the presence of others is learned rather than biologically rooted, and is acquired because the presence of others frequently is paired with reward or punishment. Thus other people become secondary sources of drive, inducing positive incentive motivation or conditioned fear. Because it has proven exceedingly difficult to establish secondary positive motivators of behavior, Cottrell's theoretical analysis of social facilitation emphasizes the anticipated aversive consequences, or the elicitation of anxiety and fear, in the presence of others. Thus the "mere presence" of others is not a sufficient explanation of social facilitation, according to Cottrell. Rather, facilitation (or impediment) occurs because others are potential evaluators, and individuals experience apprehension or anxiety in situations in which evaluative judgments about them may be made.

Cottrell et al. (1968) included a crucial experimental condition in their pseudorecognition experiment to differentiate their position from that of Zajonc. In that condition the subjects were tested in front of an audience of two blindfolded confederates. These experimental stooges supposedly were waiting for a perception experiment and were adapting to darkness. As shown in Figure 3.19, subjects performing in front of a blindfolded audience (the "mere presence" condition) behaved similarly to subjects in the "alone" condition. That is, the "mere presence" of others is not sufficient to induce drive.

While Cottrell (1972) maintains a drive (anxiety) interpretation, it is evident that evaluative apprehension involves cognitive awareness and higher mental processes. Thus his position is not consistent with the mechanical viewpoint of humans espoused by Hull. Furthermore, the notion of evaluative apprehension is irrelevant to studies of, for example, infrahuman eating and nest-building behavior. Thus Cottrell's position has less generality than the theory proposed by Zajonc.

Subsequent research substantiated that the social facilitation effect is associated with increased evaluative apprehension and uncertainty in the presence of others (see Guerin, 1986). These indeed may produce increases in arousal, but the arousal is based on a "more fundamental need to present the self to others in such a way that a desired impression will be made" (Geen, 1991, p. 382).

Word Associations

The study of word associates also offers both positive evidence and difficulties for the drive theory analysis of social facilitation (see Blank, Staff, & Shaver, 1976). In these experiments, the subjects give word associations either in the presence or in the absence of others who are competitors or mere observers (see Matlin & Zajonc, 1968). The word associates can be classified as common or unique on the basis of norms established in the research literature, or by comparison to the total responses that are given in the particular experiment. According to drive theory, the response associates should be more common in the "observer" condition than in the "alone" condition, for common responses are dominant in the subjects' habit hierarchies and are augmented by the increased level of drive. Long ago, Allport (1955), and more recently Matlin and Zajonc (1968), reported data that apparently support the drive theoretical position.

However, Blank et al. (1976) provide evidence that calls into question the drive theory analysis. In their experiment, subjects were asked to say "the first word you think of" in response to a stimulus word. On one-half of the trials, subjects responded when alone; on the other half, an observer was present. In the presence of the observer, the subjects gave fewer idiosyncratic responses. Hence it appears that subjects avoid giving personal or "strange" responses when someone is watching them. Thus the data again seem best suited to a "social impression" rather than a pure drive theoretical explanation. Machines typically are not concerned with the impressions they make.

The drive interpretation of social facilitation, as indicated above, has many challengers, for some data contradict drive theoretical predictions while other data fall beyond the range of a conception generated by a machine metaphor. In addition to a social impression interpretation, other explanations have focused on imitation and learning. For example, it has been suggested that experiences in life may teach organisms to respond with greater vigor in group settings. Of course, this is instrumental to obtaining food and surviving.

Still another explanation of social facilitation focuses upon the reduction of avoidance motivation, rather than the onset of anxiety or the augmentation of approach strivings. It has been contended that many infrahumans are frightened during feeding experiments. The presence of others is a signal that reduces fear. The reduction of fear, in turn, facilitates other responses, such as pecking (Rajecki, Kidd, Wilder, & Jaeger, 1975). In support of this interpretation, Rajecki et al. (1975) report that in the presence of other chicks, both dominant and subordinate responses increase during feeding. This contradicts the drive theoretical analysis, which states that the dominant response will replace the subordinate response given heightened drive. Further, Rajecki et al. (1975) also suggest that "animals will consume more in any sort of situation that contains familiar components" (p. 509). Thus socially reared animals should consume more when placed in social situations. Conversely, the consumption of animals reared alone should be enhanced in isolated conditions. There are many data available to support these hypotheses (see Rajecki et al., 1975).

Cognitive Dissonance

It is evident from the prior pages that the sources of drive have greatly expanded since the time of Hull's original conception. Initially, drive was defined as a tissue deficit, so that the onset of drive had negative survival consequences for the organism. Then, because of the Miller-Mowrer studies of fear, any strong internal stimulus became considered a drive. The proposed drive-arousing stimuli were typically aversive and were often linked to anxiety—they specifically included nonattainment of an expected reward and the presence of (evaluating) others.

But when one considers the amount of generated research, one can see that cognitive dissonance, which is one aspect of the study of "cognitive dynamics," was the most visible and widely investigated source of drive. It is generally acknowledged that the problem of cognitive dynamics was *the* social psychological problem of the 1960s (Zajonc, 1968, p. 338). *Cognitive dynamics* refers to the tendency toward change brought about when cognitions are in conflict—that is, when they are inconsistent or "do no fit." In the last 40 years a number of theories of cognitive consistency have been formulated. These theories, although labeled differently, "all have in common the notion that the person tends to behave in ways that minimize the internal inconsistency among his inter-personal relations, among his intra-personal cognitions, and among his beliefs, feelings, and action" (McGuire, 1966, p. 1).

The best known of the consistency approaches is the theory of cognitive dissonance (the following chapter examines the next most popular consistency conception, balance theory). Dissonance theory is concerned with the motivational effects of the relations among cognitive elements. The elements in dissonance theory refer to "beliefs" or "knowledge." These elements may be unrelated to each another or can be related in a consonant or dissonant manner. According to Festinger (1957), two cognitions are postulated to be in a state of dissonance if "the obverse of one element would follow from the other" (p. 13). For example, the knowledge that one smokes and that smoking causes cancer are dissonant cognitions. Similarly, if one decides to buy a car knowing that the model has a bad reputation, and the car indeed turns out to be a "lemon," then the cognitions do not fit. If one believes smoking causes cancer or perceives that a particular car model is poorly made, then it follows that one should not smoke or buy that make of car.

Festinger postulates that dissonance is a motivating state. Dissonance is treated as a drive, with the same conceptual status as hunger, thirst, and other physiological states of deprivation. Like other drives, dissonance is postulated to energize and direct behavior, and its offset is reinforcing. Festinger (1957) states: "Successful reduction of dissonance is rewarding in the same sense that eating is rewarding" (p. 70). Further, like other deprivation states, dissonance is aversive, and the theoretical optimal state is one of zero dissonance. Hence it is evident that the study of dissonance, although not directly derived from Hullian theory, is appropriately considered within the study of drive theory even though it concerns cognitive equilibrium. Recall again that not all aspects of a metaphor are applicable to the phenomena that the metaphor is called upon to help explain.

The way in which the "discrepant parts" are reduced will depend, in part, on the resistance to change of the relevant cognitions. Opinions and beliefs are clearly easier to alter than are actual prior behaviors (Wicklund & Brehm, 1976). However, for instance, if the individual in the car example above continues to believe that he has purchased a lemon, then he may more easily accomplish dissonance reduction by coming to believe that the purchase was a mistake and selling the car than by convincing himself that the automobile is really not that bad.

The proposed magnitude of dissonance is a function of the proportion of dissonant to consonant cognitions. Thus, for example, if the lemon was cheaply purchased, and other cars also require much repair, then the dissonance of the car purchase is lessened. In addition, dissonance is determined by the importance of the cognitions under consideration. It is manifestly more disturbing to discover that the car one purchased is a lemon than to find that one bought a poorly made article of clothing. According to Wicklund and Brehm (1976), the formula for the magnitude of aroused dissonance is as follows:

$$\frac{\text{dissonant cognitions} \times \text{importance of cognitions}}{\text{consonant cognitions} \times \text{importance of cognitions}}$$

The rather straightforward principles outlined by Festinger have led to a number of interesting observations of "real-life" behavior. For example, Festinger (1957) notes that one way of reducing the dissonance created by smoking when it is generally believed that smoking causes cancer is to persuade oneself that the latter cognition is false. (Of course, another way to reduce this dissonance is to discontinue smoking, but that often is not easily accomplished.) In one government survey study, individuals classified according to the strengths of their smoking habits were asked whether they thought that the alleged link between smoking and cancer had been sufficiently proven. The respondents were categorized into four groups: nonsmokers, light smokers, medium smokers, and heavy smokers. The proportions of respondents reporting that they did not think that the evidence was conclusive totaled 55% of the nonsmoking group and 68%, 75%, and 86%, respectively, for light, medium, and heavy smokers. Apparently, when cognitions are not in harmony, processes are instigated to help bring cognitive structures into consonance.

Attaining social support for one's beliefs is another method employed to reduce the dissonance between cognitions. In the book *When Prophecy Fails*, Festinger, Riecken, and Schachter (1956) report on the behavior of a group of cultists who predicted the world was about to come to an end. When their expectation was not confirmed, they dramatically increased their proselytizing behavior. By so doing, they apparently could bolster their own belief systems and reduce the dissonance created between their beliefs and their cognitions of the events in the real world. There are not many data available supporting the idea of proselytizing after a belief has been invalidated, but, as McGuire (1966) notes, "This notion would explain some historical occurrences of more than a little importance that have puzzled many. It is an appealing proposition that deserves to be true" (p. 18).

Although some evidence gathered in field studies supports predictions from dissonance theory, by far the vast majority of the investigations have been conducted in laboratory settings, under controlled experimental conditions. Many of the studies involve engaging subjects in behavior that normally would be avoided. The negative aspects of the action are dissonant with the knowledge that the behavior was performed. These are known as "forced compliance" or "insufficient justification" studies.

The research studies included within the forced-compliance paradigm often examine the effects of public actions that are discrepant with the private opinions of the actor. Further, the actions are performed for relatively small rewards. It is hypothesized that in such situations forces are aroused that act upon the individual to justify the prior action.

This hypothesis was first tested in a classic (and controversial) study by Festinger and Carlsmith (1959). In that study, subjects participated in an extremely boring "psychological experiment." The subjects were then requested to tell future participants that the experiment was interesting and fun. For this task, half the subjects were offered $20 and the rest were offered

$1. Afterward, the experimenters asked the subjects to rate how interesting the experiment actually had been. The results indicated that the subjects in the $1 condition rated the objectively boring experiment as more interesting than did subjects in the $20 condition. That is, the smaller reward produced greater liking of the experiment than did the larger one. Festinger and Carlsmith argued that behavior contrary to one's beliefs is not very dissonant when there is a strong external inducement (a large reward) to commit the action, for the external reward creates a consonant cognition. However, if the reward is small, then the discrepant behavior is seen as not sufficiently justified and much dissonance is created. In the Festinger and Carlsmith experiment this dissonance apparently initiated processes that modified the cognitions (attitudes) concerning the intrinsic value of the experiment.

The insufficient justification paradigm was later extended to the study of punished actions. Aronson and Carlsmith (1963) reason that

> if a person is induced to cease the performance of a desired act by the threat of punishment, his cognition that the act is desirable is dissonant with his cognition that he is not performing it. A threat of severe punishment, in and of itself, provides ample cognitions consonant with ceasing the action. If a person ceases to perform a desired action in the face of a mild threat, however, he lacks these consonant cognitions and, therefore, must seek additional justification for not performing the desired act. One method of justification is to convince himself that the desired act is no longer desirable. Thus, if a person is induced to cease performing a desired action by a threat of punishment, the milder the threat the greater will be his tendency to derogate the action. (pp. 584-585)

To test this hypothesis, Aronson and Carlsmith (1963) prevented children from playing with attractive toys, using either mild or severe threat. Both before the threat and after a period of not playing with the toys, the children's attractiveness ratings of the toys were ascertained. Table 3.5 indicates that the relative attractiveness of the toys was greater in the severe than in the mild threat condition, supporting the prediction of Aronson and Carlsmith.

The general advice offered by Festinger (1957) for both rewarding and punishing situations is as follows: "If one wanted to obtain private changes in addition to public compliance, the best way to do this would be to offer just enough reward or punishment to elicit overt compliance" (p. 95). This proposition contradicts the reinforcement approach to attitude change, which states that opinions vary monotonically as a function of their perceived reward value, and inversely as a function of their perceived aversive consequences. Thus a lively debate has ensued between dissonance and reinforcement theorists, for it appears to be the case that both dissonance and reinforcement affect attitudes, and in opposing directions (for a discussion of this issue, see Wicklund & Brehm, 1976).

TABLE 3.5 Change in Attractiveness of Forbidden Toy

Strength of Threat	Increase	Rating Same	Decrease
Mild	4	10	8
Severe	14	8	0

Source: Aronson and Carlsmith (1963, p. 586).

Traditional Motivational Research

Hunger-Thirst

Investigations demonstrating the motivational consequences of dissonance on consumption employ some variation of the public compliance-insufficient justification paradigm first introduced by Festinger and Carlsmith (1959). Brehm (1962) reports a series of studies in which feelings of hunger and thirst, as well as actual water consumption, were assessed following an insufficient justification procedure. In one of these investigations, subjects were asked to refrain from eating breakfast and lunch, under the guise of examining the effects of deprivation on intellectual and motor functioning. Prior to the expected task performance the subjects rated their degree of hunger. After completion of the required tasks, the subjects were asked to undergo continued deprivation and to return later for additional testing. In the low-dissonance condition $5 was offered as a reward for further participation, while in the high-dissonance condition no additional incentive was offered. Thus conditions of sufficient and insufficient justification were established. After a volitional commitment to continue deprivation, hunger ratings again were obtained. Figure 3.20 shows the results for subjects equal in their initial hunger ratings. The figure indicates that low-dissonance subjects perceived themselves as hungrier after the commitment, while high-dissonance subjects reported feeling less hungry. Presumably, in the high-dissonance condition continued deprivation is justified by altering the cognition related to the perceived discomfort of hunger.

Pain and Fear

Experimental paradigms similar to those reported by Brehm also have demonstrated the cognitive control of pain. In one illustrative study, subjects were given 20 trials of classical aversive eyelid conditioning (Grinker, 1967; reported in Zimbardo, 1969). Recall that in this procedure a conditional stimulus, such as a tone, is paired with an aversive puff of air to the eye, and subsequent responses to the stimulus are measured. Following the 20 trials, the subjects were told that on future trials the air puff would be

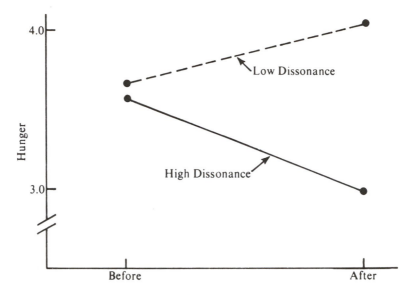

Figure 3.20. Mean self-ratings of hunger for selected subjects, before and after the dissonance manipulation. (From Brehm, 1962, p. 62. Reprinted from the 1962 *Nebraska Symposium on Motivation*, by permission of University of Nebraska Press. Copyright © 1962 by the University of Nebraska Press.)

more intense. Earlier studies had demonstrated that this stress warning increases classical aversive conditioning.

To create high- and low-dissonance conditions, different degrees of verbal justification and choice were given for participating in the experiment, although all subjects did agree to participate. A control group was given neither choice nor justification.

Figure 3.21 shows that in this investigation the change in response strength from the pre- to the postdissonance trials is an inverse function of the degree of aroused dissonance. Because of the increased stress, conditioning increased for all groups of subjects. However, it appears that dissonance suppresses the fear response, and conditioning, by inducing subjects to *think* that the puff is not very intense. That is, choosing to participate in an aversive experiment with minimal justification seems to decrease the emotionality that is caused by the unpleasant air puff and this, in turn, retards eyelid conditioning.

Resistance to Extinction

One further area of dissonance research deserving mention concerns resistance to extinction. The insufficient justification paradigm used by Festinger and Carlsmith and others is created by having the extrinsic rewards for "forced" behavior not congruent with the significance of the action. This analysis has been extended to situations in which the subject performs instrumental responses that are somewhat aversive and the in-

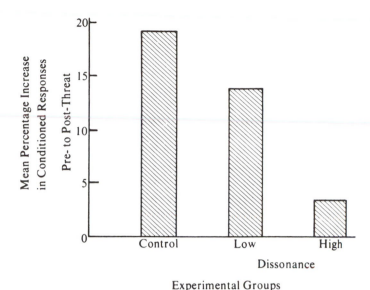

Figure 3.21. Mean percentage increase of conditioned responses from trials 11-20 to trials 21-30 (pre- and postthreat) for control and dissonance groups. (From Grinker, 1967; reported in Zimbardo, 1969, p. 130.)

trinsic value of the reward is not sufficient given the "output" of the subjects. It is postulated that in such situations dissonance is aroused and can be reduced if the reward or incentive value of the goal is perceived as greater than it really is. In the first demonstration of this principle, Aronson and Mills (1959) had females volunteer to join a group discussion concerning sex. Half of the volunteers first participated in a lengthy and embarrassing "initiation" that included the repeating of "dirty" words (high dissonance). A second group was given an easy initiation procedure (low dissonance). The girls then listened to a rather boring group discussion about sex. Aronson and Mills found that the subjects in the high-dissonance condition rated the discussion more interesting, liked the participating girls more, and so forth than did subjects in the low-dissonance condition. In sum, the cognition "I have experienced pain to attain an unattractive object" is dissonant; dissonance is reduced by perceiving the attained object as attractive.

Lawrence and Festinger (1962) applied this analysis to experimental procedures that apparently arouse dissonance in research on infrahumans. Included among these dissonance-creating procedures is the requirement of effortful responses to obtain a reward. These are situations that infrahumans (and humans) would avoid, if possible. Thus responses under these conditions are dissonance arousing relative to conditions in which there is an "easy" response. Again, the dissonance may be reduced by

TABLE 3.6 Average Running Time During Extinction (in seconds) for Different Effort Conditions

	Effort Condition	
	25° Incline (N = 31)	50° Incline (N = 31)
Last day of acquisition	1.8	2.0
First day of extinction	7.1	3.8
Second day of extinction	26.1	16.4
Third day of extinction	37.2	31.0

Source: Lawrence and Festinger (1962, p. 43).

perceiving "extra" rewards in the goal situation and thus experiencing a resulting increase in the attractiveness of the goal object.

In one experiment demonstrating the effects of effort on performance, rats were required to traverse inclines differing in steepness to receive a food reward. The group expending the greater effort took longer to extinguish, and ran faster during the extinction period, than the group expending less effort during the learning period (see Table 3.6). Subsequent experiments conducted by Lawrence and Festinger demonstrated that effort results in greater resistance to extinction regardless of the reward schedule, and that with minimal effort the absence of reward still increases resistance to extinction.

Is Internal Arousal Necessary for the Dissonance Experience?

A number of investigators have asked whether internal arousal (drive) is necessary for dissonance to be experienced. To examine this question, in one experiment Zanna and Cooper (1976) gave some subjects a tranquilizer or amphetamine prior to having them write an opinion that was counter to their beliefs. In the tranquilizer condition a dissonance effect was not displayed, while in the amphetamine condition attitude change was augmented. On the basis of these findings and other research, Zanna and Cooper concluded that aversive arousal does accompany cognitive inconsistency.

Since these early experiments, other conditions necessary to produce cognitive dissonance have been identified. These include free choice, perceived personal responsibility, recognition of consequences, and other cognitive appraisals that have seemed to erode the machine metaphor. For our purposes, however, it can again be seen that the notion of being driven toward equilibrium was a valuable and heuristic jumping-off point.

SUMMARY

In this chapter, the drive theoretical approach to motivation has been examined. The main theoretical concepts reviewed were drive, learned drive, incentive, and nonspecific energizer. These are the components, or the functions of the components, included in Hull's theory of action. The theory states that behavior is determined by drive × habit; with later elaborations, learned drives and incentives came to be included among the determinants of performance.

Five related areas were examined: anxiety, conflict, frustration, social facilitation, and cognitive dissonance. Each of these was interpreted from the perspective of drive theory.

Following are some of the chapter's main points:

(1) Anxiety is conceptualized as a nondirective drive. The emotional reaction to a stressor, which is the drive mechanism, is a function of both the aversiveness of that stressor and individual differences in reactions to aversive events. The learning of individuals classified as high in drive is enhanced at easy tasks but inhibited at complex tasks.

(2) The study of conflict has been clarified by a model proposed by Miller. This model postulates that the change in the strength of avoidance motivation as a function of the distance from the goal (the "steepness" of the gradient) is greater than the change in the approach gradient. This postulate, derived from drive theory considerations, enables the model to account for behavioral ambivalence.

(3) There are two drive theories of motivation that can account for the energizing effects of not attaining a goal: the Brown-Farber theory and Amsel's conception. Both view frustration as a source of drive.

(4) The drive theoretical approach to social facilitation suggests that the presence of others increases drive level, and thus interacts with habit in enhancing or interfering with performance.

(5) Festinger has postulated that inconsistent cognitions also have the properties of drive, motivating the organism to reduce this equilibrium by changing behaviors and/or attitudes.

It appears to me that the main contribution of drive theory has been the systematic and precise exploration of motivated behavior from a mechanistic position. Drive theorists provided an exemplar for the scientific and experimental study of motivation. They carefully identified the determinants of behavior, created a mathematical model, and then deduced predictions from this model. These predictions were tested in carefully controlled laboratory investigations. This approach contrasts sharply with Freudian psychology although as previously indicated, it paradoxically shares much with Freudian theory, including an acceptance of the principles of hedonism, homeostasis, and psychic determinism, and a reliance on energy constructs to provide the motor for action.

Drive theory is no longer dominant in psychology. However, it has played an important role in furthering our understanding of motivated behavior and has documented the power of a careful use of the machine metaphor.

Gestalt Theory and Its Derivatives:

Field Theory and Balance

Gestalt psychology generated two related yet clearly distinct theories of motivation: field theory as proposed by Kurt Lewin (1935, 1938) and the less inclusive balance theory formulation most associated with Fritz Heider (1958). Lewinian field theory, like Freud's psychoanalytic theory and Hull's drive conception, flourished around the 25-year period between 1930 and 1955. Balance theory, on the other hand, was dominant during the 1960s. Although balance was not in the tradition of a "grand" theory, it may be considered the last of the influential mechanistic conceptions of motivation (I also include in this context Festinger's [1957] popular theory of cognitive dissonance, which was not derived from Gestalt principles but is closely related to Heider's balance theory.)

In this chapter, some general principles of Gestalt psychology will first be presented briefly, and then discussion will turn to Lewinian field theory and the balance-focused conceptions.

Gestalt Psychology

deal w/ whole

Structuralist deal w/ broken down parts

The founder of Gestalt psychology is believed to have been Max Wertheimer (1912), who first called attention to the "phi phenomenon," although Kurt Koffka and Wolfgang Köhler are equally associated with the origin of the Gestalt movement. Wertheimer noted that if two lights are flashed in close temporal and spatial contiguity, then there is perceived movement. This is well known to us because of such eye-catching advertising displays as the ever-present movie marquee. To understand this perceived motion, one must consider not only the onset of a particular light, but also its relation to the onset of neighboring lights. According to the Gestaltists, the general significance of this observation is that the comprehension of perceptual phenomena is not possible if sensations are broken down or analyzed into component parts, as the structuralists had championed. Rather, one must deal with wholes, or the total situation as perceived by the person. The whole is different from the mere sum of the parts. This point is clearly illustrated in the study of chemical compounds, for the

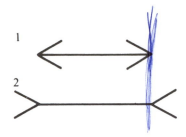

Figure 4.1. The Müller-Lyer illusion. Both lines are about one inch in length. However, Line 2 appears longer than Line 1.

force = FG/e

combination of elements, such as hydrogen and oxygen, gives rise to something entirely different (e.g., water). Gestalt ("whole") principles also are evident in the study of music, for listeners hear a melody, not just a succession of individual notes.

In attempting to formulate the laws of perception, the Gestaltists called upon field conceptions originated by physicists. Rather than treating perception as a static process corresponding to a stimulus pattern, they asserted that perceptions adhere to the laws of physical dynamics. They considered perceptual processes to be similar to an electrical network with voltage imposed across it. The Gestaltists made use of concepts such as tension, force, and equilibrium, and subsequently also applied this language to the study of learning and motivation.

Consider, for example, the Müller-Lyer illusion (see Figure 4.1). In this illusion, two lines of equal length are perceived as being unequal. According to the principles of Gestalt psychology, this is caused by differing fields of forces around the judged lines. That is, perception is determined by the total context in which an object is embedded.

The Gestaltists additionally argued that the perception of a stimulus pattern will be as "good" (regular, symmetrical, and simple) as the stimulus pattern "will allow" (Koffka, 1935, p. 151). Hence, for example, faces are perceived as symmetrical, although this is not exactly the case. Furthermore, even though a circular form is not quite closed, it nonetheless is perceived as a circle. There is, then, a tendency toward simplicity in the perceptual system, just as there is in physical systems, as may often be observed in nature. For example, if a drop of oil is surrounded by some other liquid, the play of internal and external forces gives it a symmetrical form. This pattern represents both an equilibrium of forces and a simple regular pattern; that is, "macroscopic physical states tend to develop in the direction of maximum regularity and simplicity and to become as stable as possible because in such distributions forces balance one another more exactly than in irregular patterns" (Allport, 1955, p. 132).

The Gestaltists proposed that there are laws of form—parts become organized (e.g., separate lines are seen as belonging together, as in the perception of a square, or a fence), and groupings form a particular structure. This is inevitable and not subject to conscious control or awareness by the lay perceiver. Rather, brain forces are automatically operative in a manner similar to the forces in magnetic and electrical fields.

The Gestaltists also were interested in learning, and it is instructive to contrast their analysis of learning with that proposed by Thorndike (1911). The type of learning they investigated can be considered a subset of perception and again illustrates the importance of the psychological field and the interrelationships among the parts of the field. In Köhler's book *The Mentality of Apes* (1925), experiments are reported that demonstrate insight learning in animals. The general procedure in these studies was to place a stick in one corner of an ape's cage and food outside the cage at an opposite corner. The animal could reach the food only if it used the stick as a tool. Köhler reports that the apes were able to perceive the correct solution to the problem and reached the food with the aid of the stick. Köhler contrasted this insight learning with the blind trial-and-error learning exhibited by Thorndike's cats and chicks, which so heavily influenced Hull's theory of behavior.

In Köhler's experiments, learning seems to involve perceptual processes. Although the path to the stick is physically opposite to the path toward food, it must be perceived as lying in the direction of the goal. Thus the delivery of the correct response in this situation depends upon the way in which the animal organizes the field; the solution to the problem requires the correct perception of the relation between the parts.

Turning to motivation, the Gestaltists argued that in the behavioral field, as in physical and perceptual fields, the organism seeks a particular arrangement. To illustrate this, the Gestaltists pointed out that if there is a light presented in a dark context, the eye is drawn to it. A tension arises in the visual field and some action is taken to reduce the tension that has arisen. According to Koffka (1935), "Theoretically, there is no difference between eye movement and such movements of the whole body as are executed in order, say, to quench one's thirst" (p. 626). A person attaining a goal corresponds to a simple figure, the Gestaltists suggested.

Field Theory

The language of Gestaltists, developed primarily to account for perceptual phenomena, was adopted by Lewin for the interpretation of motivated behavior. Terms such as *structure of the field*, *relation between the parts*, and *forces* form the foundation of Lewin's theory. It will be seen that Lewin employed a mechanistic conception, particularly making hydraulic comparisons. Regarding his adoption of mechanical concepts, Lewin (1935) wrote:

> When the concept of energy is used here and when later those of force, of tension, of systems, and others are employed, the question may be left quite open as to whether or not one should ultimately go back to physical forces and energies. In

KURT LEWIN

Kurt Lewin was born in Prussia in 1890. He received his doctorate in 1914 from the University of Berlin, where he came under the influence of the Gestalt psychologists, particularly Max Wertheimer, Wolfgang Köhler, and Kurt Koffka. At the time of Hitler's rise to power, Lewin was returning to Berlin via Russia after a trip to the United States. He wisely decided that arrival in Germany would be unsafe and returned to settle in the United States. After a brief period at Cornell University, Lewin went to the Child Welfare Station at the University of Iowa (1935-1945). In 1945, he became director of the Research Center for Group Dynamics at the Massachusetts Institute of Technology. Lewin died in 1947, at the age of 56.

Lewin's untimely death of a heart attack was long feared by his colleagues, for his life was one of constant activity. His thoughts encompassed theoretical models of motivation as well as the solution of social problems. His applied interests ranged from the study of adolescence and "feeble-mindedness" to an analysis of national character and food preferences.

Lewin was a warm person who actively worked with his students and colleagues. Students tell stories of Lewin ringing their bells late at night, carrying a bottle of wine, and then discussing psychology until dawn. His students, including Leon Festinger and many others, have dominated the field of social psychology.

Lewin strongly identified with America and the American way of life, but he also was a strong supporter of the state of Israel. Prior to his death, he was entertaining the idea of settling in the then relatively new Jewish state.

(Photograph courtesy of AP/Wide World Photos)

any event, these concepts are, in my opinion, general logical fundamental concepts to all dynamics. . . . They are in no way special to physics. . . . the treatment of causal dynamic problems compels psychology to employ the fundamental concepts of dynamics. (p. 46)

However, like Freud's, Lewin's theory is not entirely mechanistic; he made use of other metaphors as well. Indeed, he proposed an extremely influential Godlike metaphor that is examined in Chapter 5.

The conceptual framework advocated by Lewin is called field theory. Field theory starts with the assumption that behavior is determined by the field as it exists at a moment in time. This approach is *ahistorical*, and is contrasted with a genetic or historical analysis. Assume, for example, that an individual has a compulsion to wash his hands every ten minutes. To explain this behavior, a psychologist advocating the historical approach, such as Freud, would investigate the person's past history, particularly the pattern of child rearing and the events that occurred during the early stages

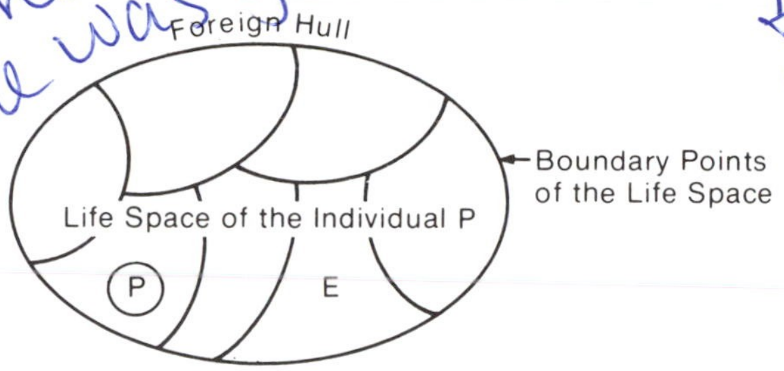

Freud
what forces drives the person when he was growing up?

what forces drives the person now (past + future)

↑ consider whole situation

Figure 4.2. Representation of a life space. *P* represents the person and *E* represents the psychological environment. (From Lewin, 1936, p. 73.)

of development. Ideally, it could then be ascertained how these historical antecedents influence the present action. Lewin, on the other hand, would determine the forces acting on the person in the immediate present. He might represent the individual as avoiding dirt, or the soap as having a positive attraction. The antecedent historical conditions, or the reasons the individual perceives the situation as he does, would not be essential. What is important is to specify the contemporary or immediate determinants of behavior. The past, as well as the future, is thus incorporated into the present. This ahistorical approach also characterizes Hull's theory, although Hull did not explicitly discuss this aspect of his conception.

A second fundamental position of Lewin already alluded to is that an analysis of behavior must consider the whole situation. As the Gestalt psychologists prior to Lewin emphasized in their study of perceptual events, one must represent the entire field of forces. Each part within a field interacts with the other parts. The use of this principle will become evident as we examine Lewin's concept of the "life space."

The Life Space

$$B = f(P,E)$$

Lewin's most basic theoretical statement is that behavior is determined by both the person (*P*) and the environment (*E*): $B = f(P,E)$, where *f* represents some function or relationship. The person and the environment together comprise the life space (see Figure 4.2).

The life space represents *psychological* reality; it depicts the totality of facts that determine behavior at a moment in time. Thus the life space encompasses the environment as it is perceived by the person. The psychological environment is not identical with the physical environment. To illustrate this point somewhat dramatically, Lewin related the story of a horseback rider lost in a snowstorm. The rider saw a light in the distance and rode directly toward it. Upon arrival at his destination, he was told that

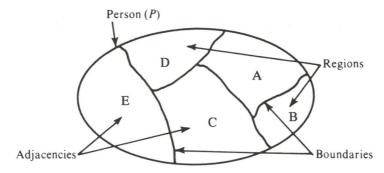

Figure 4.3. Representation of the structural properties of the person. The regions are separated by boundaries, which differ in their permeability. Adjacent regions border one another.

he had just crossed a barely frozen lake. This rider's behavior certainly would have been altered if the danger involved in crossing the lake had been a psychological, as well as a physical, reality.

The perceived environment is influenced by many properties of the person, such as needs, values, attitudes, and motives. In a similar manner, the perceived environment influences the person. The sudden appearance of a threatening event, or a physically attractive person, may change the needs or tensions of the individual. According to Lewin, to understand behavior we must conceive of the person and the environment as a constellation. The two jointly determine action.

For purposes of discussion, it is convenient to divide Lewin's conceptual scheme into categories that correspond to the person and the environmental components of the life space. Furthermore, both the person and the environment can be described as having structural as well as dynamic properties.

Concepts Related to the Person

Structural concepts. The person can be thought of either as a point in the life space or as a region. In Figure 4.2 the individual is conceived as an undifferentiated point. In many instances Lewin was concerned primarily with an individual's position or place in the life space, and in these cases it is not convenient to differentiate the person into subparts. But in other situations it is necessary to think of the person as a region in the life space. When conceptualized as a region, the person has structural properties. The structures of greatest importance are the subregions, boundaries, and adjacencies (see Figure 4.3).

The regions within the person are "containers"; they represent "vessels with walls." The walls, or boundaries, of the vessels differ in their permeability; some allow more "leakage" than others. This characteristic of regions is important because it, in part, determines the fate of the tension that is contained within the regions. Tension is the dynamic inner-personal construct.

Dynamic construct. The dynamic construct of tension is the state of a region. When a need exists, a region is represented as in a state of tension. For ease of understanding, it often is helpful to think of tension as a fluid contained in the inner-personal regions. (Recall that this metaphor also was used by ethologists in their discussion of instinct.) The amount of this tension varies as a function of the strength or the magnitude of the needs.

When tension is contained within a region, the region tries to change itself so that it becomes equal in tension to the surrounding regions. Recall that the boundaries of the vessels differ in their permeability. If the boundary between two regions is not completely permeable, then some minimal difference in the degree of tension between the two regions will be maintained. And if the regions have a common permeable boundary (adjacent regions in Figure 4.3), or if they are in "dynamic communication" (tension from one can flow to the other via an intermediate region), then a need corresponding to one region will become a need in another region. For example, because of the communication between regions, the desire to see movie X may also result in the desire to see movie Y. Adjacent regions thus may be thought of as depicting similar potential needs.

Within the person there are an unspecified number of inner-personal regions that correspond to different needs or intentions. Whenever a need or intention arises, a new region is characterized as in a state of tension. Thus Lewin has a pluralistic conception of needs, as opposed to the early Freudian and Hullian notions of a nondirective or pooled source of energy or drive. In the Lewinian system, different regions in tension do not combine to influence all behaviors. Rather, each tense region is associated with a particular goal object or class of objects.

Realization of a goal reduces the level of tension within a region. Goal attainment need not involve the consumption of the desired object. Thinking, remembering, going to a movie, and so on can reduce the level of tension in a region. Note again the difference between the Lewinian and the Freudian or Hullian ideas about goal attainment. For Lewin, needs exist that are not related to bodily functions and survival; this is not true of the early Hullian or Freudian theories.

Integrating dynamic and structural aspects. A need or an intention creates tension in a region of the person. The disequilibrium in tense states between regions causes tension to flow from one region to another. The interchange of tension between the regions depends, in part, on the firmness of the boundaries. If the boundaries are not completely permeable, then a region can remain in a relatively fixed tense state. Tension is postulated to dissipate following goal attainment, which reestablishes equilibrium between the regions.

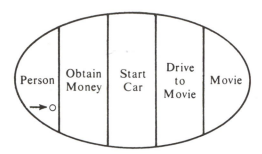

Figure 4.4. Representation of an environment. Regions represent instrumental activities and a path through which *P* locomotes to reach the goal.

Concepts Related to the Environment

Structural concepts. The structural characteristics of the environment are identical to those of the person. There are regions, barriers, and adjacencies. However, the meanings of the environmental and personal constructs differ. Environmental regions are primarily coordinated with activities. For example, if individual *P* wishes to attend a movie, then she may have to obtain money from her father, start the car, drive to the movie, and so on (see Figure 4.4). Regions are therefore instrumental actions. But note that the regions also can be considered as "spaces" through which one locomotes to get to the goal.

The number of regions in the life space at any one time is determined by the number of extant psychological differentiations. For each psychological distinction there is a separate region in the life space. The life space may thus change from moment to moment. For example, if the car needed to reach the movie theater fails to start, new regions (such as calling a mechanic) are manifested in the life space.

Regions are surrounded by boundaries that may act as barriers or as impediments to locomotion, just as the boundaries of the inner-personal regions can be impediments to the flow of tension. The boundaries determine the "space of free movement," which Lewin defined as the regions that are accessible to the person. This is limited by what is externally forbidden (environmental constraints) as well as by personal limitations, such as a lack of ability. The space of free movement may be narrow or quite extensive. For example, for a person in prison the number of accessible regions is small. In other situations the space of free movement may be virtually unlimited, yet the individual still may be unable to attain his or her goal. For example, consider the student who is accepted to many colleges, but not the one he or she most desires to attend.

The regions in the life space are represented in what is called a "topological" or, more correctly, "hodological" space (the Greek stem *hodos* means "path"). Hodological space is embraced within a nonquantitative,

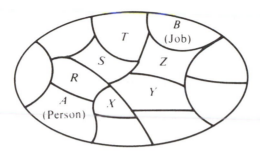

Figure 4.5. Representation of a life space with various paths from *A* to *B*.

mathematical analysis that does not require certain assumptions about distance. For example, in hodological space, the distance between two points, A and B, is not necessarily equal to the distance from B to A. This might be the case if one feels that the difference between, for example, home and school is greater or less than the distance from school to home. Lewin believed that a hodological language makes it possible to take seriously the idea of a psychological space. The concept of psychological space is necessary for many additional reasons. For example, passing an examination or getting married involves psychological movement, although there may be no change in physical location. Psychological direction at times may even be opposite to physical direction, as when one runs toward a burning room in order to escape from the fire, or when Köhler's ape went in the direction of the stick to reach the food.

Direction in the life space. Direction in the life space connotes a relationship between two regions. For example, assume that an individual located in region A (see Figure 4.5) wants to locomote in the direction of region B ($d_{A,B}$). The various linkages between regions A and B are considered to be "paths." There might be many paths between any two regions. Figure 4.5 indicates that one path uniting A with B is X, Y, Z; a second path is R, S, T; and still a third path might be X, R, S, T. Recall that the regions in the life space often represent instrumental acts, as well as a "medium" through which one locomotes to reach a goal. Hence Figure 4.5 could represent an individual in (or doing) A who wants to be in (or to obtain) B (e.g., a new job). To gain this position, the person might either go to school (X, Y, Z) or become an apprentice for the job (R, S, T). Either of these two paths will lead to the desired end state (activity).

Taxonomy of direction. Lewin provided a relatively simple yet useful taxonomy of the direction of behavior (see Table 4.1). Directions are depicted as either "toward" or "away from" a region, and as either including or not including a region other than the one in which the person is contained. The combination of these two dimensions yields four classes of direction. The

TABLE 4.1 Lewinian Taxonomy of the Direction of Behavior

| | Direction of Behavior | |
Number of Regions	Toward	Away From
One	(A, A) consummatory behavior	(A, –A) escape behavior
Two	(A, B) instrumental behavior	(B, –A) avoidance behavior

"toward" direction may be from a given region (A) to a second region (B), as just discussed, or from A in the direction of A ($d_{A,A}$). The latter classification portrays situations in which the individual is in a region and wants to remain there.

Direction characterized as "away from" also may or may not have an alternative region specified. One could be in region A, locomoting in a direction away from A ($d_{A,-A}$). For example, administering shock to an infrahuman in a given setting will cause the animal to seek safety, with any no-shock region being an acceptable alternative. Finally, in a fourth type of direction, the individual is in one region, but is going away from a different region. For example, consider a criminal who committed a crime in New York and is now in Chicago, going toward Los Angeles. His direction might be characterized as either away from New York ($d_{A,-B}$) or toward Los Angeles ($d_{A,C}$), although the former designation seems to depict more accurately the dynamics of this situation.

Dynamic environmental constructs. There is a relationship between the dynamic properties of the individual and the dynamic properties of the environment. When an inner-personal region is in a state of tension, an appropriate environmental region (object) acquires a valence. According to Lewin (1935):

> The valence of an object usually derives from the fact that the object is a means to the satisfaction of a need, or has indirectly something to do with the satisfaction of a need. The kind (sign) and the strength of the valence of an object or event thus depends directly upon the momentary condition of the needs of the individual concerned; the valence of environmental objects and the needs of the individual are correlative. (p. 78)

Thus, given a need (and, therefore, a corresponding region in tension), an object that is perceived as one that satisfies the need acquires a property of attraction. For example, if one is hungry, then a steak or some other edible object gains a positive valence. Of course, it is possible that there are needs and regions in tension, but no environmental objects available that are perceived as appropriate to the need. Hence the existence of a need does not ensure the existence of valences in the environment. However, it is also the case that as the individual becomes hungrier and hungrier, for example, tension increases and there is a tendency for it to spread to more and more regions. Eventually there may be an object coordinated with these remote personal regions that has the properties necessary to acquire a positive valence—even shoes may come to be perceived as edible given great deprivation. The above discussion implicitly indicates that if an object has a valence, then there must exist a corresponding need. That is, for a steak to be attractive to a person, that individual must have some degree of hunger. In sum, given a valence, there must be a need, but given a need, there may or may not be any valences in the environment.

[handwritten margin note: V = need / need ≟ valence]

The amount of valence that an object acquires is directly related to the intensity of the need—a steak is more attractive to one who has not eaten all day than to one who has been without food for only three hours. In addition, the valence of an object depends on its intrinsic properties. For example, a thick, juicy steak will have greater valence than a thin, dried-up piece of meat. Valence, therefore, varies quantitatively as a function of the intensity of the need and the properties of the goal object. Lewin more formally stated this relation as

$$Va(G) = f(t, G)$$

where $Va(G)$ represents the valence of the goal, t symbolizes tension, and G the properties of the goal object.

Valence, however, is not a force; it is not directly coordinated with movement or locomotion. A region with a valence becomes the center of a force field (see Figures 4.6 and 4.7). A force field specifies the magnitude and direction of behavior at all points in the life space. At any given time the person is in one of the regions and thus has a specified force acting upon him or her.

In addition to need strength and properties of the goal object, the strength of force, or tendency to change, is dependent upon one other factor: the relative distance of the person from the goal. Lewin stated that force increases as the psychological distance between the person and the goal object decreases. That means, for example, that as we approach a restaurant when hungry, enter, and finally see and smell the steak, there is increasing force upon us to reach our goal (eating). Lewin acknowledged that this may not always be true. For instance, at times increased distance actually augments the force toward the goal. Lewin believed this is why faraway countries seem so attractive, as sometimes are mates who "play hard to get." However, these are atypical situations.

Lewin conceptualized the force on the person to reach the goal as follows:

$$\text{force} = f\left[\frac{Va(G)}{e}\right] = \frac{(t, G)}{e}$$

where e symbolizes psychological distance between the person and the goal. The e represents the German *entfernung*, or distance.

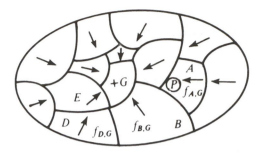

Figure 4.6. A positive central field of forces corresponding to a positive valence. The force has magnitude, represented by the length of the vector, and direction. The point of application is on P in the direction of the goal G.

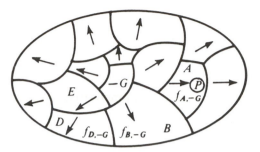

Figure 4.7. A negative central field of forces corresponding to a negative valence. The forces are away from the goal G. (Lewin, 1946, p. 933.)

Given this formula, it is possible to determine the force at every region in the life space. As already intimated, force is conceptualized as a vector. It has a magnitude or amount and a direction. In addition, force has a "point of application," the region in which the force manifests itself. Because the individual is located in this region, the point of application is on the person. When there is a psychological force acting on the person, there is likely to be locomotion in the life space. The force acts on the person in the direction of the desired goal. A goal is a region in the life space. When the goal is attained (the region entered), the tension within the tense inner-personal region dissipates. Because there is no longer any tension within the person, the environmental object loses its valence. This results in a cessation of the force acting on the individual, and goal-seeking behavior is no longer displayed. More specifically, consider a situation in which an individual has not eaten for five hours. Certain objects in that person's environment then acquire a positive valence. The magnitudes of these valences depend upon how hungry the person is and how "good" the food objects are. Because the food objects acquire a positive valence, a force field is established around them, with all forces acting in their direction. The individual is in one of the regions that contains such a force and thus locomotes to attain the goal object. Eating the food reduces hunger and tension. Thus the remaining food objects no longer are attractive and lose their positive valence. This results in the removal of the force field and the cessation of activity.

Relation to Hullian Theory

It is instructive to note the similarity between the Lewinian statement of the determinants of action and Hull's formula. The two positions include similar components in their models: needs of the person (drive D or tension *t*), properties of the goal object (*K* or *G*), and a directional variable (habit *H* or psychological distance *e*). However, Lewin's *t* is specific, *G* is dependent on the existence of *t*, and *e* is a cognitive representation of the environment, reflecting perceived distance.

Because of their conceptual similarity, it was relatively easy for Lewin to explain some phenomena that drive theorists cited in support of the drive conception. In addition, the Lewinian language provides additional insights into the dynamics of the experiments conducted or cited by the Hullians. Consider, for example, investigations employing the Columbia Obstruction Box (see Figure 3.1 in Chapter 3). To recapitulate briefly, in the experimental paradigm employing this device, an animal initially is placed in the start box. At the far end of the box is an appropriate incentive. Between the animal and the goal there is an obstacle, such as an electrified grid. In a series of systematic studies, Moss (1924) and other investigators related the amount and type of deprivation to the tendency of the animals to cross the grid. One clear finding was that as hunger increased, the animals crossed the grid with decreased latency. In addition, the properties of the goal objects also influenced behavior, with faster response for more positively valued incentives.

Lewin believed that the obstruction box aids in the measurement of psychological forces (see Figure 4.8). A force to reach the goal (*C*) is opposed by a force not to enter the shocked region (*B*). The animal is expected to locomote toward the goal when the force in the start box (*A*) toward *C* is greater than the force at *B* not to enter (−*B*). That is, locomotion will occur when $f(A,C) > f(B,-B)$. This is the familiar approach-avoidance conflict.

If there is a force from *A* to *C*, then the region *C* must be the center of a field of forces. That is, region *C* has a positive valence. The animal, therefore, must have an inner-personal region in a state of tension and be aware that an appropriate goal object exists in the environment. To establish this valence, the researcher must deprive the animal of food (or some other necessary commodity) and give it training (exposure) so it will discover that food exists in region *C*.

For one to measure the relative strengths of the approach and avoidance forces, the forces have to be opposed to one another. If the animal could circumvent region *B*, then a conflict would not occur. The physical environment in which the animal is placed ensures that the forces will act in opposition to one another. Barriers (walls) placed around the regions (runway) limit the space of free movement. The only available path to region *C* is through region *B*.

The measure of the strength of the resultant force in the early studies conducted by Moss was often the frequency of grid crossings. If the number of crossings during a given time period is greater in a specified condition (Condition 2) than in a different condition (Condition 1), then the force from *A* to *C* in Condition 2 must be greater than the force from *A* to *C* in Condition 1. But Lewin believed that the frequency of crossings generally is not a good dependent variable. If the animal crosses the grid to reach the goal, then the

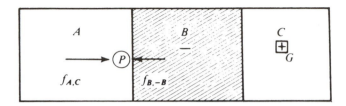

Figure 4.8. Schematic representation of the physical properties of the obstruction box, and the corresponding forces. P, the animal, is located in A; G, the goal, is located in region C; B is the electrified compartment separating A from C. There is a force on P acting in the direction from A to $C (f_{A,C})$, and a force acting on P in the direction of not entering $B (f_{B,-B})$. (Adapted from Lewin, 1938, p. 72.)

approach force must be greater than the force of avoidance. Why, then, doesn't the animal immediately cross the grid when it is replaced in the start box? If the animal remains in the start box, then there has been a change in the constellation of forces between the two trials. Lewin said that this "historical" change may have been caused by any of a number of factors, such as chance variation, loss of energy, or increased aversion to B after the initial shock. Because the frequency measure necessitates a "changing constellation of forces," Lewin did not fully accept this motivational index.

Empirical Research

We now turn from Lewin's theoretical ideas to some of the research that was initiated by his theory. Few theoretical approaches have been as fruitful as Lewinian field theory. In their well-known book *Theories of Personality*, Hall and Lindzey (1957) assert:

> One widely acknowledged criterion of a "good" theory is the measure of its fruitfulness in stimulating research. In this respect, Lewin's theory is a very "good" theory indeed. Few other theories of personality have been responsible for generating so much experimentation. Lewin himself, although he is known as a brilliant theoretician, was always a working scientist. He took the lead in formulating empirical tests of many of his basic hypotheses, and his great enthusiasm for research has been transmitted to many generations of students in Germany and in the United States. The series of articles in the *Psychologische Forschung* between 1926 and 1930 is one of the most distinguished groups of empirical studies in the psychological literature. Moreover, Lewin's ideas and his genius for devising simple and convincing demonstrations of his theoretical conceptions have acted as catalysts for many psychologists who were never personally asso-

ciated with him. It is impossible to estimate the number of investigations that bear the imprint of Lewin's influence. Their number is surely legion. Whatever may be the fate of Lewin's theory in the years to come, the body of experimental work instigated by it constitutes an enduring contribution to our knowledge of personality. (pp. 239-240)

The following research topics will be examined here: conflict, frustration, task recall and resumption, and substitution. These areas have been selected because they are most germane to Lewin's formal theory and are considered key topics in the understanding of human motivation.

Conflict

At any one moment it is likely that many competing forces are acting upon an individual, impelling the person in different directions. Thus there are "overlapping force fields" in the life space with which the person must contend. In Lewinian theory this is conceptualized as an individual being within a region that is part of more than one force field (see Figure 4.9). For example, the reader might want to go to a movie, but also wishes to finish reading this thrilling chapter; a child wants to go out and play, but her parents have told her to clean her room; and so on. Certainly the simultaneous existence of multiple wishes and needs is typical in human behavior.

Lewin provided a taxonomy of situations in which more than one force is acting upon the person at a given moment. He defined three types of conflict: approach-approach, approach-avoidance, and avoidance-avoidance. In all such conflict situations, Lewin specified (as did N. Miller) that the person will locomote in the direction of the greatest force.

Approach-Approach Conflicts (unstable)

In an approach-approach conflict the individual is included in more than one positive force field. For example, a person considers two movies worth seeing; at a restaurant, both fish and steak appear good; or a child must choose between spending his allowance on candy or a comic book. Lewin believed that approach-approach conflicts are easily resolvable and, hence, called them unstable situations.

The instability of approach-approach conflicts becomes evident when some simple numerical values are introduced into Lewin's model for the determinants of force. Assume, for example, that you are in a cafeteria line. You perceive two pies: apple on the left and cherry on the right. Both pies are equally attractive in physical properties such as size ($G = 4$), and you are fairly hungry ($t = 3$). Further, to reach either pie requires the same number of psychological steps. The apple pie requires a left turn and then an arm movement, while the cherry pie requires a right turn and a reaching

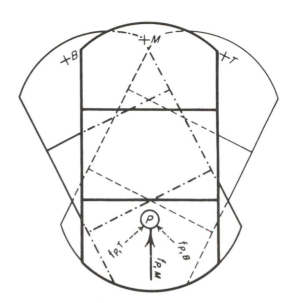

Figure 4.9. Overlapping situations. A child, P, wants to go to a movie, $f_{P,M}$; to play with his trains, $f_{P,T}$; and to read a book, $f_{P,B}$. The directions of the forces are different. The direction of the resultant force is equivalent to the direction of the dominant (i.e., strongest) force, $f_{P,M}$.

movement ($e = 2$). The strengths of the forces involved in this approach-approach conflict therefore are identical:

apple pie (left)   cherry pie (right)

$$\text{force} = \frac{4 \times 3}{2} = 6 \qquad \text{force} = \frac{4 \times 3}{2} = 6$$

Hence the outcome of the action is indeterminate; a momentary equilibrium is established. (Note that it has been assumed that G and t relate multiplicatively; Lewin did not specify this exact mathematical relationship.)

Now suddenly someone in the line behind you becomes rather impatient with the delay and gives you a slight shove. It happens that the shove is toward the right, and you find yourself confronted with the cherry pie. Now the psychological distance from the cherry pie shifts downward, say, from 2 to 1, and the psychological distance from the apple pie increases from 2 to 3. The strengths of the forces are conceptualized as follows:

apple pie (left)   cherry pie (right)

$$\text{force} = \frac{4 \times 3}{3} = 4 \qquad \text{force} = \frac{4 \times 3}{1} = 12$$

The strength of the force toward the cherry pie now is greater than the force toward the apple pie. Hence you will locomote in the direction of the red calories. The conflict is resolved; that is, the conflict equilibrium was only momentary, or unstable.

The example just presented includes only one source of tension and two valences of equal strength, but approach-approach conflicts need not be limited to such situations. Consider the conflict generated when a child has a small amount of money and is deciding whether to purchase candy or a comic book. Assume, for illustrative purposes, that the child's candy "need" is 10 units, and the jelly beans he plans to buy have a value of 3. Further, he must perform 6 psychologically distinct acts to obtain the candy (dress for the walk, walk three blocks, ask for help to cross the street, and so on). The force moving the child toward the candy has the value of 5 units $[(10 \times 3) \div 6 = 5]$. On the other hand, assume his "need" for the comic book has 2 units of strength, the book has 5 units of valence, and his psychological distance from the book has a value of 2. The forces acting upon him in the direction of the book would also have a value of 5 units $[(2 \times 5) \div 2 = 5]$. Equilibrium is thus established; the strengths of the forces acting on the child are equal.

How can this conflict be resolved? Any cognition that changes the relative attractiveness of the two goal objects will create unequal forces. Perhaps seeing a certain TV show will influence the child so that he finds the comic book more attractive. Or perhaps just vacillating in the decision will make him hungrier, increasing the tension caused by food deprivation, and thus making the force toward the candy greater than the force toward the comic book. Once the forces become unequal, the individual locomotes in the direction of the greater force. This reduces the psychological distance from the unselected alternative. The differential shifting of psychological distance further increases the differences in the strength of forces.

In sum, approach-approach conflicts represent situations in which the person is located in overlapping fields of forces generated by positively valued goals. Resolution of the conflict can be achieved if any of the determinants of force (tension, valence, or psychological distance) change. This change can be caused by a new cognition, changes in tension, or any number of other factors. Once an imbalance is created, the individual locomotes toward the goal associated with the greater force. This locomotion further increases the inequality in the magnitude of the forces because the psychological distance from the chosen alternative decreases while the distance from the unchosen alternative increases.

Avoidance-Avoidance Conflicts　　*Stable*

When a person is in overlapping fields of force generated by objects with negative valence, avoidance-avoidance conflicts are aroused. For example, a child is told she must mow the lawn or do her homework, or a town marshal has gunmen pursuing him from the left and from the right. Lewin specified that avoidance-avoidance conflicts are stable; that is, the opposing forces tend to remain in a state of equilibrium.

A simple mathematical exercise reveals why avoidance-avoidance conflicts tend to remain in a stable state. Consider for a moment the town marshal caught between two gunmen he wishes to avoid. Let us assume that his need for safety is 5 units, and that each gunman is equally despicable ($G = -3$). If the marshal perceives himself as equidistant from the gunmen as they come stalking toward him ($e = 2$), then the forces are as follows:

gunman on left

gunman on right

$$\text{force} = \frac{5(-3)}{2} = -7.5 \qquad \text{force} = \frac{5(-3)}{2} = -7.5$$

Thus there are equal and opposite forces to flee both to the left and to the right.

Now assume that the marshal suddenly remembers that the gunman on the left is a poor shot or a coward. The new field of forces then might be:

gunman on left

gunman on right

$$\text{force} = \frac{5(-2)}{2} = -5 \qquad \text{force} = \frac{5(-3)}{2} = -7.5$$

Because the negative valence is now greater away from the right, the marshal proceeds toward the left. In so doing, he alters the psychological distances; the forces might change as follows:

gunman on left

gunman on right

$$\text{force} = \frac{5(-2)}{1} = -10 \qquad \text{force} = \frac{5(-3)}{3} = -5$$

Now the force to avoid the left gunman is greater than that away from the right gunman. Even though the killer on the left does not appear as aversive, the decrease in psychological distance increases the force to avoid the confrontation. This indicates that the marshal will again shift his direction, this time to the right. In theory, the marshal will continue to oscillate between the two negative alternatives.

Does this mean that it is always impossible to solve avoidance-avoidance conflicts? This clearly is not the case, for humans are indeed placed in many such situations and usually cease their vacillation. A cognitive change might alter the strength of the avoidance forces and help to resolve the conflict. Needs can change, valences can shift in magnitude and even in direction, and psychological distance can be altered. Lewin also indicated that such conflicts are often solved by "leaving the field." This means that a person in such a conflict will frequently follow a path that increases the psychological distance from both alternatives. If the marshal ascended in a helium balloon just before the gunmen arrived, his conflict would be resolved. However, leaving the field can be employed as a method of conflict resolution only if the boundaries around the conflict situation are sufficiently permeable. For example, if a child is told to mow the lawn or do her homework, she apparently is placed in a difficult avoidance-avoidance situation. But if she knows she can escape either task by appealing to her mother or hiding in the attic, then the conflict is readily (if only temporarily) resolved. Lewin indicated that one consequence of establishing behaviors through the use of punishment and negative sanctions is that strong barriers must be erected that keep the person in the situation. And energy must be expended to ensure that these barriers persist.

In sum, avoidance-avoidance conflicts generated by multiple regions of negative valence are not readily resolvable. As one approaches the aversive region, the tendency to avoid that region becomes even stronger. Hence ambivalent behavior is exhibited; the person vacillates between the various alternatives. For such conflicts to have any degree of permanence, strong boundaries must exist to prevent the person from leaving the field and avoiding all the alternatives.

Approach-Avoidance Conflicts   Stable

The third classification of conflicts, approach-avoidance, was discussed in detail in Chapter 3. In such conflicts the same region acquires both positive and negative valence and establishes positive and negative force fields. For example, the reader might want to go to a movie, but does not want to spend the money; she might want to stop reading, but knows that a test is forthcoming. As in all conflict situations, the exhibited behavior is postulated by Lewin to be determined by needs, valences, and psychological distance. In this situation the relative steepness of the approach and avoidance slopes is an important determinant of action.

Approach-avoidance conflicts also are relatively stable. The person is expected to approach the goal, but then avoid it, because of the differential change in the strength of the approach and avoidance tendencies (see Chapter 3 for a full discussion). Again, a number of factors can lead to conflict resolution; for example, the positive aspects of the goal may gain in attractiveness, or the person may experience a reduction in the amount of fear.

Empirical Studies of Conflict

Surprisingly few studies have been generated by the Lewinian conflict taxonomy. Probably the most investigated aspect of his classification scheme concerns the relative stability and instability of the various types of conflict. A pertinent investigation is repeated here in Experiment 4.1 (please do not look at the experiment yet). The study examines the time it takes to resolve various conflicts. Two alternatives are presented, and the reader must select from between the two. To determine latencies, the reader should get a watch with a second hand. For each conflict listed, note the position of the second hand, read the conflict, make a choice, and then determine how long it took you to make the choice. Please turn to Experiment 4.1 now and complete it before reading further.

Experiment 4.1

Answer each of the following questions and write in the time it took you to reach each decision.

Decision Time

(1) Would you rather be
    (a) more intelligent
    (b) more attractive   _____

(2) Would you rather have
    (a) less social poise
    (b) less energy   _____

(3) Would you rather have
    (a) less financial security
    (b) a less positive disposition   _____

(4) Would you rather be
    (a) more self-confident
    (b) more intelligent   _____

(5) Would you rather be
    (a) less self-confident
    (b) less intelligent   _____

(6) Would you rather have
    (a) more financial security
    (b) a more positive disposition   _____

(7) Would you rather have
    (a) more social poise
    (b) more energy   _____

(8) Would you rather be
    (a) less intelligent
    (b) less attractive   _____

To determine the time to decision (stability of the conflict) between approach-approach versus avoidance-avoidance conflicts, add the latency time to Questions 1, 4, 6, and 7, and compare this to the latency time for Questions 2, 3, 5, and 8.

Total Decision Time

Approach-approach conflicts   _____
Avoidance-avoidance conflicts   _____

If the results are in accord with predictions made by Lewin, then the average time taken to choose between two positive alternatives will be less than the time taken to choose between two negative alternatives. These are the findings reported by Arkoff (1957). To attempt to control for possible experimental artifacts, within each block of four decisions, two are between positive events and two are between negative events. Further, Question 1, which involves two positive choices, is then inverted in Question 5, which involves the same type of choices phrased negatively, and so forth for all the decisions.

Frustration and Regression

One interesting scientific game is to compare how various theorists have studied identical topics. Because the behavior under investigation generally is conceptualized quite differently by the theorists, the experiments conducted and the conclusions reached often are surprisingly unrelated.

A simple examination of the principles of learning introduced in this book illustrates this point. Thorndike believed that reward and punishment are essential for response acquisition. Therefore, his experiments involved responses instrumental to the attainment of a food reward. On the other hand, Gestaltists contend that organization is an essential characteristic of the learning process. Their experiments on insight learning created situations in which perceptual reorganization apparently was necessary to reach the correct solution. In sum, each theoretical position employed a particular experimental procedure, or reference experiment, that could demonstrate each theorist's own bias. And, quite naturally, the conclusions reached were indeed disparate.

The study of frustration also exemplifies this point. Brown, Farber, and Amsel were trained within the Hullian theoretical framework. Therefore, in their studies, frustration generally was operationalized by withholding food from a previously rewarded animal. Further, it is not unreasonable to expect that in these investigations the construct of frustration would be related to drive and habits and would be used to explain phenomena such as resistance to extinction. After all, these were the problems with which Hull, Spence, and their cohorts struggled. On the other hand, Lewin was a field theorist with strong interests in personality and child development. His investigations of frustration were directed toward understanding behavior in complex settings and providing insights into the dynamics of development.

In the previous pages I have indicated that Lewin was greatly influenced by Freud and was one of the first investigators to test rigorously some of Freud's fundamental concepts, such as persisting desires, substitution, and regression. *Regression* refers to a return to an earlier mode of behavior. Freud specified that during the genetic stages of development the individual selects certain "problem solutions" to cope with conflict and stress. These behaviors tend to reduce the amount of aversive stimulation. During times of later stress, according to Freud, there is a tendency for the person to repeat these earlier modes of behavior, although they might be inadequate or maladaptive given the present situation. A mild form of regression might be "running home to mother" in difficult times, while a more extreme form of such behavior might involve thumb-sucking all day, as could be exhibited by persons in a severely psychotic state.

Barker, Dembo, and Lewin (1943) considered regression a form of "negative development" (p. 441). Hence they contended that understanding the laws of development would shed light upon regressive behavior, and vice versa. These investigators reasoned that development could be conceptualized as an increase in the degree of inner-personal differentiation and in the separation of fantasy from reality. Therefore, any state that results in a dedifferentiation of regions and a decrease in the separation of reality from unreality is regressive.

Barker et al. further contended that increasing the level of inner-personal tension could lead to a regressive state, for overriding tension might weaken the boundaries between the regions, causing dedifferentiation. Dedifferentiation indicates that the individual is making fewer psychological distinctions, leading to less sophisticated patterns of behavior.

One manner of increasing tension is to prevent the attainment of a desirable goal. The reader will recall from Chapter 3 that goal thwarting is frequently considered to be the operational manipulation that produces frustration. Similarly, frustration, or goal thwarting, was employed by Barker et al. to increase the level of tension and, in turn, to produce regression.

The experiment conducted by Barker et al. to produce regression was relatively straightforward. Children were brought into an experimental room and allowed to play with attractive toys. They were then separated from the toys by a partition, so that they could still see the toys, but were prevented from handling them. That is, there was a limitation in their space of free movement. During the separation period the children could play with other objects located in the room. Throughout the "prefrustration" and "frustration" periods the experimenters measured the "constructiveness of play." Unconstructive play was described as "primitive, simple, and with little structure" (for example, examining toys superficially), while constructive play was described as "imaginative and highly developed" (for example, using toys as part of an elaborate story). Constructiveness of play had been shown to increase as a function of mental age and thus could be used to measure regressive tendencies.

The results of the Barker et al. study revealed that the constructiveness of play activities did decrease from the prefrustration to the frustration period. During the time of frustration the play of the children was more primitive, less elaborate, and so forth. Hence the investigators concluded that frustration, or tension increment, could lead to regression. (For further discussion of this research and some methodological criticisms, the reader is directed to Lawson, 1965; Yates, 1962. The main research criticism has been that this study did not include a "no-frustration" control group. Thus the "regressive" behaviors might have been due to fatigue, boredom, or similar factors.)

Task Recall and Task Resumption

The investigations of task recall and task resumption were the first studies in which hypotheses were directly derived from Lewin's conception of motivation. Their importance within the Lewinian system cannot be overemphasized. According to Lewin (1935): "All later experimental investigations are built upon this. It was an attempt to break a first path through a primeval forest of facts and assumptions, using concepts the practical utility of which was still wholly untried" (p. 240).

Task Recall

It is said that the idea for the experimental investigation of task recall originated from observations in a restaurant. Lewin noticed that a certain waiter did not write down individuals' orders, yet was able to recall what they had selected when it was time to collect the bill. One day Lewin returned to the restaurant a few minutes after he had paid the check and asked the waiter what had been ordered. The waiter no longer retained this information. This led Lewin to believe that there is differential recall of a completed task versus an incomplete task.

Lewin (1951) employed four assumptions, which were implicitly introduced earlier in this chapter, to derive the hypothesis that there would be differential recall of finished and unfinished tasks:

Assumption 1: The intention to reach a certain goal G (to carry out an action leading to G) corresponds to a tension (t) in a certain system or region, (S^G), within the person so that $t\,(S^G) > 0$.

Assumption 2: The tension $t\,(S^G)$ is released if the goal G is reached:

$$t\,(S^G) = 0 \text{ if } P^cG \text{ [if } P \text{ completes } G]$$

Assumption 3: To a need for G corresponds a force $f_{P,G}$ acting upon the person and causing a tendency of locomotion toward G:

$$\text{if } t\,(S^G) > 0 \rightarrow f_{P,G} > 0$$

Assumption 3a: A need leads not only to a tendency of actual locomotion towards the goal region but also to thinking about this type of activity; in other words, the force $f_{P,G}$ exists not only on the level of doing (reality) but also on the level of thinking (irreality):

$$\text{if } t(S^G) > 0 \rightarrow f_{P,R} > 0$$

where R means recall. (pp. 9-10)

These assumptions logically lead to this derivation concerning differential task recall:

The tendency to recall interrupted activities should be greater than the tendency to recall finished ones. This derivation can be made as follows. We indicate the completed task by C, the unfinished one by U, and the corresponding systems by S^c and S^u respectively. We can then state:

1. $t(S^u) > 0$, according to Assumption 1.
2. $t(S^c) = 0$, according to Assumption 2.
3. $f_{P,U} > f_{P,C}$; hence, according to Assumption 3a, on the level of thinking.

In other words: there is a greater tendency spontaneously to recall unfinished tasks than finished tasks. (p. 10)

Empirical analysis. To test this derivation, Lewin and his students (e.g., Marrow, 1938; Zeigarnik, 1927) experimentally manipulated the degree of task completion in a laboratory setting. They then compared the recall of unfinished tasks with the recall of finished tasks. Subjects generally were given 16 or 20 simple puzzles (anagrams, arithmetic problems, and the like) to perform. Half of the tasks were too long to be completed within the allotted time period, while the others were relatively short and could be finished. The experimenter collected all the puzzles and, following an interval of a few minutes, unexpectedly asked the subjects to recall the tasks. Zeigarnik (1927) first demonstrated that there was greater recall of the incomplete tasks than the completed ones. The ratio of incomplete to completed tasks recalled (the Zeigarnik quotient) approached 2:1. The tendency to recall a greater percentage of unfinished tasks became known as the Zeigarnik effect.

Lewin tested a number of additional derivations from his conception of tense systems, employing differential task recall as the dependent variable. The amount of tension remaining within a tense system had been postulated to be a function of the time the region is in tension and the strength of the boundaries around that region. Therefore, the Zeigarnik quotient was expected to decrease over time and in situations in which the strength of the boundaries between the regions had been weakened. In one study, Zeigarnik found that when task recall was delayed for 24 hours, the Zeigarnik quotient dropped to 1.2:1. Further, tired subjects and individuals subjected to "strong emotional excitation" prior to recall exhibited a greatly decreased Zeigarnik quotient. The operations of fatigue and induced emotion were expected to decrease the firmness of the inner-personal boundaries. In another study, Marrow (1938) demonstrated that subjective, rather than objective, completion influences task recall. He told subjects that interruption meant they were doing well, while allowing them to finish indicated poor performance. Marrow found greater recall of the subjectively incomplete (objectively complete) tasks than of the subjectively complete (objectively incomplete) tasks.

The general pattern of results confirmed the predictions derived from Lewin's conception of tension and enhanced the validity of the theory. The results were especially supportive of his conception because they did not fit easily into any other theoretical framework.

Empirical problems. Unfortunately, a contradiction occurred when studies of task recall were conducted in the United States. Experimenters such as Rosenzweig (1943) and Glixman (1949) obtained results partially opposed to those of the previous investigations. They found greater recall of completed than incomplete tasks in "ego-oriented" or stress situations. To explain these data, Rosenzweig postulated that the incomplete tasks were "repressed." Failure was thought to represent a threat to the self or the ego; not remembering unfinished tasks was anxiety reducing. For this reason he believed there was relatively greater recall of the successful or completed tasks than the unfinished or failed tasks. (Freud's reaction to this research is shown in Figure 2.3, Chapter 2, in his letter to Rosenzweig.)

Subsequent investigators such as Atkinson (1953) attempted to reconcile the contradictory data gathered by Lewin and Rosenzweig by pointing out differences in the subject populations that were tested. However, over the years, many investigators have reported a Zeigarnik effect, many others have found "repression," and still others have found no difference in recall (see review in Weiner, 1966). Thus it is not known whether there really is a Zeigarnik effect, and a satisfactory explanation of the conflicting data has not been offered. Since the 1960s there have been very few research investigations in this area, and it is highly unlikely that this empirical issue will be resolved in the near future. Experimental psychologists certainly do not exhibit a Zeigarnik effect, for they are content to move on to new issues, leaving past problems unresolved and forgotten.

Task Resumption (only in Lewinian Theory)

The experimental paradigm used to study task resumption was very similar to the one employed for the investigation of task recall. Subjects, typically children, were given a series of tasks to complete. They were interrupted before they could finish some of these tasks, but given sufficient time for completion of others. The experimenter then removed herself from the experimental room using some pretense—answering a telephone, sharpening a pencil, or performing a similar errand. During the intervening time period, the subjects could "spontaneously" resume some of the tasks. At times the tasks remained in the subjects' immediate visual field, while on other occasions the tasks were placed out of sight, although they remained available to the subjects. In the initial investigation in this area, Ovsiankina (1928) reported a significant tendency for individuals to resume the previously unfinished tasks. This occurred whether the tasks were immediately visible or out of sight.

Further experimentation revealed that the likelihood of resumption is influenced by many factors. These include the following:

(1) *The type of activity*. Tasks having no definite end state (such as stringing beads) are resumed significantly less often than those that have a definite goal.

(2) *The point at which the activity is interrupted.* In general, the closer the subject is to the goal when the interruption occurs, the greater the likelihood of resumption.

(3) *The duration of the interruption.* As the time between the interruption and the opportunity to resume increases, the tendency to resume the task decreases. This lends support to Lewin's assumption that the amount of tension remaining within a region is, in part, a function of the time that the region is in tension.

(4) *The attitude and character of the person.* According to Lewin (1951), "Children who had the attitude of being examined and of strict obedience showed little resumption owing to the lack of involvement; they were governed mainly by induced forces" (p. 275). That is, there was no intrinsic interest among these children to undertake the activities and, therefore, no region remained in tension. The children performed the task because of an extrinsic source of motivation.

Since the 1930s there have been extremely few studies of task resumption. It is intuitively reasonable and surely an accepted observation that individuals tend to finish tasks that have been started and do not tend to "resume" completed activities. But the obviousness of an empirical fact does not minimize its theoretical importance. It is obvious that most objects fall; it is also an important empirical fact, and a sophisticated theory was required to explain this datum. Lewinian field theory specifies that unfinished tasks will be resumed. Other theoretical approaches have not focused upon the effects of attaining or not attaining a goal. Hence the derivation concerning task resumption is unique to Lewinian theory.

More sophisticated questions related to resumption that could further confirm or refute Lewinian theory remain to be raised. For example, some of the data reported by Ovsiankina actually call Lewinian theory into question. Lewin postulated that following the nonattainment of a goal the tension within the inner-personal region associated with the goal persists. Tension is defined operationally as the magnitude of a need; theoretically, it is relatively independent of psychological distance from the goal. Yet Ovsiankina found that resumption is affected by distance from the goal; the closer the goal at the time of interruption, the more likely its resumption. Because resumption is affected by psychological distance, which is a determinant of force and not tension, it is more consistent to postulate that aroused *force* persists following nonattainment of a goal. If only the magnitude of aroused tension persists, then the tendency to resume unfinished tasks should be unrelated to distance from the goal at the time of the interruption. This inference would greatly alter Lewin's theory.

Substitution

As indicated in the discussion of regression, Lewin was strongly influenced by the observations and analyses of Freud. He realized that Freud's insights were not easily put to scientific test and that experimental evidence in support of Freud's conception was indeed sparse. Lewin (1935) wrote:

> Experimental studies of the dynamic laws of the behavior and structure of personality have forced us to consider more and more complicated problems. Instead of investigating the single psychological systems which correspond to simple needs and desires, we have to deal with the interrelationships of these systems, with their differentiation and transformations, and with the different kinds of larger wholes built up from them. These interrelationships and larger wholes are very labile and delicate. Yet one must try to get hold of them experimentally because they are most important for understanding the underlying reality of behavior and personality differences. In doing this we often find facts which Freud first brought to our attention, thereby rendering a great service even though he has not given a clear dynamic theory in regard to them. (p. 180)

The study of substitution provided Lewin the opportunity to examine systematically some of Freud's most important concepts concerning the dynamics of behavior. Freud had postulated that following nonattainment of a goal the tendency to strive for that goal persists. The mechanism responsible for the persisting wish was identified as the "internal stimulus from which there is no flight." You will recall that, according to Freud, this persisting tendency often is inadvertently expressed in dreams, jokes, and slips of the tongue, when the ego is less vigilant or when social rules are more permissive. Lewin incorporated this idea into his theory by including the concept of persisting tense regions.

Within Freudian theory, the object of a desire may change; there are "vicissitudes of the instincts." A forbidden, unfulfilled wish can, for example, become directed toward (attached to) objects that have some similarity to the desired goal. Freud stated that ultimately a sexual tendency might even be expressed in cultural activities such as painting or composing. In his analyses of Michelangelo and Leonardo da Vinci he contended that these great artists had strong unfulfilled sexual urges toward their mothers, which were deflected into socially acceptable channels. Freud labeled this defense "sublimation"; it typically is included in lists of defense mechanisms, along with repression, perceptual defense, denial, intellectualization, and regression.

Lewin (1935) likewise noted that goal objects may change. Substitution, the term Lewin used rather than sublimation, is manifested in many different ways:

> There is, for instance, the man who dreams of a palace and brings a few pieces of marble into his kitchen. There is the man who cannot buy a piano, but who collects piano catalogs. Again, we find the delinquent boy who knows that he will not be allowed to leave his reform school but who asks for a traveling bag as a birthday present. And the little boy who threatens and scolds the larger boy whom he cannot beat on the playground. These and a hundred other examples make us realize how important and far-reaching the problem of substitution is in regard to psychological needs as well as with reference to bodily needs such as hunger and sex. (pp. 180-181)

Experimental Studies

Ovsiankina and Zeigarnik provided the foundation for the experimental investigation of substitution. It was believed that these investigators had demonstrated that tension persists in a region and is reduced with goal attainment. The question asked in the study of substitution is: Can tensions in regions be discharged through some compensatory activity? That is, will there be a decrease in the recall or the resumption of previously interrupted tasks following completion of other activities? If so, then this would be a valid experimental demonstration that one goal has substitute value for another.

The general experimental paradigm used in the study of substitution follows closely the methodology first employed by Ovsiankina. Subjects were given tasks to complete and were interrupted before completion. The experimenter then allowed the subjects to undertake and finish some interpolated activity. Finally, subjects were tested for the spontaneous resumption of the previously unfinished tasks. Resumption, therefore, became the behavioral criterion for the identification of goal substitutes. That is, if the individual resumed the previously unfinished activity, then the interpolated activity did not serve as a substitute goal. But if the originally unfinished activity was not undertaken following the interpolated activity, then the second activity had substitute value.

One of the first experimental studies of substitution was conducted by Lissner (1933). In her experiment, children were interrupted while they were making figures from clay. Then, after making different figures, they were tested for resumption. Lissner identified two factors that influence the substitute value of an activity: its similarity to the first activity and its level of difficulty. The more similar and difficult the interpolated task, the greater its substitute value. In another study, Lissner told the children that the interpolated activity was "completely different" from the one they had just attempted. In that situation the interpolated activity had little substitute value for the original activity. That is, the percentage of task resumption following the activity did not decrease.

Mahler (1933), another of Lewin's students, gave subjects an interpolated activity that could be completed in ways that differed in their proximity to overt behavior (the level of reality). Subjects could think about doing the task, talk through its completion, or actually do it. In general, substitute value varied monotonically with the degree of reality of the action. This implies that daydreams and other such fantasy activities will have little (but *some*) value for the reduction of motivation. Recall that earlier it was indicated that the notion of a catharsis of aggression via fantasy activity has received only weak experimental support.

The experimental attitude of the subject also has been shown to be an important determinant of substitute value (Adler & Kounin, 1939). If the subject's attitude toward a task is concrete, such as "building a house for Mary," then "building a house for a different person" has little substitute value. However, if the task is conceived more abstractly, such as building a house, then an interpolated task of building another house has substitute value.

Lewin (1935) speculated about the psychological characteristics of what he called "feebleminded" individuals from their behavior in substitution experiments. Feebleminded children exhibit great variance in their behavior following completion of an interpolated task. Either they all tend to resume the original activity after the interpolated completion (no substitution), or virtually none of the children resumes the original task (complete substitution). Lewin reasoned, therefore, that feebleminded children have strong boundaries between their inner-personal regions, but fewer regions (differentiations) than normal children (see Figure 4.10). Consequently, they perceive two activities as identical (complete substitution) or as psychologically separate (no substitution). (For some objections to this formulation, see Stevenson & Zigler, 1957; Zigler, 1962.)

Additional experimental work on substitution was conducted by Henle (1944). Her work concerned the relationship of substitution, valence of the original task, and valence of the interpolated or substitute task. In Henle's studies, subjects first rated the attractiveness of various activities. They then were given a subjectively attractive or unattractive task to complete. Following interruption, an interpolated activity of high or low attractiveness was completed. Again resumption was the behavioral criterion used to infer the degree of substitution. Henle found that the greater the valence of the original task, the less the possibility that other tasks can substitute for it. Similarly, the greater the valence of an interpolated activity, the greater its substitute value.

The studies of Mahler, Lissner, Henle, and others clearly demonstrate that goals can substitute for one another. Further, these studies identified some of the relevant dimensions and determinants of substitution. The data support Lewin's contention that there are interrelationships, or dynamic

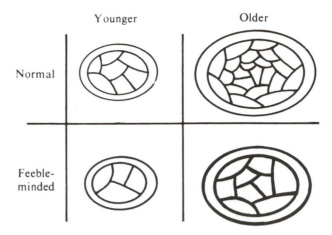

Figure 4.10. Representation of the development of normal and feebleminded individuals. Normal children are assumed to have greater differentiation and weaker boundaries between the inner-personal regions than are feebleminded children. (From Lewin, 1935, p. 210.)

communications, among psychological systems. That is, needs are not separate psychologically, or, in Lewinian language, tension spreads to neighboring regions. This body of empirical work is again uniquely Lewinian and cannot be readily accounted for within other theoretical systems.

Balance Theory

Fritz Heider (1960), the originator of balance theory, noted that this conception "is not meant to be a general theory of motivation but has been developed mainly with respect to interpersonal relations" (p. 166). Thus it was not devised to have the breadth or generality of the theories proposed by Freud, Hull, and Lewin (even though it became applied to intra- as well as interpersonal phenomena). In spite of its modest goals, balance theories were very dominant in psychology in the 1960s, playing an important role in both motivation and social psychology. There are a number of balance-type or congruity theories in addition to the one proposed by Heider (e.g., Abelson & Rosenberg, 1958; Festinger, 1957; Newcomb, 1953; Osgood & Tannenbaum, 1955; Peak, 1958), the most dominant being Festinger's dissonance theory, examined in the prior chapter. And Heider's theory was extended by Cartwright and Harary (1956) and others. Here, however, I will confine my attention to the formulations of Heider because of his important influence. I also will be content to present only briefly some of the controversies concerning these theories, which is consistent with my agenda of focusing upon the positive contributions and heuristic value of the motivational thoughts.

Balance theory is derived from the study of particular configurations. The configurations of interest to Heider (1958) involve two components: units and sentiments (affective attitudes such as liking). Entities constitute a *unit* when they are perceived as belonging together. Thus members of a club, families, and married couples are perceived as units. Similarly, a person and his or her deeds form a unit. A unit, then, is a mental clustering.

The conditions leading to unit formation were examined by the Gestaltists in their studies of object perception. For example, similarity and proximity were identified as two determinants of unit formation. Thus in the following line the asterisks are perceived in groups (units) because of their proximity:

**   **   **   **   **

Heider suggested that this rule also applies in the forming of social units: One forms a unit with a working partner because of "closeness."

Units also depend on their surrounding entities. Thus, for example, if the following two letter sequences are compared, d and e form a pair in the second but not the first sequence, although they have the same space between them in both examples.

abcd efgh   abc   d e   fgh

Heider (1958) illustrated how this principle also applies to social perception:

> The surrounding can determine the unit formation. . . . In the sequence aaaAAA the two letters [a and A] belong to different groups; in the sequence XXXaAXXX they may easily be seen as belonging to one group. If a New Yorker and a Bostonian meet in a party composed of half New Yorkers and half Bostonians they will very likely feel they belong to two different units. But if they meet in a party in which no one else is American they will feel they belong together. (p. 178)

The concept of balance concerns the relations between units and sentiments or attitudes. A balanced state designates a situation in which the perceived units and sentiments exist without stress, in equilibrium, with no pressure toward change. That is, balance means that the situation is tension free (as opposed to a state of equal opposing forces, where there might be "balance" yet tension). In contrast, given an imbalanced state, there is pressure or force toward change.

Consider, for example, a situation in which the two members of a couple dislike each other. This intuitively is an imbalanced state. In this

TABLE 4.2 Computation of Balance Within a Dyad

Numerical Value Attached to Each Relation

Unit Formation:	U = +1		−U = −1	
Liking:	L = +1		−L = −1	
			Represented as	*Multiplication*

Balanced States

(1) You like a person with whom you are associated. — pLo and pUo — $+1 \times +1 = +1$

(2) You dislike a person with whom you are not associated. — p − Lo and p − Uo — $−1 \times −1 = +1$

Imbalanced States

(1) You dislike a person with whom you are associated. — p −Lo but pUo — $−1 \times +1 = −1$

(2) You like a person with whom you are not associated. — pLo, but p − Uo — $+1 \times −1 = −1$

Note: Whenever the product of the multiplication is positive, the state is considered balanced; whenever the product is negative, the state is considered imbalanced.

situation, there would be a tendency either for the unit to break or for the sentiments to change to be more positive. There are four possible combinations to consider when examining the generality of balance principles: The persons may (+) or may not (−) be in a unit relation with one another, and they may have positive (+) or negative (−) feelings about one another. Whether a situation is balanced or not can be determined by assigning values to any situation and then multiplying the unit and attitude values (see Table 4.2). Table 4.2 shows that forming a unit with a liked other and not forming a unit with a disliked other are balanced states, whereas forming a unit with a disliked other (the example just presented) and not forming a unit with a liked other are imbalanced systems, or tense states, in which there is a tendency toward change. Action should be taken to bring these situations into equilibrium.

In accord with Gestalt principles, then, it is the whole qualities of these structures that determine their motivational effects. Just as in the perception of perceived motion and musical melodies, psychological processes associated with these configurations cannot be derived from their individual parts. In this case, the individual parts include cognitions and affects, and balance is concerned with how these work together to influence motivated behavior.

The main focus of balance theory has not been on just the sentiments of persons within a unit, but rather on how members of a unit relate to another object. Thus triads rather than dyads have received the most attention. These triads are often referred to as a "p-o-x triads" where p refers to one person, o to another individual, and x to some object. The presence of three rather than two components increases the number of

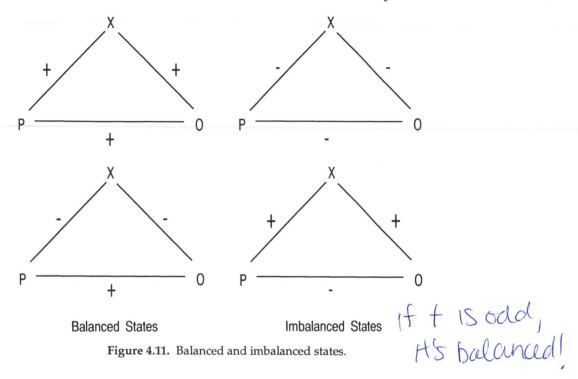

Balanced States   Imbalanced States   *If + is odd,*
                                                          It's balanced!

Figure 4.11. Balanced and imbalanced states.

possible permutations regarding the relations among the elements from four to eight: A person (p) can like or dislike an object (o) and can like or dislike another person (x), and that other person can dislike or like the object (see the examples in Figure 4.11). This results in eight possible combinations of these relations (as will be seen in Experiment 4.2).

Figure 4.11 depicts two balanced and two imbalanced states. If, for example, p likes poetry, p likes o, and o likes poetry, then this situation is considered to be balanced. Furthermore, if both p and o dislike poetry and p likes o, then again there is balance. However, if p and o both dislike poetry and yet p does not like o, or if they both like poetry but dislike one another, then the situation is not in balance. The general rule to determine if balance does or does not exist in a triad is to again assign positive and negative values to the three entities and multiply. If this product is positive, then the situation is believed to be balanced. Subsequent extensions of this theory by Cartwright and Harary (1956) and others expanded the conception to determine not only the existence or absence of balance, but also its magnitude.

In the most extensive test of this theory, situations are created that, according to the mathematical rule, are or are not in balance, and subjects rate their pleasantness (Jordan, 1953). The reader can do this now, in Experiment 4.2. In accord with balance predictions, balanced states should be (and have been) rated as more pleasant than unbalanced states.

Experiment 4.2

Rate, from 1-10, how pleasant each of the following situations is, with 1 the least pleasant and the 10 the most pleasant.

(1) You like person X, you like sports, and that person likes sports.   _____

(2) You like person X, you like sports, and that person dislikes sports.   _____

(3) You like person X, you dislike sports, and that person likes sports.   _____

(4) You like person X, you dislike sports, and that person dislikes sports.   _____

(5) You dislike person X, you like sports, and that person likes sports.   _____

(6) You dislike person X, you like sports, and that person dislikes sports.   _____

(7) You dislike person X, you dislike sports, and that person likes sports.   _____

(8) You dislike person X, you dislike sports, and that person dislikes sports.   _____

To determine if you rate balanced situations as more pleasant than unbalanced ones, add up your ratings for Situations 1, 4, 6, and 7 and compare the total with the sum of your ratings for Situations 2, 3, 5, and 8. The former are all balanced situations (note that multiplication of the signs will produce a positive value), whereas the latter are all unbalanced.

Total balance pleasantness score   _____

Total imbalance pleasantness score   _____

Some Doubts

While the results of the judgment studies regarding pleasantness have been as predicted, some problems also have arisen. Not all balanced triads are considered pleasant. For example, if p dislikes o and disagrees with that person (Situations 6 and 7 in Experiment 4.2), then this situation is not considered very pleasant, although it is one of balance. In general, only situations in which x is liked and there is agreement with o (Situations 1 and 4 in Experiment 4.2) are differentiated from the others in terms of positiveness. Other research has examined the pleasantness ratings only of situations in which there is agreement between the persons on their attitudes, and this results in as high pleasantness ratings as do general balanced states. This can be determined in Experiment 4.2 by comparing Situations 1, 4, 5, and 8 (agreement) with those depicted in 2, 3, 6, and 7 (disagreement). In addition, individuals prefer positive to negative relationships (see Zajonc, 1968). This can be ascertained in Experiment 4.2 by comparing the first four situations with the last four. These tendencies tend to be confounded with the motivational properties of balance, particularly inasmuch as Situation 1 is balanced, there is agreement between the persons, and the relationship is positive. It is usually rated as most pleasant. This confounding has placed the status of the balance conception in some question (see Insko, 1984). Nonetheless, in spite of such unresolved issues, it does appear that there is a general preference for overall balance.

Comparison to Field Theory

Both field and balance theory are partially derived from Gestalt principles, but they also differ in fundamental respects. Foremost among these is that, according to balance theory, motivation is derived from the properties of the structure (configuration), which imposes forces. These dynamic forces then change the structure itself (from one of imbalance to one of balance). That is, the structure that develops from disequilibrium differs from the one of equilibrium. This is not a matter of tension being "drained" from a system. Further, in field theory tension release does not necessarily change environmental or personal structure; rather, it alters the forces acting on the person. Perhaps the fundamental difference between field and balance theory is that the former makes use of a hydraulic metaphor, with the dynamics most closely associated with tension, whereas an electrical field metaphor is associated with balance theory, with the dynamics most closely associated with the configural state. Note, however, that both make use of machine metaphors.

Summary

Before moving on, let's again take stock of the Gestalt position regarding motivated behavior. Gestaltists first noted that in the physical world there is a tendency toward simplicity and balance of forces. Hence, for example, a drop of oil in water takes on the form of a circle. Gestaltists then contended that the perceptual world follows similar rules. That is, perception is an active process in which the stimulus world is structured into "good" forms; there is a tendency to alter incoming sensations so that they are regular and in balance. For example, faces are perceived as symmetrical and a somewhat opened circle is nonetheless identified and classified as a circle. Then Heider carried these ideas one step further, stating that these principles also capture interpersonal processes. Thus if I like Mary and the president, while she does not like the president, then this is not a "simple" or "balanced" state. Processes therefore are activated to bring the structure into balance. I may break my relationship with Mary, change my perception of the president, or convince her to accept my viewpoint. Once equilibrium is established, there is no further force toward change.

It was indicated that, unlike the theories of Freud, Hull, and Lewin, balance is a more limited principle that applies to a relatively narrow base of data. However, there are other observations that can be incorporated within balance theory, although these phenomena have not been examined by Gestaltists or balance theorists, and indeed those interested in these phenomena do not necessarily associate their research endeavors with Gestalt psychology. One current example of such an area of research concerns self-consistency—that is, the congruence between the self and experience.

Self-Consistency

The desire for self-consistency has played a role in some of the major theories of personality. For example, Carl Rogers (1951) has stated that "most of the ways of behaving which are adopted by the organism are those which are consistent with the concept of the self" (p. 507). Others, such as Lecky (1945), have contended that people want to preserve their self-concepts and so behave in ways that are consistent with their self-views. These ideas can be readily incorporated within a balance viewpoint: A system is out of balance when one's view of oneself and one's experiences are contradictory. This should initiate forces either to change self-perception or to disconfirm or minimize the experience that has occurred. Hence, for example, if Mary views herself as sincere but another calls her insincere, then she might consider either altering her self-conception or discounting that feedback. Similar examples were noted in the discussion of the theory of cognitive dissonance.

There recently has been an active debate revolving around individuals' desires for self-consistency experiences (e.g., Swann, 1987; Swann, Pelham, & Krull, 1989). In opposition, it has been argued that people want to maximize their self-esteem and hence seek opportunities to acquire positive feedback. This is known as self-enhancement theory. Hence if a person high in self-esteem, or high in self-perception regarding a particular characteristic, seeks out positive feedback from others (e.g., you are a good person; you are good at math), then such behavior not only supports self-enhancement theory, but also is in accord with predictions based on balance theory. Consider, however, those low in personal esteem or holding negative views about themselves in particular domains. Self-enhancement theory apparently predicts that these individuals would desire positive feedback about themselves regarding the attitude in question, whereas self-consistency theory suggests that they would prefer negative feedback.

That is, they should prefer, actively search for, elicit, and recall knowledge that will confirm their unfavorable self-perceptions.

Unfortunately, the data necessary to resolve this theoretical controversy, as well as the explanations of the data that have been gathered, are not definitive. Concerning those low in self-esteem or with specific negative self-views, it is yet undetermined whether and under what conditions they might prefer negative to positive information about themselves. Furthermore, even if they do prefer self-consistent feedback, it is unclear whether this is due to a mechanistic tendency or force toward balance or because of more cognitive mediators. For example, if a person perceives herself to be poor at math but others believe that she is a good mathematician, then those others could approach her for help with their math homework, call on her to perform tasks that she cannot do, and so forth. Thus realistic perceptions by others may be desired not because of mechanical balance principles, but rather because of conscious calculations regarding the consequences of inaccurate perceptions. From the perspective of this book, however, regardless of the outcome of this controversy, it is evident that balance theory is being applied to a variety of motivation-related observations.

SUMMARY

Gestalt psychology gave rise to two theories of motivation: Lewinian field theory and the less general balance theory proposed by Heider. The Gestaltists argued that the perception of an object is influenced by the field of forces surrounding that object and the interrelationships among the forces in the field. Furthermore, there was a tendency for the force field to reach equilibrium. Guided by these presumptions, the theories of Lewin and Heider presumed that behavior occurs within a psychological field and that many interacting forces determine behavior at any one moment.

Lewin's field theory includes structural and dynamic constructs for the person and the environment. The concept of tension integrates the person and environmental constructs. Tension, which results from a need state, is necessary in order for an environmental object to acquire a valence. The creation of a valence also establishes a force field around the valued object. This force acts to locomote the person in the direction of the goal object, with the intensity of the force increasing as the person approaches the desired goal. If the goal is attained, tension is released, thus reducing the valence of the environmental object and, in turn, decreasing the force acting upon the person. The reduction in force leads to a cessation of behavior. Lewin's conception of motivation thus incorporates hedonism and homeostasis. However, unlike other tension reduction theorists, Lewin is a phenomenologist, stressing the perceived, rather than the real, world.

A number of research investigations grew out of Lewin's theory. Among the areas of study are (a) conflict, with emphasis on the instability (approach-approach conflicts) or the stability (avoidance-avoidance conflicts) of behavior that results from being in a field of overlapping forces; (b) frustration and the relation between lack of goal attainment and regression (dedifferentiation); (c) task recall and resumption, which tested the notion that persisting tense regions will be manifested in the recall and resumption of unfinished tasks; and (d) substitution, a concept that captured Freud's idea of an overlap between needs and his belief that some goals derive their value because other more desirable goals are not attainable. It is evident that Lewin's theory was a great stimulant for psychological research.

Many similarities and differences among the Freudian, Hullian, and Lewinian schemes have been pointed out. Considering now only Hull and Lewin, it can be seen that both theorists attempted to identify the immediate determinants of action and specified a quasi-mathematical model of behavior. In their models both Hull and Lewin included concepts representing motivational states of the person (drive, tension), the incentive value of the goal (labeled K and G), and a directional or steering variable (habit, psychological distance). But drive theorists primarily gathered their data in experiments with infrahumans, whereas Lewinians were concerned almost exclusively with complex human behavior, at times guided by the insights of Freud. Thus drive theorists excelled in demonstrating how motivational theorists ought to operate as experimenters, conducting well-controlled investigations in the laboratory. On the other hand, the main contribution of the field theorists was pointing out the broader goals of a theory of motivation, which include understanding complex human behavior through an experimentally testable theory that can also explain the simpler behavior of infrahumans.

Heider's balance theory was less ambitious than Lewinian field theory and brought the Gestalt balance principles to bear on interpersonal relationships. Heider demonstrated that particular structural configurations are in or out of balance; in the latter instances individuals are activated to bring the structure back into balance. Unlike Lewinian theory, in Heider's theory force was derived from structure per se, and concepts such as tension within regions or tension being drained from regions were not included in the analyses of Heider and other consistency theorists. Balance principles were particularly dominant in the 1960s.

Epilogue to the
Machine Metaphor

The machine metaphor for the study of human motivation developed from the initial belief that the behavior of subhumans could be attributed entirely to bodily processes. That is, the behaviors were instinctive and/or reflexive. The postulation by Darwin of a human-subhuman continuity then gave rise to the metaphor that humans also are machines. This viewpoint helped to free psychology from its philosophical and theological roots and provided a basis for carefully conducted research on the workings of the human machine.

As far as its influence on the psychology of motivation is concerned, the machine metaphor had a rather meteoric rise and fall. This metaphor dominated the study of human motivation for approximately 25 years, between 1930-1955. However, it also found important expression in Freud's theory of motivation in the early 1900s and in the consistency theories that were so prevalent in the 1960s. The machine metaphor also certainly can be found in the contemporary study of human motivation, although with much diminished emphasis and influence.

Recall that the "associated implications" of a machine were said to include inflexible behavior, lack of volitional responding, predetermined reactions to input, use of energy, an aim or function, and coordinated subparts or a structure that is instrumental to the function. Various aspects of these machine characteristics can be found in the theories that have been reviewed thus far. Freudian psychoanalytic theory makes use of energy principles and considers the structure and functions of the human machine. The biological perspectives of ethology and sociobiology, like Freudian psychology, postulate basic urges that are unknown to the organism and are not subject to volitional control. Rather, motivation is a product of a long evolutionary history, and behaviors have survival significance. Hullian theory is guided not only by the principle that drive energizes behavior and is necessary for activation, but also that the growth of habits is based on automatic strengthening of stimulus-response bonds. Thus when an organism is in a particular environment, a response must follow that is dictated by prior reinforcement contingencies. The notion of an organism striving for equilibrium by reducing drive level also is found in Festinger's theory of cognitive dissonance. Finally, the concluding chapter in this section showed that Lewin's field theory made use of hydraulic concepts, as had the ethologists, and that balance theory is based on Gestalt notions regarding "good" figures, which were, in turn, derived from the observation of characteristics of physical objects and the interpretation of perceptual phenomena. In sum, there is no doubt that the machine metaphor has played a prominent role in a variety of psychological theories of motivation.

An extremely impressive and instructive aspect of the use of the machine metaphor has been its ability to account for phenomena that exemplify behavioral flexibility, surely not a characteristic of machines. Freud addressed issues of displacement and catharsis, Lorenz and Tinbergen considered vacuum behavior, Hull and Spence examined those remote associates to a stimulus that had been raised above threshold, and Lewin investigated substitution. The basic principles of the machine metaphor have been retained even as theorists have accounted for behavioral plasticity.

In addition, the machine metaphor can capture a surprising array of phenomena. Freudian theory has attempted to predict the consequences of fantasy activity; sociobiologists are able to predict various facets of sexual, reproductive, and altruistic actions, as documented in Experiment 2.1 in such specific illustrations as mate preferences and decisions about the targets of altruism; drive theorists are able to predict the relative speed of conditioning and verbal learning, as well as the nature of the mathematical relation between the terms in their theory, as documented in Experiment 3.1; dissonance theories have identified the types of cognitive states that result in the initiation of activity to reduce that dissonance; field theorists have anticipated the relative recall of incomplete and completed tasks; and balance theorists have pointed out those interpersonal conditions that are most satisfying, according to equilibrium notions, as documented in Experiment 4.2. Some of these hypotheses assume that the machine must feel and think. This certainly contradicts the associated implications of a machine, but, as has been emphasized throughout, not all aspects of the known must fit the unknown in order for the metaphor to shed some light upon it. That is, when one refers to a person as a shark, the metaphor does not lose its value because the target person has no tail or sharp teeth.

A metaphor is not an explanation; calling a human a machine does not explain human behavior. But it is evident that some aspects of our behavior are amenable to a machinelike analysis. And, if it is accepted that many metaphors can exist side by side at the same moment in time, perhaps even when they are contradictory, then it behooves us as motivational theorists to maintain the metaphor as a window for the explanation and interpretation of human behavior.

In my first book on motivation, written about 20 years ago, I concluded as follows: "It is argued that a mechanistic psychology is no longer adequate to account for the very data it generated" (Weiner, 1972, p. 419). This was written at a time when this metaphor still had some impact and visibility. I believe now that I was taking the metaphor too literally, and prefer to restate the conclusion as follows: It is argued that a mechanistic theory can parsimoniously account for some of the vast variety of data that it generated, although other aspects of human behavior must be examined with other metaphors. There is reason to admire what the metaphor has accomplished in terms of the generation of sophisticated theories and impressive research.

GODLIKE METAPHORS IN HUMAN MOTIVATION:

Humans as All-Knowing

I think, therefore I am.
RENÉ DESCARTES

The Historical Context of Metaphorical Transition

As previously indicated, the machine metaphor dominated psychology during the period 1930-1955. It then exhibited a rather rapid decline in popularity (although it did make a comeback in the balance theories of the 1960s and remained visible in specific areas such as behavior modification). There are many reasons for this diminution in influence, although it is difficult and speculative to understand such basic shifts in science, and in particular the waxing and waning of guiding metaphors as well as topics of study in psychology.

One apparent reason for the decline of the machine metaphor was that psychologists with opposing viewpoints took the metaphor quite literally—that is, persons are *indeed* machines. Not only was this a personal affront, as brutalizing as Darwin calling humans mere animals, it contradicted everyday observations, such as human emotional expression, the onset of language, and the use of higher-order symbolic processes. Hence the challengers contended that people are *not* machines; the depiction was declared to be incorrect. The overused phrase "throwing the baby out with the bathwater" seems appropriate to describe what happened. The heuristic value of this metaphor, the theories that it spawned, and the behaviors that it was able to explain parsimoniously became victims of the purge, put in the psychological closet, perhaps for airing at some unspecified later date.

As eulogized by Bolles (1967):

> The drive concept is like an old man that has had a long, active, and yes, even useful life. It has produced a notable amount of conceptual and empirical work; it has, perhaps indirectly, made a great contribution to our understanding of behavior. But the fruitful days are nearly gone. The time has come when younger, more vigorous, more capable concepts must take over. So, as sentimental as we may feel about our old friend, we should not despair at his passing. (pp. 329-330)

A second reason for the metaphorical decline was the general *Zeitgeist*—that is, the general intellectual trends in the field or the "spirit of the time"—that was permeating psychology toward the end of the 1950s. Psychology was entering (or, more accurately, reentering) a mental or cognitive phase. There was growth of projective testing (how persons perceive an ambiguous stimulus), interest in thought processes and language, concern with person perception among social psychologists, and so on. Furthermore, the advent of information theory and computer models lent scientific respectability to the examination of mental events. The earlier union of cognitive psychology with philosophy and theology was no longer to be feared. Clearly, the study of mental processes was incompatible with or at least inconsistent with the machine metaphor that had been used (which was not that of a computer).

Yet another reason for the fading away of the machine metaphor, one previously indicated in the discussion of the hydraulic metaphor used by the ethologists, was that psychological energy, one of the associated implications of a machine, was nowhere to be found. Physiological psychologists at one time thought they were able to identify the brain location of a purely nondirective drive, but that proved untrue. And different measures of general arousal, such as galvanic skin response and heart rate, did not relate highly to one another. Indeed, not all needs were drives (consider oxygen deprivation), and not all drives had a viscerogenic representation, so that not all drive states were functional, aiding the organism to survive. Humans often are "dying to see a movie," but not attaining the goal typically does not result in death.

Finally, and perhaps of greatest importance, was that psychologists embracing the machine metaphor were in part guided by Morgan's Canon:

"In no case is an animal activity to be interpreted as the outcome of the exercise of a higher psychical faculty if it can be fairly interpreted as the outcome of an exercise which stands lower on the psychological scale" (Morgan, 1896, p. 59). The essence of this principle is demonstrated in the early explanation of why moths fly into fire. While the followers of the machine metaphor argued that the act was innately determined and the moth has no control over the behavior (a mechanistic explanation), the early cognitivists (circa 1900) contended that moths fly into flames because they are curious!

But later opponents of the machine metaphor called upon other observations and data that provided a greater challenge. These data were generated in so-called crucial experiments that pitted a machine-generated explanation against interpretations that were based on other metaphors. One pertinent arena of argument concerned the apparent tendency to seek change and stimulation. This certainly is not readily compatible with concepts such as homeostasis, drive reduction, equilibrium, and balance, which were proposed in the mechanistic theories of Freud, Hull, Festinger, Lewin, Heider, and others.

One of the most interesting controversies between opposing camps concerned the desire for varied stimulation and involved a phenomenon labeled "spontaneous alternation." In a typical investigation utilizing a T-maze, an organism, such as a rat, is placed in the alleyway and then must turn either right or left at the choice point for a reward. It has been noted that if the rat turns left on the first trial, then it is more likely to turn right on the second trial, and vice versa. This phenomenon has been called spontaneous alternation because the organism alters its choice on the two successive experiences. Alternation is not reduced by the receipt of a reward following the initial choice, although the alternation tendency is masked after a few trials because there is repetition of the response that has resulted in a reinforcement (see Dember, 1960).

The Hullians had a simple and parsimonious explanation of alternation. They asserted that after the initial response the muscles connected with the action undergo a temporary state of fatigue. Thus on the next trial a different response is made. This explanation is consistent with the Hullians' mechanistic conception of action: The machine was "wearing out."

On the other hand, psychologists with cognitive orientations postulated a process of stimulus satiation (Glanzer, 1953). That is, there is a reduced responsiveness to a stimulus as a consequence of prior exposure to that stimulus. The stimulus satiation position leads to identical predictions as the response fatigue notion: There should be alternation on successive trials. Furthermore, the greater the time between trials, the less likelihood of alternation, for both fatigue and stimulus satiation decrease over time. This prediction also has been confirmed.

In an attempt to resolve the alternation question, a critical experiment was devised that permitted a choice between the two explanations (Glanzer, 1953; Montgomery, 1952). A maze was constructed with two different

Figure II.1. Schematic diagram of the stimulus versus response alternation test. If the rat is started from the south on the first trial, it is started from the north on the second. When one starting alley is used, the other is blocked by a gate, as represented by the dotted lines. The arrows indicate the behavior on two successive trials. On the first, the animal turned right, and thereby went into the black arm. On the second trial, the animal also turned right, thereby entering the white arm. Turning responses were repeated, but maze arms were alternated. (From Dember, 1960, p. 345. Figure from *The Psychology of Perception* by W. Dember, copyright © 1960 by Holt, Rinehart and Winston, Inc. and renewed 1988 by W. Dember, reprinted by permission of the publisher.)

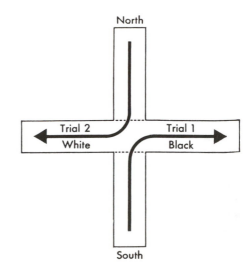

starting points (see Figure II.1). One arm of the maze was painted black; the other arm was white. After an initial trial, the animal was placed in the opposite start box. Thus, if response fatigue had built up, the organism should make a different response on the next trial, which would lead to the same stimulus as in the initial trial. But if stimulus satiation had occurred, then the organism should make the identical muscular response, for this would now expose it to a different stimulus than the one viewed on the previous trial. The results of investigations using this procedure clearly supported the stimulus satiation position. For example, an animal turned right on two successive trials, exposing itself to both black and white stimuli.

It should be noted, however, that the stimulus satiation explanation, as well as the response fatigue notion, is a "reaction against" theory. It does not propose that organisms are attracted to stimulation in the external environment. Rather, there is a decrease in the attractiveness of some stimulus due to satiation, which makes an alternative stimulus relatively more engaging.

A stimulus-seeking explanation of alternation was then proposed by Dember (1956) and Dember and Earl (1957). These investigators contended that organisms are attracted to novel stimuli and to changes in their environment. To test this hypothesis, Dember (1956) examined the behavior of rats in a Y-shaped maze. One arm of the maze was white, the other black. When the animals were placed in the start box, they were delayed before being allowed to enter the arms of the maze. During this delay the white arm was changed to black. Given a stimulus satiation conception, the animals should display no systematic choice preferences because both arms of the maze are identical in color. But if organisms are attracted to change, then they should enter the black arm that previously had been white. The data substantiated this prediction. In a similar experiment, the arms of the

Y-maze initially were black and gray and then were both changed to white. In this situation the animals entered the black-to-white arm, which represented the greater change.

Reintroducing a Metaphor

In the face of a general *Zeitgeist* change, everyday observations, and "crucial" experimental data, motivational psychologists turned to a pre- as well as post-Darwin metaphor—the person is Godlike, possessing a mind, with complete rationality and full knowledge. In Part II of this book this metaphor is examined, as represented in the expectancy-value theories of Lewin, Atkinson, and Rotter (Chapter 5), and the person-as-scientist theories of G. Kelly and the attribution theories of Heider, H. Kelley, and this writer (Chapter 6). It will then become evident that Lewin and Heider used constructs and held beliefs consistent with a Godlike, as well as a machine, metaphor. To reiterate, theorists may embrace more than one metaphor, even though the metaphors at times are conflicting.

Expectancy-Value Theories:

Humans as All-Knowing Decision Makers

CHAPTER

5

$\mathbf{M}$etaphors do not merely fade away, in spite of the admonition of Bolles (1967) that we should let drive, the "old man," peacefully pass away. Rather, a substitute or alternative way of thinking must be available to fill a void that would otherwise leave investigators unsure about the direction for their research. The study of motivation did have a replacement metaphor available, one that had existed even prior to the notion that a person is a machine. This was that humans are Godlike, that is, fully informed about all possible behavioral options, with complete rationality, and able to calculate their most hedonic course of action. Recall that this resembles the guiding view of human behavior prior to Darwin, as evident in Cartesian dualism.

Just as was true in the case of the machine metaphor, all of the associated implications of God are not applicable to humans. Indeed, the very definition of a metaphor assumes that not all the characteristics of the known will apply to the unknown. We do not, for example, think that humans created the Earth. In addition, God certainly is not conceived as hedonistic, nor must God calculate the possible results of behavioral options. Nonetheless, the conception of God, and hence of humans, as fully knowledgeable and rational is one of the essential "associated implications" of God that guided subsequent motivational research.

Criticisms of the Mechanistic Concepts of Habit and Drive

The antimechanists in the field of motivation set their sights of attack on Hullian theory, inasmuch as this was the dominant theory of action. (Neither Freudian nor Gestalt theory captured the mainstream of experimental research.) Recall that drive theory included two main concepts: habit, which was described as a learned response strengthened when that response was followed by a reward; and drive, which energized or activated the learned structure.

The main criticisms originating from motivational theorists regarding the mechanistic conception of learning were first voiced by Tolman and his colleagues. In Chapter 3, the investigations of latent learning directed by Tolman were introduced. These experiments revealed that if animals are placed in a maze without any initial reward and then reward is suddenly introduced, performance immediately improves and is virtually identical to the performance of other animals who had received repeated rewards from their initial commerce with the maze (see Figure 3.8). These observations revealed to Tolman that incentive value, or what is placed in the goal box, must be considered a determinant of performance, one that had been ignored by the drive theorists. But these data also provided evidence that learning had been occurring in the maze even prior to the introduction of the reward. The animals, Tolman and his colleagues claimed, were learning about the characteristics of the maze, or what leads to what. That is, a cognitive map was being formed. Once food was introduced, then the organism engaged in the action that led to goal attainment, with the instrumental response guided by the prior knowledge or internal representation of the maze. As stated by Tolman (1932):

> Our final criticism of the trial and error doctrine is its fundamental notion of stimulus-response bonds, which is wrong. Stimuli do not, as such, call out responses willy nilly. Correct stimulus-response connections do not get "stamped in," and incorrect ones do not get "stamped out." Rather learning consists in the organisms' "discovering" or "refining" what all the respective alternative responses lead to. And then, if, under the appetite-aversion conditions of the moment, the consequences of one of these alternatives is more demanded than the others . . . then the organism will tend, after such learning, to select and to perform the response leading to the more "demanded-for" consequences. But, if there be no such difference in demands there will be no such selection and performance of the one response, even though there has been learning. (p. 364)

Tolman also contended that animals learn expectancies—what will follow if and when a particular response is made. If reward follows a particular response in a particular setting, then the animal will come to expect to receive this incentive following the response in that setting. The concept of expectancy slowly began to replace that of habit in descriptions of the learning process, which was consistent with the more general cognitive emphasis exhibited by learning theorists.

In addition, as revealed in the introduction to Part II, the concept of drive came under increasing doubt. It was evident that the absence of certain factors necessary for survival, such as oxygen, did not always activate the organism; for instance, the organism might not respond if the oxygen was removed so slowly that the change was undetected. In addition, most human activities undertaken are unnecessary for survival. And finally, there was a conceptual shift toward the idea that organisms are always active—what is of interest is not what turns them on or off, but the direction of behavior or what choices are made. These doubts about drive resulted in increased attention being paid to incentives, which Tolman had documented are necessary for performance and even drive theorists came to accept as determinants of motivated behavior.

The growing recognition of expectancies and incentives resulted in, as well as was the product of, what is known as *expectancy-value theory*. This approach dominated the study of motivation for nearly 20 years, between approximately the early 1960s and the early 1980s.

Theoretical Assumptions and Relation to Decision Theory

The basic assumptions of expectancy-value theory are in accord with our commonsense thinking about motivated behavior: What behavior is undertaken depends on the perceived likelihood that the behavior will lead to the goal and the subjective value of that goal. Hence the greater the belief that the goal will be attained and the higher the incentive value of that goal, the greater the motivational tendency to engage in the appropriate instrumental behavior.

Furthermore, it is assumed that at any given moment in time individuals are faced with an array of alternative goals. For example, a person may wish to go to any of a number of movies, and at the same time may wish to study, or to eat. It is presumed that for each of these incompatible goals there is a likelihood that the instrumental response will lead to the goal (in these examples most of the goal likelihoods are one, although the actor may wonder if the restaurant is open, if there will be a place to park, and so on). In addition, each goal has an assigned value. Then expectancies and values are combined to yield a motivational tendency; the strongest motivational value "wins"—that is, is expressed in action.

The assumptions made by expectancy-value theories are similar to those imposed by decision theorists in their analysis of action (see Atkinson, 1964). For example, assume that one wants to predict what decision a gambler will make at a horse race. Decision theorists contend that choice will depend upon the expectancy or subjective likelihood that each horse has of winning the race, and the differential payoffs for winning. Then the expectancy and payoff values for each alternative are combined in a multiplicative manner and a decision is made based on *subjective expected utility* (SEU), or the expected personal value associated with each choice.

Consider, for example, Figure 5.1, which captures a situation in which two horses (Option A and Option B) are competing in a race. Option A has a 1/6 chance of winning, and the payoff for victory is $1.80. Option B has a 5/6 chance of winning, with a payoff for victory of $.42. If it is presumed that expectancy and value relate multiplicatively, then the expected payoff for Option A is determined by the value of $1/6 \times \$1.80$, or $.30, while the

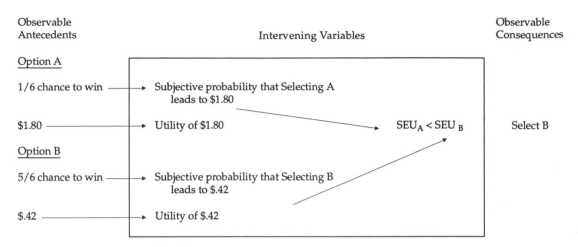

Figure 5.1. Subjective probability, utility, and subjectively expected utility (*SEU*) conceived as intervening variables and determinants of choice.

expected payoff for Option B is 5/6 × $.42, or $.35. Hence the motivational tendency toward Option B exceeds that of Option A, and therefore Option B will be selected. One implication of having the expectancy and value variables relate in a multiplicative manner is that if the likelihood of attaining an option is zero, then that option will not be selected regardless of its value. In a similar manner, although the likelihood of obtaining a goal is one, it will not be selected unless that goal has some value.

In many respects, the expectancy-value theory of motivation is comparable to the mechanistic conception of the drive theorists. Both camps represent learning (habit versus expectancy) among the determinants of behavior, and both specify that another variable (drive versus incentive value) interacts with learning in a multiplicative function. However, it also is evident that, for the Godlike theorists, the learning component involves calculation of expectancies and comparisons of alternatives, and there is an absence of an energylike concept such as drive.

When the machine metaphor gave way to the Godlike metaphor, it was not "business as usual," with Tolman's cognitive maps merely replacing Hull's habit strengths. Rather, researchers began to concentrate on human rather than infrahuman behavior. It became just as respectable to generalize from human to nonhuman behavior as vice versa. So, just as Hull speculated about human motivation from studies of rats, later the behavior of rats was derived from the study of humans. Furthermore, of the many possible topics for human research, issues associated with success and failure and achievement strivings, particular level of aspiration and the goals for which one was aiming, formed the heart of the empirical study of motivation. This was in part because of the manifest importance of achievement strivings in our lives. In addition, success and failure could be readily manipulated in the laboratory and their effects on subsequent performance determined. This was perhaps no more difficult than depriving or not depriving lower organisms of food and testing the effects of deprivation on performance. Finally, there were many naturally occurring instances of achievement outcomes that could be subject to field research, including the classroom. In sum, motivational research became almost synonymous with achievement motivation research.

With this background in mind, then, I turn to the dominant expectancy × value conceptions proposed by Kurt Lewin, John Atkinson, and Julian Rotter. Although all three have much in common, they also differ in fundamental ways. Recall that this also was the case with the biological conceptions represented by psychoanalytic theory, ethology, and sociobiology.

Lewin's Resultant Valence Theory

In Chapter 4, Lewin's hydraulic theory of motivation was introduced— his concepts of tension and force reflected the influence of mechanism and Gestalt principles derived from a consideration of electrical force fields. But, as I have indicated many times, theorists embrace multiple metaphors. Freud not only accepted energy concepts and laws regarding the conservation of energy, he also used spatial and geographical metaphors in his analysis of consciousness, thus revealing his acceptance of higher processes as well as nonmechanical guides to the understanding of these processes. In a similar manner, Lewin accepted both the mechanistic metaphor described in Chapter 4 as well as a Godlike metaphor, which is introduced next.

typical = ↑ aspiration after succ.
↓ aspiration after fail
atypical = ↑ '' fail
↓ '' succ

Level of Aspiration

Lewin developed a variant of expectancy-value theory, known as resultant valence theory, within the context of the study of level of aspiration. *Level of aspiration* typically is defined as "the level of future performance in a familiar task which an individual, knowing his level of past performance in that task, explicitly undertakes to reach" (Frank, 1935, p. 119). Level of aspiration thus pertains to goal striving and the perceived difficulty of the goals that one wishes to attain. It is aroused by such tasks as choosing a competitor at an athletic event, determining the amount of sales that one wants to make in a given month, or deciding the distance one will walk on a hike. Because many goals (levels of difficulty) are possible in all these situations, level of aspiration involves a choice among various alternatives.

In a typical experimental study of aspiration level, an individual is asked to toss rings over a peg from any of a number of specified distances.

The experimenter then attempts to predict the choices the subject will make. In this situation, all the potential choices are known to the participant. In addition, the subject is reasonably able to calculate the likelihood of success of each choice at the varying distances. In general, the further from the peg, the lower that estimate will be. Furthermore, successful completion of each toss is associated with a particular value. In the situation just described, it also is the case that the value of a success is greater as distance from the peg increases. Then, it is assumed that a decision or choice is made based on calculations of expectancy and value.

It is instructive to note how this paradigm captures a Godlike metaphor. First, all conceivable choices, all probabilities, and all values are known by the participant. That is, there is complete knowledge. Furthermore, a totally rational choice is made by combining the expectancy and the value estimates and then comparing the strength of the motivational tendency associated with each potential choice. The choice associated with the greatest value is assumed to be selected. Considering the guiding metaphor, God surely need not calculate estimates of success and is not thought of as maximizing personal hedonism. But God is construed as all-knowing and all-rational, which is captured in the aspiration situation.

In an aspiration setting the question of activation, or getting behavior started, is not at issue. Rather, the focus is on what choices are made. When a rat runs down a straight alley for food, it requires little knowledge (other than the presence or absence of what kind of food), and the investigator will examine response intensity (if and how fast the animal runs) rather than choice behavior. Hence it is evident that the research paradigms used capture or reflect the metaphors that gave rise to them.

Four temporal boundaries have been distinguished within a level of aspiration sequence (see Figure 5.2). In the ring-toss example, the subject typically first becomes familiar with the task and undertakes, say, 10 "practice" attempts. During the practice performance the number of successful tosses is counted. In this particular illustration, assume that there was success on 6 of the 10 trials. The individual then specifies an aspiration level for the next series of 10 tosses. If this were an experimental situation, this question generally would be phrased as follows: "How many are you going to try to get over the peg in the next series?" Assume that the individual responds, "Eight." This response, in relation to the level of prior performance, defines the goal discrepancy score. In this case the person is striving for more (+2) than the previous performance; the discrepancy is therefore described as positive. Of course, one could be striving for less than the prior performance, in which case the discrepancy score would be negative. The individual then tosses the rings 10 more times. The difference between the number of successes and the stated goal is the attainment discrepancy. If the thrower gets only 7 rings over the peg, the discrepancy is –1; the stated goal was not reached. Presumably, affective reactions are related to the goal discrepancy: This individual will probably feel "bad" because the desired level of achievement was not reached.

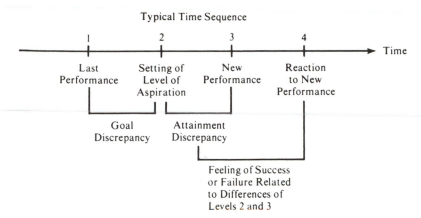

Figure 5.2. Four main points in a typical sequence of events in a level of aspiration situation: last performance, setting of the level of aspiration for the next performance, new performance, and the psychological reaction to the new performance. (From Lewin, Dembo, Festinger, & Sears, 1944, p. 334.)

Empirical Research

Numerous clear empirical findings have emerged from level of aspiration research. It has been demonstrated that feelings of success and failure are determined primarily by the attainment or nonattainment of the goal for which one is striving, as opposed to the absolute level of performance. For example, a student with a very high aspiration level might be unhappy upon receiving a grade of B, while an equally bright student with lesser aspirations would be satisfied with this grade. Perception of success and failure involves subjective, rather than objective, levels of attainment. (William James stated that feelings of success or self-esteem are a direct function of actual success and an inverse function of pretensions.) Further, the subsequent aspiration level is, in part, dependent upon the prior attainment discrepancy (subjective success or failure). In most instances, the goal level increases after success and decreases following failure. However, "atypical" reactions are sometimes observed; that is, sometimes an individual lowers his or her aspiration level after goal attainment or raises it after failure. Level of aspiration has been shown to be influenced by individual differences, group standards, and cultural factors. For example, individuals with high ability, or those classified as ambitious, tend to set higher aspiration levels (Hoppe, 1930). In addition, the level that is set tends to be guided by, and conforms to, group goals and performance (Festinger, 1942).

Experimentation with level of aspiration also has increased our knowledge about defensive reactions to failure. Failure generally leads to more variable performance and aspirations (Sears, 1942), and is more likely to result in psychological withdrawal from the task. These findings have led some investigators to consider aspiration level more an index of defensiveness than of goal striving.

Resultant Valence Theory

A theoretical analysis guided by the research findings briefly reviewed above was first presented by Escalona (1940) and subsequently elaborated and clarified by Festinger (1942) and Lewin, Dembo, Festinger, and Sears (1944). This analysis, *resultant valence theory*, characterizes level of aspiration as a choice (conflict) situation in which one locomotes toward (chooses) the alternative with the greatest resultant approach force.

Resultant valence theory specifies the determinants of the valence, and force, of the various alternative goals that make up the possible choices. It is postulated that anticipated success has positive valence and that potential failure has negative valence. Further, the valences of success and failure are assumed to be dependent, in part, upon the difficulty of the task. "The attraction of success seems to increase with the level of difficulty . . . while the negative valence of failure is greater the less difficult the task" (Atkinson, 1964, p. 99).

Given only the specification that choice is a function of valence, and that positive valence is greater for more difficult tasks and negative valence less for more difficult tasks, the greatest force would be in the direction of the most difficult goal. Yet individuals often select tasks of intermediate difficulty or even tasks that are very easy to perform. Therefore, other determinants of behavior must be influencing aspiration level.

An additional construct postulated by Escalona (1940), Festinger (1942), and Lewin et al. (1944) as a determinant of aspiration level is the Lewinian notion of potency. *Potency* refers to subjective expectancy or certainty; there is a potency associated with success and a potency linked with failure. A more contemporary view might use the term *probability* rather than potency. The concept of potency also can be compared with psychological distance; a low potency could be considered an indication of great psychological distance (many steps intervening between the person and the goal), while a high potency could indicate that few instrumental actions are necessary to reach the goal. Lewin, however, did not use the constructs of potency and psychological distance interchangeably. Clearly, one could be many steps from the goal, but each step might have a very high probability of being consummated.

Corresponding to each level of difficulty there is a potency of success (Po_s) and a potency of failure (Po_f). The approach force toward a goal is postulated by Lewin et al. (1944) to be a function of the valence of success (Va_s) multiplied by the potency of success, while the force away from the goal is postulated to be the negative valence of failure (Va_f) multiplied by the potency of failure. Therefore, the resultant force toward the goal is conceptualized as follows:

valence
potency

$$\text{resultant force} = (Va_s \times Po_s) - (Va_f \times Po_f)$$

In sum, each alternative can be considered to involve an approach-avoidance conflict between positive and negative forces determined by valences and potencies. Choice involves a comparison of all the available alternatives; the alternative that has the greatest resultant approach force is expected to be selected.

A numerical example adapted from Lewin et al. by Atkinson (1964, p. 101) indicates some of the power of this conception. In the example shown in Table 5.1, the valence of success and the valence of failure are given arbitrary values that increase and decrease, respectively, with the level of task difficulty. Similarly, the potencies of success and failure, which range in value from 0 to 100, vary with objective task difficulty. In the illustration it is assumed that, on the prior task, performance was at level 7. The subsequent choice—that is, the alternative associated with the greatest resultant value—is level 8. Hence there is a positive goal discrepancy of 1.

As indicated previously, motivational dispositions also influence level of aspiration. Table 5.2 portrays a situation in which an individual has great anxiety associated with failure. In Table 5.2 the negative valence of failure is double that shown in the prior illustration. The table indicates a surprising result. Although fear of failure increases, the level of aspiration actually rises three steps from past performance. This captures the unrealistic goal striving that is exhibited sometimes by individuals with histories of failure and motivational deficiencies in the area of achievement (this will be discussed in greater depth below).

Aspiration Level in Social Contexts

The concept of level of aspiration has been modified and used for the analysis of social interaction and interdependence. Thibaut and Kelley (1959) assumed that individuals can assess their degree of satisfaction with a relationship, just as one can determine the valence of an achievement-related success or failure. They introduced the concept of "comparison level" (CL) to define "a neutral point on a scale of satisfaction-dissatisfaction" (p. 81). If the average of "outcomes" from a relationship is above the CL, the relationship is "rewarding"; however, if the outcome average is below the CL, the relationship is relatively "punishing." However, even if the relationship is negative, individuals may remain interdependent. The continuation depends, in part, on the alternatives that are available, or the potential satisfactions expected from equivalent relationships or opportunities.

In sum, Thibaut and Kelley assume a rational person striving to maximize gains, capable of comparing a number of potential satisfiers, and deciding which "goal" (relationship) to pursue. This is clearly a direct extension of aspiration work into the sphere of interpersonal relations.

TABLE 5.1 Numerical Illustration of the Determinants of Level of Aspiration

Levels of Possible Objective	Force to Approach Success			Force to Avoid Failure			Resultant Force[c]
	$Va_{succ} \times$	$Po_{succ} =$	fp_{succ}[a]	$Va_{fai} \times$	$Po_{fai} =$	$fp_{,-fai}$[b]	
↑ 15	10	0	0	0	100	0	0
Too 14	10	0	0	0	100	0	0
difficult 13	10	0	0	0	100	0	0
12	10	0	0	0	100	0	0
11	10	5	50	0	95	0	50
10	9	10	90	0	90	0	90 Level
9	7	25	175	−1	75	−75	100 of
8	6	40	240	−2	60	−120	120 ← aspiration
7	5	50	250	−3	50	−150	100 ⟍ Goal ⟋ discrepancy
6	3	60	180	−5	40	−200	−20 Level of
5	2	75	150	−7	25	−175	−25 past
4	1	90	90	−9	10	−90	0 performance
Too 3	0	95	0	−10	5	−50	−50
easy 2	0	100	0	−10	0	0	0
↓ 1	0	100	0	−10	0	0	0

Source: Atkinson (1964, p. 101).
a. Force toward success.
b. Force away from failure.
c. Force on the person toward the goal.

Atkinson's Theory of Achievement Motivation

The starting point of the development of Atkinson's theory of achievement motivation is most clearly the contributions of Henry Murray. Murray played a dual function in the history of achievement research. On the one hand, he first called attention to a *need* for achievement. Historically, the concepts of drive and need were often used interchangeably or were closely linked. For example, Hull considered drive the psychological manifestation of a need state. Over time, however, drives became identified with states of deprivation, behaviorism, and research employing subhuman organisms, while the concept of need became identified with molar personality theorists and signified more stable characteristics of individuals.

Murray (1938) devised a taxonomy that included 20 basic human needs. This taxonomic approach was not unlike some of the earlier, unsuccessful attempts by McDougall and others to develop lists of instincts. One of these needs, called achievement, was conceived as the desire

to accomplish something difficult. To master, manipulate or organize physical objects, human beings, or ideas. To do this as rapidly and as independently as

TABLE 5.2 Determinants of Level of Aspiration When the Negative Valence of Failure Is Relatively High

Levels of Possible Objective	Force to Approach Success $Va_{succ} \times$	$Po_{succ} =$	$fp_{succ}{}^{a}$	$Va_{fai} \times$	Force to Avoid Failure $Po_{fai} =$	$fp_{-fai}{}^{b}$	Resultant Force^{c}
Too difficult 15	10	0	0	0	100	0	0
14	10	0	0	0	100	0	0
13	10	0	0	0	100	0	0
12	10	0	0	0	100	0	0 Level
11	10	5	50	0	95	0	50 of
10	9	10	90	0	90	0	90 ← aspiration
9	7	25	175	-2	75	-150	25
8	6	40	240	-4	60	-240	0 \ Goal
7	5	50	250	-6	50	-300	-50 / discrepancy
6	3	60	180	-10	40	-400	-220 Level of
5	2	75	150	-14	25	-350	-200 \ past
4	1	90	90	-18	10	-180	-90 performance
Too easy 3	0	95	0	-20	5	-100	-100
2	0	100	0	-20	0	0	0
1	0	100	0	-20	0	0	0

Source: Atkinson (1964, p. 102).
Note: The values of subjective probability of success and failure are the same as in Table 5.1, but the negative valence of failure is doubled.

possible. To overcome obstacles and attain a high standard. To excel one's self. To rival and surpass others. To increase self-regard by the successful exercise of talent. (p. 164)

These desires, according to Murray, are accompanied by the following actions:

To make intense, prolonged and repeated efforts to accomplish something difficult. To work with singleness of purpose towards a high and distant goal. To have the determination to win. To try to do everything well. To be stimulated to excel by the presence of others, to enjoy competition. To exert will power; to overcome boredom and fatigue. (p. 164)

Murray's second contribution to the study of achievement motivation was the development of an instrument to assess need states. This measure, the Thematic Apperception Test (TAT), supposedly revealed "covert and unconscious complexes" (Murray, 1938, p. 530). The TAT was almost universally adopted by subsequent investigators to assess achievement needs.

A vast number of studies were conducted in the 1940s and 1950s in which the TAT was administered and scored for the presence of imagery thought to reflect the need for achievement. These scores were then related to a host of other variables, such as grade point average and task performance and persistence.

Subjects taking the TAT are shown pictures to which they are asked to respond with stories. The pictures portray everyday scenes in life, often in a work setting, such as two men in a machine shop, two women who appear to be chemists, and so forth. Responses such as "The men are the Wright brothers, building the first airplane," or "The women want to do a perfect job" are among the indicators of the presence of achievement desires. A complex scoring scheme with 11 categories was developed by McClelland, Atkinson, Clark, and Lowell (1953) and Atkinson (1958); the categories include emotional reactions and instrumental activities that contribute to a final need for achievement score. Then, as previously indicated, these scores are related to a number of dependent variables.

The Need for Achievement

Given the importance of personality structure in the study of achievement motivation, it is necessary to review what is known about the personality disposition called the "need to achieve" before turning to achievement theory. Two questions are of special importance:

(1) What is the generality (or extensiveness, or breadth) of the need for achievement?
(2) Is this disposition stable, or at least *relatively* enduring?

Unfortunately, these questions have not been answered adequately. It is not known, for example, whether a person who strives for success in a particular occupation also exhibits achievement-type behaviors on the tennis court, in a night school literature class, or in other such situations. In the only study examining this issue, Rosenstein (1952) found that chemistry majors had a significantly higher need achievement score on the TAT than did physical education majors when responding to scenes depicting laboratory situations. It certainly seems reasonable to believe that there are circumscribed avenues or outlets of achievement expression for a given individual. That is, similar genotypes or underlying needs may have disparate phenotypic or displayed representations. But this supposition has not been investigated, and the generality (or specificity) of this motive or trait is unknown.

The stability of achievement needs has been the subject of more research than has the issue of motive generality. This is perhaps surprising, inasmuch as longitudinal studies are difficult to conduct and require a dedicated masochism. As might be anticipated, research investigations of long-term stability are, therefore, also few in number. The most-cited data concerning motive stability come from what are known as the Fels Institute studies (see Kagan & Moss, 1959; Moss & Kagan, 1961). Kagan and Moss reported low but significant positive correlations ($r = .22$) between TAT scores ages 8 and 14. Birney (1959) found a correlation of slightly higher magnitude ($r = .29$) given testing over a four-month interval, and Feld (1967) reported a correlation of $r = .38$ over a six-year period. In sum, correlations in the magnitude of roughly .25 to .35 are found in studies of long-term stability. This indicates weak, but certainly greater than chance, stability.

Given that the essential questions of generality and stability are unanswered or at least unclear, what, then, is known about people who are labeled as high in the need for achievement, or high in the desire to achieve success? There is suggestive evidence that tasks of intermediate difficulty are more attractive to individuals who are highly motivated to succeed than to those lower in achievement needs. In a similar vein, individuals high in achievement needs have been characterized as "realistic" and have occupational goals that are congruent with their abilities (Mahone, 1960; Morris, 1966). The desire for intermediate risk may be indicative of a preference for personal feedback or knowledge about oneself. This informational explanation is consistent with the high achiever's reported preference for business occupations, where feedback (profits) is evident (Mayer, Walker, & Litwin, 1961; McClelland, 1961, p. 55). In addition, individuals high in need for achievement apparently are better able to delay gratification (Mischel, 1961) and attain higher grades in school than individuals low in achievement needs, if the grades are instrumental to long-term success (Raynor, 1970). Furthermore, individuals high in achievement needs are conceptualized as "hope" rather than "fear" oriented. It has been suggested, for example, that they bias their probabilities of success upward so their subjective probabilities of success are greater than the objective probabilities (Feather, 1965). Finally, individuals high in achievement needs take personal responsibility for success and generally perceive themselves as high in ability (Kukla, 1972). The self-attribution for success increases their feelings of worth. This helps explain evidence that they volitionally undertake achievement-oriented activities when the opportunity arises (Atkinson, 1953; Green, 1963). In addition, the self-perception of high ability may account, in part, for their high self-concept, as some investigators report (Mukherjee & Sinha, 1970).

There are a host of other reported linkages to achievement needs, although, as with the prior reported findings, many of the relationships are tenuous or their theoretical meanings are unclear. For example, it has been found that achievement needs are positively correlated with resistance to social influence, preference for particular colors (blue), aesthetic tastes, lowered recognition thresholds for success-related words, selective retention of incomplete tasks, forms of graphic expression (single and S-shaped lines), and high content of serum uric acid (see the reviews cited earlier for references). Although the sampling of associations listed above increases the "relational fertility" of the need for achievement construct, the lasting significance of many of the relationships is questionable because of the absence of clear theoretical relevance of the findings and doubts concerning their replicability.

Need for Achievement and Economic Development

Numerous sociological and anthropological investigations of the need for achievement also have proceeded outside the laboratory. Foremost among these was the monumental attempt by McClelland (1961) to relate the need for achievement to economic growth. McClelland's hypotheses were guided by findings relating need for achievement to child-rearing practices. It had been reported that boys relatively high in need for achievement had mothers who retrospectively reported that they expected their sons to be self-reliant and independent at an early age. These mothers believed that their sons should know their way around the city, make their own friends, and the like, at an earlier age than mothers whose sons were low in need for achievement.

McClelland reasoned that the relationship between early independence training and the growth of achievement motivation is pertinent to the linkage postulated by Weber (1904/1958) between the Protestant Reformation and the growth of capitalism. McClelland (1955) noted:

> In the first place, he [Weber] stresses, as others have, that the essence of the Protestant revolt against the Catholic church was a shift from a reliance on an institution to a greater reliance on the self, so far as salvation was concerned. . . . As Weber describes it, we have here what seems to be an example of a revolution in ideas which should increase the need for independence training. Certainly Protestant parents, if they were to prepare their children adequately for increased self-reliance so far as religious matters were concerned, would tend to stress increasingly often and early the necessity for the child's not depending on adult assistance but seeking his own "salvation." In the second place, Weber's description of the kind of personality type which the Protestant Reformation produced is startlingly similar to the picture we would draw of a person with high achievement motivation. He notes that Protestant working girls seemed to work harder and longer, that they saved their money for long-range goals, that Protestant entrepreneurs seemed to come to the top more often in the business world despite the initial advantages of wealth many Catholic families had, and so forth. . . .
>
> What then drove him to such prodigious feats of business organization and development? Weber feels that such a man "gets nothing out of his wealth for himself, except the irrational sense of having done his job well." This is exactly how we define the achievement motive. . . . Is it possible that the Protestant Reformation involves a repetition at a social and historical level of the linkage between independence training and *n* Achievement? . . .
>
> The hypothesis can be diagrammed rather simply [see Diagram 5.1]. In terms of this diagram Weber was chiefly concerned with the linkage between A and D, with the way in which Protestantism led to a change in the spirit of capitalism in the direction of a speeded-up, high-pressure, competitive business economy. But the manner in which he describes this relationship strongly suggests that the

DIAGRAM 5.1 Hypothetical Series of Events Relating Self-Reliance Values With Economic and Technological Development

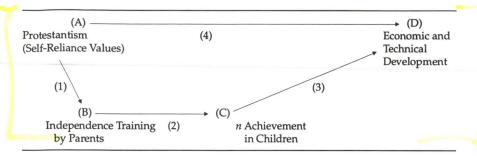

linkage by which these two events are connected involves steps B and C, namely a change in family socialization practices which in turn increased the number of individuals with high achievement motivation. Thus a full statement of the hypothesis would be that Protestantism produced an increased stress on independence training which produced higher achievement motivation which produced more vigorous entrepreneurial activity and rapid economic development. (pp. 44-46)

Diagram 5.1 indicates four relationships McClelland has examined: (1) Protestantism and early independence training, (2) early independence training and need for achievement, (3) need for achievement and economic growth, and (4) Protestantism and economic growth. The relationship between religious training and child-rearing practices (1) and the relationship between child-rearing practices and achievement development (2) remain indeterminate. McClelland cited evidence available at the time his book was written that Protestant families expect earlier mastery from their sons than Catholic families and that early independence training produces concerns about achievement. Since that time, these relations have been called into question.

The great bulk of McClelland's personal investigations concern relations 3 (need for achievement and economic growth) and 4 (Protestantism and economic growth). To investigate the hypothesis that Protestantism is related to economic growth, McClelland (1961) compared the per capita electric power consumption of predominantly Protestant societies with that of Catholic countries. McClelland contended that per capita usage of electricity is the best index of economic growth (rather than, for example, the more widely used index of gross national product) because these data are available, the figures are in comparable units from country to country, and modern societies are based upon the use of electrical energy. The findings of this investigation are given in Table 5.3, which shows the consumption of electricity per capita and the predicted electrical output based on the natural resources of the country. Deviations between the actual

TABLE 5.3 Average per Capita Consumption of Electric Power, Corrected for Natural Resources, for Protestant and Catholic Countries Outside the Tropics of Cancer and Capricorn

Countries	Consumption of Electricity kwh/cap (1950)	Predicted Output kwh/cap	Difference (predicted–obtained)	Rank of Difference
Protestant				
Norway	5,310	3,379	1,931	1
Canada	4,120	3,186	964	4
Sweden	2,580	903	1,672	2
United States	2,560	2,328	232	9
Switzerland	2,230	1,253	977	3
New Zealand	1,600	1,526	74	11
Australia	1,160	1,598	–438	20
United Kingdom	1,115	2,631	–1,566	24
Finland	1,000	652	348	6
Union S. Africa	890	1,430	–540	21
Holland	725	724	1	15
Denmark	500	74	426	5
Average	1,983	1,645	338	10.1
Catholic				
Belgium	986	1,959	–973	22
Austria	900	620	280	8
France	790	989	–199	16
Czechoslovakia	730	1,734	–1,004	23
Italy	535	227	308	7
Chile	484	764	280	18
Poland	375	2,007	–1,632	25
Hungary	304	628	324	19
Ireland	300	154	146	10
Argentina	255	251	4	14
Spain	225	459	–264	17
Uruguay	165	154	11	18
Portugal	110	82	28	12
Average	474	771	–208	15.7

Source: Adapted from McClelland (1961, p. 51).

and expected consumption are computed and are related to the religious affiliation of the country. The table reveals that the level of economic activity (as measured by McClelland) of Protestant countries exceeds that of Catholic countries.

The crucial question McClelland then attempted to answer was whether the association between Protestantism and economic activity is mediated by achievement needs. He hypothesized that achievement needs precede economic growth, and he gathered indicators of these two variables over a wide array of societies and historical periods.

A major problem faced by McClelland and his colleagues was how to assess the level of achievement motivation of a society. Perhaps TAT stories could be collected and scored for a representative sample of the population, or from a sample of business entrepreneurs (who, McClelland believed, are most responsible for economic advancement). But this is not possible when examining the achievement motivation of earlier societies. To assess the level of achievement concerns in past generations, McClelland and his colleagues gathered samples of the written products of the societies. They then scored the samples for achievement motivation, using the general procedure mentioned earlier in this chapter. Frequently the written material is from children's readers, but folktales, speeches of the leaders of the countries, poems and songs, and even the shapes of lines on vases have been used as indicators of achievement motivation.

In a large study of 22 contemporary societies, for example, McClelland compared the differences between the expected and actual gains in electric power consumption per capita between 1929 and 1950 as a function of achievement motivation. Achievement needs were assessed from children's readers published in 1925. The data revealed a dramatically high correlation ($r = .53$) between the achievement score of a society in 1925 and subsequent economic growth.

In a similar manner, achievement needs assessed from children's readers published in 1950 predicted economic growth from 1952 to 1958. Table 5.4 shows the countries in the latter study, the level of achievement concerns in 1950, and the deviation from the expected rate of growth. The index of achievement motivation in 1950 did not predict growth rate from 1929 to 1950, but did predict development from 1952 to 1958. Thus McClelland contended that achievement motivation precedes economic development.

A similar examination was made of the growth and decline of the Greek empire. Level of achievement needs was ascertained by scoring the literary content of leading writers of that era. Three periods of economic growth and decline were identified: 900-475 B.C. (growth), 475-362 B.C. (climax), and 362-100 B.C. (decline). The respective achievement scores in the three periods were 4.74, 2.71, and 1.35. Thus the period of climax was preceded by the highest achievement score, and the decrease in economic development followed the decrease in achievement needs.

The reader might now be wondering about the achievement motivation in our culture. Figure 5.3 indicates that achievement needs in the United States, ascertained from children's readers, increased from 1800 to 1910. Since 1910 the indicators of achievement concerns have steadily decreased. Does this hint that our economy also is going to decline? Figure 5.3 shows that the patent index, one indicator of unique accomplishments, also is falling. The conclusions from this study by de Charms and Moeller (1962) are evident.

Achievement Change

The data reported by McClelland (1961) provide more than suggestive evidence that need achievement is an important factor influencing

TABLE 5.4 Rate of Growth in Electrical Output (1952-1958) and National *n* Achievement Levels in 1950 (deviations from expected growth rate in standard score units)

National n Achievement Levels (1950)	Above Expectation	National n Achievement Levels (1950)	Below Expectation
High *n* achievement			
3.62 Turkey	+1.38		
2.71 India	+1.12		
2.38 Australia	+ .42		
2.33 Israel	+1.18		
2.33 Spain	+ .01		
2.29 Pakistan	+2.75		
2.29 Greece	+1.18	3.38 Argentina	− .56
2.29 Canada	+ .06	2.71 Lebanon	− .67
2.24 Bulgaria	+1.37	2.38 France	− .24
2.24 United States	+ .47	2.33 Union S. Africa	− .06
2.14 West Germany	+ .53	2.29 Ireland	− .41
2.10 Soviet Union	+1.62	2.14 Tunisia	−1.87
2.10 Portugal	+ .76	2.10 Syria	− .25
Low *n* achievement			
1.95 Iraq	+ .29	2.05 New Zealand	− .29
1.86 Austria	+ .38	1.86 Uruguay	− .75
1.67 United Kingdom	+ .17	1.81 Hungary	− .62
1.57 Mexico	+ .12	1.71 Norway	− .77
.86 Poland	+1.26	1.62 Sweden	− .64
		1.52 Finland	− .08
		1.48 Netherlands	− .15
		1.33 Italy	− .57
		1.29 Japan	− .04
		1.20 Switzerland	−1.92
		1.19 Chile	−1.81
		1.05 Denmark	− .89
		.57 Algeria	− .83
		.43 Belgium	−1.65

Source: McClelland (1961, p. 100).
Note: Correlation of *n* achievement level (1950) × deviations from expected growth rate = .43, $p < .01$.

economic development. Therefore, it would be of utmost importance to determine whether the economic growth of a nation could be accelerated by increasing the achievement motivation of some members of the society. As McClelland and Winter (1969) put it:

> The book [*The Achieving Society*] ends with the scientist's traditional hope that the knowledge so painstakingly collected will somehow be useful in helping man shape his destiny. At the time it was little more than a pious hope, since it was not at all clear how a developmental specialist or a leader of a new nation could make use of knowledge accumulated about the achievement motive. (pp. 1-2)

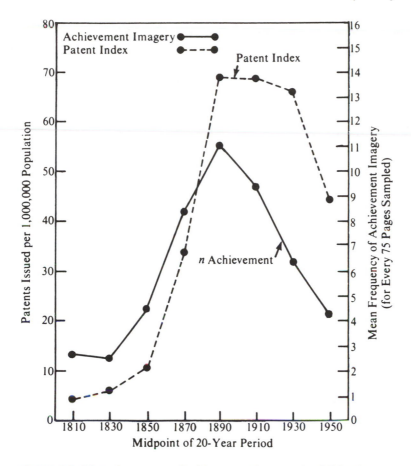

Figure 5.3. Mean frequency of achievement imagery in children's readers and the patent index in the United States, 1800-1950. (Adapted from de Charms & Moeller, 1962, p. 139.)

Indeed, if achievement-related dispositions are formed during early childhood, and if they are relatively enduring, then attempts to modify an adult's level of achievement needs are fruitless. The only practical way to alter the achievement needs of the members of a society and, as a possible consequence, enhance the economic development of that society would be to change child-rearing practices and then wait some time to determine whether or not the changes were effective.

This is a somewhat pessimistic position, rather incompatible with the optimism of American environmentalism. Although McClelland originally believed that needs are learned early in life as a result of particular child-rearing practices and are stable, he subsequently discarded this position and initiated short-term motivational change programs designed to increase the level of achievement needs of the participants (see McClelland & Winter, 1969).

To increase achievement needs, McClelland and Winter (1969) designed a three- to six-week training course in which the participants become acquainted with the thoughts and actions associated with achievement behavior. They learn to score TATs for achievement motivation, and they are taught the beneficial consequences of intermediate risk taking and future time perspective. In addition, the participants undergo a program of self-study in which they describe their life goals, values, self-images, and so forth. The training program assists in the establishment and setting of career goals, and suggests means to assess progress toward these goals. These program "inputs" take place in a warm and permissive atmosphere in the company of others, who it is hoped will become part of a new reference group. McClelland (1965) has described this as an eclectic method, using all the psychological principles believed to be effective in behavioral change.

However, the effectiveness of motive change training is uncertain. Positive results with underachievers (Kolb, 1965), schoolteachers (de Charms, 1972, pp. 255-256), and businessmen (McClelland & Winter, 1969) have been reported. But data that question the effectiveness of change programs also have been reported (see McClelland & Winter, 1969), and the amount of research is small. There certainly is some hope that achievement needs can be altered, given appropriate intervention techniques. However, more evidence is needed before this hope can be accepted as truth.

Achievement Needs Among Females

McClelland (1958) contended that for an instrument to have validity in assessing motive strength, it must reflect temporary arousal states of the organism. That is, like a thermometer, if the "motive temperature" is turned on, then the instrument should register a high reading. Achievement motive arousal, accomplished via failure induction or "ego-involving" instructions, indeed generates higher TAT need achievement scores than those registered under nonarousal conditions. But this is true only for males; females have not exhibited motive score differences between arousal and neutral conditions. Therefore, it was believed that the TAT motive measure was not valid for females, and females tended to be neglected in early achievement research. Of course, some studies did include females and combined the data from both sexes, but an equally large number of research investigations either did not test females or reported systematic data for the male, but not the female, subjects.

It is uncertain why the few motive arousal studies were unsuccessful for women and why males appear to yield more systematic data than females in studies of achievement motivation. Achievement may be a more complex motivational system for females than for males because of cultural inhibitions and social norms that at one time restricted females to the home. But little has been done to substantiate this intuitively reasonable supposition.

Another plausible explanation of the mysterious findings for females was offered by Horner (1968), who postulated a motive to "avoid success," or a "fear of success," for females. She suggested that as a consequence of success, the threat of social rejection and fear concerning a perceived lack of femininity are aroused in women. These fears inhibit achievement strivings. To test this notion, Horner had both male and female subjects write stories to this cue: "At the end of the first-term final, Anne finds herself at the top of her medical school class." Horner found much greater fear-of-success imagery in females' responses than in males'.

These data caused immediate excitement among many psychologists and others. The data meshed with the feminist movement and were immediately incorporated into courses on the psychology of women. But the generated enthusiasm may have been more a symptom of an extant void and the desire for understanding than a consequence of the establishment of a scientific truth. Subsequent research has revealed that males exhibit as much fear of success in projective imagery as do females (see, for example, Brown, Jennings, & Vanik, 1974; Tresemer, 1974). Thus the findings first reported by Horner are very much in doubt.

Personality Measurement, the Need for Achievement, and Theory Construction

It is reasonable for the reader to ask why so much space has been devoted to the discussion of the need for achievement and why equal space has not been allotted for the discussion of, for example, the Manifest Anxiety Scale as used by drive theorists. The answer to both questions is that achievement theory, in contrast to the conceptions of Freud, Hull, and Lewin, has focused upon the role of individual differences in achievement needs in attempting to understand motivational processes.

Both Hull and Lewin recognized that they had to deal with individual differences. Hull, however, paid relatively little attention to this issue because

> behavior theorists have inherited from their empiricist and associationist forebears of previous centuries a bias towards environmentalism. . . . Behavior theorists spend most of their time studying learned behavior and feel that to understand the behavior of higher mammals means, above all, to understand how learning works. . . .
>
> Preoccupation with learning may lead one to disregard innate differences, which must seem the logical starting point to anyone who wishes to throw light on the dissimilarities among human beings. . . .
>
> It is perfectly obvious that human beings are different from one another in some respects but alike in other respects. The question is whether we should first

look for statements that apply to all of them or whether we should first try to describe and explain their differences. The behavior theorist feels that research for common principles of human and animal behavior must take precedence. This, he would point out, is how scientific inquiry must proceed. . . . Until we can see what individuals of a class or species have in common, we cannot hope to understand how their dissimilarities have come about or even to find the most fruitful way to describe and classify these dissimilarities. (Berlyne, 1968, pp. 639-641)

In a similar manner, Lewin sought to discover general laws, and the person was usually considered "a mass point of indifferent constitution" (Murray, 1959, p. 29). As Atkinson (1964) pointed out:

In the theoretical conception and experimental analysis of motivation, Lewinians consider only the momentary and temporary condition of the person, which is represented at $t(S_G)$ [a system in a state of tension]. And in most cases, $t(S_G)$ is assumed to be roughly equivalent for all subjects exposed to the same experimental instructions and arrangements in the course of conducting the experiment. (p. 103)

Achievement theory, on the other hand, is built upon the idea of individual differences, and personality structures are essential determinants of behavior. Atkinson's philosophy is illustrated in the following quotation:

A most encouraging development in recent experimental analysis of motivation . . . is the use of tests to assess individual differences in the strength of theoretically-relevant motivational dispositions of humans. Here again, the broad implication of Lewinian ideas is apparent. The guiding hypothesis, $B = f(P,E)$, is now represented in a methodological development that may provide a means of bridging the gap between the study of individual differences in personality and the search for basic explanatory principles. [This gap] has so far seriously handicapped both enterprises in psychology's relatively short history. (p. 271)

I now turn from this discussion of personality measurement and the need for achievement to Atkinson's theory of achievement motivation. It will be seen that this conception is intimately linked with the measurement of achievement needs and is guided by the resultant valence conception proposed by Lewin et al. (1944).

A Theory of Achievement Motivation

In the tradition of Hull and Lewin, Atkinson (1957, 1964) attempted to isolate the determinants of behavior and then specify the mathematical relations among the components of his theory. As already intimated, Atkinson differs from other such theorists in his concentration on individual

JOHN W. ATKINSON

John Atkinson first became acquainted with the field of motivation as an undergraduate philosophy major at Wesleyan University. There he participated with David McClelland and others in developing a scoring system for the TAT that would be useful for research purposes. This interest in individual differences persisted throughout his career, and he is most responsible for pointing out the importance of personality structure for the understanding of motivational processes.

Atkinson received his Ph.D. at the University of Michigan, and he remained at that university for virtually his entire career. His work had a number of rather distinct phases. After the refinement of the TAT, he developed a theory of achievement motivation using an expectancy-value framework. This cognitive theory was introduced at a time when drive theory dominated psychology, and thus Atkinson found relatively little support from others in the field at the time. The history of motivation, however, vindicated his beliefs. He later collaborated with David Birch and others in constructing a general theory of behavior.

Atkinson has been one of the nation's most productive psychologists, publishing numerous books and many journal articles. He also is recognized as an outstanding teacher. He was responsible for the training of many well-known psychologists, including Norman Feather and Joseph Veroff. (He was also this writer's Ph.D. supervisor.)

(Photograph courtesy of J. W. Atkinson)

differences. But in spite of this difference in emphasis, his conception of behavior is very similar to the mechanistic theories of Hull and Lewin. These earlier motivational theorists conceptualized behavior to be a function of a temporary state of the organism (drive or tension), the properties of the goal object (incentive value or valence), and an experiential or learning factor (habit or psychological distance). Atkinson included a very similar set of individual, environmental, and experiential variables among the immediate determinants of action.

Further, Atkinson's theory of achievement motivation was influenced by Miller's conflict model. Achievement-oriented behavior was viewed by Atkinson as a resultant of a conflict between approach and avoidance tendencies. Associated with every achievement-related action is the possibility of success (with the consequent emotion of pride) and the possibility of failure (with the consequent emotion of shame). The strengths of these anticipated emotions determine whether an individual will approach or avoid achievement-oriented activities. That is, achievement behavior is viewed as the resultant of an emotional conflict between hopes for success and fears of failure.

However, as part of the expectancy-value tradition, Atkinson was primarily guided by the Godlike metaphor of motivation. Consistent with the just-completed discussion of Lewin's resultant valence theory, the person is viewed as totally rational, knowing all expectancies and all values associated with all choices, and making a choice that maximizes personal hedonism.

An Experimental Demonstration

Before turning to the theory itself, I would like the reader to complete Experiment 5.1, in which a choice situation is presented and the reader is asked to select the difficulty of the task that he or she would prefer to undertake. Please do that now, before reading further.

Based on prior research, I expect that the reader selected the alternatives where the likelihood of winning was between 40% and 60%. That is, most of us want to undertake tasks of intermediate difficulty. Heightened motivation at intermediate tasks also is evident in involvement with sporting activities. When the score is tied between our favorite team and the opponent, then we are most engaged and excited. On the other hand, if the game is one-sided, either a clear victory or a clear defeat, then involvement lessens. Why is it that most individuals prefer and are motivated by tasks of intermediate difficulty? What kind of theory has evolved to explain this empirical fact? That is the empirical focus of Atkinson's theory of achievement motivation (although it will be seen that he anticipated that some individuals also are maximally motivated given very easy or very difficult tasks).

Hope of Success

The tendency to approach an achievement-related goal (T_s) was conceived by Atkinson to be a product of three factors: the need for achievement, also known as the motive for success (M_s); the probability that one will be successful at the task (P_s); and the incentive value of success (I_s). It is postulated that these three components are multiplicatively related:

$$T_S = M_s \times P_s \times I_s$$

The Need for Achievement

In the equation of approach motivation, M_s represents a relatively stable or enduring disposition to strive for success. The definition and measurement of this concept, as well as its historical linkage to the work of Murray and McClelland, have already been discussed. Atkinson (1964)

Experiment 5.1

Imagine yourself in this situation:

You are planning to engage in a certain activity (such as tennis, a card game, or chess). You must select an opponent in this activity (for example, a person who is easy or difficult to beat). The choice can be made from among nine persons. You have seen them compete against each other, so you can estimate how well you might do as follows:

You think you might beat Opponent 1 in your matches 10% of the time.
You think you might beat Opponent 2 in your matches 20% of the time.
You think you might beat Opponent 3 in your matches 30% of the time.
You think you might beat Opponent 4 in your matches 40% of the time.
You think you might beat Opponent 5 in your matches 50% of the time.
You think you might beat Opponent 6 in your matches 60% of the time.
You think you might beat Opponent 7 in your matches 70% of the time.
You think you might beat Opponent 8 in your matches 80% of the time.
You think you might beat Opponent 9 in your matches 90% of the time.

Considering both the possibility of winning and losing, which *one* of the above levels would you select?   Opponent ___5___

---

defined the need for achievement as a "capacity to experience pride in accomplishment" (p. 214). That is, the achievement need is an affective disposition.

The Probability of Success

The probability of success, P_s, refers to a cognitive goal expectancy or the anticipation that an instrumental action will lead to the goal. Atkinson's use of this concept was guided by Tolman's earlier analysis. Tolman contended that when a reward follows a response, response-reward contingencies, or expectancies, are formed. The animal becomes aware that making the same response to the stimulus will be followed by a reward. In discussing his usage of P_s, Atkinson (1964) explained:

> What Tolman originally called the *expectancy of the goal* and conceived as a forward-pointing cognition based on prior experience is represented as the subjective probability of attaining the goal. . . . The two terms *expectancy* and *subjective probability* have been used interchangeably in the theory of achieve-

ment motivation which . . . calls attention to the fact that the concept of expectancy . . . serves to represent the associative link between performance of an act
and the attainment of the goal. (p. 275)

According to Tolman, expectancy increases as a function of the number
of rewarded trials. Further, he stated that early and late trials exert special
influence on the formation of goal anticipations. Atkinson, however, working with human rather than subhuman subjects, took much more liberty in
the specification of operations that alter expectancy, or subjective probability. Any information or contrived stimulus situation that influences a
subject's beliefs about winning or performing well can be used to define
operationally the magnitude of P_s. The most frequently adopted strategy
to manipulate P_s is to supply subjects with some normative information
about the difficulty of the task they are attempting. For example, the subject
might be told: "Our norms indicate that ____ % of the students of your age
level and ability are able to solve these puzzles" (see Feather, 1961; Weiner,
1970). Another procedure used to influence P_s is to have subjects compete
against varying numbers of others. For example, Atkinson (1958) told some
of the subjects that they had to perform better than only 1 other person to
win a prize, while others were informed that they were in competition with
20 others. Still a further operation employed to alter P_s is to vary the actual
difficulty of a task. For example, many studies of achievement motivation
employ a ring-toss game requiring that rings be thrown over a peg. It is
generally assumed that the farther one stands from the peg when playing
this game, the lower the subjective expectancy of success. Finally, the
altering of reinforcement history also is used to produce varying levels of
P_s. In one experiment, subjects received puzzle booklets varying in the
number of soluble puzzles (Weiner & Rosenbaum, 1965). The perceived
percentage of success at these tasks determined the P_s.

The Incentive Value of Success

The third determinant of approach behavior specified by Atkinson is
I_s, or the incentive value of success. Guided by resultant valence theory,
Atkinson postulated that I_s is inversely related to P_s: $I_s = 1 - P_s$. Thus the
incentive value of success increases as P_s decreases. Atkinson contended
that the incentive value of an achievement goal is an affect, labeled "pride
in accomplishment." He argued that greater pride is experienced following
success at a difficult task than after success at an easy task. For example,
little pride should be experienced by a student receiving a grade of A in an
easy course, but that student would feel much pride if this grade were
earned in a difficult course. In a similar manner, strong positive affect
should be experienced by an athletic team when defeating a superior, rather
than a poor, opponent.

Because the incentive value of success is conceived as an affect, it
complements the concept of the achievement motive, which is an affective

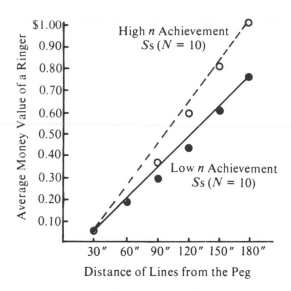

Figure 5.4. Judged mean reward for success at varying distances from the peg. (Reported in McClelland, 1961, p. 236.)

disposition or a capacity to experience pride in achievement. Thus, as in the mechanistic Lewinian scheme, the final valence of a goal is a function of both the properties of the person (motive strength) and the properties of the goal (task difficulty).

Although the inverse relationship between I_s and P_s may be considered a postulate within Atkinson's system, it has been the subject of experimental investigation. For example, Litwin (1958/1966; reported in Atkinson & Feather, 1966; McClelland, 1961) found that the farther one stands from a peg in a ring-toss game, the greater the reward assigned for success (see Figure 5.4). In a similar manner, occupations in which the attainment of success is believed to be difficult are accorded greater prestige and salary (I_s) than occupations in which success is believed to be relatively easy (Strodtbeck, McDonald, & Rosen, 1957). Note, however, that in these instances it is not "pride" that is being assessed as the incentive value of success.

Fear of Failure

Achievement-related activities *elicit positive affective anticipations* because of past successful accomplishments and experienced pride, as well as *negative affective anticipations* learned from prior failures and experienced shame. Thus both a fear of failure and a hope of success are aroused in achievement-related situations.

The determinants of fear of failure, or the tendency to avoid achievement tasks, are conceived by Atkinson as analogous to those of the hope of success. It is postulated that the tendency to avoid failure (T_{AF}) is a multiplicative function of the motive to avoid failure (M_{AF}), the probability of failure (P_f), and the incentive value of failure ($-I_f$):

$$T_{AF} = M_{AF} \times P_f \times (-I_f)$$

The Motive to Avoid Failure

Just as M_s is conceived as a capacity to experience pride in accomplishment, M_{AF} is considered a capacity to experience shame given nonattainment of a goal (failure). The conception of an avoidance motive, independent of the approach motive, was introduced well after the TAT assessment studies, and a supporting measurement program was not initiated. Generally, Atkinson and other researchers employ the Mandler-Sarason Test Anxiety Questionnaire, or TAQ (see Mandler & Sarason, 1952), to define operationally the strength of M_{AF}. The TAQ is an objective self-report measure of anxiety. Atkinson therefore employs a projective instrument to assess M_s and an objective self-report measure to assess M_{AF}. This asymmetry is of interest, inasmuch as self-report measures of M_s generally are ineffective, and they were rarely used by Atkinson and his coworkers (see Atkinson, 1964).

The items on the TAQ pertain only to the anxiety aroused in test-taking situations (as opposed to the Manifest Anxiety Scale, which includes items related to general anxiety). Typical items on the TAQ are as follows:

While taking an intelligence test, to what extent do you worry?
Before taking a course examination, to what extent do you perspire?

The questions are answered on rating scales anchored at the extremes (for example, perspire a lot—perspire not at all), and a total score is attained by summing the scores on the 39 test items. Mandler and Sarason (1952) reported a correlation of $r = .59$ between scores on the TAQ and behaviors such as hand and body movements, inappropriate laughter, and talking during an exam. These actions interfere with task performance because the responses are incompatible with, or irrelevant to, exam-taking behavior. Anxiety as measured by the Manifest Anxiety Scale and test anxiety assessed by the TAQ correlate from $r = .40$ to $r = .55$.

Probability and Incentive Value of Failure

Two environmental factors influence the avoidance of achievement activities: the probability of failure (P_f) and the incentive value of failure ($-I_f$). It is assumed that the incentive value of failure is a negative affect, "shame." Greater shame is believed to be experienced following failure at an easy task than after failure at a difficult task. Therefore, I_f is conceived as equal to $-(1 - P_f)$. In contrast to the empirical work concerning the determinants of I_s, there have been few successful attempts reported to support the presumed I_f and P_f relation.

It is further assumed by Átkinson that the probabilities in the model total unity: $P_s + P_f = 1$. Thus $P_f = 1 - P_s$. It previously was noted that I_s also is equal to $1 - P_s$. Hence numerically $I_s = P_f$.

Resultant Achievement Motivation

The resultant tendency to approach or avoid an achievement-oriented activity (T_A) is postulated to be a function of the strength of the tendency to approach the task minus the strength of the tendency to avoid the task:

$$T_A = T_S - T_{AF}$$

or

$$T_A = (M_S \times P_s \times I_s) - (M_{AF} \times P_f \times I_f)$$

It has been indicated that $I_s = 1 - P_s$, $P_f = 1 - P_s$, and that $I_f = P_s$. Simple arithmetic substitution yields

$$T_A = (M_S - M_{AF}) [P_s \times (1 - P_s)]$$

Inasmuch as M_S and M_{AF} are uncorrelated within the general population, Equation 3 reveals that there are two degrees of freedom among the personal determinants of behavior. However, there is only one degree of freedom among the four environmental determinants of action. Given that P_s is assigned a value, the numerical strengths of I_s, P_f, and I_f are determined. Whether, then, these four variables all can be considered determinants of behavior is a point of theoretical contention.

Further Elaboration of the Model

It is evident from Equation 3 that when $M_S > M_{AF}$, T_A has a positive value. Individuals with this motive constellation, labeled high in resultant achievement motivation, therefore should approach achievement-related activities when given the opportunity. On the other hand, when $M_{AF} > M_S$, T_A has a negative value. Individuals with this motive constellation, labeled low in resultant achievement motivation, should not approach achievement-related activities. Atkinson believed that negative motivation merely indicates what an individual will not do. That is, avoidance motivation is conceptualized as an inhibitory tendency.

It is evident that in our culture the vast majority of individuals engage in some achievement-related actions, such as attending school or working at a job. This apparently contradicts the achievement avoidance behavior expected among individuals in whom $M_{AF} > M_S$. However, achievement-oriented activities are not necessarily initiated to satisfy achievement needs. Motivation may come from some other source, such as attempts to avoid punishment, to gain power, or to satisfy affiliative tendencies. For example, one might study hard at school to impress a potential mate or to win parental favors. This is merely belaboring the self-evident truth that behavior is overdetermined and that many sources of motivation may cause an action.

To capture the overdetermination of achievement behavior, Atkinson specified that the final tendency to undertake achievement activities is determined by the strength of the resultant achievement-oriented tendency, plus the strengths of all other tendencies elicited in the situation but unrelated (extrinsic) to achievement needs per se:

$$\text{achievement behavior} = T_A + \text{extrinsic motivation}$$

It is therefore possible for the model to account for achievement-type behavior exhibited by individuals in whom $M_{AF} > M_S$. Such actions are attributed to sources of motivation unrelated to achievement. The strengths of these extrinsic motivations presumably are a function of the magnitudes of other motives, goal expectancies, and incentives.

Combining the Motives

Some readers might reasonably ask: How can one be classified as high or low in the resultant tendency to strive for success? How can the strengths of M_S and M_{AF} be compared if they are conceived as independent dimensions and assessed with different instruments? The procedure generally followed by Atkinson and other researchers in this area is to assign each individual standard scores, or Z scores, computed from TAT and TAQ scores using deviations from the means of the population under investigation. By transforming scores on both the TAT and TAQ into Z scores, it is possible to compare the relative strengths of these motives within any individual. Thus if an individual scores high on the TAT relative to his or her comparison group and low on the TAQ relative to this group, he or she is classified as high in resultant achievement motivation, or as one in whom $M_S > M_{AF}$. One shortcoming of this procedure is that persons scoring high on both measures and those scoring low on both measures are grouped into a common "intermediate" classification (see Table 5.5). It is likely that these two intermediate groups have differentiating characteristics.

TABLE 5.5 Resultant Achievement Motivation Classification as a Function of Strength of the Hope of Success (generally assessed with the TAT) and Strength of the Fear of Failure (generally assessed with the TAQ)

Hope of Success (Need for Achievement)	Fear of Failure (Anxiety)	Resultant Achievement Motivation
High	Low	High
High	High	Intermediate
Low	Low	Intermediate
Low	High	Low

Derivations from the Theory and Supporting Evidence

We turn now from the rather abstract analysis of Atkinson's theory to some hypotheses derived from his conception and to empirical studies testing these hypotheses. Two experimental topics will be examined first: level of aspiration and persistence of behavior. Following the format of prior chapters, critical analyses of these bodies of research are not undertaken. Rather, the experiments will serve simply to elucidate the theory. Finally, a third area of investigation, choice behavior, is examined in detail. Task selection has been the main testing ground of Atkinson's theory.

Hypotheses in all of these areas of study can be made clear by substituting numerical values for the theory shown in Equation 2 (see Table 5.5). In Table 5.5 it is assumed that when $M_S > M_{AF}$, $M_S = 2$ and $M_{AF} = 1$; when $M_S = M_{AF}$, the value assigned to both motives is 1; and when $M_{AF} > M_S$, $M_{AF} = 2$ and $M_S = 1$. The rows in the table indicate the value of the resultant tendency to strive for success as a function of the difficulty (P_s) of the task. In this example, extrinsic motivations are neglected.

It can be seen in Table 5.6 that when $M_S > M_{AF}$, T_A is positive; when $M_S = M_{AF}$, $T_A = 0$; and when $M_{AF} > M_S$, T_A is negative. Thus the motive scores may be considered relative weights brought to bear upon the environmental sources of motivation. When $M_S > M_{AF}$, greater weight is given to the combination of $P_s \times I_s$ than to $P_f \times -I_f$. On the other hand, when $M_{AF} > M_S$, the negative affect linked with failure is more salient to the individual than is the positive affect associated with success.

More detailed analysis of Table 5.6 yields some rather complex hypotheses. The table reveals that achievement motivation varies systematically as a function of the P_s at the task. Among those in whom $M_S > M_{AF}$, motivation is maximum when $P_s = .50$. Further, the strength of motivation decreases symmetrically as P_s increases or decreases from the level of intermediate difficulty. Neither the incentive value of success nor the expectancy of success is greatest at tasks of intermediate difficulty. But the postulation that $I_s = 1 - P_s$ and the specification that I_s and P_s relate multiplicatively mean greatest motivation occurs when P_s, and therefore I_s, is equal to .50.

TABLE 5.6 Strength of Resultant Achievement Motivation Related to Task Difficulty (probability of success) for High-, Intermediate-, and Low-Achieving Groups

	Motive Classification	
High $(M_S > M_{AF})$	*Intermediate* $(M_S = M_{AF})$	*Low* $(M_{AF} > M_S)$
M_S P_s I_s M_{AF} P_f I_f	M_S P_s I_s M_{AF} P_f I_f	M_S P_s I_s M_{AF} P_f I_f
$2 \times .1 \times .9 - (1 \times .9 \times .1) = .09$	$1 \times .1 \times .9 - (1 \times .9 \times .1) = 0$	$1 \times .1 \times .9 - (2 \times .9 \times .1) = -.09$
$2 \times .3 \times .7 - (1 \times .7 \times .3) = .21$	$1 \times .3 \times .7 - (1 \times .7 \times .3) = 0$	$1 \times .3 \times .7 - (2 \times .7 \times .3) = -.21$
$2 \times .5 \times .5 - (1 \times .5 \times .5) = .25$	$1 \times .5 \times .5 - (1 \times .5 \times .5) = 0$	$1 \times .5 \times .5 - (2 \times .5 \times .5) = -.25$
$2 \times .7 \times .3 - (1 \times .3 \times .7) = .21$	$1 \times .7 \times .3 - (1 \times .3 \times .7) = 0$	$1 \times .7 \times .3 - (2 \times .3 \times .7) = -.21$
$2 \times .9 \times .1 - (1 \times .1 \times .9) = .09$	$1 \times .9 \times .1 - (1 \times .1 \times .9) = 0$	$1 \times .9 \times .1 - (2 \times .1 \times .9) = -.09$

Turning attention to those in whom $M_{AF} > M_S$, it can be seen that among these individuals motivation is most inhibited at tasks of intermediate difficulty. All achievement tasks are aversive in that they predominantly elicit fear. But tasks that are very easy or very difficult are mildly aversive in comparison to tasks of intermediate difficulty.

Finally, the resultant achievement tendency for individuals in whom positive and negative affective anticipations are equal is 0. Motivation is unaffected by task difficulty. However, the degree of absolute approach-avoidance conflict decreases as task difficulty departs from the intermediate level. At high or low P_s levels, little approach and little avoidance motivation are aroused, while at more intermediate P_s levels, both high approach and high avoidance tendencies are elicited.

Several within- and between-group hypotheses follow from the above analysis. Inasmuch as highly achievement-oriented individuals are most motivated by tasks of intermediate difficulty, they should select such tasks when given the opportunity and should exhibit the greatest intensity of motivation when performing activities of intermediate difficulty (such as competing against an opponent of equal skill). Conversely, individuals highly fearful of failure are theoretically expected to select easy or difficult tasks (if they must undertake achievement-oriented activities), and should exhibit the greatest intensity of performance at tasks of extreme probabilities (such as competing against an opponent of greater or lesser comparative ability). The derivations concerning task preferences have generated the most research in the achievement area and are responsible for the "risk-preference" label applied to Atkinson's model.

Level of Aspiration

The analysis of task preference described above has been related to the conceptualization of level of aspiration proposed by Lewin et al. (1944). *Level of aspiration* refers to the setting of a performance goal. It can be contended that goal setting necessitates a comparison among a number of possible alternatives differing in P_s level and a selection of one of these alternatives as the subjective goal. For example, when establishing a level of aspiration for a series of arithmetic problems, individuals may believe that the probability of completing 10 problems within the allotted time is .70; 15 problems, .50; 20 problems, .30; and so forth. They then select the level for which they will strive, knowing that easier tasks are more likely to be attained, but that success at easier tasks is less attractive than success at more difficult tasks. Hence the setting of an aspired level of performance is similar conceptually to a risk preference in which selection is made among a number of alternatives differing in difficulty.

An experiment by Moulton (1965) combined a modification of the usual level of aspiration paradigm with achievement theory. Moulton's subjects were first introduced to three tasks that differed in level of difficulty. Task difficulty was manipulated by presenting fraudulent norms indicating that one of the tasks was easy ($P_s = .75$), a second of intermediate difficulty ($P_s = .50$), and a third difficult ($P_s = .25$).

After receiving the normative information, all the subjects were given the task of intermediate difficulty to perform and received either success or failure feedback. The task involved rearranging letters to form a word.

Following the success or failure experience, the subject was asked to select a second task, the choice being between the two remaining tasks that originally had been introduced as easy or difficult. Moulton reasoned that if an individual was successful on the first trial, he or she would now perceive the "difficult" task as closer to the $P_s = .50$ level than the "easy" task. Success should increase P_s, and the probabilities initially symmetrical around the intermediate level (.25 and .75) would now be, for example, .35 and .85. Thus the difficult task ($P_s = .35$) is closer to .50, or more intermediate in difficulty, than the easy task.

Given this new asymmetry in probability levels, subjects high in resultant achievement motivation were expected to choose the initially difficult task, and subjects low in resultant achievement motivation were expected to select the easy task. Selection of the easy task following success when $P_s = .50$ was considered an atypical response, for the subject would be lowering his or her aspiration level following goal attainment.

In a similar manner, it was assumed that P_s decreases following failure. The subjective probabilities may have shifted from .25 and .75 to, for example, .15 and .65. Thus the task introduced as easy would now be perceived as more intermediate in difficulty than the task introduced as difficult. Individuals in whom $M_S > M_{AF}$ were expected, therefore, to select the easier task, while those in whom $M_{AF} > M_S$ were expected to make an atypical response by selecting the more difficult task after failure.

The results of this study are shown in Table 5.7. As can be seen, subjects in whom $M_{AF} > M_S$ exhibited more atypical responses than did those in the intermediate or high motive groups. Thus Moulton's hypotheses were confirmed, additional support was provided for Atkinson's conception of

TABLE 5.7 Type of Shift in Level of Aspiration as Related to Resultant Motivation

		Type of Shift	
Motive Classification	Resultant Motivation	Atypical	Typical
$M_{AF} > M_S$	avoidance oriented	11	20
$M_{AF} = M_S$	ambivalent	3	28
$M_S > M_{AF}$	approach oriented	1	30

Source: Adapted from Moulton (1965, p. 403).

motivation, and a rapprochement was made between level of aspiration and the study of risk preference.

Persistence of Behavior

Persistence of behavior, along with choice, has been a widely used dependent variable in motivational research. An experiment conducted by Feather (1961), which examined how long an individual would continue to work at an achievement-related task, perhaps best captures the predictive value of Atkinson's theory of achievement motivation.

Feather created a free-choice situation in which subjects were given an achievement-related puzzle to perform. They were instructed that they could work on the task for as long as they desired and could quit whenever they wished to undertake a different puzzle. The task required subjects to trace over all the lines on a complex figure without lifting the pencil from the paper or retracing a line. Although the subjects did not know it, the task was impossible.

Feather introduced false norms to establish a P_s at the task. In one experimental condition the task was presented as quite difficult ("At your age level, approximately 5 percent of the college students are able to get the solution"). In a second condition the task was introduced as relatively easy ("70 percent of the college students are able to get the solution"). Feather then examined the number of trials attempted by the subject, or the persistence of behavior, before quitting the task. Persistence was predicted to be a function of the initial P_s at the task and individual differences in the strength of achievement-related needs.

The derivations of Feather's hypotheses are similar to those outlined in the level of aspiration study conducted by Moulton. Table 5.8 shows the strength of motivation toward the achievement tasks in the two experimental conditions for subjects in whom $M_S > M_{AF}$ and for those in whom $M_{AF} > M_S$. Again, for ease of presentation, it is assumed that when $M_S > M_{AF}$, M_S = 2 and M_{AF} = 1, and vice versa when $M_{AF} > M_S$. In addition, extrinsic motivation is assumed equal to .50, and the decrement of P_s following failure is .10 in the P_s = .70 condition and .01 in the P_s = .05 condition. The table shows that among subjects in whom $M_S > M_{AF}$, motivation on Trial 1

TABLE 5.8 Strength of Motivation to Undertake the Activity in Progress Among Subjects High or Low in Resultant Achievement Motivation, Given the Two Experimental Conditions Employed by Feather (1961)

| | | | *Strength of Total Motivation (achievement + extrinsic motivation)* | |
| | | | *Subject Classification* | |
Experimental Condition	Trial	P_S	$M_S > M_{AF}$	$M_{AF} > M_S$
$P_s = .70$	1	$.70^a$	$2 \times .7 \times .3 - (1 \times .3 \times .7) + .50^c = .71$	$1 \times .7 \times .3 - (2 \times .3 \times .7) + .50 = .29$
	2	.60	$2 \times .6 \times .4 - (1 \times .4 \times .6) + .50 = .74$	$1 \times .6 \times .4 - (2 \times .4 \times .6) + .50 = .26$
	3	.50	$2 \times .5 \times .5 - (1 \times .5 \times .5) + .50 = .75$	$1 \times .5 \times .5 - (2 \times .5 \times .5) + .50 = .25$
$P_s = .05$	1	$.05^b$	$2 \times .05 \times .95 - (1 \times .95 \times .05) + .50 = .55$	$1 \times .05 \times .95 - (2 \times .95 \times .05) + .50 = .45$
	2	.04	$2 \times .04 \times .96 - (1 \times .96 \times .04) + .50 = .54$	$1 \times .04 \times .96 - (2 \times .96 \times .04) + .50 = .46$
	3	.03	$2 \times .03 \times .97 - (1 \times .97 \times .03) + .50 = .53$	$1 \times .03 \times .97 - (2 \times .97 \times .03) + .50 = .47$

a. It is assumed that P_s decreases .10 following failure when the initial $P_s = .70$.
b. It is assumed that P_s decreases .01 following failure when the initial $P_s = .05$.
c. Extrinsic motivation is assumed constant and equal to .50.

is greater when $P_s = .70$ than when .05 (.71 versus .55). Further, following initial failure, motivation rises in the $P_s = .70$ condition, for P_s decreases and moves closer to the level of intermediate difficulty. Assuming that the decrement in P_s remains .10, motivation also should increase after the next failure. On the other hand, motivation immediately decreases following failure in the $P_s = .05$ condition, for P_s moves from the level of intermediate difficulty. Further, motivation continues to decrease given repeated failures. Thus Feather predicted that persistence, or the number of choices of the activity in progress, would be greater in the $P_s = .70$ than in the $P_s = .05$ condition among subjects in whom $M_S > M_{AF}$.

The right half of Table 5.8 portrays the hypothetical strength of motivation among subjects in whom $M_{AF} > M_S$. The total motivation for these subjects is positive only because the strength of the assumed extrinsic sources of motivation exceeds the achievement inhibition aroused by the task. When $M_{AF} > M_S$, motivation initially is greater in the $P_s = .05$ than in the $P_s = .70$ condition (.45 versus .29), for .05 is further from the level of intermediate difficulty than .70. In addition, following failure the motivation in the $P_s = .70$ condition decreases, while it increases in the $P_s = .05$ condition. This is again due to the respective shifting of P_s toward or away from the .50 level. Because repeated failures are experienced, it would be expected that motivation continues to increase in the $P_s = .05$ condition and approaches asymptote (the strength of extrinsic sources) as P_s approaches 0. Hence Feather predicted that subjects in whom $M_{AF} > M_S$ would persist longer in the $P_s = .05$ than in the $P_s = .70$ condition.

In sum, an interaction was hypothesized between level of resultant achievement needs and task difficulty. Among subjects in whom $M_S > M_{AF}$,

TABLE 5.9 Number of Subjects Who Were High and Low in Persistence in Relation to Stated Difficulty of the Initial Task and the Nature of Their Motivation

			Persistence Trials	
n Achievement	Test Anxiety	Stated Difficulty of Task	High (above median)	Low (below median)
High	Low	$P_s = .70$ (easy)	6	2
		$P_s = .05$ (difficult)	2	7
Low	High	$P_s = .70$ (easy)	3	6
		$P_s = .05$ (difficult)	6	2

Source: Adapted from Feather (1961, p. 558).

greater persistence was predicted in the easy than in the difficult condition. On the other hand, among subjects in whom $M_{AF} > M_S$, greater persistence was expected at the difficult than at the easy task. The data from the experiment, shown in Table 5.9, confirmed Feather's hypotheses (see Weiner, 1972, for a more detailed analysis of some of the conceptual issues raised by this experiment).

Choice Behavior

As already indicated, choice among achievement tasks varying in difficulty has been the main testing ground of Atkinson's theory of achievement motivation. The general procedure in these studies is illustrated in an experiment by Atkinson and Litwin (1960). In this investigation the subjects attempted to toss rings over a peg. The subjects were allowed to stand at varying distances from the peg and could change positions following each toss. It was assumed by Atkinson and Litwin that a position close to the target corresponded to a high P_s level and that P_s decreased as the distance from the peg increased. Thus distance from the peg was the observable indicator of choice and of task difficulty.

The subjects were given the TAT and the TAQ and were classified into resultant achievement motivation subgroups. The data on choice from this study are shown in Figure 5.5, which reveals that intermediate task preference is greatest for the high motive group, least for subjects in whom $M_{AF} > M_S$, and intermediate for subjects either high or low in both motives. Intermediate difficulty in this study was defined either as intermediate physical distance from the peg or the median of the actual distribution of shots. The two measures yielded comparable results.

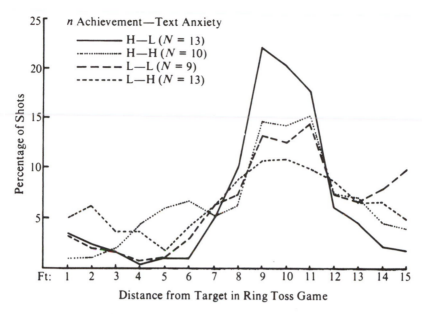

Figure 5.5. Percentage of ring-toss attempts as a function of distance from the peg, with subjects classified according to strength of resultant achievement motivation. (Adapted from Atkinson & Litwin, 1960, p. 55.)

The data reported by Atkinson and Litwin are typical of most of the findings in the study of risk preference. Three research questions that guided these studies, and their answers, are as follows:

(1) Do individuals high in achievement needs exhibit a preference for tasks of intermediate difficulty? Absolutely yes!
(2) Do individuals low in achievement needs exhibit a preference for tasks that are comparatively easy or comparatively difficult? Convincingly not!
(3) Do individuals high in achievement needs exhibit a greater preference for tasks of intermediate difficulty than individuals low in achievement needs? Most likely yes. (See a review in Meyer, Folkes, & Weiner, 1976.)

In sum, all individuals seem to prefer intermediate difficulty, although this preference may be more evident among individuals highly motivated to achieve. These data pose some problems for Atkinson's theory, yet they do tend to support the broad (and often tested) hypothesis that groups classified by the strength of achievement needs will display differential preference for intermediate difficulty tasks.

Atkinson and Feather (1966, pp. 22, 342) acknowledge that individuals classified as highly fearful of failure do not avoid intermediate tasks. They contend that in the populations tested (such as college students) the subjects generally are high in need for achievement. Hence extreme risks should not be chosen, although differential preference for intermediate difficulty tasks is still expected among groups differing in their level of achievement needs. However, this argument is weakened by the fact that even when high school and grammar school students are subjects, persons low in achievement needs do not avoid intermediate difficulty.

An alternate explanation. Atkinson's prediction of disparate motive-group preferences is based upon the belief that choice among achievement tasks follows the principle of maximization of positive affect for the highly achievement-oriented person and minimization of negative affect for individuals low in achievement needs. That is, anticipatory emotions and hedonic concerns determine what tasks an individual will attempt to perform.

An alternative interpretation of risk preference appeals to informational rather than hedonic principles. Research has demonstrated that outcomes at tasks of intermediate difficulty provide performers with the most information about their efforts and capabilities. There are logical reasons that performance at intermediate difficulty tasks provides a maximum of personal information. Selection of easy tasks typically results in success, and that outcome is attributed to the ease of the task (see Weiner & Kukla, 1970). In a similar manner, selection of a very difficult task typically results in failure, and the blame is placed on the characteristics of the task. Thus selection of easy or difficult tasks generally confirms one's knowledge about the external world. Conversely, tasks of intermediate difficulty are just as likely to produce success as they are to produce failure. Thus performance at such tasks provides information about the efforts and abilities of the *person* undertaking the activity. Given this conception, differential risk-preference behavior between groups differing in achievement needs would indicate disparate desires for personal feedback or self-evaluation (see McClelland et al., 1953). Of course, it is quite functional and adaptive to have a realistic or veridical view of oneself.

To disentangle the hedonic versus informational determinants of choice, Trope and Brickman (1975) simultaneously varied the difficulty of tasks as well as their "diagnosticity," or the difference between the proportion of individuals designated as high or low in ability who succeed at the task. Thus, for example, a task at which 90% of the high-ability group and 60% of the low-ability group succeed has greater diagnostic value (30) than a task accomplished by 52% versus 48% of the individuals respectively high and low in ability. However, the 52-48 task is more intermediate in difficulty than is the 90-60 task.

Trope and Brickman (1975) created a choice setting in which tasks that varied in difficulty levels also varied in diagnosticity. For example, subjects were asked to choose either a task at which 90% of the high-ability and 60% of the low-ability subjects succeeded or a task at which 52% of the high-ability and 48% of the low-ability subjects succeeded. They reported that in

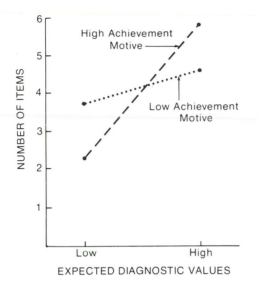

Figure 5.6. Mean number of items chosen from tests varying in expected diagnostic value by subjects varying in achievement motive. (From Trope, 1975, p. 1008.)

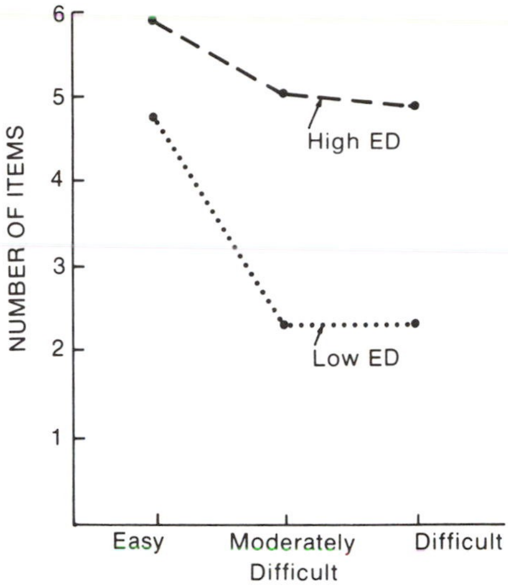

Figure 5.7. Mean number of items chosen from six tests varying in difficulty and expected diagnostic value (ED). (From Trope, 1975, p. 1008.)

this situation the subjects chose to perform the tasks of greater diagnosticity (90-60) rather than the tasks more intermediate in difficulty (52-48). This suggests that the preference for intermediate difficulty reported by so many investigators is attributable to the high diagnostic value of these tasks.

In a replication and extension of this investigation, Trope (1975) again gave subjects a choice between tasks varying in difficulty as well as in diagnosticity. In addition, measures of achievement motivation were taken. The results of this investigation are shown in Figure 5.6, which reveals that subjects in both motive groups prefer to undertake high- rather than low-diagnosticity tasks. However, this preference is significantly greater among high achievement-oriented subjects. Thus the two motive groups apparently differ in their information-seeking desires. Figure 5.7 depicts choice as a function of task difficulty. As can be seen, at all levels of difficulty, tasks of high diagnosticity are preferred. Furthermore, there is no differential preference for tasks of intermediate difficulty when diagnosticity is controlled. Indeed, there is a general trend to choose easier tasks.

Investigations by Meyer et al. (1976) demonstrated more directly the informational value of intermediate difficulty choice. These researchers examined the phenomenology of choice behavior by assessing the perceived affective and informational determinants of risk preference. Subjects classified according to their level of achievement needs expressed preferences among tasks varying in difficulty. In one of the experimental conditions the instructions conveyed that performance at the task chosen should

TABLE 5.10 Mean Objective Difficulty Level and Subjective Certainty Rating for Feedback Choice

| Ability Group | n | Target Shooting | |
		Objective Difficulty (%)	Subjective Certainty
Very high	18	15[a]	5.22[b]
High	16	39	6.12
Average	50	47	5.42
Low	23	75	6.69

Source: Adapted from Meyer, Folkes, and Weiner (1976, p. 420).
a. Mean percentage of policemen specified as hitting the target.
b. Scale: 0 = certainly will not succeed; 11 = certainly will succeed.

maximize satisfaction, while in a second condition the instructions specified that the choice should maximize the information gained about the subject's ability and effort expenditure. It was found that the majority of all subjects preferred to undertake tasks of intermediate difficulty and that both positive affect and information gain were perceived to be optimal at or near this difficulty level. As already noted, the finding that intermediate risk taking is displayed by subjects regardless of their magnitude of achievement needs is consistent with a great amount of prior research.

Two additional experiments investigated at what level of task difficulty individuals most desire information about their performance. Police trainees and high school students with disparate self-concepts of their abilities in target shooting and high-jumping, respectively, were able to receive limited but self-selected performance feedback at a series of shooting or jumping tasks that varied in difficulty. More specifically, in the police study, Meyer et al. (1976) first had police rate their general shooting abilities prior to a target practice. Targets of varying objective difficulty were then presented, and the policemen rated their subjective probability of success at each of the targets. Finally, the subjects were told they would shoot at each of the targets, but they could learn the results of their performance on only one of these targets. The policemen were allowed to choose the target at which feedback was desired.

The results of this study are given in Table 5.10, which indicates the target for which the feedback was desired and the subjective likelihood of success at that target. Among all the policemen, feedback was chosen for the target for which the subjective probability of success was intermediate. Thus policemen perceiving themselves as poor shots requested feedback at the objectively easy (subjectively intermediate) target, while policemen who perceived themselves as high in shooting ability desired performance information at the objectively difficult (also subjectively intermediate) tar-

TABLE 5.11 Comparison of the Determinants of Behavior Specified in the
Motivational Models of Atkinson, Hull, and Lewin (including both
Lewin's hydraulic and resultant valence conceptions)

| | Construct | | |
Theorist	Person	Environment	Learning
Atkinson	motive[a]	incentive of success[b]	probability of success
Hull	drive	incentive	habit
Lewin (hydraulic)	tension[c]	valence[d]	psychological distance[e]
Lewin (resultant valence)		valence of success[f]	potency[g]

a. Represents a stable personality disposition.
b. Is equal to 1 – the probability of success.
c. Did not specify the mathematical relations among all the components in the theory.
d. Determined by properties of the goal object.
e. Defined by the "steps in the path."
f. Related to the probability of success, but not in an exact manner.
g. Considered here as the subjective certainty of success.

get. The intermediate ability groups fell between these extremes in their
choice behavior.

In sum, the data from choice studies indicate that there is a general
tendency to select intermediate difficulty tasks, probably because of their
informational (diagnostic) value. However, intermediate preference may
be more evident among individuals highly motivated to succeed.

Comparison with Hullian and Lewinian Theory

As indicated throughout this chapter, there are important similarities
and differences in the approaches to the study of motivation advocated by
Atkinson, Hull, and Lewin. Consider first the determinants of action specified by these three theorists when considering Lewin's hydraulic theory
presented in Chapter 4. Table 5.11 shows that all three postulate that
behavior is a function of the properties of the person (motive, drive, or
tension), the properties of the goal object (incentive or valence), and an
experiential or learning variable (probability of success, habit strength, or
psychological distance). However, the property of the person is a stable
personality attribute in Atkinson's conception, but a temporary state of
drive or tension in the Hullian and Lewinian theories. Further, in the
Hullian and Lewinian conceptions the incentive value of the goal object has
an independent operational existence. But for Atkinson, I_s is determined by
the value of P_s. (Atkinson, however, does consider achievement to be a
special case of a general model in which I_s and P_s are not necessarily related.)
Finally, in the Hullian model the learning or associative variable represents a mechanical strengthening of an S-R bond, while for both Atkinson

and Lewin the experiential component is conceptualized as cognitive and involves foresight concerning the goal event or the consequences of a response. That is, Atkinson and Lewin contend that mental events (expectancies) intervene between stimulus input and the final response, even though Lewin is a mechanist.

There are other points of convergence and divergence among the three motivational models. All are hedonistic conceptions. Individuals are believed to act to maximize pleasure and minimize pain. Most theories of motivation link hedonism to homeostatic processes; pleasurable events return the organism to a state of equilibrium. For Hull, as well as for Freud, a state of equilibrium involves no stimulation. All internal stimuli are considered unpleasant and are to be eliminated. Lewin also asserts that motivational processes are derived from homeostatic imbalance. In contrast to the above theorists, Atkinson abandons the concept of homeostasis. It plays no formal role in his theory. Further, because the motivational property associated with the person is a stable trait, rather than a drive or tense state, attainment or nonattainment of a goal cannot dramatically increase or decrease its strength.

There are also differences between the actual and stated breadths of the theories under consideration. Although the Hullian conception is formulated as a general behavioral theory, the data cited in support of the conception primarily were generated by hungry rats running down a straight alley. It is only with difficulty and great ingenuity that the theory can be used to explain other behavioral data. Lewin, on the other hand, is more of a general theorist. He attempts to explain the data gathered by Hullians and offers his own research in a variety of areas in support of his theory. In contrast to both Hull and Lewin, Atkinson has limited his theory to the area of achievement-related behavior. Virtually all of the data cited in support of his conception involve success or failure at some achievement activity, or a decision in an achievement-related context. Thus his conception follows the general trend in psychology to predict and understand more circumscribed domains of behavior. It also is true that Atkinson's model may be considered a general theory of action. But when considered as such, the implicit breadth of the theory is greater than its data base. Whether the model of achievement behavior can also serve as a model for power seeking, affiliative actions, and the like remains to be demonstrated.

When Atkinson's conception is compared with Lewin's resultant valence theory, it can be seen that both include valence and expectancy-type constructs among the determinants of action. However, Lewin, in contrast to Atkinson, does not have a person component in his model and, although he specifies that incentive and expectancy (potency) are related, he does not make the one-to-one correspondence that is specified by Atkinson.

Finally, both the Lewinian resultant valence conception and achievement theory as specified by Atkinson conceptualize persons as perfectly rational, able to compare all alternatives, and thus as "super-beings" (God-like). They also do not include an energizing construct, as it is assumed that people are always active. Hence they concentrate on the prediction of choice behavior, or what alternatives are selected.

Summary of Achievement Theory

The experimental study of achievement motivation has its origins in Murray's taxonomy of need systems and his development of a projective instrument, the TAT, to infer an individual's motivational concerns. The TAT was refined by McClelland and his colleagues for use as a research tool to assess the strength of achievement needs.

The need for achievement was then included as one component of a theory of achievement motivation. This theory was formulated by Atkinson and specifies that achievement-related behavior is a result of a conflict between a hope of success (approach motivation) and a fear of failure (avoidance motivation). The approach and avoidance tendencies, in turn, are a function of achievement-related needs (need for achievement and anxiety about failure), the expectancy of success and failure, and the incentive value of success and failure. A special assumption of the model is that the incentive value of achievement tasks is determined by the probability of success.

The main derivation of this theory is that individuals high in resultant achievement needs are particularly attracted to tasks of intermediate difficulty, while those low in achievement needs avoid tasks that have a probability of success near .50. Investigations by Moulton, Feather, and Atkinson and Litwin employing, respectively, the dependent measures of level of aspiration, persistence, and choice, support the general hypothesis that differential attraction toward tasks of intermediate difficulty is displayed by groups high and low in achievement motivation. However, persons low in achievement needs do not avoid tasks of intermediate difficulty, thus contradicting Atkinson's theory. Rather, they also are attracted to intermediate probability, but less so than individuals high in achievement needs.

The risk-preference data also have been interpreted from an informational point of view. It has been contended that achievement choice is in part motivated by the individual's desire to discover his or her level of competence. Tasks of intermediate difficulty provide the most information about the performer, while easy or difficult tasks merely tend to confirm knowledge about the environment.

It was suggested previously that drive theorists demonstrated that motivational psychologists could proceed in a scientific and mathematical manner, while Lewin and his colleagues directed attention to the subject matter motivational theorists should investigate. The study of achievement motivation was guided by both these methodological and content concerns. Investigators adopted the procedures and mathematical orientation developed by Hullians, but applied this approach to the study of complex human behaviors observed in "everyday" life. Thus achievement theory represents the most precise of the cognitive, Godlike motivational models.

Rotter's Social Learning Theory

Rotter's social learning theory is concerned primarily with the choices that individuals make when confronted with a number of possible alternative ways of behaving (Phares, 1976). To explain choice, or the direction of behavior, Rotter (1954) attempted to integrate two major approaches in American psychology: the S→R, or reinforcement, position as exemplified primarily by Skinner and, to a lesser extent, by Hull, and the cognitive or field position advocated by Tolman and Lewin.

Rotter stresses *learned* social behavior, giving relatively little attention to the unlearned, biological determinants of action focused upon by Freud. For this reason, Rotter is categorized in the tradition of social learning theorists. Because learning (the strengthening and weakening of expectancies, or beliefs about reinforcements) is so central to Rotter's theory, the psychological situation also becomes of paramount importance, inasmuch as expectancies are elicited in particular situational contexts. However, Rotter also assumes that on the basis of a variety of learning experiences, general belief systems develop that influence behavior in any specific situation. These general beliefs, such as the conviction that one has control over one's fate, are similar to what are typically meant by traits, or personality characteristics. Rotter's social learning theory, therefore, emphasizes the general (trait) and the specific (situational) determinants of action, with both being the product of learning experiences. Hence, in a manner similar to Lewin, Rotter (1954) contends that "the unit of investigation for the study of personality is the interaction of the individual and his meaningful environment" (p. 85).

Basic Concepts

There are four basic concepts in Rotter's theory: behavior potential, expectancy, reinforcement value, and the psychological situation. These are linked with more general concepts (need potential, freedom of movement, and need value) and provide the foundation for still other constructs, including generalized expectancy. Rotter's basic motivational statement is that the potential of any behavior is determined by the expectancy that the

JULIAN ROTTER

Julian Rotter received his undergraduate education at Brooklyn College, his master's degree at the University of Iowa, and his doctoral diploma at Indiana University in 1941. Each of these settings had an important impact on his theory. In New York he attended a series of seminars given by the then aging Alfred Adler. Adler's teachings convinced Rotter of the importance of considering the perceived social context of behavior, rather than concentrating solely on the intrapersonal

determinants of action (see Mosher, 1968). At Iowa and Indiana, he was influenced by the Hull-Spence behavioral theory and the ideas of Skinner concerning the significance of reinforcement (and, thus, the situation) in determining the direction of behavior. In addition, Rotter's theory was greatly shaped by Edward Tolman, who championed the concept of "expectancy" in psychology.

Some years after his graduate training, Rotter became chairman of the program in clinical psychology at Ohio State University. For many years Ohio State was one of the largest clinical psychology training centers in the United States, and the department included three famous clinicians: George Kelly, Carl Rogers, and Rotter. (Kelly's ideas are examined in detail later in this volume.) Rotter subsequently moved to the University of Connecticut.

Rotter is perhaps best known for his development of a locus of control scale. The popularity of this work took even him by surprise. Alluding to the widespread use of this scale, Rotter once confided: "I was walking in the woods, lit my pipe and threw away the match, and when I looked behind me there was a forest fire."

(Photograph courtesy of J. B. Rotter)

behavior will lead to a reinforcement and by the reinforcing value of the goal:

$$\text{behavior potential} = f \text{ (expectancy of reward and reward value of the goal)}$$

This approach is similar to that advocated by Hull, Lewin, and Atkinson in that an attempt is made to identify the immediate determinants of behavior, and the formulated model "explains" why persons behave as they do.

Behavior Potential

Behavior potential is the likelihood for any given behavior to occur "as calculated in relation to any single reinforcement or set of reinforcements" (Rotter, Chance, & Phares, 1972, p. 12). For example, at a party a man might desire to meet a particular person of the opposite sex. To do this, he might walk up and introduce himself, wait for an opportunity to be introduced, or promote a meeting by taking part in an activity or game that involves mutual interaction. Each of these actions has a particular potential or likelihood of being undertaken, given the party setting. Behavior potential is a relative concept, for it involves a comparison among many possible behaviors. Furthermore, the term *behavior* is used in its broadest sense and includes cognitive activity, such as further planning or even invoking a psychological defense. It also includes both molecular and molar overt actions, such as smiling or engaging in one of the relatively complex sequences listed above to meet another person. In all cases, however, the totally knowledgeable person selects the course of action perceived as "best."

###

Expectancy is the key concept in Rotter's theory. It is defined as the "probability held by the individual that a particular reinforcement will occur as a function of a specific behavior on his part in a specific situation" (Rotter, 1954, p. 107). Rotter considers expectancy to be a subjective probability: It may or may not be identical to the true or objective likelihood of reaching one's goal. For example, the person at the party might believe that if he introduces himself, he will be considered "impolite" or "forward." This will minimize the subjective likelihood of establishing a friendship (the reinforcer). However, such a conviction may be objectively quite false. Theoretically, expectancies can be measured on a scale that ranges from zero (no likelihood of reward) to one (reward is certain to follow).

The concept of expectancy as used by Rotter has much in common with the prior use of the term by Tolman (1932), the Lewinian concept of potency, and Atkinson's concept of subjective probability. Rotter contends that in the study of motivation, often behavioral predictions are made entirely on the basis of the assumed needs or traits of the person, while the likelihood of goal attainment given an action is ignored. According to Rotter and Hochreich (1975):

> Simply knowing how much an individual wants to reach a certain goal is not sufficient information for predicting his behavior. A student may want very badly to finish school and qualify himself for a well-paying job. But if his past experiences have led him to believe that no amount of studying will result in passing grades—if his expectancy for success in this situation is low—he is unlikely to study, despite his strong desire to graduate. A fellow student may share the same strong goals, and as a result of a different set of past experiences in school, have a high expectancy that studying will lead to academic success. In this instance, one could safely predict that the second student would be likely to study in order to obtain his goals. As you can see, the goals in these two cases are

identical, but the expectancies differ, and as a result, the behavior of the two students is likely to differ. (p. 95)

Generalized expectancy. It is assumed that an individual's beliefs about reinforcements are determined, in part, by his or her past history in the specific situation under consideration. However, it is evident that reinforcement expectancies are influenced not only by the prior behavior-outcome experiences in the same situation, but also by experiences in similar circumstances. For example, a person's beliefs about making a friend at a party will be influenced by his or her prior experiences at parties and by the outcome of friendship attempts made in a wide variety of social settings; that is, expectancies generalize from similar behavior-reinforcement sequences. More formally, Rotter proposes that

$$E_{S1} = f\ (E_{S1} + GE)$$

This formula conveys that the expectancy of reinforcement in Situation 1 (E_{S1}) is determined on the basis of expectancies in that particular situation, as well as by generalized expectancies (GE) from similar situations. The more novel a situation, the greater the importance of generalized expectancies in determining immediate beliefs. On the other hand, given a great deal of experience in a specific situation, generalized expectancies may have little significance in influencing behavior. Phares (1976) illustrates these statements with the following example:

> Suppose a college student who has never taken any work in chemistry is asked to state her expectancy for receiving an "A" on her first quiz in the course. Her statement might be determined by her overall experience in those science-related courses that she regards as similar. That is, she has no specific expectancies based on prior chemistry experience. However, if that same question were posed at the end of the chemistry course, her answer would be based almost entirely on her specific experience with chemistry quizzes and hardly at all on expectancies generalized from related courses. (pp. 16-17)

Reinforcement Value

Reinforcement value refers to "the degree of preference for any reinforcement . . . if the possibility of their occurring were all equal" (Rotter, 1954, p. 107). Thus reinforcement value, like behavioral potential, is a relative or comparative term. Furthermore, some reinforcements gain in value because of their association with or relevance to other reinforcements. For example, receiving an A in a course is desired in and of itself, but the value of this grade may be enhanced if it is also perceived as aiding the person in being admitted to graduate school.

The reinforcement value of a goal is clearly linked with the needs of an individual. As Lewin previously noted, an object does not acquire a valence, or reinforcement value, unless the person is in a state of need and is desirous of the object. Rotter has contended that most human needs are learned. He suggests six very broad need categories: recognition-status, dominance, independence, protection-dependency, love and affection, and physical comfort. These needs supposedly influence most of the learned psychological behaviors because of their role in determining perceived reinforcement.

The Psychological Situation

Throughout the prior discussion, the importance of the individual's situational context has been stressed. Rotter and Hochreich (1975) state: "Because of its basic learning theory assumptions, [social learning theory] emphasizes that a person learns through past experiences that some satisfactions are more likely to be obtained in certain situations than in others" (p. 98). The situation discussed by Rotter is the psychological situation, or the subjective meaning of the environment. Behavior takes place in this environment and thus the social context of behavior must be described in order to understand and predict action.

The Determinants of Action

With this discussion in mind, the motivational model formulated by Rotter may be specified in greater detail. His basic formula is as follows:

$$BP_{x,s_1,r_a} = f(E_{x,r_a}s_1 + RV_{a,s_1})$$

This formula states: "The potential for behavior x to occur in Situation 1 in relation to the reinforcement a is a function of the expectancy of the occurrence of reinforcement a following behavior x in Situation 1, and the value of reinforcement a in Situation 1" (Rotter et al., 1972, p. 14). This formula includes the notion that the expectancy of a reinforcement is a composite of both specific and generalized expectancies, and that the value of a reinforcement is determined by its own reinforcement properties as well as its relation to other potential reinforcers.

Rotter also suggests a more general formula that conveys the same meaning, but is less situation specific. That formula is as follows:

$$N.P. = f(F.M. + N.V.)$$

This reads: "The potentiality of occurrence of a set of behaviors that lead to the satisfaction of some need (need potential) is a function of the expectancies that these behaviors will lead to these reinforcements (freedom of movement) and the strength or value of these reinforcements (need value)" (Rotter, 1954, p. 110).

Relation Between the Constructs

Expectancy and reinforcement value have been presented as independent constructs. Expectancy is assumed to be determined, in part, by the number of reinforced experiences relative to total experiences, whereas value is related to the properties of the goal object and one's needs. It is evident, therefore, that Hull's concept of habit (H), Lewin's notion of potency (P_o), and Atkinson's use of probability (P_s) resemble expectancy, while Hull's incentive (K), Lewin's concept of valence (Va), and Atkinson's incentive of success (I_s) are similar to what Rotter means by the "value" of the goal.

However, Rotter also notes (as did Lewin and Atkinson) that the expectancy and value constructs are not entirely independent. Rotter et al. (1972) suggest that if one fails to attain a goal, then the "reinforcement itself may become associated with the unpleasantness of failure and diminish in value" (p. 19). Conversely, it is often true that difficult goals have high values. For example, it is more rewarding to defeat a good athletic competitor than a poor one, or to complete a difficult rather than an easy puzzle. That is, high expectancy at times is associated with low value, and vice versa.

Low expectancy and high value. According to social learning theory, one cause of personal difficulties is to experience a low expectancy of success for a highly valued goal. For example, one might want to go to college, but perceive oneself to be low in ability, or one might desire to date a person who does not reciprocate one's warm feelings. In these situations individuals may learn to avoid the punishment of failure by using maladaptive defenses, such as withdrawal into a fantasy world. The psychological withdrawal decreases subsequent chances of success even further, because the chosen behavior is not constructive.

Deviant behavior. The effects of a discrepancy between expectancy and value also have been analyzed at a social level. Merton (1957) has pointed out that in American society material success is a goal for all individuals. This goal is realized when one has a home, one or two automobiles, and other indicators of a high income. On the other hand, many members of our society have only limited access to the "opportunity structure," or the means to achieve such goals. These means include a high education, influential friends, appropriate manners of behavior, and so on. A discrepancy between values and expectancies, Merton argues, causes individuals to adopt deviant or illegitimate means to attain success. Jessor, Graves, Hanson, and Jessor (1968) report some evidence in support of Merton's ideas. They found that persons with the lowest access to the opportunity structure are most likely to engage in deviant behavior, such as drinking and crime.

Implications for Psychotherapy

Social learning theory was originally formulated by Rotter (1954) to supply a new language for clinical psychologists. Some of the implications of social learning theory for the understanding of psychopathology and psychotherapeutic techniques already have been alluded to in the discussion of the adverse effects of a discrepancy between expectancy and reward value. Social learning theory states that maladjustment represents a learning problem; the goals of psychotherapy are to lessen the occurrence of undesirable actions and to increase the occurrence of desirable actions through new learning (Katkovsky, 1968). Two questions are of special importance to the therapist when considering what the patient should unlearn and learn: (a) What does the client expect? (b) What does the client value?

Expectation and maladjustment. Low expectancies are one source of personal problems. Expectancy may be low for any number of reasons. For example, the individual may not have learned the necessary skills or appropriate goal-directed behaviors. In this case the therapist may actively suggest new and more instrumental behaviors. The therapist is therefore a teacher, and helps the client to develop competencies. Contrasting this approach with more traditional analytic theory, Rotter and Hochreich (1975) state:

> This emphasis on the acquisition of new and more effective behaviors distinguishes the social learning theory approach from other kinds of psychotherapy which are based on the assumption that once a person is free from internal conflict and understands himself better, he will automatically be able to find healthier ways of achieving his goals. Insight into one's problems may be very useful but does not always lead to actual changes in a person's behavior. (p. 107)

Expectancies also may be low because of erroneous generalizations. For example, a person's self-image during an unattractive adolescent period may persist into adulthood when it is no longer suitable, or an individual who does poorly in school might also expect to do poorly in nonacademic settings, even though different skills are involved in these two areas. In these cases the therapist must help the client to discriminate among different situations and to make more adaptive differentiations. The therapist might also suggest a change in environment so the client can escape the cues that promote low expectancies. Thus, for example, the therapist might advise the client to seek a new job, a different college, or an altered set of acquaintances.

Value and adjustment. Values also play an important role in problems of maladjustment. For example, the individual may place too much importance upon a particular goal. This could lead to perceptual-cognitive distortions, such as interpreting all situations as relevant to this particular need (e.g., the paranoid patient who perceives the clanging of the radiator as a signal that someone is watching him). The therapist can aid the patient in altering goals or selecting more appropriate targets of action. In a similar manner, a person's goal level may be too high, thus promoting dissatisfaction. Alternatively, the person may have several highly valued needs and goals that are incompatible. For example, an individual with both high independence and protection needs may find that the same behavior positively reinforces one need but is a negative reinforcer for the other.

In sum, social learning theory suggests an eclectic approach to psychotherapy. The theory stresses

> the development of problem-solving skills on the part of the patient, such as looking for alternative ways of reaching goals, analyzing the consequences of behavior, and trying to analyze how situations differ from one another. The goal of therapy is not only to help the person solve his immediate problems, but to provide him with skills which will be useful to him in meeting life's difficulties in the future. (Rotter & Hochreich, 1975, p. 109)

Representative Research

It should come as no surprise that the research generated by Rotter's social learning theory primarily concerns the measurement of expectancy and value and the effects of these factors on a wide variety of behaviors and personal adjustment. In this section of the chapter a few characteristic research studies examining the antecedents and consequences of expectancy of reinforcement are reported to acquaint the reader with the research methods and goals of Rotter's approach.

Expectancy Generalization

Crandall (1955) developed a projective method of assessing expectancy of success and then examined the effects of failure on the generalization of expectancies. Subjects made up stories in response to nine different TAT-type pictures. The pictures depicted three need areas: recognition for physical skill, recognition for academic skill, and love and affection from the opposite sex. On the basis of stories about these pictures, Crandall inferred the subjective expectancy of satisfaction of these needs.

The subjects in an experimental group then were given a failure experience at a physical coordination task, while subjects in a control group received no such experience. Following the failure (or neutral control activity), subjects made up stories to a second set of pictures.

The results of this investigation are shown in Figure 5.8, which indicates that there was a lowering of expectancy in the experimental group relative to the control group. This is in accordance with the supposition that expectancies are determined by behavioral outcome histories. Furthermore, the decrement in expectancy of success depends upon the similarity

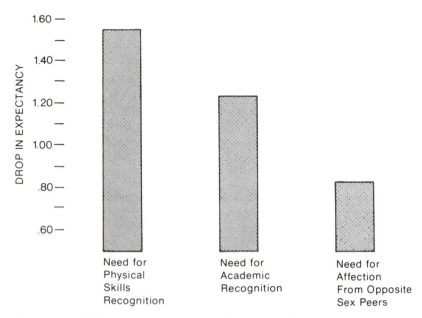

Figure 5.8. Difference in the amounts of lowering of expectancy in Crandall's experimental subjects compared with his control subjects. (From Rotter, 1954, p. 122; based on data reported in Crandall, 1955.)

between the need that was frustrated and the need-related area that was depicted in the pictures. Nonetheless, expectancies did generalize from one need area to another; that is, failure in a skill-related area lowered expectancies even for academic recognition and physical affection.

Expectancy and Delay of Gratification

Because of the apparently close association between the important topic of ego control and delay of gratification, delay behavior has been the subject of study from many perspectives, including the theoretical position espoused by Rotter. The research shows the value of Rotter's theoretical position in the understanding of ego control.

Guided by social learning theory, Mahrer (1956) demonstrated that delay behavior is, in part, determined by the expectation of reinforcement following the delay interval. Children 7 to 9 years old were offered a choice between a smaller immediate reward and a more attractive delayed reward. Prior to the choice dilemma, three levels of expectancy were induced for the receipt of the promised reward. On each of five consecutive days the experimenter told the children that for performing an activity they would receive a small balloon on the following day. To develop groups of high, moderate, and low expectancy for delayed reward, this promise was kept 100%, 50%, or none of the time. Three days later these same subjects were offered the choice between the immediate and delayed rewards. Further-

TABLE 5.12 Choices of Immediate and Delayed Reinforcement

Reinforcement Choice	High		Moderate		Low	
	Expectancy					
	E_A	E_B	E_A	E_B	E_A	E_B
Immediate	6[a]	6	15	5	18	7
Delayed	19	14	11	15	6	15

Source: Adapted from Mahrer (1956, p. 104).
a. Number of subjects.

more, the experimenter offering the choices was either the same one (Experimenter A) who conducted the training session or a person differing from A in sex and age (Experimenter B).

The results of this study are given in Table 5.12, which shows that the groups of subjects tested by Experimenter B (E_B) all exhibited the same delay behavior, regardless of prior training. On the other hand, responses to Experimenter A (E_A) were consistent with the expectancies based on the prior experiences. Thus in this setting the expectancies did not generalize, for the highly different experimenters created disparate social situations and served as cues for different expectancies. In sum, prior training influences the choice of delayed reinforcements, and one of the important cues for the expectancy of delayed reinforcement is the social agent responsible for the reinforcer.

Expectancy and Drinking Behavior

Recall that Merton (1957) has suggested that discrepancies between expectancy and value are one cause of deviant behavior. Jessor, Carman, and Grossman (1968), guided by Merton's ideas, proposed that in a college population two goals are of special importance: academic achievement and social affection. Failure at these goals should lower expectations, which, in part, might cause deviant behavior such as the drinking of alcoholic beverages. Consumption of alcohol not only produces an avoidance of both prior failures, but also might enhance possible satisfactions of other goals, such as dominance and independence, which could partially compensate for failure in the other domains.

To test these ideas, Jessor, Carman, and Grossman (1968) assessed expectancies of need satisfaction in academic achievement and peer affection by means of a questionnaire in which subjects indicated the likelihood that, for example, they would be "in the top half of their class" or would "have many friends in different groups." In addition, three aspects of drinking behavior were assessed: amount of alcoholic intake, frequency of drunkenness, and reported drinking-related complications (accidents, loss of job, and so on). The results of the investigation supported the hypothesis that drinking is related to low expectancy of success, and is particularly predictive of the drinking behavior of women.

In this experiment the function that alcohol was perceived to serve also was examined. Individuals with low expectancy of success reported that drinking offered physical relief and was an escape from personal short-comings, thus further supporting the predictions derived from Merton and social learning theory. These data again were clearer for the female participants.

Personal Responsibility

Locus of Control

Social learning theory assumes that "man is a categorizing animal" (Rotter et al., 1972, p. 39), and that individuals subsume diverse situations within the same class or category. These categories represent the under-lying, shared properties of situations. One such category or dimension of situations concerns whether a potential reinforcer can be attained through one's own actions or follows from luck or other uncontrollable external factors. That is, situations can be grouped according to the perceived cause of a reinforcement, or the locus of control.

Definition. Rotter (1966) describes two views people may have of their control over outcomes:

> When a reinforcement is perceived by the subject as . . . not being entirely contingent upon his action, then, in our culture, it is typically perceived as the result of luck, chance, fate, as under the control of powerful others, or as unpredictable because of the great complexity of the forces surrounding him. When the event is interpreted in this way by an individual, we have labeled this a belief in *external control.* If the person perceives that the event is contingent upon his own behavior or his own relatively permanent characteristics, we have termed this a belief in *internal control.* (p. 1)

Locus of control thus refers to the belief that a response will or will not influence the attainment of a reinforcement. Therefore, locus of control is conceived as one determinant of the expectancy of success. However, locus of control is not an expectancy concerning a particular type of reinforce-ment. Rather, it is considered a "problem-solving" generalized expectancy, addressing the issue of whether behaviors are perceived as instrumental to goal attainment, regardless of the specific nature of the goal or reinforcer. Perceived locus of control is believed to influence the individual's specific goal expectancy in any given situation, with the extent of the influence in part dependent upon the novelty and the ambiguity of the setting, as well as the degree of reinforcement that the individual has directly experienced in that setting.

Skill versus chance. A series of systematic investigations were undertaken by Rotter and his colleagues to demonstrate that perceptions of control as internal or external influence expectancy of success. These studies compared expectancy of success in situations that were perceived as skill determined (internal control) or chance determined (external control). Before continuing with the examination of the consequences of perceptions of skill and chance environments on expectancy of success, the reader should now complete Experiment 5.2.

The intuitive rationale guiding investigations that manipulate skill versus chance instructions or perceptions has been described by Rotter, Seeman, and Liverant (1962):

> It is a matter of common sense that most individuals who would find a $5 bill on a given street would not return and walk up and down the street many times to find more $5 bills, because they consider the event that occurred to be a matter of chance. On the other hand, should someone take up ping-pong and be told that he plays an excellent game for someone just learning, he is quite likely to increase the number of times he plays ping-pong. In the first case, the reinforcement appears to be a matter of chance, controlled in some way by people or forces outside the individual, and in the second instance, the reinforcement appears to be dependent on some characteristic or quality of the person, which he can label as a skill. In the latter case, the reinforcement, in a sense, is understood as occurring because of his own behavior. (p. 474)

The first of the skill versus chance experiments was conducted by Phares (1957), who contended that in skill situations, success and failure indicate to the individual that he or she "can" or "cannot" perform the task. Hence Phares hypothesized that in a skill situation there would be relatively large increments in the perceived likelihood of future success after a success experience and large decrements in expectancy after a failure. On the other hand, in situations determined by chance, success and failure are beyond the control of the individual. Therefore, expectancies should change little following success or failure. Phares also suggested that in chance-related tasks there occasionally would be increments in expectancy of success after a failure and decrements following a success, inasmuch as the direction of luck might be anticipated to change by the subject (these are atypical expectancy shifts).

To test these hypotheses, researchers gave subjects a task that was ambiguous with respect to the objective determinants of success and failure. In one condition the outcome was described as determined by skill, while in a second condition performance was said to be entirely a matter of luck. Prior to each trial the subjects indicated how many of 10 chips they would be willing to bet on their next performance. Expectancy of success

Experiment 5.2

(1) Imagine the following situation. You have just taken part in a coin-tossing game. You have been informed that the outcome on this is entirely determined by chance. On the first five guesses your record is as follows: wrong, right, wrong, wrong, wrong. How *sure* are you that you will get the next problem *right*? Circle a number from 1 to 10 on the scale below to show your answer.

1 2	3	4	5	6	7	8	9	10
Sure I			uncertain					Sure I
will *not*								will be
be right								right

(2) Imagine the following situation. You have just taken part in a coin-tossing game. You have been informed that the outcome on this is entirely determined by chance. On the first five guesses your record is as follows: right, wrong, right, right, right. How *sure* are you that you will get the next problem *right*? Circle a number from 1 to 10 on the scale below to show your answer.

1 2	3	4	5	6	7	8	9	10
Sure I			uncertain					Sure I
will *not*								will be
be right								right

(3) Imagine the following situation. You have just taken a problem-solving test. You have been informed that your performance on this test is entirely dependent on your skill in this type of problem solving. On the first five problems your record is as follows: wrong, right, wrong, wrong, wrong. How *sure* are you that you will solve the next problem? Circle a number from 1 to 10 on the scale below to show your answer.

1 2	3	4	5	6	7	8	9	10
Sure I			unsure					Sure I
will *not*								*will*
solve it								solve it

(4) Imagine the following situation. You have just taken a problem-solving test. You have been informed that your performance on this test is entirely dependent on your skill in this type of problem solving. On the first five problems your record is as follows: right, wrong, right, right, right. How *sure* are you that you will solve the next problem? Circle a number from 1 to 10 on the scale below to show your answer.

1 2	3	4	5	6	7	8	9	10
Sure I			unsure					Sure I
will *not*								*will*
solve it								solve it

was inferred from the magnitude of the reported bet. Subjects in both the skill and the chance conditions received the same relatively random reinforcement schedule on 13 test trials.

Phares found that his hypotheses generally were confirmed. In the skill condition the expectancy shifts were of greater magnitude than in the chance condition. For example, following success, subjects in the skill condition were more likely to increase their bets on the next trial, and by a greater amount, than subjects in the chance condition. On the other hand, there were more "atypical" shifts in the chance condition. These atypical shifts often are known as the "gambler's fallacy." This refers to a perceived dependence imposed on independent outcomes; that is, a loss is expected to be followed by a win, and vice versa.

With these results in mind, the reader should now return to analyze the data from Experiment 5.2. The first two situations depict failure and success at a chance (coin-tossing) game, whereas the next two situations describe failure and success at a skill (problem-solving) task. According to the prior analysis, expectancies at skill tasks are more affected by prior experience than are outcomes at chance tasks. Hence the expectancy of success should be lower when comparing the responses after failure in Situation 3 to Situation 1. Guided by the same logic, the expectancies following success should be greater in Situation 4 in comparison with Situation 2. Another way of stating these hypotheses is that the difference between the expectancies in Situation 1 versus Situation 2 should be less than the difference between the expectancies in Situation 3 versus Situation 4. Indeed, it might even be the case that the expectancy of future success in a chance task is greater following failure than after success, because one thinks that good or bad luck might change in the future. On the other hand, it should certainly be found that in a skill game expectancies are higher following a positive outcome than they are after a negative outcome. Again, based on past research, I am fairly confident that the reader's responses will replicate this pattern.

Individual differences in perceived control. The data collected by Rotter and his associates demonstrate that chance and skill environments differentially affect behavior. The question then raised by this research group was whether, in identical environments, some individuals would act as if the task were more influenced by chance (or skill) than others. If so, then individual differences would be a determinant of generalized expectancies, and thus would influence the subjective probability of goal attainment and subsequent behavior.

Beliefs concerning personal responsibility for a reward have been postulated to constitute a personality dimension. That is, it is anticipated that some persons perceive greater internal (or external) control over potential reinforcers across a variety of situations than do others. Individual differences in locus of control have been the subject of hundreds of research investigations.

Lefcourt (1976) cites a passage from an interview reported in Oscar Lewis's classic book on Mexican culture to illustrate the thoughts of a person who would be labeled as having an external locus of control:

> To me, one's destiny is controlled by a mysterious hand that moves all things. Only for the select, do things turn out as planned; to those of us who are born to be tamale eaters, heaven sends only tamales. We plan and plan and some little thing happens to wash it all away. Like once, I decided to try and save and I said to Paula, "Old girl, put away this money so that some day we'll have a little pile." When we had ninety pesos laid away, pum! my father got sick and I had to give all to him for doctors and medicine. It was the only time I had helped him and the only time I had tried to save! I said to Paula, "There you are! Why should we save if someone gets sick and we have to spend it all!" Sometimes I even think that savings bring on illness! That's why I firmly believe that some of us are born to be poor. (Lewis, 1961, p. 171)

It is worth noting that many research efforts in the field of motivation first demonstrate the importance of environmental influences on behavior, and then examine whether individuals will differ in their relations to these environments. For example, in Chapter 3 it was revealed that individuals condition faster when the intensity of an aversive stimulus (a puff of air to the eye) is increased. Then the Manifest Anxiety Scale was developed to determine whether, given the same puff intensity, some individuals would react as if it were more intense than others. If so, then these persons would be identified as high in general level of drive (emotional reactivity). Likewise, in achievement research, it was first demonstrated that arousal conditions produce more achievement-related imagery on the TAT than neutral conditions. Then researchers investigated the hypothesis that, under neutral conditions, some individuals are more aroused to achieve than others. In a similar manner, the locus of control research first examined expectancy shifts under skill versus chance conditions. Researchers in this area then ascertained whether, given the same setting, some individuals would react as if that environment were more chance (or skill) determined than would other persons.

It also is worth noting that, for Spence and Atkinson, individual differences refer to drive level or need, somewhat related concepts. However, for Rotter, individual differences influence expectancy of reinforcement, rather than need, drive, or some other intrapsychic motive construct.

Assessment procedure. Individual differences in the tendency to perceive events as being internally or externally controlled are assessed with a 29-item self-report inventory. The test, the Internal-External Control Scale (I-E Scale), has a forced-choice format with an internal belief pitted against an external belief in each item. The items on the scale are classifiable into six general subcategories on the basis of the types of needs portrayed and the characteristics of the described goals: academic recognition, social recognition, love and affection, dominance, social-political beliefs, and life philosophy. Some sample items, and their keyed responses (underscored letters represent externality choices), are as follows:

(1) (a) Many of the unhappy things in people's lives are partly due to bad luck.
    (b) People's misfortunes result from the mistakes they make.
(2) (a) The idea that teachers are unfair to students is nonsense.
    (b) Most students don't realize the extent to which grades are influenced by accidental happenings.

It is evident that the questions on the scale are very broad. As Rotter (1975) indicates, the scale "was developed not as an instrument . . . to allow for a very high prediction of some specific situation, such as achievement or political behavior, but rather to allow for a low degree of prediction of behavior across a wide range of potential situations" (p. 62). That is, typically the situational cues in a setting most influence the perceived expectancy of a reinforcement. However, generalized beliefs about control also are presumed to affect the expectancy of success to some extent, with this influence displayed across a wide array of environments.

Validity. It is reasonable to anticipate that the validation of the scale would involve resistance to extinction and expectancy shifts. But this has not been the case. The few published studies that relate I-E scores to resistance to extinction have failed to find significant results (see, for example, Battle & Rotter, 1963). In addition, the expected greater frequency and magnitude of typical shifts, which have been clearly shown to distinguish chance from skill situations, have not been differentially exhibited by subjects high or low on the I-E scale.

As a general rule, the closer the test-taking situation to the situation in which behavioral data are gathered, the more likely it is that the test will be "validated." Responses to a measure that includes, for example, questions about happiness in life bear little immediate relevance to investigations of expectancy shifts. Thus it is not surprising that the I-E Scale has not successfully predicted expectancy change. This is not to say that internality-externality is or is not a trait, or a personality dimension having some transsituational predictive power. Rather, there is too great a gap between the I-E test items (predictor variable) and expectancy changes on some laboratory task, such as guessing an X or an O on a tachistoscope. This sentiment is in accord with the analysis of Rotter and his associates, who might contend that the situational cues in the skill or chance settings override any differences in behavior that could be generated by personality dispositions, or generalized expectancies.

Phares (1976) states:

> The best single indicator of the validity of the I-E scale would undoubtedly be evidence showing that internals are more active, alert, or directive in attempting to control and manipulate their environment than are externals. Since locus of control refers to expectancies for control over one's surroundings, a higher level of coping activity would be anticipated from internals. (p. 60)

There is scattered evidence that this indeed is the case.

Summary of the Social Learning Approach

Julian Rotter has formulated an expectancy-value theory of behavior from the perspective of social learning. He postulates that behavior potential is determined by the expectancy of goal attainment and the value of the goal or reinforcer. Expectancy, in turn, is believed to be a product of the prior reinforcement history in a specific stimulus situation and a generalized belief about reinforcers learned from behaviors in similar situations. Although expectancy and value are independent, the interrelationships between these constructs greatly affect personal adjustment. A low expectancy of success coupled with a highly valued goal is particularly likely to generate behavioral problems.

One area of research that developed from Rotter's conception of behavior concerns locus of control. Rewards can be perceived as the result of personal ability or effort, as in skill-related tasks, or controlled by external factors, as in chance tasks. Perceptions of environments as skill or chance determined influence shifts of expectancy following success and failure. In addition, there are individual differences in the perception of environments as personally or externally controlled.

In the previous chapters, I indicated the fruitfulness of psychoanalytic theory, the precision of Hullian theory, the real-world concerns of Lewinian theory, and the combination of these values in achievement theory. Social learning theorists advocate a more careful use of concepts, thus bringing more restraint into motivation research. They also have demonstrated the importance of environmental, rather than intrapsychic, determinants of action. In so doing, they have brought more balance to the generally accepted belief that behavior is a function of both the person and the environment. And by initiating the study of personal control, social learning theorists have identified a major psychological issue. It is of interest to note that while concerning themselves with psychology as a science, advocates of social learning theory have prompted a major philosophical debate: the meaning of free will.

GENERAL SUMMARY

In this chapter, three expectancy-value conceptions of motivation have been introduced: Lewin's resultant valence theory, Atkinson's theory of achievement strivings, and Rotter's social learning approach. All are based on the principle that individuals maximize their hedonic pursuits by selecting those activities with the highest likelihood of reaching the most valued goal. I contend that these approaches are based on a Godlike metaphor. Obviously, God need not calculate likelihoods, and God is not maximizing personal hedonism. But humans, like God, are given complete rational powers. They are assumed to possess knowledge of all alternatives, the likelihoods of attaining these potential choices, complete capability of assigning each goal a value, and the capacity not only to merge expectancy and value into a single numerical figure, but to compare this figure with all others. Then humans selfishly select the goal that will produce the "highest" pleasure.

There also are some shared empirical or research concerns among the theorists. First, they concentrate primarily on achievement strivings, with goal attainment captured by "success" and nonattainment of a goal synonymous with failure. Second, level of aspiration, or the difficulty of the goal for which one is striving, is a key research issue for all. Third, expectancy shifts play a dominant role in their empirical investigations. And finally, individual differences assume a much more dominant role than was the case in the machine-based conceptions. This is because, as the metaphors for the study of human motivation changed, the research shifted from the study of subhumans to the testing of humans, where these individual differences are so prominent.

The theories presented in the chapter also have their differences and uniquenesses. For example, individuals differ in motive strength in Atkinson's theory but in an expectancy-related construct within Rotter's conception. Further, Rotter is linked with social learning theory, reinforcement, and the importance of the situation (in spite of his championing a cross-situational individual difference variable). Atkinson, on the other hand, is more closely tied with Freud (using a projective testing instrument), Tolman (with his emphasis on cognitive learning), and Lewin (for Atkinson elaborated resultant valence theory by adding an individual difference term).

The theories of Atkinson and Rotter remain influential today, and the TAT measure of achievement needs and the I-E Scale are still used. But certainly the theories and the measures are fading in their impact. This was evident to me when I decided to include Atkinson and Rotter, as well as Lewin's resultant valence theory, within a single chapter in this book. In my prior motivation book, written a little more than a decade ago, Atkinson and Rotter were discussed in separate chapters, and neither chapter contained Lewin's resultant valence theory, which appeared elsewhere. Again it must be stated that theories do not fade and leave a vacuum—they are replaced, or supplemented. One of their most serious scientific competitors has been attribution theory, which also is guided by a Godlike metaphor, yet differs in substantial respects from the expectancy-value approaches.

Attributional Theories of Motivation:

Persons as Scientists

It is evident that most motivational psychologists have accepted the belief that behavior is in service of the pleasure-pain principle. That is, organisms seek to maximize pleasurable stimulation and to minimize painful experience. This should come as no surprise for, as Freud (1920/1955) noted, "the impressions that underlie the hypothesis of the pleasure principle are so obvious that they cannot be overlooked" (p. 1).

Although Freud often is considered to be the staunchest advocate of the hedonistic position, acceptance of the pleasure-pain principle is found in most of the theories guided by either the mechanistic or the Godlike metaphor. Paradoxically, this is the case in spite of the fact that neither machines nor God is affectively guided by or seeks to attain pleasure or avoid pain. That is, the very basic principle and foundation of motivational theory is inconsistent with both of the directing metaphors. I will return to this point later in the book.

Within the theories that embrace the machine metaphor, pleasure typically is derived from returning to a state of equilibrium or balance, which also connotes that needs have been satisfied. Expectancy-value theories, on the other hand, generally eschew homeostatic concepts and assume that pleasure or some other more specific positive affect such as pride is experienced when valued goals are attained.

Freud did, however, consider a second "motive force" akin to what we now know as mastery behavior, or competence seeking. Some behaviors of interest to psychoanalytic theorists, including traumatic dreams, games of disappearance (peekaboo), and transference (the patient acting as if the analyst were a parental figure), are engaged in even though they apparently do not increase pleasure. Freud (1920/1955) therefore concluded:

> We shall be forced to admit that . . . the whole ground is not covered by the operation of the familiar motive forces [the pleasure principle]. Enough is left unexplained to justify the hypothesis of a compulsion to repeat—something that seems more primitive, more elementary, more instinctual than the pleasure principle which it overrides. (p. 17)

Freud went on to suggest that this compulsion to repeat or return was part of the functioning of the death instinct. But Freud also considered an alternate explanation. Concerning disappearance games, he stated:

> One gets an impression that the child turned his experience into a game from another motive. At the outset he was in a *passive* situation—he was overpowered by the experience, but, by repeating it, unpleasurable though it was, as a game, he took on an *active* part. These efforts might be put down to an instinct for mastery that was acting independently of whether the memory was in itself pleasurable or not. (1920/1955, p. 10)

Freud also applied the principle of mastery to explain transference and traumatic dreams. On the subject of traumatic dreams, he suggested:

> But it is not in the service of that principle [pleasure] that the dreams of patients suffering from traumatic neuroses lead them back with such regularity to the situation in which the trauma occurred. We may assume, rather, that dreams are here helping to carry out another task, which must be accomplished before the dominance of the pleasure principle can even begin. These dreams are endeavoring to master the stimulus retrospectively. (1920/1955, p. 26)

In sum, Freud recognized two fundamental principles of action, or motive forces: (a) hedonism (pleasure-pain), and (b) understanding the environment and oneself. Pleasure-pain has been the principle guiding the field of motivation, and it seems reasonable to expect that it will not be supplanted as a source of action. But in recent years it has increasingly been supplemented by mastery and information-gain notions. Similar ideas were suggested for the explanation of intermediate risk taking in achievement-related contexts, where the concept of "diagnosticity" was introduced.

The belief that persons are motivated to understand and master their environments is consistent with the Godlike metaphor, for humans are considered to be scientists, completely rational in their search for understanding, dispassionate and objective as God would be if understanding were in question. Again the metaphor is not totally consistent, inasmuch as God need not test hypotheses—all is already known. Instead, humans are striving for perfection, striving for complete knowledge, and hence are not "Gods," but Godlike.

Personal Construct Theory

Perhaps the clearest proponent of the "person as scientist" metaphor is George Kelly. However, Kelly (1955) rejected the notion of motivational constructs. He believed that individuals are continuously active and that the concept of motivation "can appear only as a redundancy" (Kelly, 1958, p. 50). To clarify this position, Kelly (1962) stated:

> Suppose we began by assuming that the fundamental thing about life is that it goes on. It isn't that something *makes* you go on; the going on *is the thing itself.* It isn't that motives *make* a man come alert and do things; his alertness is an aspect of his very being. (p. 85)

It would therefore seem inappropriate to examine personal construct theory in this book. However, Kelly equated the concept of motivation exclusively with an energizing or an activating function and the associated constructs of drive and tension. If the field of motivation is broadened to include the more general and correct question of "why organisms behave as they do," it is quite evident that Kelly's conception contains a clear statement about motivation. The underlying goal of the individual, Kelly contended, is to predict and to control the events that are experienced. Hence Kelly can be included among the mastery theorists.

Scientific Behavior as a Model for Human Behavior

It is puzzling that while psychologists try to explain the behavior of their clients, or people in general, the theories they have formulated cannot account for their own scientific activity. For example, if persons are impelled by sexual and aggressive instincts, and if all behavior is directed toward the reduction of these primary urges, as the Freudians argue, then what motivated Freud to formulate his theory of personality? Freud did contend that higher intellectual activities, such as scientific pursuits, are derivatives of instinctual drives and are in service of these basic drives. However, this analysis is far from convincing. In a similar manner, if humans are mere robots, as the behaviorists such as Hull would have us believe, then how did the new ideas formulated by Hull and Spence originate? Freudian and Hullian theory, which dominated psychology for so many years, cannot account for the scientific behavior of Freud and Hull.

Kelly's theory of personal constructs can explain scientific endeavors, for Kelly considered the average person an intuitive scientist, having the goal of predicting and understanding behavior. To accomplish this aim, the naive person formulates hypotheses about the world and the self, collects data that confirm or disconfirm these hypotheses, and then alters personal theories to account for the new data. Hence the average person operates in the same manner as the professional scientist, although professional scientists may be more accurate and more self-conscious in their attempts to achieve cognitive clarity and understanding.

For example, assume that a woman (Nancy) believes that a man (John) has strong negative feelings toward her. When Nancy meets John at a party, she anticipates that he will ignore her, make an insulting remark, or embarrass her in front of friends. However, assume that, to Nancy's surprise, John acts in a friendly manner and appears to be happy to see her. Assume also that this unanticipated behavior is repeatedly experienced by Nancy, so that John's friendliness at the party cannot be ascribed to a temporary mood state or to the immediate social pressure. On the basis of the new data, Nancy should reformulate her hypothesis and perceive that John likes her. The new construction more accurately predicts behavior and allows her to anticipate correctly her interactions with John.

In discussing his conception of the person as a seeker of truth, Kelly (1955) asserted:

> It is customary to say that *the scientist's ultimate aim is to predict and to control.* This is a summary statement that psychologists frequently like to quote in characterizing their own aspirations. Yet, curiously enough, psychologists rarely credit the human subjects in their experiments with having similar aspirations. It is as though the psychologist were saying to himself, "I, being a *psychologist,* and therefore a *scientist,* am performing this experiment in order to improve the prediction and control of certain human phenomena; but my subject, being merely a human organism, is obviously propelled by inexorable drives welling up within him, or else he is in gluttonous pursuit of sustenance and shelter." (p. 5)

Many other psychologists implicitly accept the conception of the individual as an intuitive scientist. Of great concern to experimental psychologists is the possibility that the subject will infer what the experimenter is trying to prove and then will consciously or unconsciously comply with the hypothesis (Orne, 1962). The "demand characteristics" of the experiment, therefore, must be carefully controlled or concealed in many psychological investigations, particularly in the field of motivation. But the very existence of such controls implies that subjects search for meaning in their environment, formulate hypotheses, and act on the basis of these belief systems.

Bannister and Fransella (1971), commenting on the "human as scientist" formulation, note:

> One of the effects of this is to make the model man of personal construct theory look recognizably like you: that is, unless you are the very modest kind of man who can see himself as the stimulus-jerked puppet of learning theory (or) the primitive infant of psychoanalytic theory. . . . If you do not recognize yourself at any point in personal construct theory, you have discovered a major defect in it and are entitled to be suspicious of its claims. (p. 16)

As a consequence of the "human as scientist" model, both the psychologist and the client ("subject") are now equal parts of a dyad. That is, the psychologist is not "higher" than the "naive" person and the person is not a mere "lower object" of study. Rather, as Bannister and Fransella (1971) suggest:

Construct theory sees each man as trying to make sense out of himself and his world. It sees psychology as a meta-discipline, an attempt to make sense out of the ways in which men make sense out of their worlds. This not only puts the psychologist in the same interpretive business as his so-called subject—it makes them partners in the business, for on no other basis can one man understand another. (p. 42)

Philosophical Position: Constructive Alternativism

Kelly (1966/1970) labeled his basic philosophical assumption *constructive alternativism*, or "epistemological responsibility" (p. 31). Meaning, Kelly asserted, is not inherent in an event, but depends upon how the person construes or interprets that event:

The events we face today are subject to as great a variety of construction as our wits enable us to contrive. . . . All our present perceptions are open to question and reconsideration. . . . The most obvious occurrences of everyday life might appear utterly transformed if we were inventive enough to construe them differently. (p. 28)

Thus there is no "reality"; reality depends on the eye of the beholder. Hence some of Kelly's ideas are closely associated with the psychoanalytic notion that needs, values, and similar factors influence "reality."

Because meaning is subject to change, Kelly reasoned that individuals are personally responsible (i.e., *able* to respond) for their own future. Nature does not dictate an individual's life; as Kelly contended, "No one needs to be the victim of his biography."

Formal Theory

Kelly's formal theory consists of a fundamental postulate and 11 corollaries. I will briefly examine the postulate and some of the corollaries, selecting those that shed the most light on his conception of behavior.

Fundamental Postulate: A person's processes are psychologically channelized by the ways in which he or she anticipates events. By this Kelly means that an individual's *life* (conduct) is guided by how he or she construes the world. Furthermore, the predictive power of the construal is demonstrated or proven by how much sense has been made out of the world, that is, the accuracy with which the individual is able to predict future events. Kelly (1966/1970) asserted that "confirmation or disconfirmation of one's predictions are accorded greater psychological significance than rewards, punishments, or . . . drive reduction" (p. 38).

Individual Corollary: Persons differ from each other in their construction of events. Since individuals perceive the same objective stimulus situation in a different manner, it follows that their behaviors also will differ. Furthermore, because no two constructions are exactly alike, each person is unique.

Dichotomy Corollary: A person's construction system is composed of a finite number of dichotomous constructs. Kelly asserted that all constructs are bipolar, or dichotomous. Hence if we perceive someone as honest and sincere, we implicitly deny that the individual is dishonest and insincere. A construct, therefore, also involves a contrast.

Range Corollary: A construct is convenient for the anticipation of a finite range of events only. A given knowledge is not appropriate for all events. For example, the construct tall-short may be appropriate for the anticipation of play on a basketball court, but is likely to be quite irrelevant in predicting an individual's honesty. Kelly distinguished between the range of convenience and the focus of convenience of a construct. The *range of convenience* indicates the breadth of different phenomena to which a construct may be applied. The *focus of convenience* refers to the area in which the construct is maximally useful. Thus the focus involves those events for which the construct was developed.

The range and focus notions frequently are employed by scientists in describing and evaluating psychological theories. Freudians, for example, argue that the range of convenience of their theory includes war, wit, and neurosis; such generalizability is a positive attribute of a theory. But perhaps the focus of convenience of the Freudian model is intrapersonal conflict. A similar description of the range and focus of convenience of all the theories presented in this book could be made and would prove useful for purposes of comparison and evaluation (see Chapter 8).

Experience Corollary: A person's construction system varies as he successfully construes the replication of events. Since a construct is akin to a hypothesis, the confirmation or disconfirmation of a hypothesis may result in the changing of constructs. Kelly suggested that confirmation may lead to as much future change as disconfirmation because confirmation prompts the exploration of new experiences, which expose the person to situations that require the alteration of the present construct system.

Psychotherapy, in Kelly's perspective, is a process in which a person's construct system is altered with the aid of a therapist. The therapist first must discover how the client is perceiving the world and then assist the client in reorganizing the old system and in finding new constructs that are more functional. The therapist might help the client design and implement "experiments" that test particular hypotheses. For example, if an individual perceives a parent or a spouse as "aggressive" or "dominating," the therapist might suggest special behaviors to test whether this perception is "valid," that is, aids in the anticipation of events. Role playing and modeling frequently are used to help alter construct systems. The therapist might suggest, for example, that the client act as if the parent or the spouse were not aggressive or not dominant in order to test an alternative hypothesis. (Earlier in his life Kelly taught drama, and that may in part account for his selection of role playing as a technique for altering construct systems.)

In one social experiment involving the change of constructs, the subjects were teachers who believed that their students were not learning because the children were "lazy" (Kelly, 1958). Experimenters suggested that the teachers give the children nothing to do in the classroom and see what happened. Of course, the pupils would not sit without activity. On the basis of this contradictory evidence, the teachers began to consider the school environment and their own inadequacy as causes of poor learning, rather than blaming the problems entirely on the children.

The Role Construct Repertory Test

Kelly devised a particularly ingenious testing instrument to ascertain an individual's personal construct system. The test reflects Kelly's belief that the psychologist should not impose constructs on the test taker as, for example, is the case in tests of internal-external locus of control. This particular construal or dimension of thought may be irrelevant to the test taker. Rather, the respondents should be allowed to display the constructs that they naturally use to give meanings to the world.

In the Role Construct Repertory (Rep) Test, the test taker first lists the names of individuals who play or have played certain roles in his or her life—mother, father, rejecting person, threatening person, and so on. On the standard Rep Test, three roles are considered together. For each triad the subject determines the construct, such as cold-warm or dominant-submissive, that links two individuals in the triad and differentiates them from the third member. This procedure clearly is guided by Kelly's belief in the bipolarity of constructs. The construct selected is assumed to represent a dimension along which significant people in the respondent's life are ordered, or compared.

Using sophisticated but not difficult mathematical techniques akin to factor analysis, the tester can reduce the constructs chosen to just a few basic ones that represent the respondent's typical way of perceiving and classifying others.

Thus far the Rep Test has been used sparingly, primarily in clinical rather than research settings. Some reliability studies suggest that grid responses have reasonable test-retest stability, but there has been limited assessment of the test's reliability and validity (see Bannister & Fransella, 1971). This is true for the entire theory proposed by Kelly. It has had little heuristic value or generative power, in spite of its apparent usefulness and its provision of another language for psychological understanding.

Emotions

Critics have charged that Kelly's theory ignores affective states, or "the human passions." Bruner (1956), for example, stated: "I wish Professor Kelly would treat most religious men in their most religious moments" (p. 357). In defense of Kelly, Bannister and Fransella (1971) countered that Kelly has not ignored the emotions. Rather,

> Kelly did not accept the cognition-emotion division as intrinsically valid. It is a jargon descendant of the ancient dualities of *reason* versus *passion*, *mind* versus *body*, *flesh* versus *spirit* which had led to dualistic psychologies. . . . In order to avoid this dualism, Kelly focuses our attention on certain specific constructs, namely *anxiety, hostility, guilt, threat, fear,* and *aggression,* but defines them all as "awareness" that construct systems are in transitional states. (pp. 34-35)

Hence for Kelly even emotions are logical in that they follow particular thoughts or cognitive appraisals.

Anxiety, according to Kelly, occurs when one's construct system provides no means for dealing with an experience. Bannister and Fransella (1971) elaborate this as follows:

> We become anxious when we can only partially construe the events which we encounter and too many of their implications are obscure. Sex for the chaste, adulthood for the adolescent, books for the illiterate, power for the humble and death for nearly all of us tend to provoke anxiety. It is the *unknown* aspect of things that go bump in the night that gives them their potency. (p. 35)

In a similar manner, interacting with a person whom we cannot understand often gives rise to vague feelings of uneasiness. And even greater anxiety is experienced when starting a new job or confronting a new environment. If anxiety reactions are frequent and severe, the range of constructs must be broadened so that more phenomena can be incorporated. Disconfirmation of a belief also arouses anxiety because it reveals an inadequacy in the construct system. Anxiety, therefore, is not necessarily bad, for this affective experience is one precondition for construct change.

Kelly distinguished between threat and anxiety, although both result from defective, and therefore transitional, conceptual systems. *Threat* is experienced when a fundamental change is about to occur in one's construct system. For example, threat is experienced "when our major beliefs about the nature of our personal, social, and practical situation are invalidated and the world around us appears to become chaotic" (Bannister & Fransella, 1971, p. 37). Thus, for example, questioning the purpose of life is threatening, for it is likely to lead to basic conceptual changes. In a similar manner, a deeply involving extramarital affair may alter one's conception of what it is to be a parent or a spouse, and thus may engender a threat. Psychotherapists have to be aware of the possibility that they may be viewed as threatening inasmuch as they are perceived as agents of construct change.

Finally, in Kelly's system *guilt* results from a discrepancy between one's ideal self and one's actions. Thus "if you find yourself doing, in important respects, those things you would not have expected to do if you are the kind of person you always thought you were, then you suffer from guilt" (Bannister & Fransella, 1971, p. 36). It therefore follows that if you value dishonesty and see yourself as dishonest, then honest actions should produce feelings of guilt.

Summary: Kelly's Theory

Kelly asserted that humans are intuitive scientists, construing the world in idiosyncratic ways to give it meaning. Meaning is the interpretation of events with dichotomous constructs; it enables one to predict (anticipate) the future. Construct systems are not immutable; individuals are able to produce alternate constructs, and they are personally responsible for their own well-being. Finally, certain emotions, such as anxiety, threat, and guilt, are products of construct systems that are inadequate and undergoing change.

Attribution Theory

The mastery, or understanding, position today finds its most conspicuous expression among psychologists identified with attribution theory. For example, Harold H. Kelley (1967), one of the leading psychologists in this area, assumes that humans are motivated to "attain a cognitive mastery of the causal structure of [the] environment" (p. 193). One wants to know why an event has occurred—to what source, motive, or state it may be ascribed. Fritz Heider (1958), the acknowledged "founder" of attribution theory, explained:

> The causal structure of the environment, both as the scientist describes it and as the naive person apprehends it, is such that we are usually in contact only with what may be called the offshoots or manifestations of underlying core processes or core structures. For example, if I find sand on my desk, I shall want to find out the underlying reason for this circumstance. I make this inquiry not because of idle curiosity, but because only if I refer this relatively insignificant offshoot event to an underlying core event will I attain a stable environment and have the possibility of controlling it. Should I find that the sand comes from a crack in the ceiling and that this crack appeared because of the weakness in one of the walls,

then I have reached the layer of understanding conditions which is of vital importance for me. The sand on my desk is merely a symptom, a manifestation that remains ambiguous until it becomes anchored. . . . The search [for causality] may carry us quite far from the immediate facts or . . . may end hardly a step from them. That is, there exists a hierarchy of cognitive awarenesses which begins with the more stimulus-bound recognition of "facts," and gradually goes deeper into the underlying causes of these facts. . . . Man is usually not content simply to register the observables that surround him. . . . The underlying causes of events, especially the motives of other persons, are invariances of the environment that are relevant to him; they give meaning to what he experiences and it is these meanings that are recorded in his life space, and are precipitated as the reality of the environment to which he then reacts. (pp. 80-81)

There is no unified body of knowledge that neatly fits into one specific attribution theory; there are many types of attribution theorists and theories. Nevertheless, there are some central problems that guide the thoughts of all investigators in this field (e.g., Heider, 1958; Jones et al., 1972; Kelley, 1967; Weiner, 1985, 1986). Attribution theorists are concerned with perceptions of causality, or the perceived reasons for a particular event's occurrence. Three general programs of research have emerged from the analysis of perceived causality. First, the perceived causes of behavior have been specified, with particular consideration given to a distinction between internal or personal causality and external or environmental causality, as reviewed in the prior chapter. Second, general laws have been developed that relate antecedent information and cognitive structures to causal inferences. And third, causal inferences have been associated with various indexes of observed behavior. For example, assume that one's toes are stepped on while one is riding the subway. Attribution theorists are likely to ask: (a) What are the perceived causes of this event (e.g., an intentional aggressive act, an accident, a result of standing too near the door)? (b) What information influenced this causal inference (e.g., the clenched fist of the aggressor, the observation that other people's toes are being stepped on, the observation that only people standing near the door were stepped on)? and (c) What are the consequences of the causal ascription (e.g., hitting the aggressor, deriding the public transportation system, moving away from the door)?

It should be noted that the perception of causality is an ascription imposed by the perceiver; causes per se are not directly observable. You can only infer, for example, that an individual stepped on your toes because "he is aggressive" or because "it was an accident." Hume (1739/1888) argued that causality is not an inherent property of sensory events. To use Hume's example, one can see that upon impact of ball A, ball B moves. One might then conclude that A caused B to change location; that is, one can attribute the moving of B to the impact of A. But one does not "observe" causes. Hume (and later Kant, 1781/1952) contended that causes are constructed by the perceiver because they render the environment more meaningful.

FRITZ HEIDER

The attributional approach to psychology received its impetus from the writings of Fritz Heider. Heider was born in Austria in 1896 and received his Ph.D. from the University of Graz in 1920. It is interesting to note that Heider's dissertation adviser was Professor Meinong. Meinong had written his dissertation under the direction of Professor Brentano, who is closely identified with the pleasure-pain principle of motivation.

After completing his dissertation, Heider moved to Berlin, where he came under the influence of the Gestalt psychologists, particularly Kurt Lewin and Max Wertheimer. In 1930, Heider went to the school for the deaf at Smith College for what was supposed to be a year-long visit. However, there he met another psychologist, Grace Moore, whom he subsequently married; he established residency in the United States after his marriage. In the late 1940s Heider left Smith College for the University of Kansas, where his work continued for many years. He died in 1989.

Heider's insights into interpersonal relations and commonsense psychology were relatively neglected by psychologists until publication of his book *The Psychology of Interpersonal Relations* (1958). Heider is responsible for two seminal contributions to psychology: balance theory, which gave rise to theories of cognitive organization, and the study of attribution processes.

Heider's writings are sparked with warmth and wit. He is perhaps unique among academic psychologists in drawing heavily on works of literature for his scientific insights. He exemplifies the scholor-humanist-scientist ideal.

(Photograph courtesy of K. G. Heider)

The prevalence of causal constructions was dramatically illustrated in experiments reported by Heider and Simmel (1944). They created a "movie" consisting of three moving figures: a large triangle, a small triangle, and a circle. Interpersonal dramas unfolded from the movements of the figures. For example, impacts were interpreted as fights, joint movements generated themes of "belonging," and so forth. Heider and Simmel noted the "great importance which causal interpretation plays in the organization of events" (p. 251). This organization is largely determined by motives that were attributed to the figures. Perceived self-induced actions led to different interpretations than behaviors perceived as induced by others.

Heider and Simmel's experiment erased the distinction between perception of physical objects and perception of persons. Objects were perceived as "people," with motives, emotions, and so forth. Well before this experiment, Hume had reasoned that there was no difference between causal analyses of physical events and causal analyses of psychological events.

Attribution and Motivation

The discussion of attribution theory in relation to motivation that is now undertaken will follow a different course from that taken in prior chapters. In reviewing drive theory, for example, or achievement strivings, the basic theory was first presented, followed by empirical evidence, theoretical nuances and issues, and so forth. However, attributional approaches to motivation involve a number of concepts and processes so that initially presenting the entire theory is not feasible. This may be especially true because of my personal involvement with this approach, which makes it more difficult for me to take a step back and see the entire forest rather than the individual trees.

I begin the presentation of attribution theory as related to motivation by outlining the antecedents that give rise to a causal ascription. Then some specific causes are identified in the domain of achievement striving, as well as in regard to other "outcomes" such as poverty. Following this, the underlying properties of these causes are examined. These properties or characteristics, in turn, are related to the proximal determinants of motivation—expectancy and "value" (which in this case relates to emotional reactions). Then some motivational sequences, such as a student dropping out of school after an exam failure, are examined from this perspective.

Thus I slowly present the building blocks of the theory, and finally present the overall conception. The reader therefore must exhibit patience and accept being led by small steps, without immediately looking for the motivational significance of the issue under consideration.

Causal Antecedents

How do we know what caused an event? Attribution theorists have been particularly concerned with how causal attributions are reached—the information used or the processes or structures activated that enable one to reach a causal ascription, and thus to attain "deeper" knowledge. Heider (1958), guided by Mill's method of inquiry, contended that attributions are reached according to the following rule: "That condition will be held responsible for an effect which is present when the effect is present and which is absent when the effect is absent" (p. 152). That is, covariation is the foundation of the attribution process and enables one to infer the cause of an effect.

Consider, for example, an early experiment by Michotte (1946/1963), in which a red disk and a black disk (A and B) were presented as moving on a screen. Object A approached and "bumped" B. If B immediately moved, then individuals had the "causal impression" that the withdrawal was due to A. Michotte labeled this the "launching effect." Perception of

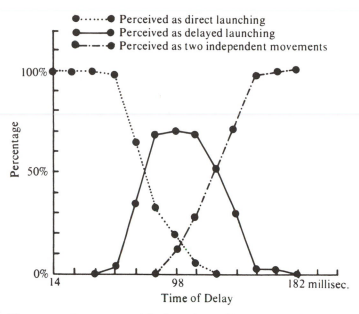

Figure 6.1. Perception of the launching effect as a function of the interval between the bumping by *A* and *B*'s departure. (From Michotte, 1946/1963, p. 94.)

the launching effect is greatly influenced by the interval between the arrival of *A* and the departure of *B*. Figure 6.1 shows that if the interval between *A*'s arrival and *B*'s departure was shorter than 75 milliseconds, a "direct launching" interpretation was given by the subjects. "Delayed launching" was the most probable interpretation if the delay interval approximated 100 milliseconds. If the delay time was longer than 200 milliseconds, subjects did not perceive that *A* caused *B* to move. Michotte also noted that if *B* moves together with *A* after impact, *B* was believed to be "carried along" by or to have "joined" with *A*. He labeled this the "entraining effect."

In interpersonal relations, and in the area of motivation, preconceived causality is more complex, requiring an analysis of many determinants that may be changing over time. Heider (1958) discussed how covariation analyses may proceed in these situations:

> If I always experience enjoyment when I interact with an object, and something other than enjoyment when the object is removed (longing, annoyance, or a more neutral reaction, for instance) then I will consider the object the cause of the enjoyment. The effect, enjoyment, is seen to vary in a highly coordinated way with the presence and absence of the object. . . .
>
> If I sometimes enjoy the object and sometimes do not, then the effect varies, not with the object, but with something within me. I may or may not be able to define that something, but I know that the effect has to do with some fluctuating personal state. It may be my mood, my state of hunger, etc. which though

temporary in character, are often detectable as the conditions highly related to the effect. Notice that in this type of attribution, a temporary state and therefore a more or less nondispositional property of the person is singled out as the source of the pleasure. . . .

When enjoyment is attributed to a dispositional property of the person, additional data pertaining to the reactions of other people are necessary. Concretely, if I observe that not all people enjoy the object, then I may attribute the effect to individual differences. . . . That is to say, the effect, enjoyment in this case, depends upon who the person is. With o enjoyment is present, with q it is absent. We sometimes, then, speak about differences in taste. The important point is that the presence and absence of the enjoyment is not correlated with the presence and absence of the object, but rather with the presence and absence of different people. Therefore o is felt to enjoy x, and q to be dissatisfied with x, because of the kind of person each is. (pp. 152-153)

Kelley (1967) then systematized the factors that result in causal attributions to either person or environmental factors. He also assumed that covariation is the foundation of the attribution process and likened the ascription of causality to the more formal statistical procedures employed by scientists. Assume, he wrote, that an individual enjoys a movie. The question then raised is whether the enjoyment, or "raw data," is attributed to the person (for example, she is easily pleased) or to the perceived properties of the entity (it is a good movie). Kelley (1967) reasoned that the responsible factor may be determined through an examination of the covariation of the effect and causal factors over "a) entities (movies), b) persons (other viewers of the movie), c) time (the same person on repeated exposures), and d) modalities of interaction with the entity (different ways of viewing the movie)" (p. 194). Attribution of the enjoyment to the entity (movie) rather than to the person or self is most likely if the individual responds differentially to movies, if the response to this movie is consistent over time and modalities, and if the response agrees with the social consensus of others. Thus the probability of attribution to the movie is maximized when the individual enjoys only that movie (high distinctiveness), when she enjoys it on repeated occasions and over different modalities (high consistency), and when all others also like the movie (high consensus). On the other hand, if the individual likes all movies—that is, her response to the entity is not distinctive—and if no one else likes this particular picture (low consensus), then we would ascribe the enjoyment to stable attributes of the viewer (see Försterling, 1989).

Consider, for example, a simple experiment by Weiner and Kukla (1970) that examined the effects of social norm information on causal attributions. Subjects were given information about the outcome of an achievement task (success or failure) as well as social norm information revealing the percentage of others successfully completing the task (99, 95, 90, 70, 50, 30, 10, 5, 1). The subjects then rated whether the outcome in the 18 conditions (2 levels of outcome × 9 levels of social norms) was attributable to the hypothetical person who attempted the task. Ascriptions were

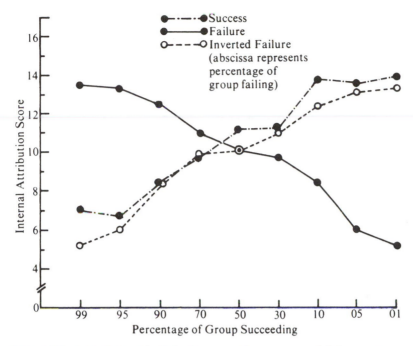

Figure 6.2. Mean internal attribution score for success and failure outcomes as a function of task difficulty. (From Weiner & Kukla, 1970, p. 18. Copyright 1970 by the American Psychological Association. Reprinted (or adapted) by permission of the publisher.)

indicated on a rating scale anchored at the extremes (outcome due/not due to the person).

The results of this investigation are shown in Figure 6.2. It is evident from the figure that the greater the consistency between outcome and the performance of others, the less the attribution to the person (or the greater the inferred attribution to the task). That is, if one succeeds when most others do likewise, or fails when most others fail, the outcomes are ascribed to an easy or hard task, respectively. But if one succeeds when others fail, or fails when others succeed, the outcomes are attributed to the person. Social norms are, therefore, one source of information that allows an individual or an observer to determine whether an effect is attributable to the person or the environment.

Another way of characterizing these data and attributional inferences is that the attribution made "stands out" or is the "abnormal condition." For example, if all individuals except John succeed, then John's failure is attributed to him. Similarly, if individuals succeed at all exams but the one in chemistry, then John's failure at chemistry will be ascribed to that class or subject matter, and not to John (see Hewstone & Jaspers, 1987). This approach does not require the complex task that the Kelley model gives to the perceiver.

Although these predictions have been confirmed in many contexts, difficult issues about attributions remain to be resolved that need not be discussed here (see, for example, Hewstone & Jaspers, 1987; Hilton & Slugoski, 1986). One issue, however, that will be returned to later is that the attributions people make depend on many factors, including the contextual features of the situation (e.g., the same interpersonal shove can be perceived as an intentional push or an unintentional jostle), enduring beliefs and expectancies of the attributor (such as personal esteem), and hedonic factors that result in ascriptions favorable to the attributor.

Attributions in Animal Experiments

Some of the experiments discussed in prior chapters that have been conducted with subhumans can be interpreted from the attributional (co-variation) perspective just presented. Of course, one question immediately raised is whether subhumans can make causal ascriptions and differentiate, for example, attributions to the self from attributions to external factors in the environment. In discussing the cognitive capacities of infrahuman organisms (rats), Festinger (1961) stated:

> All that is meant by cognition is knowledge or information. It seems to me that one can assume that an organism has cognitions or information if one can observe some behavioral difference under different stimulus conditions. If the organism changes his behavior when the environment changes, then obviously he uses information about the environment and, equally obviously, can be said to have cognitions. (p. 4)

A simple taxonomy aids in the selection of animal investigations pertinent to attribution theory. The proposed taxonomy includes two dimensions: the subjective (perceived) and the objective (veridical) origins of causality. A combination of these two dimensions yields four experimental classifications, as shown in Table 6.1.

Following Heider and Kelley, assume that causation is inferred from a systematic covariation of antecedents and consequents. If an effect occurs given one set of antecedents and does not occur when those antecedents are absent, it is assumed that the effect is perceived as caused by those particular antecedents. For example, if food always follows a lever press and does not appear when the lever is not pressed, it is postulated that the responding organism will ascribe the presence of food to the instrumental lever press. Thus a simple instrumental-learning paradigm is classified within quadrant I in Table 6.1: The outcome objectively is controlled by the organism, and causation is perceived as due to personal factors.

Now consider quadrant IV. Inasmuch as outcomes are externally controlled, any response the animal makes should not covary with an effect. The effect sometimes occurs in the presence of a particular response,

TABLE 6.1 Taxonomy of Experimental Paradigms (Infrahuman Subjects) Pertinent to Attribution Theory

Objective (Veridical) Causality	Subjective (Perceived) Causality	
	Self	*Environment (External Agent)*
Self	(I) simple instrumental learning	(II) instrumental escape learning following classical aversive conditioning (learned helplessness)
Environment (External Agent)	(III) reward following experimenter-established time interval (superstitious behavior)	(IV) simple classical conditioning

sometimes in the absence of that response, and at other times in the presence of differing responses. This apparently corresponds to the classical conditioning paradigm. In a classical conditioning procedure the reward or punishment, or the presentation of an unconditioned stimulus, is independent of the organism's response, and is presumed to be so perceived.

The remaining two quadrants in Table 6.1 represent situations in which attributional errors are made. Quadrant III includes experimental paradigms that induce the outcome to be perceived as caused by the self when, in fact, the outcomes are under environmental control. Beliefs labeled *superstitious* can be described as attributional errors, and are included in quadrant III. The experimental paradigm resulting in such misattribution generally involves the presentation of food to a hungry animal following some experimentally determined time interval. Prior to the reception of the food the animal happens to be engaging in some response, and errs in ascribing the appearance of the reward to this behavior. Subsequently, this "superstitious" response is repeated.

In sum, because a response has inadvertently preceded a reinforcement—that is, there is covariation—the animal makes the false (but not unreasonable) inference that the reward was *caused* by the response. This attributional error receives repeated confirmation, for repetition of the behavior is at times accompanied by reception of the reward. But rather than calling this superstitious behavior, it may be better understood as an honest error in information processing and inference making. The animal apparently weights the response-reward covariation more heavily than the information gained during response-nonreward sequences. What is needed to correct this false causal inference is information that the reward will also appear in the absence of the "superstitious" response. The animal may then discover that the reward is not contingent upon any self-generated behavior.

A reverse attributional error is shown in quadrant II: There is attribution of an outcome to external circumstances when the outcome is, or may be, self-determined. In studies of learned helplessness, discussed later in this chapter, dogs first trained with a classical aversive conditioning procedure did not display performance gains over trials in a subsequent instrumental avoidance learning situation. Indeed, the majority of the previously conditioned animals never learned the escape response. Apparently, the dogs were making attributional errors; they were generalizing their prior conclusions about the inescapability of shock and making the incorrect inference that in the new situation, shock termination was independent of their personal behavior.

Causal Schemata

Even in the absence of complete information, individuals are able to use partial evidence to reach logical causal inferences. Indeed, in the typical situation all the information needed to perform a complete covariation analysis is not available. In these instances, causal schemata, or general rules that relate causes and effects, are elicited. These rules, which are built up from prior experiences, are activated by appropriate environmental cues and enable the person to transcend situations in which the available information is limited (see Kelley, 1972).

An example of a *compensatory* schema—that is, a rule in which one cause can compensate or, in effect, make amends for the absence or weakness of another cause—is seen in the formal analysis of achievement performance proposed by Heider (1958). Heider postulated that the outcome of an action is a function of both "can" (the relation of ability to task difficulty) and "try" (execution). Whether "can" is exhibited in action depends on motivation, or "try." Heider (1958) summarized:

> Relating the roles of "can" and "try" we can state the following: When we say, "He can do it, but fails only because he does not try sufficiently" then we mean that the effective personal force is smaller than the restraining environmental force only because the exertion is not great enough; with greater exertion he would succeed. (p. 86).

That is, "try" can compensate when there is low "can"—high effort can make amends for low ability and/or a difficult task.

Kelley (1972) has suggested two other causal rules, although they both may be variants of the compensatory schema outlined by Heider. Kelley hypothesized that extreme or atypical events elicit "multiple necessary" causal rules, whereas mild or typical events elicit "multiple sufficient" causal rules. To understand what is meant by necessary and sufficient causality, consider a simple situation in which two causes (X and Y) are associated with an effect (Z). For example, eating or not eating (the observed

TABLE 6.2 Multiple Sufficient and Multiple Necessary Causal Schemata Showing the Presence or Absence of Two Causes (X and Y) and the Presence of an Effect (Z)

Multiple Sufficient Schema

		Cause X	
		Absent	Present
Cause Y	Present	Z	Z
	Absent	—	Z

Multiple Necessary Schema

		Cause X	
		Absent	Present
Cause Y	Present	—	Z
	Absent	—	—

Source: Kun and Weiner (1973, p. 199).

effects) may be associated with the presence or absence of hunger and/or the presence or absence of attractive food (the perceived causes of eating or not eating). An individual may believe that the presence of either hunger *or* attractive food will produce eating behavior. This *disjunctive* set of causal relations, coded linguistically as an "or" relationship, is referred to as a multiple sufficient causal schema. Each cause in and of itself is capable of producing the effect. On the other hand, the person may believe that both hunger *and* the availability of desirable food are required to produce eating behavior. This *conjunctive* set of causal relations, coded as an "and" relationship, is referred to as a multiple necessary causal schema. Both causes are needed to produce the effect (see Kelley, 1972).

The significance of causal schemata is that they permit the individual to predict effects from the presence or absence of certain causes. Furthermore, given an effect, they generate inferences about the underlying causes. For example, if an individual observes someone eating, a multiple necessary schema would lead to the deduction that the person was hungry *and* that the food was attractive. This inference obviously has functional significance.

Necessary schemata and sufficient schemata generate different attributions and beliefs about the world (see Table 6.2). As already indicated, if the attributor knows that Z has occurred, a multiple sufficient schema allows him or her to infer that either X or Y was present. Further, if it is known that X was present when Z occurred, there should be uncertainty about the presence of Y, provided that X and Y are independent. As shown in Table 6.2, Z occurs given X regardless of the presence or absence of Y. Thus, for example, if a person eats when hungry, we should be uncertain about the attractiveness of the food, given a sufficient schema relating eating behavior and the presence of hunger. On the other hand, if a multiple necessary schema is used, the occurrence of Z in the presence of X provides unequivocal evidence for the presence of Y. As depicted in Table 6.2, with a necessary schema, Z occurs only when both X and Y occur. Thus, if a necessary schema is used, we infer that the food is attractive when eating behavior is observed.

Lest the reader think that these analyses do not capture "real-life" situations, Cunningham and Kelley (1975) offered the following examples of situations where we must make similar decisions or causal inferences:

> When a person reads in a sports page account of a football game that the defensive guard knocked the opposing quarterback unconscious, he may wonder what to make of the event. Does it say something about the guard's skill, size, and aggressiveness, or does it reflect more on the ineptitude and fragility of the quarterback? Similar questions about the causes of the event may occur to the reader when he learns that the local mayor enthusiastically endorses an unknown upstate politician in the senatorial race, that a movie director is madly in love with the ingenue, or that a business man is extremely critical of the director of a particular government agency. (p. 74)

To demonstrate the effects of causal schemata on causal inferences, Kun and Weiner (1973) created situations to elicit necessary or sufficient causal schemata. More specifically, subjects were provided information regarding success and failure at tasks varying in difficulty. After receiving the outcome and task difficulty information, the subjects were informed about the presence or absence of one cause (ability or effort). They then had to decide whether the complementary cause (effort or ability) was present or absent. For example, the subjects were told that an individual performed excellently on an exam, and that 90% of the other students also performed excellently (an easy task). Furthermore, the pupil was described as high in ability. The subjects then judged whether the pupil also tried hard. Judgments were made on a scale ranging from "definitely tried hard" to "definitely did not try." Prior to discussing the results from this study, the reader should respond to Experiment 6.1, which examines perceived causality for a successful achievement experience. Please do that now, before reading further.

Figure 6.3 shows the judgments in the Kun and Weiner (1973) study. In that investigation there were three levels of task difficulty (success by 90%, 50%, or 10% of other students), two levels of outcome (success or failure), and information regarding ability or effort. The given cause was characterized as present or absent. As already indicated, the subjects had to judge the presence or the absence of the other cause. For success outcomes, the reported causes were high ability and high effort, while for failure outcomes, ability and effort were always described as low.

Figure 6.3 shows that when told of success at the most difficult task and the presence of ability (or effort), subjects indicated that effort (or ability)

Experiment 6.1

An exam has been graded with only two possible outcomes, pass or fail. You will be given information about a person's outcome on the exam. In addition, you will be told what percentage of the other students passed the exam. Finally, you will be told whether the person has ability or not. Your task is to infer in each case whether effort was present or absent, or note that you are uncertain about how hard the person tried.

(1) A pupil passed the exam, and 90% of the other pupils also passed. The pupil is able. Do you think he or she also tried hard?
   (a) definitely tried hard
   (b) probably tried hard
   (c) am not certain if the person did or did not try hard
   (d) probably did not try hard
   (e) definitely did not try hard

(2) A pupil passed the exam, and 10% of the other pupils also passed (that is, 90% of the other pupils failed). The pupil is able. Do you think he or she also tried hard?
   (a) definitely tried hard
   (b) probably tried hard
   (c) am not certain if the person did or did not try hard
   (d) probably did not try hard
   (e) definitely did not try hard

---

was also present. Hence in Question 2 of Experiment 6.1, you probably chose answer a or b. Thus a multiple necessary schema is used. Conversely, given success at the easiest task, subjects infer that the complementary cause was absent. Hence in Question 1 you were likely to answer c, d, or e. According to Table 6.2, you would be uncertain about the presence of effort, inasmuch as high ability is a sufficient cause for success at an easy task. But many believe that ability compensates for effort; that is, the two causes are not independent, so that exertion is not necessary if one has ability.

Turning to the failure condition (which is not included in Experiment 6.1), given failure at the most difficult task and low ability (or low effort), subjects expressed the belief that low effort (or low ability) was not a cause. And given failure at the easiest task, there was a slight tendency to infer the presence of both low ability and low effort.

In sum, when performance outcomes are uncommon, attributions tend to include multiple causes; when performance outcomes are common, attributions are made to only one cause. Thus causal schemata elicited in

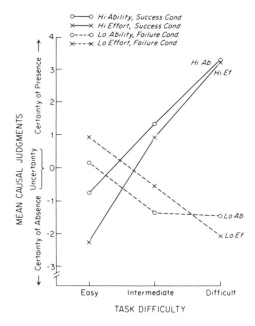

Figure 6.3. Mean certainty judgments of ability or effort given information concerning the complementary cause (effort or ability), task outcome, and the difficulty of the task. The labels indicate the cause being judged. (From Kun & Weiner, 1973, p. 203.)

achievement-related contexts by information concerning the commonness of an event influence the attribution process and perceptions of causality.

Figure 6.3 also shows that over an extended range of task difficulty levels, both ability and effort are believed to be necessary to attain success. This is evident in the figure because both the intermediate- and difficult-task judgments are above the uncertainty point in the success condition, indicating the presence of the complementary causal factor. On the other hand, over an extended range of task difficulty levels, either low ability or low effort is believed to be sufficient to produce a failure. As shown in Figure 6.3, both the intermediate and the difficult task causal judgments are below the uncertainty point, indicating the absence of the complementary causal factor. One is reminded of the saying that a chain is only as strong as its weakest link; that is, all components must be strong for "success," and the absence of strength in any of the subparts is sufficient for "failure." It therefore appears that the attributions for success and failure might be governed by somewhat different psychological rules.

Discounting

Given a multiple sufficient schema, individuals may discount or disregard the extent to which a second cause has contributed to an effect. For example, individuals offered a reward to undertake an intrinsically interesting task may come to believe that they performed the task only for that reward. That is, their intrinsic interest is discounted.

Another example of discounting has been demonstrated in a study of surveillance carried out by Strickland (1958). In Strickland's experiment, a subject was assigned to be a supervisor over two (fictitious) students supposedly performing a task. The supervisor had the power to observe and punish one of the workers more than the other. The supervisor was given feedback that the two workers exhibited identical satisfactory performance, and punishment was not administered. The causal determinants of the subordinates' performances were then indicated by the supervisor. In addition, a subsequent task was performed in which the supervisor was free to monitor the performance of either worker. Trust was inferred from the relative amount of time spent observing the two subordinates and from self-reports obtained in a questionnaire.

The results of the study indicated that the supervisor ascribed the performance of the more monitored worker to the external threat of punishment, verbalized less trust in him, and monitored him more on the subsequent task. Thus the worker's role as a cause was discounted in this context. Power over another, even if not used, often results in attributions of successful outcomes to the power source. Attributions of confidence and trust to another person apparently are not made unless there has been an opportunity to exhibit positive performance under nonpower conditions.

The Actor-Observer Perspective

Throughout the discussion of attribution theory it has been indicated that a distinction between dispositional factors and situational factors is especially prevalent. It has been contended that there are systematic differences in attributions to dispositions versus situational factors as a function of the perspective of the attributor. More specifically, Jones and Nisbett (1972) have stated that "there is a pervasive tendency for actors to attribute their actions to situational requirements, whereas observers tend to attribute the same actions to stable personal dispositions" (p. 2). Statements such as "I hit him because he provoked me" and "You hit him because you are an aggressive person" exemplify the anticipated actor-situation and observer-person inferential biases.

Jones and Nisbett (1972) offer a number of plausible reasons for these judgments. They contend that actors have knowledge about how they acted across diverse situations. Their variance in behavior across different settings diverts them from making dispositional attributions about their own actions. (Note that this explanation assumes that individuals indeed behave differently in disparate environmental settings.) On the other hand, the absence of distinctiveness information may bias observers toward a dispositional attribution. Second, Jones and Nisbett suggest that actors focus their attention upon the environment, but observers concentrate on the actors and their behavior. Hence actors will perceive the environment as salient, while observers perceive the person as prominent. In sum, actors and observers base their inferences on disparate information and, hence, may reach incongruous judgments.

If attention or focus is responsible for attributional biases, then it should be possible to alter these biases by manipulating relative self-awareness. A number of research investigations have demonstrated that altering perspective does change causal ascriptions. For example, Duval and Wicklund (1973) had subjects read several scenarios such as the following:

> Imagine that you have selected and purchased a race horse. You enter the horse in a major race and hire a good jockey to ride him. The horse wins first place. To what degree did your actions cause the victory and to what degree did the actions of the jockey cause the victory?
>
> Imagine that a friend of yours wants to get you a date. You tell her what characteristics you like in a date and she selects one of her friends. You go out with him and have a very good time. To what degree did your actions cause the successful date and to what degree did the actions of your friend cause the successful date? (p. 26)

Half the subjects read these stories under normal conditions; the rest read the passage while in front of a conspicuous mirror. The presence of the mirror was expected to alter the subjects' focus of awareness to themselves, and thus bias the attribution toward the self. In accordance with the reasoning of Jones and Nisbett, individuals in the "mirror" condition made relatively more self- than situation attributions.

However, the status of the actor-observer hypothesis remains uncertain (see Monson & Snyder, 1977). Part of the problem is that self- and environmental attributions are not always clearly separable. For example, if female X states that she dates male Y because he is sensitive, does that indicate a situational attribution or that she likes sensitive people, a trait attribution?

In addition to this confounding, reversals in the actor-observer biases also have been found (see review in Monson & Snyder, 1977). In achievement-related contexts, for example, actors typically ascribe success and failure to ability and/or effort, which are personal factors. In sum, although the actor-observer hypothesis has attracted much attention, the effects of perspective on attributional biasing are unclear and complex. What is very clear, however, is that observers tend to underestimate the effects of the situation and overestimate the effects of personal dispositions on behavior (Ross & Nisbett, 1991).

The Hedonic Bias

The hedonic bias (or error) also is known as the self-serving attribution bias, ego enhancement, ego-defensiveness, and beneffectance. The concept refers to people's tendency to take more credit for success than they do responsibility for failure. It is presumed that this pattern of ascriptions maximizes the pleasure linked with success and minimizes the pain generated by failure. Hence the hedonic bias is one manifestation of the underlying pleasure-pain principle.

Many personality theorists have contended that we are motivated to see ourselves in a positive light. But Heider (1958) first applied this principle to the formation of causal ascriptions, suggesting that the perceived reasons for an event or outcome tend to "fit the wishes" of the person. In opposition to the cognitive antecedents outlined by Kelley and the presumed rationality of the attribution process, the hedonic bias intimates that causal beliefs also are determined by "irrational" forces, or by rationalization as well as rationality.

The existence of a self-serving attributional pattern has been amply demonstrated in a variety of settings (see reviews by Bradley, 1978; Miller & Ross, 1975; Tetlock & Levi, 1982; Zuckerman, 1979). For example, prototypical studies in achievement-related contexts have revealed that in athletic settings, players in a competitive game attribute their wins to skill and effort and their losses to bad luck (Snyder, Stephan, & Rosenfield, 1976; see review in Mullen & Riordan, 1988); in school environments, teachers ascribe improved performance of students to good teaching, but lack of improvement to students' low ability and/or effort (Beckman, 1970; Johnson, Feigenbaum, & Weiby, 1964); and in gambling situations, following a loss but not a win, gamblers search for possible external reasons (Gilovich, 1983). Similar findings also have been observed in the political arena. For example, politicians ascribe victories to personal characteristics but losses to party labels (Kingdon, 1967).

Three mechanisms have been proposed to account for the observed hedonic biasing of causal attributions. The most obvious possible mechanism underlying self-serving biases is that the individual wants to "look good." That is, attributions are conscious devices used by individuals to appear favorably in the eyes of others.

A second postulated mechanism already has been introduced—hedonic biasing is in service of the pleasure-pain principle. It is ego enhancing to take credit for success rather than to ascribe success externally, and it is ego-defensive to place fault externally rather than on the self. Such a motivational interpretation of self-serving ascriptions assumes that attributions influence emotions (see review in Weiner, 1986). That is, internal ascriptions for success enhance self-esteem more than external ascriptions, while external ascriptions for failure maintain self-worth relative to internal ascriptions. The fact that this assumption is well supported by research does not confirm that self-serving biases are *caused* by motivational factors, however. The ego-defensive consequences of self-serving biases provide no evidence that a desire or need to defend one's ego produces the biases, just as the lung cancer consequences of smoking provide no evidence that a desire to die produces smoking behavior.

A third mechanism proposed to account for hedonic biasing relies on principles of rational inference making (see Miller & Ross, 1975). It has been suggested that most individuals (and particularly the oft-tested college students) have had general success in life and expect further success. If success is anticipated, then actual success will tend to result in an internal ascription, inasmuch as the behavior is consistent with the past. On the other hand, failure is inconsistent with prior outcomes and thus promotes an entity (external) attribution. In sum, the self-serving bias can be explained by using principles of attribution proposed by Kelley (1967) without postulating "irrational forces."

The self-serving pattern can also exact a price. Most obviously, sometimes the pattern will allow people to hold positive beliefs about themselves that simply are not true. Some of those beliefs may be self-defeating. An untalented student may incur considerable financial and emotional costs in pursuing an impossible career goal kept active by self-serving attributions. Further, Jones and Berglas (1978) have uncovered a phenomenon in which people create situations so that failure is nondiagnostic of their ability. For example, a student may party the night before an important exam, so that poor performance on the exam tells nothing about his or her actual ability. Jones and Berglas (1978) also reason that self-destructive behaviors such as alcoholism may in some instances be instigated by a self-handicapping strategy. Although this phenomenon is not well documented (and one wonders about its pervasiveness—after all, most individuals prefer success to failure), Jones and Berglas's analysis could provide novel insights into some apparently dysfunctional behaviors (see Arkin & Baumgardner, 1985; Berglas, 1989).

Summary and Conclusion

Attribution theorists contend that individuals are scientists, trying to understand the causal structure of the world. To reach a veridical understanding of causation, they gather data such as consistency and consensus information, apply causal rules, and use other contextual information. Then they reach a rational causal decision. Hence, although God surely need not gather information to understand causality, humans act in a systematic and rational manner that is characteristic of a perfect being (although some hedonic biasing also plays a role in this process).

The Content of Causal Thinking

It has been documented that individuals use a variety of information and processes to reach causal decisions. But what are the answers to the causal questions? What are the perceived causes of, for example, success and failure in school or at sports, for being accepted or rejected for a social

TABLE 6.3 Summary of Perceived Causality in Selected Domains

Wealth	*Poverty*	*Sickness*
Family background	Individualistic	Common illness
inheritance	lack of effort	being worn out
good schools	lack of intelligence	exposed to germs
	won't move to new	weather
Social factors	places	poor eating habits
unions	lack of thrift	stress and nerves
high wages in certain	loose morals and	
trades	drunkenness	Surgery
		bad habits
Individual effort	Societal	heredity
	policies of government	physical history
Luck and risk taking	influx of immigrants	personality
	weak unions	stress
	prejudice and discrimination	fatigue
	taken advantage of by rich	
	poor schools	
	Fatalistic	
	bad luck	
	sickness and physical	
	handicap	

engagement, for winning and losing an election, and so forth? As already intimated, the answers will depend on many factors, such as the particular event under consideration, the outcome, the information available, who is responding, and on and on.

In spite of the warnings given above, it appears that in achievement domains, and particularly school contexts, there is a fairly well agreed-upon set of causes of success and failure: ability, immediate and long-term effort, task characteristics, intrinsic motivation, teacher's competence, mood, and luck. In particular, in achievement settings ability and effort are the dominant perceived causes of performance; that is, success is attributed to high ability and/or effort expenditure, and failure to low ability and lack of trying.

Although achievement strivings have elicited most attention regarding causality, a number of researchers also have examined other "outcomes," including the causes of wealth and poverty and illness. The major causes of these states are shown in Table 6.3, which reveals a potpourri of causes that should strike the reader as familiar, such as family background as a cause of wealth and exposure to germs as a cause of illness. In these domains some causes are similar to those associated with achievement success and failure, such as ability, effort, and luck. However, each domain is characterized by some unique causes, such as "influx of immigrants" being perceived as a cause of poverty.

Causal Dimensions (Properties)

The study of causal attributions then moved away from a description of what the particular causes of events are to the development of a taxonomy or classification of these causes. A reasonable question to raise is: Why does one want to create a classification system for perceived causes? What purpose or role does this play in the goal of theory construction? In response, consider that within any particular activity myriad distinct causal explanations are possible. Furthermore, as already indicated, the causes of, for example, success and failure at achievement-related activities, such as ability and effort, may be quite unlike the perceived causes of social acceptance or rejection, such as personality or physical characteristics. One puzzle that arises is the relationship or the comparability between the various causal explanations: In what ways are ability and effort, or ability and physical beauty, alike? In what ways do they differ? A taxonomy enables us to answer these questions, for when finding the underlying properties of causes we are no longer confronted with incomparable qualitative distinctions. Rather, quantitative comparisons can now be made. This facilitates empirical study so that other relations may be uncovered that contribute to the meaning and significance of a cause. A taxonomy also permits the imposing of order; parsimony is certainly one of the accepted goals of science.

There have been two approaches in the attempt to find the underlying properties or the structure of perceived causality. The first method that was employed is best labeled as *dialectic* (see Rychlak, 1968). The general procedure was to group logically a set of causes (thesis), discover an apparent contradiction in reasoning by demonstrating that causes within the same grouping differ in some respect (antithesis), and then resolve the inconsistency by postulating an additional causal dimension to capture this dissimilarity (synthesis). This approach was guided by the prior intuitive analysis of Heider (1958). The second method is best labeled as *experimental* or *empirical*. The empirical procedure has involved an analysis of responses from subjects primarily using the quantitative methodologies of factor analysis or multidimensional scaling.

The Logical Analysis of Causal Structure

The first systematic analysis of causal structure was proposed by Fritz Heider. The most fundamental distinction between causes made by Heider (1958) was stated as follows: "In common-sense psychology (as in scientific psychology) the result of an action is felt to depend on two sets of conditions, namely factors within the person and factors within the environment" (p. 82). A simple example clarifies the person versus environment differentiation. Assume that one has successfully rowed across a lake on a windy day. The final outcome (reaching the other side) can be perceived as due to factors within (internal to) the person (ability, effort, strength) and/or external or environmental factors (wind, waves). In a similar manner, success at a task can be conceived as due to personal factors (ability, study habits) or factors residing in the environment (an easy task, a good instructor).

The domination of the internal-external distinction arrived in psychology with the work of Rotter (1966), presented in the prior chapter. The classification of individuals into internals and externals became a dominant focus in psychology. Hundreds of studies related scores on the measure of this proposed personality dimension to other psychological indexes.

A number of subsequent distinctions were guided by the contrast between a perception of internal versus external control. Most closely related to Rotter's contribution was the typology offered by de Charms (1968), which classified individuals as origins (internally directed) or pawns (externally driven). In addition to these classifications of persons, environments also have been categorized with associated concepts such as those promoting freedom versus constraint (Brehm, 1966; Steiner, 1970), or fostering intrinsic as opposed to extrinsic motivation (Deci, 1975; Lepper, Greene, & Nisbett, 1973). This simple classification allows one to consider where causes are perceived on an internal-external continuum. Thus not only does effort qualitatively differ from the wind as a cause of rowing success, but one can specify the precise way in which the two differ—in other words, how they are perceived in terms of locus of causality. In addition, it can be concluded that, in some respects, ability and effort are the same, as are ability as a cause of math success and personality as a cause of social success, although these obviously differ phenotypically.

The argument was then made by Weiner et al. (1971) that a second dimension of causality is required. The reasoning was that, among the internal causes of behavior, some fluctuate while others remain relatively constant. For example, as Heider had previously noted, ability (or, more appropriately, aptitude) is perceived as a constant capacity, whereas such causal factors as effort and mood are perceived as more variable, changing from moment to moment or from one time interval to the next. Among the external causes the same reasoning applies: Success in rowing across the lake may be perceived as due to the narrow width of the lake or the presence of wind. The structure of the lake is fixed, but the wind might vary from hour to hour or from day to day. In a similar manner, success or failure at an exam might be perceived as dependent on the university's grading policy, a relatively fixed external criterion, and/or on lucky or unlucky guessing during the exam, a fluctuating external cause. Because causes within an identical grouping (internal and external) differ in some respect, an additional causal dimension is needed to capture this dissimilarity.

Figure 6.4 depicts four dominant causes of achievement success and failure as classified on the two dimensions of locus and stability. It is evident from the figure that aptitude is considered internal to the actor and stable,

	Internal	External
Stable	Aptitude	Objective task characteristics
Unstable	Temporary exertion	Chance

Figure 6.4. Locus × stability classification scheme, with the entries within the cells altered. (From Weiner, 1986, p. 47.)

objective task characteristics are external and stable, effort expenditure is internal and unstable, and chance (luck) is perceived as external and unstable. In addition to representing four causes within two dimensions, this classification system sheds light on some of the shortcomings of Rotter's dichotomy. Rotter (1966) had defined internal control as the perception that rewards are determined by skill (ability), whereas an external orientation in part indicates that reinforcements are perceived as decided by luck or fate. Figure 6.4 points out that ability and luck differ not only in locus, but also in stability. Thus the Rotter classification system is deficient or inadequate in that it blurs two dimensions of causality. Some of the consequences of this confusion are examined in detail later in this chapter.

A third dimension of causality was established with the same deductive reasoning that led to the naming of the stability dimension. Causes were first identified within each of the four cells shown in Figure 6.4. The causes within a cell were then discriminated on a particular property, and this property was used to describe all the remaining causes.

The third dimension recognized that mood, fatigue, and temporary effort, for example, all are internal and unstable causes. Yet they are distinguishable in that effort is subject to volitional control—an individual can increase or decrease expenditure of effort. This is not typically true of mood or the onset of fatigue, which under most circumstances cannot be willed to change. The same distinction is found among the internal and stable causes. So-called traits such as laziness, industriousness, and tolerance often are perceived as under volitional or optional control. This is not characteristic of other internal and stable causes of success and failure, such as mathematical or artistic aptitude and physical coordination.

This dimension is called controllability (Weiner, 1979). Among the topics illuminated was again the distinction by Rotter between internal and external perceptions of control of reinforcement. Within the three-dimensional taxonomy, two of the proposed independent causal properties are labeled locus and control. A cause therefore might be internal, yet uncontrollable. Art aptitude and physical coordination, as already indicated, are examples of such causes. Failure ascribed to poor aptitude reveals that this outcome is perceived as determined by skill and ability which, according to Rotter, would also indicate that the task outcome is perceived

	Stable	Unstable
Uncontrollable	Aptitude	Fatigue
Controllable	Long term effort Laziness Industriousness	Temporary exertion

Figure 6.5. Internal causes of success and failure, classified according to stability and controllability. (From Weiner, 1986, p. 49.)

as subject to internal control. Yet aptitude, which often is perceived as genetically inherited, is not be considered controllable. Thus confusion is again evident in the Rotter classification. To avoid confounding, throughout this chapter the locus dimension is labeled *locus of causality*. Locus *and* control, not locus *of* control, describe causal perceptions.

A major problem created with this reasoning concerns the factorial nature of the taxonomy, or the idea that there are eight identifiable causal distinctions or "cells." Eight causal distinctions may not be possible. It will be recalled from Figure 6.4 that all the causes could be classified as internal or external, and as stable or unstable. Logically an internal cause could be stable (e.g., aptitude) or unstable (e.g., fatigue), and the same is true of external causes (contrast the width of the lake with the wind as perceived causes). But thus far in this chapter in the discussion of controllable versus uncontrollable causes, distinctions have been made only among internal causes. For example, aptitude was contrasted with laziness, for although both are internal and stable, only the latter is perceived as controllable. In a similar manner, contrasts were made between fatigue and temporary exertion, both being internal and unstable, with only the latter considered controllable. The *internal* causes are more specifically represented in Figure 6.5 with examples of causes of success and failure in achievement-related contexts.

But what about the external causes? From the perspective of the successful or failing person, external causes seem by definition to be uncontrollable, for they are not willfully changeable by the actor. Although all external causes are then uncontrollable, not all uncontrollable causes are external.

However, a decision to label all external causes as uncontrollable may be ill advised, inasmuch as causes external to the actor may be perceived as controllable by others. For example, assume that a student failed an exam because of perceived lack of help from negligent friends, or because the teacher was biased. These external causes are uncontrollable by the student, but they are perceived by the student as subject to volitional change by the friends or the teacher. The student would hold these individuals responsible for his or her failure.

	Stable	Unstable
Controllable	Prejudice of people doing hiring	Temporary lack of governmental support
Uncontrollable	Jobs replaced by machines	Temporary recession

Figure 6.6. Perceived external causes of unemployment. (From Weiner, 1986, p. 50.)

Consider, more specifically, an economist viewing the unemployment of a particular group of individuals, such as adolescents or women. He or she attributes this negative outcome to four causes external to these groups, shown in Figure 6.6, which reveals quite credible *external* causes that are perceived as controllable. The obviously difficult problem that remains to be solved is whether controllability implies "controllable by me" or "controllable by anyone."

Review

The logical analysis of causality yields three dimensions: locus, stability, and controllability. Each of these properties is conceived as a bipolar continuum, labeled at the extremes with the phrases *internal-external, stable-unstable,* and *controllable-uncontrollable.* For present purposes, however, we assume that causes fall within discrete categories such as internal or external. Table 6.4 presents eight causes for achievement failure and eight causes for social rejection that intuitively represent the meanings of these dimensions. As shown in Table 6.4, one can fail because of such internal causes as low aptitude or lack of effort, or because of external causes such as a biased instructor or friends who failed to help. For illustrative purposes, in the social situation the external causes primarily refer to the rejector. Hence one can be rejected for a date because of internal causes such as appearance or because of such external factors as the rejector preferring not to go out. The dimensions equally apply in the achievement and affiliative contexts and permit direct comparisons between phenotypically distinct causes across disparate motivational domains.

Empirical Confirmation

The dimensions of locus, stability, and controllability were derived from the intuitions of psychologists such as Heider and Rotter. A number of investigators have employed empirical techniques to discover whether the dimensions generated by logical analysis also will emerge with experimental methodology. Different mathematical techniques have been used to analyze the responses of research participants for underlying causal

TABLE 6.4 Perceived Causes of Achievement Failure and Social Rejection on the Basis of a Locus × Stability × Controllability Classification Scheme

Dimension Classification	Motivational Domain	
	Achievement	Social
Internal-stable-uncontrollable	low aptitude	physically unattractive
Internal-stable-controllable	never studies	always is unkempt
Internal-unstable-uncontrollable	sick the day of the exam	coughing when making the request
Internal-unstable-controllable	did not study for this particular test	did not call sufficiently in advance
External-stable-uncontrollable	school has hard requirements	religious restrictions
External-stable-controllable	instructor is biased	rejector always prefers to study at night
External-unstable-uncontrollable	bad luck	rejector must stay with sick mother that evening
External-unstable-controllable	friends failed to help	that night the rejector wants to watch television

structure. In one methodology, subjects are given numerous pairs of causes, such as ability and effort, and are asked how similar they are. These ratings are then subjected to sophisticated analyses that permit the experimenter to group causes together and to identify the properties on which these groupings are based.

The data from these empirical approaches support the contention that there are three dimensions or properties of perceived causality (see review in Weiner, 1986). These data also indicate that the structure of causality is not merely a convenient classification system imposed by attribution theorists. Rather, these dimensions are part of lay psychology, indicating that there is a relative simplicity in the organization of causal thinking, just as there is in the selection of specific causes.

Motivational Dynamics of Perceived Causality: Expectancy of Success

Thus far it has been documented that individuals search for causality and that a relatively small number of causes are particularly salient. In addition, causes share three properties: locus, stability, and controllability.

I now turn from causal description and causal structure to the dynamics of behavior. Hence I turn back to key problems in motivation.

Recall that when motivational metaphors shifted from a machine conception of human behavior to the metaphor of humans as Godlike, the concept of expectancy played a key role. Rather than conceiving human behavior as guided by "cemented" stimulus-response bonds, theorists contended that organisms calculate their goal expectancies, determining likelihoods of attaining their preferred goals. This was the heart of the expectancy-value motivational theories that dominated motivation during the late 1950s until the 1980s. Thus all the major "Godlike" conceptions of motivation included expectancy of goal attainment among the determinants of action.

Attribution theorists also have directed much attention to expectancy of success and its change as a consequence of success and failure. Three pertinent literatures discussed in prior chapters guided their reasoning. One set of investigations is associated with level of aspiration, the second concerns the effects of outcomes at skill and chance tasks on probabilities of future success, and the third research endeavor is linked with resistance to extinction and beliefs about locus of control.

Level of Aspiration

A number of quite replicable findings emerged from level of aspiration research. Among the most important for present purposes is that subsequent aspiration level is in part dependent on the prior outcome. In the vast majority of instances, aspiration increases after goal attainment and decreases if a prior aspiration has not been fulfilled. These so-called goal discrepancies are referred to as "typical" aspiration shifts.

It has been assumed that aspiration level in good part reflects the subjective expectancy of success: The higher the expectancy, the higher the aspiration level. Hence the aspiration literature can be interpreted as revealing that increments in expectancy follow success, whereas expectancy decrements follow failure. This conclusion also has been documented extensively in contexts where expectancy is directly measured, rather than inferred from statements about goal aspiration (see, e.g., Montanelli & Hill, 1969; Zajonc & Brickman, 1969).

This is not the complete story, however, for in games of skill "atypical" reactions also are sometimes observed. In these instances, there is a decrease in aspiration level following success and an increase after failure. For example, Lewin et al. (1944) noted that "in the case of nonachievement which is linked, for instance, to outside disturbances, the subject is not likely to lower his aspiration in a way that he would if he believed that the nonachievement reflected a genuine decrement in his performance ability" (p. 367).

Task Characteristic

	Skill	Chance
More common observation	Typical shift	Atypical shift
Less common observation	Atypical shift	Typical shift

Figure 6.7. Observation of expectancy change at skill and chance tasks. (From Weiner, 1986, p. 83.)

Chance Tasks

A divergent pattern of data emerged from research on the subjective probability of success at games of chance. Here the gambler's fallacy often is observed. That is, after a win, a loss is expected, and after a loss, a win is anticipated (see Cohen & Hansel, 1956). A related phenomenon at games of chance is labeled the *negative recency effect*. This is illustrated in the increased expectancy of a *heads* after the appearance of a *tails* on a coin toss. Hence, atypical shifts are frequent at games of chance. There are, however, some exceptions to this general rule. At times, gamblers exhibit the belief that they are on winning or losing streaks and anticipate repetitions of prior wins or losses. Thus typical shifts also are observed in chance settings, but with less frequency than are atypical shifts. Note that this is the mirror image of the data pattern given skill tasks.

Expectancy Shifts at Skill Versus Chance Tasks:
The Social Learning Theory Integration

In skill-related tasks, then, expectancies tend to increase after success and to decrease after failure. These are called typical expectancy shifts. On the other hand, in chance tasks there are frequent occurrences of atypical shifts, or what is called the gambler's fallacy: The future is perceived as having a reasonable likelihood of differing from the past. There also are less frequent instances of the opposite pattern of data: atypical shifts at skill-related tasks and typical shifts at chance tasks. These data are summarized in Figure 6.7.

The problem that social learning theorists have attempted to solve involves the creation of a conceptual framework able to incorporate all these observations. As one step in this endeavor, experiments were conducted that manipulated both skill and chance perceptions within the identical situational context (see Phares, 1957). As reviewed in the prior chapter, the data revealed that typical expectancy shifts were more frequent and of greater magnitude in the skill condition, whereas atypical shifts were more evident in the chance condition. However, there were some observations of atypical shifts in the skill setting and of typical shifts in the chance setting. The data therefore were entirely consistent with the scheme in Figure 6.7.

To explain these data, Rotter and his colleagues used principles from social learning theory and the concept of locus of control introduced in the prior chapter. They reasoned that the magnitude of expectancy change following a success or failure was influenced by the perceived locus of the event, with internal or personal causal ascriptions for an outcome producing greater and more typical shifts than environmental or external perceptions of control (causality).

This theory therefore could explain the predominant typical shifts observed in skill settings (internal control) and the atypical shifts evident in chance settings (external control). In addition, given that some individuals might perceive skill tasks as determined by chance, and chance tasks as affected by personal factors, occasional reversals in the usual pattern of data could be accounted for.

A Confound

Earlier in the chapter, however, it was reasoned that Rotter and his colleagues gave insufficient attention to the richness of causal explanation and confounded dimensions of causality. Ability (skill), in addition to being perceived as internal, also is relatively stable. On the other hand, in addition to being perceived as external, luck is unstable. Hence ability and luck differ in subjective stability and not just on the locus dimension of causality (see Figure 6.4). The observed differences in expectancy shifts given skill versus chance tasks (or perceptions), which can be regarded as an empirical fact, may then be ascribed to either the locus (ability as internal versus luck as external) or the stability (ability as stable versus luck as unstable) dimension of causality. Attribution theories contended that Rotter and his colleagues erred in selecting locus rather than stability as the causal property linked with expectancy and expectancy change (see Weiner, 1986).

An Attributional Approach to Expectancy Change

The attributional position is that the stability of a cause, rather than its locus, determines expectancy shifts. If conditions (the presence or absence of causes) are expected to remain the same, then the outcomes experienced on past occasions will be expected to recur. A success under these circumstances would produce relatively large increments in the anticipation of future success, and a failure would strengthen the belief that there will be subsequent failures. On the other hand, if the causal conditions are perceived as likely to change, then the present outcome may not be expected to repeat itself in the future, or there may be uncertainty about subsequent outcomes. A success therefore would yield relatively small increments, if any, and perhaps decrements in the expectancy of subsequent success, whereas a failure need not necessarily intensify the belief that there will be future failures.

Just as with social learning theory, these principles are able to explain all the data thus far presented. Success and failure at skill tasks are usually ascribed to ability and effort. Ability is thought to be a fixed property, such as visual acuity, and the belief that success was caused by hard work usually results in the intent to work hard again in the future. Inasmuch as the causes of a prior success are perceived as relatively stable given skill-related tasks, future success should be anticipated with greater certainty, and there will be increments in aspiration level and expectancy judgments. Occasionally, however, outcomes at skill tasks are ascribed to unstable factors, such as the "outside disturbances" noted by Lewin et al. (1944). In addition, if failure is attributed to low effort, then the failing person may plan to work harder in the future. In these situations, there would be atypical or minimal shifts in expectancy following the outcome. Note that this shows the importance of the phenomenology of the subject, or how the world appears to him or her. Thus it is quite reasonable to propose that effort is perceived as a stable cause in situations of success, yet an unstable cause in situations of failure. However, for any individual at any given time, these causal interpretations might change.

On the other hand, success or failure at a chance task tends to be ascribed to an unstable factor. The person is likely to reason, "I had good (or bad) luck last time, but that may not happen again." Expectancy or level of aspiration therefore should not rise and indeed could drop following a positive outcome or rise after a negative outcome. On occasion, however, given a chance task, a person might conclude that he or she is lucky or unlucky (a trait), or is riding a winning (or losing) streak. In these instances, the cause of the outcome is perceived as stable, so that typical shifts are displayed. In sum, the attributional position also can account for the pattern of data summarized in Figure 6.7.

One test of the competing theories can be made by the reader, as shown in Experiment 6.2. The reader should complete that exercise before reading further.

In Experiment 6.2, expectancies are recorded after failure due to four causes: ability, effort, task difficulty, and luck. If locus of control determines expectancies, then the values following ability and effort should differ from those following task difficulty and luck as the causes, for these pairs are internal and external in locus of control (causality), respectively. On the other hand, if causal stability influences expectancy of success, then the expectancies after the unstable causes of effort and luck should differ from

Experiment 6.2

You have just failed at an exam, and you think the failure was due to a certain factor. The responsible cause will be indicated below. You expect to take a similar exam in the near future. Indicate your subjective expectation of succeeding at the next exam.

(1) The prior failure occurred because you do not have ability in the subject matter (for example, you think you are poor at math, art, etc.).

Likelihood of future success:

1	2	3	4	5	6	7
very low			intermediate			very high

(2) The prior failure occurred because you did not study enough.

Likelihood of future success:

1	2	3	4	5	6	7
very low			intermediate			very high

(3) The prior failure occurred because this teacher makes up difficult exams and the class is very difficult for you.

Likelihood of future success:

1	2	3	4	5	6	7
very low			intermediate			very high

(4) The prior failure occurred because of bad luck (unlucky guessing, happened to study the wrong material, etc.).

Likelihood of future success:

1	2	3	4	5	6	7
very low			intermediate			very high

(be greater than) the expectancies given the ability and task stable attributions. From past experience, I believe that will reflect the reader's responses.

A large number of research studies have supported the contention that the perceived stability of a cause influences expectancy of success. These empirical findings were sufficiently strong to result in my proposing the following "fundamental psychological laws" (Weiner, 1985, p. 558):

Expectancy Principle: Changes in expectancy of success following an outcome are influenced by the perceived stability of the cause of the event.

This principle has three corollaries:

Corollary 1: If the outcome of an event is ascribed to a stable cause, then that outcome will be anticipated with increased certainty, or with an increased expectancy, in the future.

Corollary 2: If the outcome of an event is ascribed to an unstable cause, then the certainty or expectancy of that outcome may be unchanged or the future may be anticipated to be different from the past.

Corollary 3: Outcomes ascribed to stable causes will be anticipated to be repeated in the future with a greater degree of certainty than are outcomes ascribed to unstable causes.

Practical Implications of a Stability-Expectancy Linkage

In addition to the many laboratory research studies supporting these propositions, the relation between causal stability and expectancy of success finds interesting applications in field research or laboratory research with a "real" component. For example, Folkes (1984) examined what consumers intend to do after purchasing a defective product. According to Folkes, this depends on the perceived cause of the deficiency. If the cause is perceived as stable, then the consumer expects poor products in the future and wants a refund. On the other hand, if the cause is unstable, such as a freak heat wave damaging the product, then the consumer prefers an exchange rather than a refund.

In another research program with practical implications, Anderson and Jennings (1980) told subjects that the Red Cross was examining persuasion techniques used by telephone solicitors when asking others to donate blood. The subjects were tricked into believing that they would be phoning individuals for blood donations and were asked to prepare a sales pitch. In fact, the calls were made to a confederate who refused to donate.

To manipulate causal ascriptions, another confederate (thought to be a subject by the real research participants) commented on his or her perceptions of the causes of success and failure in this situation. Two attributions were manipulated: task strategy (unstable) and ability (stable). In the strategy condition the confederate remarked:

> It seems to me that we could do all right if we approach this thing in the right way. I have a friend in Oakland who is a salesman for Bristol-Meyers. At first he didn't do too well. Then, he started using different tactics until he found one that worked. He's developed a strategy that's pretty successful. I think we should try the same type of thing. (p. 397)

On the other hand, in the ability condition the confederate said:

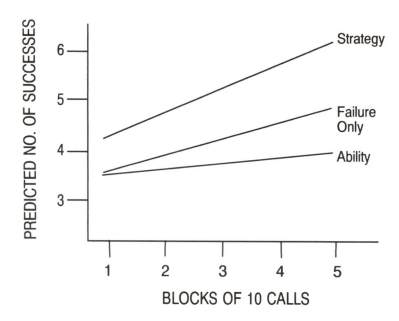

Figure 6.8. Predicted number of successes as a function of antici-pated number of calls for the experimental and control (failure) con-ditions, following an initial failure. (From Anderson & Jennings, 1980, p. 403. "When Experiences of Failure Promote Expectations of Success: The Impact of Attributing Failure to Ineffective Strategies" by C. A. Anderson and D. L. Jennings in *Journal of Personality, 48.* Copyright 1980, Duke University Press. Reprinted by permission.)

I think that the problem is exactly what that guy [the experimenter] said it was: some people do well, others do poorly. I had some friends calling for the Cancer Research Foundation. One guy was really good. He could talk just about every-body into contributing. The other guy couldn't get anybody to contribute. It is sort of like either you've got it or you don't. (p. 397)

The key dependent variable was a judgment, after initial failure, of how many donations would be solicited in the next 50 calls. Success expectancies were stated in terms of five blocks of 10 calls each and are shown in Figure 6.8. The figure unambiguously reveals that persons in the strategy condition expected continual improvement, whereas those in the ability condition did not anticipate increments in volunteer rates. A control group of subjects not given any feedback following their failure fell in between these extremes.

Parole Decisions

Now consider an antisocial behavior, crime, rather than the prosocial investigation of blood donations. A criminal act is certainly negative from the standpoint of society and is at variance with normative behavior. Thus

TABLE 6.5 Attribution and Recidivism Ratings by Inmates and Staff

Rated Variable	Inmates	Staff
Externality	2.87	2.12
Stability	2.72	3.54
Recidivism	1.70	3.49

Source: Saulnier and Perlman (1981, p. 561). Reprinted by permission.
Note: Higher scores reflect more external (fewer internal) attributions, more stable attributions, and a greater perceived likelihood of recidivism.

it should elicit an attributional search to determine why the crime was committed. The results of this attributional decision have far-reaching consequences for the length of the criminal sentence, the treatment during incarceration, and the decision to release or not release the prisoner early (parole).

Saulnier and Perlman (1981) asked criminal inmates as well as prison staff acquainted with the prisoners about the causes of their crimes. The participants then responded to the following causal dimension questions (which were slightly varied for each population):

(1) Overall, think about the causes of the crime. Did it occur mainly because of something about you (such as your personality or habits), or was it due to something about the situation or another person or persons?

(2) Did the crime occur because of something that changes easily (such as luck, fate, person's mood)—or because of something pretty unchanging (such as long-term lack of a job, or other unchanging qualities of a person or situation)? (p. 560)

In addition to the locus and stability ratings, both groups were asked about the possibility of the criminal taking part in a similar crime again (recidivism).

The results of this study are given in Table 6.5. The staff rated the cause of the crime as less external (more internal) and more stable than did the inmates. Thus they tended to attribute criminal behavior to traits. The staff also had a higher expectancy of recidivism than did the prisoners. Within both groups there was a positive correlation between causal stability and expectancy of another crime.

Inasmuch as the expectancy of future criminal behavior appears to be in part determined by the perceived stability of the cause of the prior crime, the decision to release or not release a prisoner early should be guided by perceptions of causality. After all, one of the main concerns of a parole board is whether or not the criminal is a risk to society, where risk implies a reasonable probability that a crime might be repeated.

According to Carroll and Payne (1976), a parole decision is a complex judgment in which causal attributions play a major role. Figure 6.9 in part

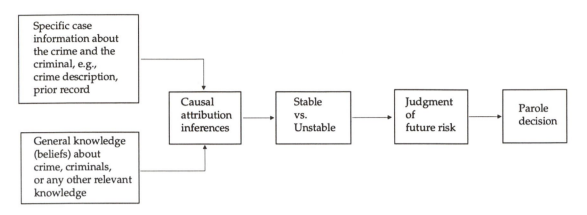

Figure 6.9. An attribution framework for the parole decision process for parole board members. (From Carroll & Payne, 1977, p. 200. Adapted by permission.)

depicts the parole decision process as conceptualized by Carroll and Payne (1976, 1977). The figure indicates that the decision maker is provided with information about the criminal, the crime, and other pertinent facts. This information is combined and synthesized, yielding attributions about the causes of the crime and their stability. The causal perceptions, in turn, influence judgments about social risk, which is believed to be the main determinant of the final parole decision (see Carroll, 1978).

Carroll and Payne (1976, 1977) and Carroll (1978) have furnished support for this line of reasoning, examining professional parole decision makers as well as the judgments of college students when given simulated criminal cases. In the research most closely approximating a field (i.e., nonintervention) study, Carroll (1978) designed a two-page questionnaire to be completed by members of a parole board immediately following a parole hearing. The questionnaire included the recommendation decision, 22 possible factors influencing this decision, and an open-ended assessment of the causal attribution for the crime. The experimenter coded the attributions on the three causal dimensions. Carroll (1978) reported:

> Parole recommendations did not depend upon sentence, crime type, or record, but did depend on the individual decision maker and upon the stability of the offense cause. More stability is associated with less favorable recommendations. (p. 1506)

He went on to conclude:

> The Board seems to take the viewpoint that the judge *evaluates* the seriousness of the crime and assigns punishment, whereas the parole board predicts the benefits to the client and the risks to the community in deciding upon release. As we have previously shown, the stability of causal attributions regarding the offense appears to affect recommendations by mediating predictions of the risk of future crime. (pp. 1507-1508)

Characterological Versus Behavioral Blame

In addition to studies of criminal behavior, attention also has been devoted to the victims of crime, examining their reactions from an attributional perspective. For example, Janoff-Bulman (1979) examined perceptions of personal causality among rape victims:

> In the case of rape, for example, a woman can blame herself for having walked down a street alone at night or for having let a particular man into her apartment (behavioral blame), or she can blame herself for being "too trusting and unable to say no" or a "careless person who is unable to stay out of trouble" [characterological blame]. (p. 1799)

Janoff-Bulman went on to explain how this distinction relates to attributional dimensions:

> This . . . corresponds to the distinctions drawn by Weiner and his colleagues in their scheme of attributions in the area of achievement. In attributing failure to oneself (internal attribution) one can point to his/her own lack of ability or effort, attributions that have very different implications for perceived control. Individuals who make an attribution to poor ability believe that there is little they can do to control the situation and succeed, for ability is stable and relatively unchangeable. Effort attributions, on the other hand, will lead one to believe that as long as he/she tries harder, he/she will be able to control outcomes in a positive manner. (p. 1799)

Research investigators studying these experiences report evidence substantiating the two types of self-blaming tendencies. For example, Janoff-Bulman was able to gather attributional data from 38 rape victims. She found that 74% of these women partially blamed themselves for the rape. Of these, nearly 70% blamed their behavior (e.g., "I shouldn't have let someone I didn't know into the house," "I shouldn't have been out that late"). Conversely, about 20% blamed themselves characterologically (e.g., "I'm a weak person," "I'm too naive and gullible"). There is very little evidence, however, concerning the differential consequences of these divergent blaming tendencies.

The differentiation between characterological and behavioral self-blame has been applied not only to reactions to rape, but also to such outcomes as unwanted pregnancy (Major, Mueller, & Hildebrandt, 1985). In research using a population of women about to undergo abortions, Major et al. (1985) found evidence of self-blame for the pregnancy. Of these women, 96% blamed some aspect of their behavior (which seems more reasonable for pregnancy than for rape), whereas 57% made some attributions to their character. This replicated the preponderance of behavioral self-blame also reported by Janoff-Bulman. Furthermore, women who were classified as high in characterological self-blame for their pregnancy coped significantly less well immediately following the abortion (i.e., had more physical complaints, were in a worse mood, expected greater negative consequences, and were more depressed) than women who were low in characterological self-blame. The differences between the self-blaming groups were also reported three weeks after the abortion, although they were much less evident.

In sum, the distinction between characterological and behavioral self-blame is logical and quite consistent with attributional thinking. It is an important differentiation to make among those who do self-blame, surely as critical as the separation of ability and effort in the achievement domain.

Attributional Change (Therapeutic Intervention)

Application-oriented investigations particularly have been carried out by psychologists and educators concerned with personal adjustment and improving the lives of others. To effect these positive changes, therapeutic programs have been developed that attempt to replace maladaptive or dysfunctional causal ascriptions with other attributions that better aid coping and increase the likelihood of the attainment of desired goals. The underlying principle guiding such intervention attempts is that if causal attributions do influence achievement strivings, then a change in attributions should produce a change in behavior (see Försterling, 1985, 1988).

But what "bad" attributions have these programs attempted to replace, and what "good" attributions do they attempt to induce? The answers to these questions are somewhat complex, for different theoretical approaches have given rise to attribution-change attempts, and these conceptions do not fully agree on what are the functional and dysfunctional ascriptions. However, there are important areas of consensus, and the great majority of the attribution-change attempts, in spite of theoretical disagreement, have focused on the identical causal ascriptions.

As indicated many times in this chapter, an attribution of failure to a stable factor is dysfunctional inasmuch as hopes about future success are minimized. On the other hand, ascriptions of failure to unstable causes would then be functional. These principles lead attributional researchers to alter attributions from stable factors (usually low ability) to unstable factors (primarily lack of effort) (see Försterling, 1985, 1988). Other researchers have broken from the lack-of-effort mode and manipulated causal attributions by providing information regarding the increasing ease of college success as one progresses past the freshman year (Wilson & Linville, 1982, 1985).

The achievement-change programs that have been conducted follow a rather similar format. Subjects are chosen for training on the basis of some maladaptive cognition or behavior. The maladaptive cognition is merely assumed to be the tendency to ascribe failure to lack of ability, or the tendency not to ascribe achievement outcomes to effort. The maladaptive behaviors include a variety of indicators, from poor school performance to judgments of teachers. These students are then selected to participate in the change program. In this program, most often the experimenter merely informs participants that induced failure at a laboratory task was caused by insufficient effort. But models voicing that they failed because they did not try, reinforcement when the participants communicate that failure was due to lack of effort, and false attribution-relevant information also have been used. These programs often last for two or three weeks. Then the retrained subjects are tested for persistence in the face of failure or task performance relative to a control group of subjects who did not undergo the training manipulation.

A review of the findings of the attributional change research has revealed that "it can be concluded ... that attributional retraining methods have been consistently successful in increasing persistence and performance" (Försterling, 1985, p. 509).

As already indicated, in a particularly interesting variation of the usual change technique, Wilson and Linville (1982, 1985) induced task difficulty ascriptions. They identified students who felt that their first-year performance in college was a failure. The researchers then merely presented an experimental group of subjects with information indicating that the school grading policy became more lenient as students progressed through school. This was conveyed by means of video interviews with students sharing their experiences about the increasing ease of school. The data indicated that the students receiving the unstable task difficulty manipulation were less likely to drop out of school (although the absolute number of comparison students was quite small) and attained better grades than students not exposed to the manipulation.

Learned Helplessness

An area of research generating much interest is identified by the label of *learned helplessness*. This topic of study brings together both the notion of perceived responsibility, as examined in the prior chapter concerned with locus of control, and causal stability. The analysis of learned helplessness has undergone much historical shift since its inception, so a brief history of the area will first be helpful before we examine how this research became subsumed within attribution theory and causal stability.

The previous chapter introduced the idea that individuals may believe that they are unable to control their lives. This belief may be quite harmful. Two experimental investigations employing rats as subjects dramatically illustrated some of these adverse effects. The procedures used and the consequences observed were so injurious in these experiments that lower organisms had to be the experimental subjects.

In one of these investigations, Mowrer and Viek (1948) gave hungry rats the opportunity to eat food 10 seconds prior to the onset of a shock. For one-half of the animals, the shock could be terminated by a jump into the air. This response was readily learned by the rats. The second group of rats could not terminate the shock through their own actions. Rather, each was paired with a "controlling" rat and received the same amount of shock that the "partner" had received before the partner jumped to terminate the shock.

The experimenters measured the eating behavior of the two groups to examine the effects of the helplessness experience. It was known from prior experimental research that fear inhibits eating. The data revealed that the noncontrolling, or "helpless," rats were inhibited in their eating, whereas the consummatory behavior of the controlling rats was not greatly affected. Thus rats who could terminate shock through their own actions apparently were less fearful, even though the two groups experienced an identical amount of shock.

In the course of subsequent research, Richter (1958) observed many cases of "sudden death" among rats during experimentation. For example, in a study of swimming endurance many unexplained drownings occurred after the rats swam for only a short period of time. Richter (1958) speculated:

> The situation of these rats is not one that can be resolved by either fight or flight—it is rather one of hopelessness: being restrained in the hand or in the swimming jar with no chance of escape is a situation against which the rat has no defense. Actually, such a reaction of apparent hopelessness is shown by some wild rats very soon after being grasped in the hand and prevented from moving. They seem literally to give up. (pp. 308-309)

Thus it was inferred that a loss of control has adverse effects on the well-being of the organism (see Lefcourt, 1973).

Learned Helplessness and Depression

Perhaps the most systematic and influential analysis of the loss of control is that conducted by Seligman (1975) and his colleagues. The majority of their research investigations initially were conducted with subhumans, although humans are now being increasingly used as research subjects.

Seligman (1975) contends that organisms are helpless when their actions do not influence outcomes. Seligman's analysis of the antecedents of helplessness is depicted in Figure 6.10. In the figure the horizontal axis shows the probability of a reinforcement when a response is made, $p(RF/R)$. The vertical axis shows the probability of the reward, given no response, $p(RF/\overline{R})$. According to Seligman, if $p(RF/R) = p(RF/\overline{R})$ (the diagonal line in Figure 6.10), that is, if the response does not increase the likelihood of receiving a reinforcement, then the conditions for helplessness have been established. For example, assume that a baby goes to sleep after crying for one hour. The harried parents try to shorten this aversive period by rocking, or feeding, or even playing music to the baby. Despite all actions, however, the baby still falls asleep after one hour of crying. Thus the reinforcer (the offset of crying and the onset of sleep) is independent of

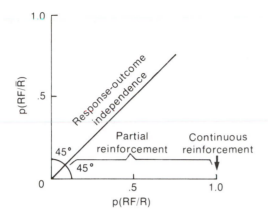

Figure 6.10. Portrayal of the antecedents of learned help-lessness. (Adapted from Seligman, 1975, p. 17.)

the behavior of the mother and father. The parents, therefore, are helpless in this situation.

To study helplessness in the laboratory, researchers first administered inescapable shock to dogs for a period of time. The dogs were in a harness-type device, and the shock was administered to one of their back legs. Then these animals, as well as other dogs not given inescapable training, were placed in the shuttle boxes used by Miller in the study of fear. In this situation a conditioned stimulus came on, signaling to the animals that shock would follow. However, unlike in the harness procedure, the dog could terminate the shock by crossing a barrier in the middle of the shuttle box that separated the "safe" and "unsafe" compartments.

Seligman and his colleagues (e.g., Seligman & Maier, 1967) observed that many of the dogs given prior inescapable aversive training did not attempt to terminate the shock in the shuttle box. Rather, they passively accepted their supposed fate; they appeared to have "learned helpless-ness." This behavior contrasted markedly with the actions of dogs not exposed to the prior shock treatment. The untrained dogs engaged in a variety of behaviors until they learned the escape response. Similar differ-ences in behavior have been reported in experiments using inescapable training on a variety of other infrahumans, including fish, rats, and cats.

It must be added, however, that not all animals exposed to inescapable shock exhibit helplessness, and deficits are displayed on some subsequent tasks but not on others. Furthermore, in some cases helplessness is exhib-ited if testing immediately follows training, while a waiting period erases the helplessness effect. And finally, there is some question as to whether the animals are unable to learn the new responses or are motivationally de-pressed and, therefore, do not engage in activities that might lead to new learning (see Levis, 1976). Hence the distinction between learned helpless-ness as a training condition and learned helplessness as a response pattern or reaction to the conditions is important to make.

To explain the observations of learned helplessness, Seligman (1975) initially proposed a three-stage theory that asserted the following:

(1) Information is gained about the contingency between outcome and responding. In the case of helplessness training, this information reveals that there is no contingency or association between instrumental actions and reward.

(2) This information results in the development of the expectation that responses and outcomes will remain independent in the future. That is, the organism perceives or believes that there is nothing it can do to alter events or alleviate its plight. (Note that the theory therefore fits within the general framework of expectancy-value formulations.)

(3) The low expectation causes deficits in future learning as well as motivational and emotional disturbances.

This program of research then expanded to include the use of human subjects. In one of the first research investigations, Hiroto and Seligman (1975) demonstrated the phenomenon of learned helplessness in humans. Subjects were exposed to either an escapable or an inescapable aversive tone. The subjects then were given a "finger shuttle box" task in which they could escape the noise by moving their hands. Hiroto and Seligman reported that in this situation the individuals exposed to the prior inescapable tone performed poorly compared with groups without prior training or with escapable noise training. Hiroto and Seligman also found that failure at solving a discrimination problem (response-outcome independence at a cognitive task) caused decrements in subsequent anagram-solving behavior. Again, however, these findings are not unambiguous, for it is well known from research on achievement strivings that failure often enhances, rather than retards, subsequent learning and performance.

Finally, the research of Seligman and others called attention to a parallel between helplessness learning in the laboratory and human depression. It certainly does appear fruitful to think of some kinds of depression as akin to learned helplessness. Seligman's model, originally derived from laboratory work with animals, therefore may aid in the understanding of complex human problems.

Learned Helplessness and Causal Beliefs

A theoretical framework proposed to explain learned helplessness suggested that (a) an objective noncontingency between responding and outcome (b) produces an expectation that outcomes are uncontrollable, which is (c) sufficient to generate cognitive (e.g., negative beliefs about oneself), emotional (e.g., sadness), and motivational (e.g., passivity) consequences, or a syndrome resembling depression. This theory therefore can be represented as follows:

$$\text{noncontingency} \longrightarrow \begin{array}{c} \text{expectations of} \\ \text{future noncontingency} \end{array} \longrightarrow \begin{array}{c} \text{symptoms} \\ \text{of helplessness} \\ \text{(depression)} \end{array}$$

A so-called reformulated theory of helplessness was then proposed that gave causal attributions a central place. It was contended:

> We argue that when a person finds that he is helpless, he asks *why* he is helpless. The causal attribution he makes then determines the generality and chronicity of helplessness deficits as well as his later self-esteem. (Abramson, Seligman, & Teasdale, 1978, p. 50)

The theory therefore was expanded to

$$\text{noncontingency} \longrightarrow \begin{array}{c} \text{attributions for} \\ \text{noncontingency} \end{array} \longrightarrow \begin{array}{c} \text{expectations} \\ \text{of future} \\ \text{noncontingency} \end{array} \longrightarrow \begin{array}{c} \text{symptoms of} \\ \text{helplessness} \end{array}$$

According to Abramson et al., the attribution for a response-outcome noncontingency can be classified on three dimensions of causality: locus, stability, and globality. *Globality* refers to the cross-situational generality of a cause so that, for example, failure at math because of perceived low intelligence would be considered more global than failure at math because of low math aptitude. It is yet unclear whether this is a basic dimension of causality, but it has been considered as such by some investigators who have examined depression.

The stability and globality dimensions of causality influence the expectancy of future noncontingency and therefore have implications for the chronicity and the generality of helplessness. The more stable and global the perceived cause of noncontingency, the more likely it is that the noncontingency will be expected in the future, and the greater the variety of situational cues that also will elicit perceptions of noncontingency. Inasmuch as expectations of a lack of covariation between responses and outcomes determine helplessness (depression), the linkages between causal dimensions and expectancy play key parts in this theory.

Abramson et al. (1978) summarized their attributional approach to depression as follows:

1. Depression consists of four classes of deficits: motivational, cognitive, self-esteem, and affective.
2. When highly desired outcomes are believed improbable or highly aversive outcomes are believed probable, and the individual expects that no response in his repertoire will change their likelihood, (helplessness) depression results.
3. The generality of the depressive deficits will depend on the globality of the attribution for helplessness, the chronicity of the depression deficits will depend on the stability of the attribution for helplessness, and whether self-esteem is lowered will depend on the internality of the attribution for helplessness. (p. 68)

Helplessness Versus Hopelessness

It was specified that learned helplessness involves a low expectancy generalized on the basis of prior noncontingent responding in an aversive setting. However, the more accurate designation for a low expectancy of goal attainment is learned *hopelessness.* Clearly one may be helpless (probabilities of reward are not increased by personal responding) without being hopeless. Positive anticipations may be sustained by the knowledge that someone else is going to help or by ascribing the current noncontingency to unstable causes. If one assumes that a low expectancy of goal attainment is the key antecedent of depression, then hopelessness, rather than helplessness, is the appropriate concept to stress. Helplessness would then be a necessary, rather than a sufficient, antecedent of depression (see Weiner, 1980b, p. 402).

This has recently been recognized and a hopelessness theory of depression has been formulated (Abramson, Metalsky, & Alloy, 1989) that proposes hopelessness as one subtype of depression. Guided by the documented linkage between causal stability and expectancy of success, Abramson et al. (1989) liken hopelessness to generalized pessimism and state that

> a proximal sufficient cause of the symptoms of hopelessness depression is an expectation that highly aversive outcomes will occur coupled with an expectation that no response in one's repertoire will change the likelihood of the occurrence of these outcomes. . . . [This is likely to occur when] negative life events are attributed to stable (i.e., enduring) . . . causes. (pp. 359, 361)

In sum, the stability-expectancy linkage also has played a major role in the analysis of some types of depression. If globality were a dimension of thought, then it could certainly be used to describe the stability-expectancy linkage, which is pervasive across a wide range of psychological phenomena.

Motivational Dynamics of Perceived Causality: Self-Esteem

The discussion in Chapter 5 indicated that locus of causality was considered to be a determinant of expectancy of success. This was a key assumption in Rotter's social learning theory. This inference initially was derived from comparisons between reactions given skill versus chance tasks. But the review just completed reveals that this was an inferential error and that perceived causal stability, rather than locus, is the essential attributional determinant of task expectancies. Rotter's error in reasoning was due to a confounding of the dimensions of locus with stability when comparing skill- (internal, stable causality) versus chance-linked (external, unstable causality) attributions.

When, then, is the function or consequences of attributions due to the locus dimension of causality? In addition to Rotter, theorists including Heider, Kelley, and others have contended that a distinction between internal versus external causality is central within attribution theory.

A key to the psychological consequences of locus ascriptions was found in Atkinson's analysis of achievement strivings. Recall that Atkinson specified that motivation is in part determined by the probability (expectancy) of success, and also by the incentive value of goal attainment. The incentive value was presumed to be inversely related to probability and was conceptualized as an affective anticipation, called pride in accomplishment. Hence Atkinson reasoned that both expectancy and affect influence achievement strivings.

Following this lead, attribution theorists proposed that locus of causality, rather than being linked to probability of success, is associated with pride in accomplishment, or self-esteem and self-worth (see Weiner, 1986). Further, as Atkinson (1957, 1964) specified, achievement strivings were believed to be in part determined by both expectancy and self-related affect. A relation between causal locus and self-esteem has been long recognized by many well-known philosophers. Hume, for example, believed that what an individual is proud of must belong to that person; Spinoza reasoned that pride consists of knowing one's merits; and Kant nicely captured the locus-pride union by noting that everyone at a meal might enjoy the food, but only the cook of that meal could experience pride.

It is therefore reasoned that pride and positive self-esteem are experienced as a consequence of attributing a positive outcome to the self and that negative self-esteem is experienced when a negative outcome is ascribed to the self (Stipek, 1983; Weiner, Russell, & Lerman, 1978, 1979). Thus, for example, an "A" from a teacher who gives only that grade is not likely to generate feelings of pride because the cause of that success is external to the actor (the ease of the task, or teacher generosity). On the other hand, an "A" from a teacher who gives few high grades generates a great deal of pride. In that instance, the causes of success are likely to be perceived as high ability and/or great effort expenditure. The current movement in industry stressing that the worker be given personal credit for the product is another example that is guided by an intuitively perceived relation between causal ascriptions and affect. In sum, it is reasonable to hypothesize that there is an association between causal ascriptions for achievement outcomes and feelings about these accomplishments.

One of the initial experiments investigating this hypothesis was conducted by Feather (1967), who induced success or failure at tasks of varying perceived difficulty and had subjects report the "attractiveness" of success and the "repulsiveness" of failure. In addition, the outcome of the task was described as determined by either skill or luck. Figure 6.11 shows these ratings as a function of the perceived difficulty of the task and the chance

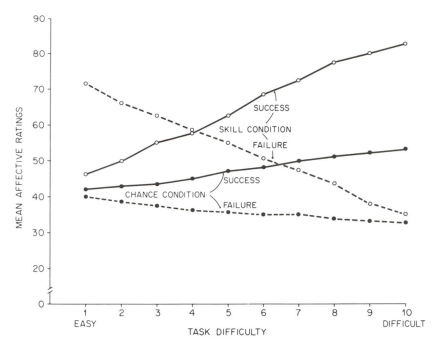

Figure 6.11. Mean attractiveness of success and repulsiveness of failure as a function of chance versus skill attributions and the difficulty of the task. High scores indicate greater positive affect for success and greater negative affect for failure. Compare the two success and the two failure functions. (From Feather, 1967, pp. 379-380.)

versus skill instructions. Feather found that when success and failure were ascribed to skill rather than luck, there were higher ratings of attractiveness for success and repulsion for failure. In addition, Figure 6.11 shows that task difficulty also influenced the rated affects. Success at difficult tasks and failure at easy tasks were rated as most attractive and most repulsive, respectively. Recall that Atkinson postulated that the incentive value of success (pride, or I_s) and failure (shame, or I_f) are inversely related to the probabilities of success (P_s) and failure (P_f) at a task; that is, $I_s = 1 - P_s$ and $I_f = 1 - P_f$. More specifically, one experiences greatest pride when succeeding at a difficult task and greatest shame following failure at an easy task. These postulates are consistent with the data portrayed in Figure 6.11.

From an attributional perspective, success at a difficult task and failure at an easy task produce internal attributions. This is because the outcomes are at variance with the social norms. Hence Figure 6.11 also documents that ascriptions of causality to self or others, as inferred from task difficulty information, influence affective reactions.

In sum, the relation between task difficulty and pride in accomplishment found by Atkinson is, according to attributional principles, mediated by self-ascriptions for success and failure. That is, success at a difficult task and failure at an easy task, respectively, maximize and minimize self-esteem because they tend to elicit self ascriptions:

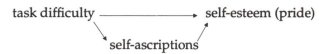

In achievement settings, pride in accomplishment has a positive motivational function, directing the person to repeat pertinent goal-directed actions and hence to reexperience this emotion. That is, pride captures a "pleasure" that strengthens the likelihood of a particular class of activities. Hence pride in accomplishment is a positive motivator, and it therefore is desirable to foster this self-directed emotion following successful goal attainment.

The Locus-Esteem Linkage in Nonachievement Settings

Earlier in this chapter, a bias toward ascribing success rather than failure to the self and failure rather than success to external factors was described. This so-called hedonic bias demonstrates that individuals may manage feelings about the self by means of causal ascriptions, with the bias such that good things are self-ascribed and bad things are externally ascribed. In addition, the linkage between locus and self-esteem is consciously used to influence the emotional lives of others and, in turn, their interpersonal behaviors. That is, the association between internal ascriptions for outcomes and self-esteem is not only recognized by philosophers and psychologists—it is an integral part of everyday interaction.

Perhaps the most evident or conscious and calculated use of the locus-esteem association occurs in affiliative contexts. Frequently, individuals are asked to take part in social engagements, such as dates or parties. A recipient of such a request may prefer to refuse and will communicate a rejection. The requester is then likely to ask "why" to determine the cause of the refusal. Most readers have surely heard the query, "Why can't you come to the party?" or "Why won't you go out with me?" The rejector may then tell or not tell the truth. One question that arises is, Under what conditions will the rejector withhold the truth and communicate a false cause (i.e., tell a lie)?

Folkes (1982) examined this issue in a simulational study. Participants in her experiment were asked to imagine that they had turned down a request for a date. A total of 16 reasons for rejection were provided, equally representing causes within the three-dimensional causal matrix (see Table 6.5). Rejection was specified as due to a lack of physical attractiveness (internal to the requester, stable, and uncontrollable), religious restrictions (external, stable, and uncontrollable), and so on. The female subjects were asked to reveal what cause they publicly would give to the requester. In

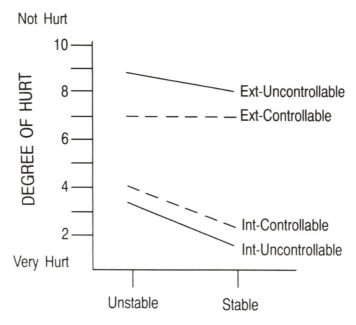

Figure 6.12. The rejector's judgments of the requester's degree of hurt feelings as a function of the dimensional classification of the reason for rejection. (From Folkes, 1982, p. 245. Reprinted by permission.)

addition, the participants indicated the extent to which the public and private (real) causes would "hurt the feelings" of the individual asking for a date, if those causes were known to him. It was assumed that "hurt feelings" captures the general meaning of personal esteem.

The relations between anticipated hurt feelings and the three causal dimensions are shown in Figure 6.12, which reveals that internal causes for rejection maximize the belief that the other's feelings will be hurt. In addition, Figure 6.12 shows that an internal cause for rejection that is stable (e.g., "His face and body type are not attractive") exacerbates these perceived reactions more than does public rejection because of an internal, unstable cause.

Other data revealed that the communications from the rejectors were guided by their beliefs about thinking-feeling associations. When the true cause of rejection was external to the requester, the participants stated that reason 99% of the time. But when the real cause of rejection was internal to the requester, the female subjects stated an external reason (withheld the truth) more than two-thirds of the time. Hence the behavior of the rejecting females was apparently benevolent, guided in part by an attempt to protect the self-esteem of others and mediated by the "naive" assumption of a causal locus-esteem relation.

The prevalence and significance of a locus-esteem relation also have been documented in the study of social stigmas conducted by Crocker and

Major (1989) and Crocker, Voelkl, Testa, and Major (1991). These authors note that it is often predicted that those with social stigmas will have low self-esteem. However, this belief has not been substantiated; for example, a host of studies have shown that blacks have levels of global self-esteem equal to or higher than those of whites. Crocker and Major contend that when stigmatized groups receive negative evaluation from others or poor feedback, they tend to attribute it to the prejudice of those others. The external attributions then act as buffers to their self-esteem. A number of experiments have confirmed this analysis and have shown, for example, that attribution to the prejudice of another minimizes negative affect following unfavorable feedback (Crocker et al., 1991).

Finally, envy of others also appears to be related to a locus-esteem linkage. Attributions of failure to personal factors promote more jealousy of others than do external attributions for those failures, in part because of the threat to self-esteem generated by internal ascriptions (Mikulincer, Bizman, & Aizenberg, 1989).

In sum, there is strong evidence confirming a causal locus-esteem union. The issue for attribution theorists has been to incorporate this linkage, as well as the stability-expectancy union, within a broader motivational theory. I will turn to this after first examining two other affects linked with internal ascriptions for failure—shame and guilt.

Shame and Guilt: Causal Controllability

In both the philosophical and social science literature, shame often is discussed along with guilt. Davitz (1969) and Wicker, Payne, and Morgan (1983) note that these two emotions have much in common. As Wicker et al. (1983) summarize, both "involve negative self-evaluations and are painful, tense, agitating, real, present, and depressing" (p. 33). On the basis of the prior discussion of locus of causality, some similarity between these emotions is anticipated in that both result from internal ascriptions for some negative act or failure, and hence both are associated with a lowering of self-esteem.

Yet differences between the two affects frequently are reported. For example, anthropologists tend to contrast guilt and shame cultures. To understand some of the differences between guilt and shame, we have to turn to the controllability dimension of causality. Attribution theorists have argued that shame results from an attribution to failure that is not only self-related, but uncontrollable. In studies testing this internal uncontrollability-shame linkage, Brown and Weiner (1984), Covington and Omelich (1984), and others have found that shame-related affects, which include disgrace, embarrassment, and humiliation, are associated with lack of ability ascriptions. In addition, it also has been documented that shame-related emotions give rise to withdrawal and motivational inhibition. As

Wicker et al. (1983) summarize, based on their own research and the findings of others:

> Shame causes one to lose control, to feel powerless and externally controlled; . . .
> with shame, one expects abandonment and attempts to change the self, to hide, or
> to run away. . . . [There is] a general picture of helplessness in the shame situation.
> (p. 27)

Considerable attention also has been devoted to the experience of guilt,
its antecedents, and its consequences. Reviewing the guilt literature, Wicker
et al. (1983) conclude: "In general, guilt is said to follow from acts that
violate ethical norms, principles of justice . . . religious codes, or moral
values. Guilt is [accompanied by] feelings of personal responsibility"
(p. 26). In a similar manner, Izard (1977) concludes:

> Guilt results from wrongdoing. The behavior that evokes guilt violates a moral,
> ethical, or religious code. . . . Guilt occurs in situations in which one feels
> personally responsible. There is a strong relationship between one's sense of
> personal responsibility and one's threshold for guilt. (pp. 423-424)

In sum, there is general agreement that guilt is produced when a person
perceives him- or herself as personally responsible for a negative outcome.
Of course, an individual may perceive a negative outcome as personally
controllable and yet not experience guilt. But if guilt is experienced, then
perceived self-responsibility seems to be a necessary antecedent (see Hoffman, 1975, 1982).

There have been a number of empirical verifications of these descriptions of guilt. For example, Davitz (1969) gave individuals a list of emotions
and 556 potentially associated descriptive statements. The subjects indicated which descriptors were pertinent to each of the emotions. The three
statements selected as most linked with feelings of guilt were "There is a
sense of regret"; "I get mad at myself for feelings or thoughts or for what
I've done"; and "I keep blaming myself for the situation" (p. 62).

Weiner, Graham, and Chandler (1982) asked college students to describe a time they felt guilty and to rate the cause of the outcome on the
three causal dimensions. The most frequent guilt-related situations involved lying to parents, cheating on exams, and being disloyal to dating
partners. Some typical stories included these:

(1) One situation in which I felt guilt was in lying to my mother about
    having a certain guest over in my apartment. She thought he was
    staying somewhere else, but he was really staying with me. . . .
(2) When I got caught cheating on a math final in high school, I had extreme
    guilt feelings.

Some 94% of these occurrences were rated as personally controllable by the
guilty person.

TABLE 6.6 Comparison of Guilt and Shame

	Guilt	*Shame*
Antecedents		
audience	not necessary	necessary
sanctions	internal	external
source	action of self	action or characteristic of self
cause	internal, controllable	internal, uncontrollable
Experience and consequence	seek control, make amends	submission, feel inferior, helpless, withdrawal
Achievement attribution	lack of effort	lack of ability

In contrast to shame, guilt-related affects, such as regret and remorse, are associated with failure due to lack of effort, which connotes personal responsibility. In addition, these affects often promote approach behavior, retribution, and motivational activation (Hoffman, 1982; Wicker et al., 1983).

Table 6.6 contrasts guilt with shame on some relevant antecedents and experiential and consequence parameters. To summarize Table 6.6, guilt arises from a particular act that is under volitional control and produces a desire to make amends (see Brewin, 1984a; Carlsmith & Gross, 1969). Shame, on the other hand, is elicited as a result of an act or a characteristic of the self that is not under volitional control and produces a desire to withdraw. Relating these differences to the dominant attributions for success and failure, Table 6.6 indicates that guilt follows when failure is ascribed to lack of effort, whereas shame is produced when failure is ascribed to lack of ability.

It is also of interest to point out that, given success, ability and effort generate common affects including pride, whereas given failure they produce partially differentiating experiences. That is, pride results whether an attribution for success is to an internal uncontrollable or an internal controllable factor, whereas for failure these ascriptions generate different affective reactions.

An Attributional Theory of Motivation

It is now possible to present an attributional theory of motivation based on the earlier discussions of the theoretical components in this theory. This theory, presented here in only partial form (see Weiner, 1985, 1986), is outlined in Figure 6.13. Note that the conception captures a historical or a temporal sequence; motivation is not conceived as an "ahistorical prob-

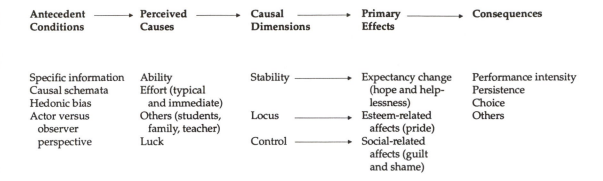

Figure 6.13. Partial representation of an attributional theory of motivation.

lem," which is the position advocated by Lewin and Atkinson. The sequence depicted in Figure 6.13 is first used to discuss the following contrived (but surely extant) achievement-related scenario:

(1) Johnny plays Little League baseball. In a recent important game Johnny struck out when batting, and his team lost. Johnny missed practice the next day, did not appear at the game that night, and quit the team.

Other scenarios, including Johnny reacting to failure by taking extra batting practice and coming early for the next game, and a depiction of enhanced motivation after success, are subsequently also used to illustrate how the theory depicted in Figure 6.13 conceptualizes an achievement-related motivational episode. But let us first turn to the failure-motivational decrement scenario.

A motivational sequence is initiated by an outcome that the person interprets as positive (goal attainment) or negative (nonattainment). A causal search is then undertaken to determine why the outcome occurred. That is, like other scientists, Johnny should overtly ask or covertly wonder: "Why did I perform so poorly?"

A large number of antecedents influence the causal ascription(s) reached. Some of the known attributional antecedents are included in Figure 6.13, such as specific information (e.g., past personal history, performance of others), causal schemata (compensatory, necessary, sufficient), hedonic biasing, and actor versus observer perspective.

The causal decision reached is biased toward a relatively small number of causes, such as ability and effort in the achievement domain. In the example, assume that Johnny played quite poorly in the past and that other children on the team are playing well. He also practiced many hours. On the basis of past outcome history, social comparison information, and effort expenditure, Johnny thinks that he is low in baseball-playing ability. That is, he decides: "I failed because I am not any good at baseball."

This cause is then located in dimensional space. The three main properties or characteristics of causes are stability, locus, and controllability. Johnny ascribed his performance to lack of ability, which is likely to be perceived as stable, internal, and not controllable.

These causal dimensions have psychological consequences, being related to expectancy and affect. The stability of a cause influences the relative expectancy of future success. In the baseball vignette, Johnny will anticipate repeated failure inasmuch as low ability is perceived as a stable cause.

Turning to the affective consequences, expectancy of success fosters feelings of hopelessness or hopefulness. In addition, the locus of a cause influences self-esteem and pride. Johnny failed because of a cause considered stable and internal; therefore he should be expecting to fail in the future (hopeless feeling) and experiencing low self-esteem. Finally, causal controllability also has impact on emotions—internal controllable causes of personal failure promote feelings of guilt, whereas internal uncontrollable causes generate shame. Inasmuch as Johnny has made an attribution to low ability, he should be feeling ashamed of himself and humiliated, but not guilty.

Finally, expectancy and affect are presumed to determine action. The actions might be in any motivational domain, whether achievement, affiliative, or whatever, and can be described according to their intensity, the persistence of behavior, and so on. In the baseball scenario, Johnny has a low expectancy of future success and is feeling low in self-worth (locus-related affect), ashamed (internal uncontrollability-linked affect) and hopeless (stability-related affect). These conditions are anticipated to decrease achievement strivings and behaviors instrumental to the attainment of the desired goal. Johnny then stays home from practice as well as from the next game, and finally quits the team.

Other Motivational Sequences

The theory illustrated in Figure 6.13 has been used thus far to explain or account for a decrement in achievement strivings after failure. I now want to explore very briefly two other vignettes that involve motivational enhancement in the achievement domain, one following failure and the other after success:

(2) Bill plays Little League baseball. In a recent important game, Bill struck out when batting and his team lost. The next morning, he went to the baseball field before all the other players and took extra batting practice. Bill looked forward to the game that night, arriving early to better prepare himself.

(3) Susan is undecided about her career goals. She enrolls in a math class and attains a very high mark on the final exam. She then decides to pursue a career in math.

How might the attributional theory be applied to these rather common types of occurrences?

Motivational Enhancement Following Failure

In Scenario 2, Bill performed poorly during a baseball game. He had performed well in the past, whereas in this game he did not do well while his teammates did experience success. He therefore ascribes his personal failure to lack of adequate preparation before the game and to poor concentration while at bat. These causes are perceived as unstable, internal, and controllable. Because they are unstable, Bill maintains a reasonable expectation of success in future games; he is hopeful about the future. Because the causes are internal, his self-esteem decreases. And because lack of preparation and poor concentration are controllable by Bill, he experiences guilt. High expectation of success, along with hopefulness and guilt, are able to overcome Bill's weakened self-esteem and results in renewed goal striving and an increase in motivation to perform. He therefore takes extra batting practice and arrives early for the game to be ready.

Motivational Enhancement After Success

In Scenario 3, Susan experiences success at math. She thinks about the causes and realizes that she has also performed at the top in other math classes. She therefore attributes the high score to her mathematical abilities. This increases her self-esteem, she anticipates future success in math, and she is proud of herself. High expectation of success, high self-esteem, and pride increase her achievement interests to pursue a career in mathematics.

Experimental Tests of the Theory Within Achievement Contexts

The achievement-related situations discussed above were crafted to be without ambiguity. There was no uncertainty regarding the perceptions of the outcomes, nor were there conflicting attributions or doubts about the dimensional classifications of the causes. Most problematic, the explanations offered were not accompanied by any experimental evidence. They were merely logical explanations of the behavior, given the framework of the theory. Observations of boys quitting baseball teams after failure, or of women motivated by achievement success, certainly exist; documentation of such events is not really necessary. What is necessary is to provide supporting evidence pertinent to the motivational significance of the factors postulated to mediate the behaviors in these scenarios; that is, evidence

TABLE 6.7 Correlations Between Attributions to Ability and Effort, Expectancy, Perceived Competence, and Persistence

	Ability Ascription	*Effort Ascription*
Expectancy	−.28**	−.04
Competence	−.39**	−.01
Persistence	−.21*	−.07

Source: Graham (1984, p. 47). Adapted by permission.
*$p < .01$; **$p < .001$.

about the roles of causal ascriptions, expectancy, and emotion in motivational sequences must be furnished.

Unfortunately, the achievement literature does not yield unambiguous proof in support of the complete attributional theory, in part because the conception has only recently been fully developed, in part because even recent investigations have not included all the pertinent variables, and in part because some of the findings have been disconfirmatory. What an overview of the research does reveal, however, is a history of studies that can be increasingly incorporated within the theory, that is, a history documenting more and more of the processes hypothesized to mediate between the task stimulus and performance.

Reviewed below are two investigations, one in the laboratory and the other a field study, that examine strivings from an attributional perspective and attempt to include some of the variables within the theory. It will be seen that neither study completely confirms the theory, although both provide some promising evidence.

One pertinent investigation by Graham (1984) used children as subjects. They were given a block-design puzzle to complete. There were four consecutive failure trials, and after each failure, ratings of causal attributions, expectancy of success, and perceived competence were made (perceived competence has been construed as an important motivational determinant in Bandura's [1986] theory of behavior). Graham manipulated causal attributions by means of experimenter feedback, with information that either lack of ability or lack of effort was the cause of failure. On a final puzzle attempt, the subjects were permitted to work for as long as they liked at an insoluble puzzle; persistence of behavior in the face of failure provided an index of strength of motivation.

Table 6.7 shows the relations between the attributions for failure to ability and effort and the expectancy, competence, and persistence measures. The table reveals that the correlations with effort ascriptions are weak, but ability attributions for failure correlate negatively with expectancy of success, perceived competence, and persistence of behavior. That is, the more one ascribes failure to low ability, the lower the expectancy, perceived competence, and persistence.

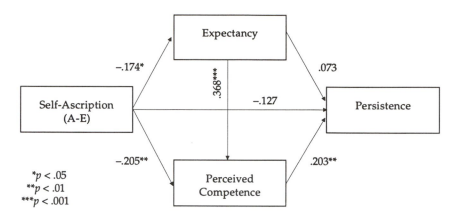

Figure 6.14. Path diagram of causal relations among attributions, expectancy, perceived competence, and persistence. (From Graham, 1984, p. 48. Adapted by permission.)

Figure 6.14 shows the path-analytic representation of these data and reveals that causal ascriptions to ability minus effort, which indicate the relative stability of the perceived cause of failure, are negatively related to expectancy of success. Again this replicates the large number of research studies showing that the stability dimension is related to hopes for the future. Figure 6.14 also indicates that causal attributions relate to perceived competence, with attributions to low ability associated with low perceived competence. However, only competence, and not expectancy, significantly predicted motivated behavior. In sum, the attributional theory depicted in Figure 6.13 is only partially supported in this investigation.

The study by Graham did not include affective reactions to failure, including guilt and shame, and therefore did not fully test the attribution theory shown in Figure 6.13. In a later study, Covington and Omelich (1984) did include affects as well as expectancy in an achievement-related investigation. In addition, their research was conducted in a classroom, thus contrasting with the laboratory approach of Graham.

Covington and Omelich (1984) gave students who considered their midterm exams a failure (regardless of the objective grade) the opportunity to retake equivalent exams three weeks later. After the initial exam feedback, the students made attributions for their subjectively unsatisfactory performance to low ability and lack of effort; they reported their feelings of humiliation, shame, and guilt; and they revealed their expectancy of success on the next exam. The index of motivation in this classroom context was actual retake exam performance.

Figure 6.15 shows the path-analytic representation of these data, retaining only the significant paths. The figure reveals that both effort and ability attributions are related to all of the affects (perhaps indicating some

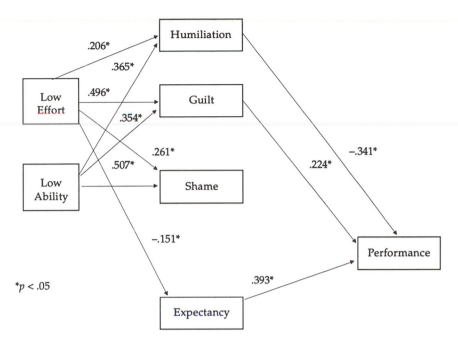

Figure 6.15. Path diagram of the effects of causal attributions, affective reactions, and expectancy on subsequent performance following failure. (From Covington & Omelich, 1984. Copyright 1984. Reprinted by permission.)

response bias), but low effort is more highly related to guilt, whereas lack of ability is more highly related to shame and humiliation. Humiliation (but not shame) negatively relates to performance, whereas guilt is positively associated with exam score. Turning next to the expectancy variable, only lack of effort is related to expectancy, and in a direction opposite to that predicted, since attribution of failure to low effort results in low expectation of success. Expectancy, however, is related to exam score—the higher the expectancy, the better the performance. In sum, in this investigation many of the key unions in Figure 6.13 were documented (attribution-affect, affect-action, expectancy-action), save the relations between attributions and expectancy (see also Platt, 1988).

The investigations by Graham (1984) and Covington and Omelich (1984) have been selected for presentation here to give a flavor to some of the complexity in theory testing when multiple terms of a theory are included for predictions. It is clearly easier to document a relation between stability and expectancy, between locus of causality and pride, between self-responsibility and guilt, and so forth, than it is to document that causal stability, causal locus, expectancy, pride, guilt, and so on are simultaneously contributing to task performance. But that is a goal toward which all motivational theories and theorists must strive.

Comparison with Expectancy-Value Theory

It is evident that expectancy-value theories, and particularly Atkinson's approach to achievement strivings, have much in common with an attributional perspective. Both are subsumed within the metaphor of the person as Godlike: perfectly rational and, if not all-knowing, at least attempting to reach that state. However, these theories also differ in some fundamental respects. Expectancy-value theory has hedonism at its foundation, along with the guiding submetaphor of the person as a rational decision maker. Attribution theory, on the other hand, presumes that understanding is the basic spring of action and is based on the submetaphor of the person as a scientist.

In addition, according to Atkinson, achievement strivings are determined by needs, expectancies, and affective anticipations (hopes and fears regarding the possible future experiences of pride and shame). Attribution theory also links behavior to expectancies, but in addition behavior is guided by experienced (rather than anticipated) emotions. Hence, considering the role of emotion as a motivator, expectancy-value might be considered a "pull" theory, whereas attribution embraces a "push" conception. Furthermore, within the attributional framework, both expectancy and affect are determined by prior causal ascriptions.

In sum, the two theoretical approaches can be depicted as follows:

Expectancy-Value Theory (Atkinson)

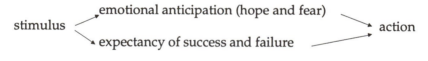

Attribution Theory (Weiner)

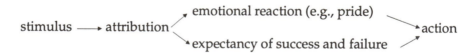

SUMMARY

In this chapter, the attributional approach to motivation has been introduced. The acknowledged "founder" of the attributional view is Fritz Heider, and the underlying assumption of this conceptual approach is that humans are motivated to attain a causal understanding of the world. That is, they want to know "why" an event has occurred.

In part because of the important consequences of causal ascription, it is essential for individuals to reach veridical causal decisions. H. Kelley has attempted to describe the rational attribution process. According to Kelley, the attribution process is akin to a scientific procedure in which covariation is examined across situations, persons, time, and modalities. In addition, in the absence of complete covariation information, persons use causal rules, or schemata, to account for events. Finally, although there is much evidence to support the conception of a rational, information-processing individual, there also is support for the belief that individuals bias perceived causation to enhance self-esteem by ascribing success to oneself and failure to external factors (the hedonic bias).

A number of causes have been identified to explain outcomes such as wealth and poverty, and success and failure in achievement-related contexts. The vast achievement literature has documented that the primary causes of achievement-related outcomes are ability and effort, but the difficulty of the task, luck, and help or hindrance from others also are often used as explanations of success and failure.

Causes have been classified within three dimensions, or as having three basic properties, labeled *locus of causality* (internal or external to the actor), *stability* (stable or unstable over time), and *controllability* (controllable or not controllable or subject to volitional change). The causal dimension of stability relates to expectancy changes after success and failure. Relatively enduring causes indicate that the past outcomes will be repeated again in the future, whereas variable causes signify that the future may differ from the past. A variety of implications and application of this principle have been subsumed within the distinction between characterological and behavioral self-blame, and have been incorporated into achievement change programs.

The causal dimension of locus relates to self-esteem and pride in accomplishment following success and failure, with internal causes magnifying positive and negative self-regard, respectively, following success and failure. The locus-esteem relation also is seen in research on excuse giving, and may account for the maintenance of self-esteem among the stigmatized, who may tend to attribute bad outcomes to the prejudice of others rather than to their handicaps.

Finally, the dimension of controllability relates to self-directed affects of guilt and shame, with guilt requiring a controllable attribution for a transgression whereas shame follows given an uncontrollable ascription for a failure or negative event.

Expectancy and affect, both of which are mediated by causal attributions, influence the choice, intensity, and persistence of behavior. Attributions of failure to a lack of ability are particularly debilitating because ability is a stable cause that also generates low self-esteem and shame given failure. On the other hand, causal attributions of failure to a lack of effort tend to enhance performance.

There are some clear differences between an attributional and an expectancy-value approach, both in terms of assumptions about the basic determinants of behavior and the role of emotion as "pulling" or "pushing" the organism. But the main values of the attributional approach to motivation have been in increasing the number of both cognitive and emotional determinants of action and in having very clear empirical linkages among the components in the theory. The theory then is richer in the postulation of the processes that mediate between a stimulus and the response to that stimulus.

.

Epilogue to the Complete Rationality Assumption (the Godlike Metaphor)

The Godlike metaphor for the study and understanding of human behavior has a long history, stemming from the belief that humans were created in the image of God, and that bodily (mechanical) processes (the "foot soldiers") could be controlled by the mind (the "general"). Hence there could be mind over matter, and behaviors were believed to be governed by higher-order thinking. This viewpoint is consistent with common sense and with the conviction that humans are more than "mere machines" or "animals."

One associated implication of the Godlike metaphor, that humans are completely rational and knowledgeable, was dominant both before the advent of the machine metaphor and after the demise of that approach. Within the field of motivation, the beliefs in rationality and complete knowledge were ushered into prominence when the concept of expectancy of success, or the perceived likelihood of goal attainment, replaced habit strength as a determinant of the direction of behavior. The expectancy construct was first championed by Tolman, but later was accepted by Lewin, Atkinson, and Rotter, the triad responsible for the visibility of expectancy-value theories. All these investigators made important use of the level of aspiration paradigm.

At a later point in time, Heider, H. Kelley, and this writer, along with other attribution theorists and G. Kelly, advanced the submetaphor of the person as a scientist, using covariation principles and other information to understand the causes of behavior and to master the environment. Here again the Godlike metaphor and the associated implications of complete knowledge, objectivity, and rationality were accepted and guided the proposed theories as well as research endeavors.

The rationality assumption was particularly invoked to explain choice behavior, rather than behavioral activation. It was believed that individuals know all the goals available to them, know the likelihood of each goal, calculate how those likelihoods change depending on what caused success or failure, and then select that goal with the highest personal utility. Research was often conducted in the achievement domain, with the choices between tasks of varying difficulty or the choice between undertaking or quitting achievement strivings. Hence persistence of behavior, typical and atypical shifts, and changes in subjective likelihoods (particularly between chance tasks as opposed to skill tasks) were often prominent foci. However, there also were a great many research investigations conducted outside the achievement domain that were guided by the expectancy construct and rational beliefs, ranging from studies of deviance, dissatisfaction, and emotional reactivity to consumer responses given product defects and treatments for dysfunctional behavior. Hence there is a tremendous empirical breadth, or range of convenience, that relates to the expectancy and attribution notions and the guiding metaphor of the person as Godlike.

In addition to incorporating expectancy or likelihood concepts into their theories, the Godlike-guided theories presented in Chapters 5 and 6 also accept other determinants of behavior. One such determinant is some type of trait, such as the need for achievement or enduring locus of control tendencies. The shift from a machine to a Godlike metaphor increased the testing of human subjects, which in turn enhanced the search for individual differences. In spite of the popularity of such measures, they seem not to have greatly added to our understanding of human motivation in these domains.

Further, the Godlike-guided theories incorporated affective reactions, which greatly increased their validity and usefulness. The affects embraced within a Godlike paradigm are decidedly rational, or appraisal driven. They follow, for example, from the perceived difficulty of the task and/or the perceived causes of success and failure. They seem less like passions than like cognitions that feel good or bad, such as pride or shame.

The associated implication of a "Godlike" person is not without contradictions. Expectancy-value theories and, to a lesser extent, attributional conceptions postulate hedonism, or the pleasure-pain principle, as a basic spring of action, although God surely is not concerned about personal pleasures. Furthermore, all the Godlike theories propose that individuals act on hypotheses, subjective likelihoods, calculations, and future predictions, and that they seek knowledge, although God need not be burdened with such mundane matters. And the somewhat problematic inclusion of affects as determinants of behavior already has been pointed out.

Hence, like all metaphors, the Godlike metaphor has limits and, as will be seen, limitations. But let me repeat what I said previously when evaluating the machine metaphor, for it is equally applicable: A metaphor is not an explanation; calling a human a machine (or calling a human Godlike, or completely rational) does not explain human behavior. But it is evident that some aspects of our behavior are amenable to a machinelike (or Godlike) analysis. And, if it is accepted that many metaphors can exist side by side at the same moment in time, perhaps even when they are contradictory, then it behooves us as motivational theorists to maintain the metaphor as a window for the explanation and interpretation of human behavior.

GODLIKE METAPHORS IN HUMAN MOTIVATION:

Humans as Judges

He sees you when you're sleeping,
He knows when you're awake,
He knows if you've been bad or good,
So be good for goodness sake.

HAVEN GILLESPIE

The Historical Context of the Associated Implication
Transition Within the Godlike Metaphor

The totally rational, knowledgeable, objective aspect of the Godlike metaphor ruled the field of motivation from approximately 1960 to 1980. Since then, it has slowly undergone a decline in popularity. One way to document this trend is to gather information from the *Social Science Citation Index*. This valuable source lists all the journal articles that reference a particular work. Thus one can determine how many times the writings of Atkinson (1957, 1964) that contain the most extensive and focused presentation of his theory

Number of Citations

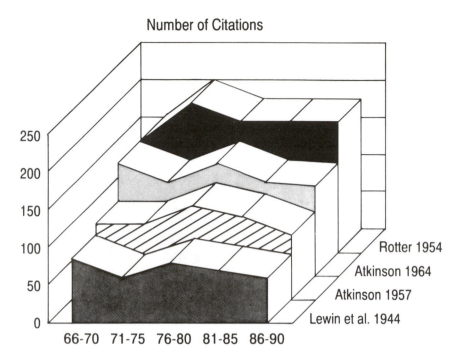

Figure III.1.

are cited by others. In a similar manner, one can count the references to the Lewin et al. (1944) level of aspiration chapter. These counts provide a rough idea of the visibility and impact of a written document.

As might be imagined, this procedure is fraught with danger. One might cite Atkinson, for example, because of his use of projective measures, so that the cited article is totally unrelated to expectancy-value theory. Indeed, in Figure III.1, which charts the citations in five-year periods beginning with 1966, I chose to analyze Rotter's 1954 book, rather than his much more popular article describing locus of control (Rotter, 1966). This is because many psychologists are interested in and make use of the locus of control construct but have no interest in social learning theory as espoused by Rotter in his earlier book. In a similar manner, it was not appropriate to gather citations concerning Heider, Kelley, or me, for we typically are referenced by social psychologists with little concern about motivational theory. Another possible confound when analyzing trends in the citation index is that some sources may no longer be cited because more current authors discuss the theories and these contemporary writers, rather than the original contributors, are included in the references.

Given these warnings, one can cautiously draw the conclusion from Figure III.1 that there is a relative decline in references to the main writings of expectancy-value theories since 1980. The trends appear to be slight, but

I believe the magnitude of the decline is masked by two facts. First, the total published literature in psychology is rising at an alarming rate, so that a small absolute drop indicates a large percentage drop in terms of the total literature. Furthermore, the *Social Science Citation Index* has been sampling more and more journals, so that again the relative drop is surely underestimated in Figure III.1.

As already indicated, it is difficult to comprehend fully why a particular conception or metaphor or implication of a metaphor undergoes a lessening of influence. Of course, investigators seek to make their own unique contributions, and theories undergo the law of diminishing returns, with activities becoming less and less possible as a theory is more and more developed. But there are other, more theory-related reasons, for the decline of the rational component of the Godlike metaphor within motivational thinking. This characterizes both the expectancy-value and the attributional conceptions.

Hedonism, Rationality, and Expectancy-Value Theory

Assume that you are at the library studying and that you are attracted to a person who is studying near you (this may, in fact, be an accurate description of your present condition). You then consider asking this person to join you for a break. What is the decision process, according to expectancy-value theory? Included in the process is calculation of the value of continuing to study, which is likely to be based in part on the importance to you of receiving a high grade. Then there is a calculation of the expectancy that continuing to study will result in attainment of your goal. In addition, there is a determination of the "value" or desirability of meeting this other person, as well as an estimation of the likelihood that asking will result in a successful outcome. But these are just the four components of approach tendencies. There also is avoidance generated by fear that the other person will reject you, with the accompanying affect of humiliation, shame, and so on, and fear that not studying will result in failure, as well as expectancies of these negative outcomes. For illustrative purposes, the following numerical values are assigned to the theoretical components specified by expectancy-value theory:

Achievement Tendency

> expectancy of success with studying = .7
> value of a high grade = 5
> expectancy of failure if leaving for an extended break = .3
> negative value associated with a low grade = –2

Affiliative Tendency

> expectancy that dating request will be accepted = .4
> value of affiliative activity = 8
> expectancy that dating request will be rejected = .6
> negative value of rejection = 4

According to expectancy-value theory, the achievement tendency is equal to $(.7 \times 5) - (.3 \times 2)$, which is 2.9. In addition, the affiliative tendency is $(.4 \times 8) - (.6 \times 4)$, which is .80. Based on these calculations, you should continue to work and ignore the other person (until the values change).

But is it likely that individuals actually engage such processes when initiating a motivational action? And what about other potential choices that are available? After all, many in the library may seem attractive, and there are numerous other courses for which to study. It seems (to me) that the individual is likely to be "buried in thought," with no decision forthcoming.

But even given calculations of expectancy and value, persons are not very adept at reaching decisions that are in their best interests, and the decisions may be quite different from those that the objective values suggest. Consider, for example, the choices in Experiment III.1. Please do that now before reading further.

In this experiment, the reader should be indifferent to—that is, should have no preference between—the two alternatives in each vignette. For both alternatives, the expected values are equal ($100 in the first vignette and –$100 in the second vignette). However, there is a great deal of evidence that individuals are risk averse in positive settings (that is, they "play it safe") and risk prone in situations of potential loss. Hence the reader is quite likely to have chosen to accept the $100 offer in the first vignette, while taking the risky choice in the second vignette and accepting the coin toss so that the loss was either $200 or nothing. Such findings call into question the generality of expectancy-value predictions (see Dawes, 1988; Tversky & Kahneman, 1974).

Finally, it is evident that decisions need not be based on the principle of maximizing gain. Many competing principles have been articulated. One is taking the most available and "easiest" choice, or "bettering" oneself. Thus, for example, when deciding which movie to see, the reader may look at the ads in the paper for the nearest theater, see that movie Y is playing, and say, "That's okay with me." There has not been a total search and selection of the "best" movie relative to the distance that has to be traveled. In a city such as Los Angeles, this calculation would take the entire day! Another possible decision principle is to minimize the possibility of the greatest loss. For example, when investing money one may want to make sure to protect one's funds, even though the investment is not the best one possible. In sum, hedonic maximization is not a necessary characterization of decision making (see Dawes, 1988).

Experiment III.1

(1) You get a call from the Internal Revenue Service. It is good news—because of the new tax laws there has been some confusion and the government is giving rebates. You are entitled to a rebate of $100. However, the IRS is giving people the opportunity to get either $200 or nothing, as determined (and you can assume honestly, with a computer coin toss) by chance. Which would you prefer?

    (a) receiving the $100
    (b) tossing the coin and getting $200 or nothing

(2) You get another call from the IRS, but they are indicating that each person needs to give $100 more income tax. Again, some choice is involved. With this fair coin toss you can either pay the $100 or take a chance and pay either $200 or nothing. Choose one.

    (a) paying the $100
    (b) tossing the coin and paying $200 or nothing

Summarizing the questions raised about expectancy-value formulations, Dawes (1988) writes:

> Psychologists and behavioral economists studying the decision making of individuals and organizational theorists studying single groups tend to reach the opposite conclusion [individuals do not make decisions based on rational or normative principles]. Not only do the choices of such unitary decision making units tend to violate the principle of maximizing expected utility, they are often patently irrational. . . . They are irrational in systematic ways. (p. 13)

The Boundaries of Rationality and Attribution Theory

There is a growing literature demonstrating that because of cognitive limitations, humans indeed are poor decision makers and poor information processors and users (see Tversky & Kahneman, 1974). Herbert Simon (1957), one of the leading decision theorists and a Nobel laureate, has stated: "The capacity of the human mind for formulating and solving complex problems is very small compared with the size of the problems whose solution is required for objectively rational behavior in the real world—or even for a reasonable approximation to such objective rationality" (p. 198).

Inasmuch as reaching a causal attribution can also be considered a complex decision problem, it should be anticipated that humans will be imperfect attributors. Hence the capabilities of the attributor appear to fall short of the conception of rationality put forth by attribution theorists. In the following pages some of these cognitive deficiencies are reviewed and related to the attribution process.

Perceptions of Randomness and Illusions of Control at Chance Tasks

It clearly is important to distinguish chance from skill situations. Any effort invested in instrumental responding in a chance situation is "wasted," whereas misperception of a skill task as one of chance could result in a failure to expend the appropriate effort needed for goal attainment. Yet investigators have demonstrated that individuals often misperceive chance and skill tasks. For example, randomness of outcome is one characteristic of a chance task, but individuals do not recognize randomness when they see it and cannot produce random patterns when asked (Bakan, 1960; Cohen & Hansel, 1956). A random sequence constructed by "naive" persons has too many alternations. For example, in a series of coin tosses, subjects expect alternate or double alternate head (H) and tail (T) sequences, such as HTHTHT or HHT and TTH, while the frequencies of sequences such as HHHTTT are underestimated.

In addition, chance events often are misperceived as skill determined, as if the outcomes at a chance-determined task were under personal control. The reader has probably observed gamblers at slot machines or dice games acting as if they were personally "responsible" for hitting a jackpot or throwing a seven. Some of the determinants of such illusions of control have been identified and include the availability of choice, familiarity with the situation, active involvement, and competition (Langer, 1975).

For example, competition typically is associated with skill-related tasks, such as tennis or bridge. Hence the introduction of competition into a luck setting could give the illusion that the game is skill determined. To test this notion, Langer had subjects compete against another person in a card selection game. The person choosing the higher card from the deck, an act that is entirely luck determined, was the winner. In one experimental condition the subject competed against a person acting in a confident manner (actually a confederate), while in a second condition the confederate "appeared rather shy, behaved awkwardly, had a nervous twitch, and was dressed in a sportcoat that was too small for him" (Langer, 1975, p. 314).

The subjects were allowed to wager up to 25 cents on each of four bets. The amount of the bets was assumed to be an index of expectancy of success. Inasmuch as the task was entirely one of chance, the characteristics of the competitor should not have altered the perceptions of winning.

However, the data revealed that the subjects wagered more when competing against the "schnook."

In other demonstrations of fallacious reasoning reported by Langer (1975), persons were less willing to sell a lottery ticket when they selected the number than when they were merely given a ticket. Thus the introduction of choice or preference seemed to create the illusion of control. In addition, individuals were less willing to sell a lottery ticket if it contained familiar letters rather than unfamiliar symbols. On the bases of these data and the personal responsibility literature, Langer concluded that there is a motivation to control events and that this desire is responsible for creating the illusion of control. Furthermore, she reasoned that the greater the similarity between chance and skill situations in terms of their stimulus properties, the more likely that this illusion will be manifested.

Illusory Correlations

Recall that both Heider and Kelley contend that covariation is the foundation of the attribution process. A covariation or a correlation between two variables means that knowledge of one variable enables prediction about the second variable. Research has shown that correlations often are misjudged because of deficiencies in the cognitive system.

A few sources of error have been uncovered in the study of correlations. Chapman and Chapman (1969) demonstrated that prior expectations about the relation between two variables can lead to the perception of a correlation that does not exist. These researchers presented subjects with information concerning several hypothetical mental patients. The information consisted of drawings by these patients and the patients' hospital diagnoses. Later the subjects estimated the frequency with which diagnostic categories (such as paranoia) had been accompanied by a specific type of drawing. In making these judgments, the subjects overestimated the covariation or association between certain of the variables. Chapman and Chapman labeled this an "illusory correlation," for subjects perceived what they expected to find (e.g., a correlation between paranoia and "suspicious eyes" drawings). The researchers pointed out that clinical diagnosticians may be victims of some of the same type of errors.

A second source of error in judgments of correlations is that individuals do not make equal use of all the information they have. Smedslund (1963) and Jenkins and Ward (1965) have demonstrated that associative beliefs primarily are based on instances of the joint positive occurrences of the judged variables. Slovic (1972) illustrates this principle with the following example:

> A woman asked Abigail Van Buren the following question: "Why do so many people say that marijuana is harmless? Our daughter began using it in January. She went on to mescaline in March, and was in a mental hospital in July." (p. 7)

This woman erred in basing her belief about a covariation between marijuana use and mental illness on only one case. But in addition, this example also illustrates an instance in which positive values of both variables under consideration were in evidence. Instances in which persons using marijuana did not become mentally ill, or in which individuals not using marijuana did become mentally ill, were ignored.

In addition to nonmotivated errors, a number of investigators have reached the conclusion that human judgments are motivationally driven so that the attributor can "look good" or be consistent. As Fiske and Taylor (1984) have concluded, "Instead of a naive scientist entering the environment in search of the truth, we find the rather unflattering picture of a charlatan trying to make the data come out in a manner most advantageous to his or her already held theories" (p. 88).

Does Thinking Help?

Given the complexity of the choices that individuals must make, including attributional decisions, it seems reasonable to believe that spending a good deal of time and devoting much thought to the alternatives will aid in the selection of the best choice. However, even this simple presumption has been called into question. Wilson and Schooler (1991) contend that reflections about reasons and explanations can actually be disruptive because the reasons that are focused upon are not the ones that are actually used or that lead to the best problem solution. When subjects were given time to analyze how they felt about different products before choosing among them, their choices corresponded less with the opinions of experts.

SUMMARY

There is a growing belief in psychology that individuals are inefficient users of information, attempting to reduce cognitive strain by taking shortcuts in mental processing (see Fiske & Taylor, 1984). Further, they are not rational decision makers. What is emerging, then, is the belief that expectancy-value and attribution theories present too positive a picture of the capacities and capabilities of humans. Their information-processing and decision-making capacities are more limited than the Godlike metaphor would have us believe. Thus the core of the Godlike metaphor has become strained such that its validity is becoming increasingly questioned. As happened with the mechanistic metaphor, psychologists are beginning to accept that the metaphor is "untrue"—individuals are not Godlike in their cognitive abilities.

A new associated implication of the Godlike metaphor appears to be emerging, one that relies more on emotionality and less on rationality, more on evaluation and less on decision making and choice, and is more focused on the external social world and less on the self and hedonic maximization. I have labeled this the "person as a judge" metaphor. God is conceived as the final judge, so this is another associated implication of the Godlike metaphor.

Humans as
Evaluating Judges

One of the main dimensions along which humans construe their world is that of evaluation (Osgood, Tannenbaum, & Suci, 1957). Objects, people, events, and even the self are thought of as good or bad—they are evaluated on a scale ranging from positive and approved to negative and disapproved. This is particularly true in our perceptions of others. Virtually all traits—sincerity, dominance, honesty, energy level, and so on—are considered "good" or "bad." An evaluation has an emotional component; it involves a subjective feeling state, having positive to negative qualities.

As already indicated, the theories of motivation that have been reviewed in this volume thus far are relatively devoid of emotion, in spite of the manifest importance of the role of feeling in motivated behavior. All of the theories do accept that individuals strive to maximize pleasure and to minimize pain, with this being a secondary rather than a primary motivational determinant within the "person as a scientist" metaphor. Emotion has perhaps played a more central role in the theories guided by the Godlike metaphor than in those based on the machine metaphor, for specific emotions—including pride, anxiety, guilt, and shame—are taken into account by expectancy-value and attribution theorists. Yet in these conceptions the motivational impact of expectancy of success was the focus of attention, with many studies devoted to ascertaining the determinants of expectancy and expectancy shift, the consequences of holding high and low expectancies of goal attainment, and so on. Only a handful of research investigations were concerned with emotions. In addition, very few among the many emotions were incorporated into these theories. As previously intimated, the relative neglect of emotion may be traced to the guiding machine and Godlike metaphors, for the behavior of neither machines nor God is driven by emotions; acceptance of these metaphors resulted in a neglect of the impact of emotions on behavior.

This neglect is now being redressed. There has been a tremendous increase in recent years in the study of emotion in psychology, including the function of emotion as a motivator (see, for example, Frijda, 1986; Roseman, 1984; Weiner, 1985, 1986). The centrality of emotion also is evident in the emergence of another metaphor introduced in this chapter: The person is a judge. Inasmuch as one of the characteristics or associated implications of God is that of being the final judge of all humans, the judge submetaphor is part of the larger and more embracing metaphor of the person as Godlike. Judges of course must be rational; they must gather data and use the information wisely in reaching their conclusions. Hence a judge metaphor includes the belief in the rationality and objectivity of humans. After reaching a conclusion, however, a judge also must render a decision that could involve punishment, forgiveness, or even reward. In reaching this decision, feelings play a central role. Judges can be compassionate or hard-hearted, sympathetic or vengeful, subject to pity or anger. These emotions influence and determine decisions and linked behaviors. Hence of key importance within the metaphor of the person as a judge are feelings and their motivational impact.

To understand the motivational function of emotions, which was briefly introduced in the Chapter 6 discussion of pride, guilt, and shame, we must first take one step back and consider, albeit briefly, the general field of emotion as it relates to motivation and judgments.

Emotion

Definition

The word *emotion* is derived from the Latin *emovere* ("to move out"). Young (1943) describes how the word *emotion* found its way into the field of psychology:

> Originally the word meant a moving out of one place into another, in the sense of a migration. Thus: "The divers emotions of that people (the Turks)" (1603). . . . The word [then] came to mean a moving, stirring, agitation, perturbation, and was used in a strictly physical sense. Thus: "Thunder . . . caused so great an Emotion in the air" (1708). . . . This physical meaning was transferred to political and social agitation, the word coming to mean *tumult*, popular disturbance. Thus: "There were . . . great stirres and emocions in Lombardye." . . . Finally, the word came to be used to designate any agitated, vehement, or excited mental state of the individual. Thus: "The joy of gratification is properly called an emotion." (p. 1762; quoted in Cofer & Appley, 1964, p. 25)

An array of emotion-related terms have been distinguished by psychologists, including *affect, feeling, evaluation, mood,* and, of course, *emotion.* In this chapter I will use these words synonymously, with the exception of *mood.* A mood is considered of longer duration than an affect, and it is not centered around a particular object or event.

Averill (1982) points out that emotions are interpreted as passions, rather than actions. An action is something a person does deliberately. A passion, however, is something the person suffers. Thus a disease is a "passion," and it is of interest to note that the words *passion, patient,* and *passivity* all stem from the same root. Hence a person is "gripped" by fear, "falls" in love, is "torn" by jealousy, is "dragged down" by grief, and so on. In these examples, something happens to the person that does not appear to be subject to volitional control.

This does not mean, however, that emotions do not follow their own logic and are not guided by thoughts, for it is evident that feelings follow from certain construals or perceptions of the world. The fear associated with the sight of a large dog can quickly change to laughter as the docility of the dog becomes evident. On the other hand, given a particular emotional experience, some behaviors may automatically follow, so that fear promotes flight in addition to bodily activity such as sweating, rapid heartbeat, and so forth.

A number of distinguishing characteristics are associated with emotions. Not all emotions are described by all the characteristics, but if all the characteristics are evident, then an emotional state can be inferred with some certainty.

(1) Emotions have a positive or negative experiential quality. That is, they are something the person likes and wants to get more of (joy, love, pride) or something the person dislikes and wants to be rid of (sadness, hatred, guilt).

(2) The positive and negative characteristics of emotions vary in magnitude. Thus one can feel a little or a great deal of happiness, somewhat sad or very sad, and so on.

(3) The feelings might be accompanied by certain facial expressions and body postures. Smiling often accompanies positive emotions, curled lips and tightened facial muscles are linked with anger, and pride may be displayed with an upright posture.

(4) The emotions are signals for certain types of behavior. Thus, for example, one strikes out in order to "eliminate" the object of anger, gratitude gives rise to a reciprocal favor, and so on. This point will be considered in detail in this chapter. Tomkins (1970) has proposed that emotions, not drives or desires, are the chief movers of behavior. He makes his point powerfully with the following anecdote:

Consider anoxic deprivation. Almost any interference with normal breathing will immediately arouse the most desperate gasping for breath. Is there any motivational claim more urgent than the demand of one who is drowning or choking to death for want of air? Yet it is not simply the imperious demand for oxygen that we observe under such circumstances. We also are observing the rapidly mounting panic ordinarily recruited whenever the air supply is suddenly jeopardized. We have only to change the rate of anoxic deprivation to change the nature of the recruited affect. . . . Thus, in the Second World War, those pilots who refused to wear their oxygen masks at 30,000 feet suffered a more gradual anoxic deprivation. They did not panic for want of oxygen. They became euphoric. It was the affect of enjoyment which the more slowly developing anoxic signal recruited. Some of these men, therefore, met their death with smiles on their lips. (pp. 101-102)

(5) As suggested earlier, emotions often follow particular thoughts. For example, if you fail an exam because you believe that others hindered you, anger is a likely reaction; success ascribed to help from others elicits gratitude; both success and failure believed to be due to luck bring about surprise; and so on. Thus one's feelings are determined in part by one's thoughts. The subjective interpretation, not the objective facts, determines emotions. For example, one may fail because of insufficient studying, yet anger (rather than, say, guilt and self-blame) is experienced if the failure is believed to be due to the teacher's bias. This position also will be examined in detail in this chapter.

The complexity in the definition and determination of an emotion brings to mind a story about a new student's first visit to a university. The student is given a tour and told, "This is the administration building, this is the student union, this is the gymnasium, . . ." After the tour is over, the student asks, "But where is the university?" In a similar manner, the antecedent thoughts, the facial expressions, the behavioral consequences, and so on of an emotion can be pointed out, but the emotion itself is an amalgam; it represents the entire system and the way in which the components are organized.

One final definitional issue should be addressed, namely, the distinction between a "cold" thought ("This is a table") and a "hot" emotion ("I feel angry"). Intuitively, the condition of the person in these two contexts differs. But what if the person is described as relaxed, or curious, or tired, or interested, or abandoned? When these terms are applied, is the individual in a "cold" cognitive state or in a "hot" emotional state?

Emotion theorists differ on the answer to this question. For example, some have considered "interest" to be a very basic emotion, while others do not even classify "interest" as an emotion. In one investigation attempting to resolve this issue, Clore, Ortony, and Foss (1987) searched for a criterion that distinguishes emotional labels from other words. They proposed that "genuine" emotions are equally judged as emotions when presented in the context of feeling or of being. For example, one can be described as feeling angry or being angry, as feeling proud or being proud, and in both instances the label of emotion is judged as equally applicable. But other words, such as interested, are not equally judged as emotions when accompanied by the states of feeling and being. Feeling interested, for example, is considered more of an emotional state than being interested, which is thought of as a cognitive state. Of course, there remain gray areas, but this is an attempt to distinguish between emotional and nonemotional labels.

There are two main theoretical positions in the field of emotion that relate most closely to motivation: arousal theories and structural (cognitive) theories. Perhaps surprisingly, both have been part of the attributional approach to motivation.

Arousal Theories

The concept of arousal has been one of the most dominant themes in the study of emotion and is the basis for various theories. *Arousal* refers to the intensity or state of activation characterizing an individual. It is very similar to the Hullian notion of generalized drive.

An early theory of emotion specified that too high an activation level would result in overexcitement, while too low a level would produce depression. Furthermore, emotions were believed to lead to either behavioral organization or disorganization, depending on the intensity of the emotion or the person's level of arousal. Schlosberg (1954) illustrated this position with the following vignette:

> [A sleeping man] . . . is near the zero level of action. . . . As a result of this general condition, he doesn't respond to ordinary stimuli; he is unconscious.
>
> Now let the alarm clock ring. . . . The individual is awake and responsive to stimulation. . . . Let us assume that our hero has reached an optimum level of activation by 10:00 a.m. He is alert, and responds efficiently to his environment. But now he finds that a book he needs is missing from his shelf. This frustration produces an increment in level of activation, perhaps not high enough at first to be dignified by the name of anger. But as he continues to search for the book the level of activation builds up until he is "blind with rage." (pp. 82-83)

This conception of emotions, however, proved to be inadequate. First of all, emotions do not necessarily disrupt behavior. As indicated in Tomkins's quote about pilots, even emotions of great intensity may be quite adaptive and survival relevant. Equally important, given the same level of arousal, there are different emotional reactions. For example, high arousal might be accompanied by intense hate, intense love, or excitement. Arousal is therefore not a sufficient explanation of experienced emotions; it does not provide the conceptual tools to distinguish among emotions.

Schachter (1964) and Schachter and Singer (1962) supplemented arousal theory so that it could differentiate among emotions. They proposed that emotions are a function of two factors: level of arousal and cognitions about the arousing situation. In real-life situations the situational cues that arouse an organism also provide the information necessary for understanding the event. For example, the appearance of a birthday cake may heighten arousal and act as a stimulus for positive affect (joy); the sight of a gun is likely to cause heightened arousal and act as a cue for fear. However, in laboratory settings, Schachter and his colleagues were able to manipulate arousal and cognitive factors independently and thereby study their joint effect on emotional expression.

In the best known of their studies, Schachter and Singer (1962) injected subjects with epinephrine (an activating agent that often produces autonomic arousal and a general "high" feeling) under the guise of studying "how vitamin supplements affect the visual skills" (p. 382). Some subjects were told of the effects of the drug and could thus appropriately label the source of their feelings. But other subjects were either uninformed or misinformed about the drug's effects, and control subjects were injected with a placebo. The subjects then awaited their "visual test" in the presence of a stooge subject. The stooge either acted in a very euphoric manner or feigned anger at some personal inquiries that were part of a questionnaire administered during the waiting period. During this interval, the subjects' behaviors were observed and rated for euphoria or anger. The main reported findings were that uninformed epinephrine-injected subjects (aroused but "unlabeled") were relatively angrier in the anger-inducing situation and relatively more euphoric when the stooge acted in a euphoric manner than were control subjects. Thus emotion is a function of arousal level, and individuals in an aroused state may experience disparate emotions as a function of the social (cognitive) situations in which they find themselves.

Schachter's theory suggests that emotional experience results from the following sequence:

(1) There is a bodily reaction (arousal).
(2) The individual becomes aware of this reaction.
(3) There is a need to seek a reason or explanation for the reaction, as suggested by attribution theory.
(4) An external cue is identified and the internal reaction is labeled. This labeling provides the quality or the naming of the emotional feeling and is thus a key determinant of experienced emotions.

A number of other so-called misattribution paradigms have evolved to study emotional experience. In an experiment by Nisbett and Schachter (1966), subjects were given a placebo after being told that they were about to receive a series of electric shocks. All of the subjects were informed that the placebo had side effects. In one condition, the side effects were described as tremors, shaky hands, pounding heart, and other effects identical with symptoms of fear arousal. In a second condition, the side effects were described as itching, headache, and other reactions unrelated to fear. Subjects were then given a series of shocks that progressively increased in intensity. The dependent variables included the point at which pain was first experienced and the intensity at which the shock was reported to be unendurable. The data revealed that, within the range of shock at which the subjects reasonably could attribute their arousal symptoms to the two possible causal sources (pill or shock), the individuals in the pill-attribution condition reported that they first experienced pain at a higher level of intensity and had a higher tolerance level than subjects who could attribute their arousal reactions only to the fear of shock. That is, the misattribution of the fear symptoms (which were objectively due only to the shock) to the pill resulted in a reduction of fear itself.

Studies in the aggression area have shown the influence of misattribution on hostile responding and feelings of anger (see Rule & Neasdale, 1976). In these studies, a subject is treated badly by another (typically, a confederate). In addition, there is heightened arousal from an extraneous source, such as loud noise, erotic stimuli, or physical exercise. Under the heightened arousal conditions, angered subjects acted more aggressively than subjects who lacked additional arousal. This finding is very consistent with Hullian theory and the notion of generalized drive. However, the additional arousal did not have this effect if it was attributed to its true source (see Zillmann, 1978). This finding severely calls into question the notion of persons as machines, for the effects of drive depend in part on how that drive is labeled by the organism.

The arousal-plus-cognition theory of emotions proposed by Schachter has been severely challenged by several researchers, including Marshall and Zimbardo (1979), Maslach (1979), and Reisenzein (1983). These investigators pointed out some of the weaknesses in the data analysis carried out by Schachter and Singer and were unable to replicate their reported results. In addition, Maslach and Marshall and Zimbardo offered the following strong objections to the Schachter position:

(1) Unexplained arousal is akin to free-floating anxiety and has a negative quality, rather than being a neutral state to which any emotional label can be applied.

(2) When individuals seek to explain a state of arousal, they do not use merely the behavior of others in their environment. Rather, many other sources of information are called on, particularly their own personal histories. That is, they search for prior occasions on which they felt this negative arousal state to explain its occurrence now. The behavior of others may dictate or suggest how one should behave in the situation, but it does not provide information concerning why one feels as one does. For example, if a confederate were behaving in a completely inappropriate manner, the subject would not use this action to infer something about his or her own emotional state. In this instance, the attribution for the confederate's behavior may not be at all applicable to the subject.

A number of other investigations contradict Schachter's position and suggest that cognitions are sufficient to produce emotional behavior. To demonstrate that the energizing, physiological effects of arousal do not influence emotional expression, Valins (1966) presented fraudulent information to his subjects. At times the subjects overheard bogus heart-rate information indicating that they were in a heightened state of arousal while viewing slides of seminude females. After viewing the stimuli, the subjects rated the attractiveness of the nudes. It was found that the nudes associated with a perceived change in heart rate were rated more attractive than the pictures of nudes not linked with this bogus information. Valins therefore concluded that internal events such as arousal act only as a source of

	Positive event	Negative event
Signaled increase	Hope	Fear
Signaled decrease	Disappointment	Relief

Figure 7.1. Mowrer's (1960) analysis of four emotions.

	Ideal self	Ought self
Judged by Self	Dissatisfaction	Guilt
Judged by Others	Shame	Insecurity

Figure 7.2. Four emotions as interpreted by Higgins, Strauman, and Klein (1986).

information to the actor; actual arousal is not necessary for emotional experience.

Further evidence that arousal is not necessary for the experience of emotion comes from recent studies of spinal cord-injured patients (Chwalisz, Diener, & Gallagher, 1988). This injury prevents autonomic feedback to the brain, depending on the degree of the injury. According to Schachter's theory of emotion, these individuals should not experience emotion, or should experience it in greatly reduced intensity. However, Chwalisz et al. (1988) report intense emotional feelings, thus contradicting the Schachter theory and some earlier studies that were not well controlled.

The data from Valins (1966), Chwalisz et al. (1988), and others suggest that cognitions are sufficient to produce emotional behavior. Thus we turn to the cognitive (at times called "appraisal") approach to emotional experience.

Cognitive Theories

The cognitive position concerning emotions is relatively straightforward: Emotions depend on the interpretation, meaning, or appraisal of an event. Thus "cold" knowledge or "hot" appraisal (which includes an interpretation of the personal significance of an event) determines feelings (Lazarus & Smith, 1988). Given the belief that cognitions are necessary and sufficient causes of feelings, it follows that one can be "talked into" or "talked out of" particular feeling states. Hence one can convince another to be angry by planting the suspicion that an act was intentionally engaged in to harm that person and, similarly, one can convince another not to be angry by presenting evidence that the act was accidental.

One cognitive approach to emotions is illustrated in a simple classification proposed by Mowrer (1960), who distinguished between situations connoting increases or decreases in the likelihood of undergoing positive or negative experiences. Increases in the perceived likelihood of experiencing positive events gives rise to hope, while decreases in this estimate produce disappointment. Considering negative events, increased likelihood promotes fear, while decreases in their anticipated appearance produces relief (see Figure 7.1). Note, then, that the only determinants of emotion are cognitions about the change in probability of an event and the perception of the positivity of that event. Arousal is not discussed as a determinant of these emotions.

The scheme proposed by Mowrer (1960) is obviously limited in that it addresses only four among the many, many emotions. In a similar manner, Higgins, Strauman, and Klein (1986) developed a classification scheme that examines four emotions, but the emotions are quite different from those addressed by Mowrer.

Like Mowrer, Higgins et al. first differentiated two cognitive determinants of emotion. They stated that the self is differentiated according to an "ideal" self (how one would ideally like to be) and an "ought" self (a representation of the attributes that someone "should" possess). They also distinguished between the frames of reference according to which one is judged—from the perspective of the self or from the perspective of others. This again resulted in a 2 × 2 classification scheme, as shown in Figure 7.2. Figure 7.2 reveals that if there is a discrepancy between an ideal and a perceived actual self when judged from one's personal point of view, then dissatisfaction is experienced. Thus, for example, if an individual would like to be smarter than he or she is, then the affect the person feels is dissatisfaction. However, when this shortcoming is considered from the viewpoint of others, the person experiences shame. Turning next to the ought self, if one thinks one is less honest than one should be, then one feels guilt. However, if judged from the perspective of others, then the emotional experience is labeled insecurity. Note, then, that just as Mowrer proposed, a simple division of thinking is brought creatively to bear on a small subset of feelings.

When comparing the disparate emotions addressed by Mowrer (1960) and Higgins et al. (1986), one becomes aware of the difficulties of a cognitive approach to emotion: One must be able to specify which cognitions are linked to which emotions. Inasmuch as there are myriad pertinent thoughts, there also must be classification systems that reduce the number of thoughts to underlying dimensions, yet this classification system must remain rich and diverse enough to account for a wide range of emotions. Mowrer and Higgins et al. had rather sparse classification systems based, respectively, on dimensions of changes in probability of an event as well as perceived valence of the event, and types of self and other perspectives of evaluation.

A number of other theorists have developed more complex cognitive schemes, and thus have been able to account for more emotions (e.g., Frijda, 1986; Roseman, 1984; Smith & Ellsworth, 1987; Weiner, 1985, 1986). In these theories, the investigators attempt to identify the basic dimensions of thought that determine an array of specific emotions. This approach also can be found in attribution theory (Weiner, 1985, 1986), and that will be the focus of the remainder of this chapter.

An Attributional Approach to Emotions

Recall from the prior chapter that attribution theory specifies three basic dimensions or characteristics of perceived causality: locus, stability, and controllability. Each of these dimensions of phenomenal causality has been linked with specific emotions. It was indicated in the prior chapter that attributions of causality to the locus dimension influence the pride and self-esteem that are experienced following successful goal attainment, as well as the reduction in self-worth that follows from nonattainment of a goal. Hence a grade of "A" in a class ascribed to high ability and/or high effort promotes pride and positive evaluation of the self, whereas an "A" because of good luck or because that teacher only gives high grades might produce happiness, but not pride in accomplishment.

In addition, the stability of a causal ascription, by influencing expectancy of success and failure, generates emotions such as hope and hopelessness. Hence a failure ascribed to bad luck or lack of effort, both unstable causal attributions, will give rise to the belief that success can be attained in the future, whereas a failure attributed to, for example, lack of aptitude will result in a low expectancy of future success and hopelessness.

But most important in the present context is the influence of perceived controllability on affective reactions, for this has far-reaching motivational consequences. This issue was briefly touched on in the prior chapter in the discussion of the antecedents of guilt and shame.

Causal Controllability and Social Emotions

Causal controllability pertains to the volitional control that one has over the cause of an event. If the cause is controllable, then one "could have done otherwise" (Hamilton, 1980). Further, if the cause is perceived as controllable, then the individual is held responsible and "blamed" if the event was negative and praised if the event was positive. This construal also influences a number of specific social emotions, including guilt and shame, and anger and pity.

If personal failure is due to causes perceived as controllable by others, then anger is elicited. For example, when failure is caused by an inconsiderate neighbor who kept one awake the night before an exam, one reacts with anger. On the other hand, uncontrollable causes of negative outcomes of others elicit pity. Thus if it is discovered that the neighbor was violently ill, or was being attacked by thieves and was making noise to attract attention, then pity rather than anger is likely to be experienced. As already indicated, the causal dimension of controllability also is associated with the affects of shame and guilt, as discussed in the prior chapter, although these are self- rather than other-directed emotions. Thus, for example, when one does not freely provide help to needy others, one may experience guilt. Uncontrollable causes, on the other hand, are linked with shame (embarrassment, humiliation). One is embarrassed, for example, when one fails at sports because one is shorter or less coordinated than others. Inasmuch as the perceived degree of controllability is thought to influence the very prevalent emotions of anger, pity, guilt, and shame, this causal dimension plays an important role in the maintenance of social relationships and social order.

In addition to the rational approach of attribution theory, the biological conception proposed by the sociobiologists, with its link to altruism, also has addressed the emotions of anger, pity, and guilt. As reviewed in Chapter 2, sociobiologists contend that altruism is a genetically programmed behavior in service of the preservation of one's gene pool. However, it can also be survival relevant to cheat; cheaters take unfair advantage of the general altruistic system and increase their survival fitness at the expense of others. This temptation, sociobiologists argue, has resulted in the evolution of mechanisms to protect against cheating. They point out that anger, sympathy (pity), and guilt are in service of the maintenance and regulation of the altruistic system and aid in preventing cheating (Trivers, 1971). Specifically:

- *Anger* (and the aggression that it instigates) "counteracts the tendency of the altruist in the absence of reciprocity to continue to perform altruistic acts, . . . educates the unreciprocating individual by frightening him with immediate harm or with the future harm of no more aid; and . . . select[s] directly against the unreciprocating individual by injuring, killing, or exiling him" (Trivers, 1971, p. 49).
- *Sympathy (pity)* "has been selected to motivate altruistic behavior as a function of the plight of the recipient of such behavior; crudely put, the greater the potential benefit to the recipient, the greater the sympathy and the more likely the altruistic gesture" (Trivers, 1971, p. 49).
- *Guilt* "has been selected for in humans partly in order to motivate the cheater to compensate for his misdeed and to behave reciprocally in the future, and thus to prevent the rupture of reciprocal relationships" (Trivers, 1971, p. 50).

The convergence of two quite different theoretical systems on the same set of emotions certainly encourages one to think that fundamental issues and important affective states are under consideration. I now turn to the specific emotions of anger and pity and examine in detail how attribution theory accounts for their elicitation. I will not examine guilt and shame further, although these also are social emotions with motivational significance in the interpersonal domain (see Weiner, 1986).

Anger and Pity

A large survey study by Averill (1982, 1983) illustrates the attributional antecedents of anger. Averill asked his respondents to describe a situation in which they were made angry, and then examined the characteristics of these situations. He concluded:

> The major issue for the person in the street is not the specific nature of the instigating event; it is the perceived *justification* for the instigator's behavior. Anger, for the person in the street, is an accusation. . . . Over 85% of the episodes described by angry persons involved either an act that they considered voluntary and unjustified (59%) or else a potentially avoidable accident (e.g., due to negligence or lack of foresight, 28%). . . . To summarize, the typical instigation to anger is a value judgment. More than anything else, anger is an attribution of blame. (1983, p. 1150)

Averill (1983) noted that others "have pointed out that anger involves a normative judgment, an attribution of blame" (p. 1150). For example, in one of the very first of the pertinent investigations, Pastore (1952) demonstrated that blame attributions influence the relation between frustration and aggression. He found that aggression (and, by implication, anger) is not merely the result of nonattainment of a desired goal, but rather follows when a barrier imposed by others is "arbitrary" rather than "nonarbitrary." Among the arbitrary, aggression-instigating conditions identified by Pastore (1952) was "Your date phones at the last minute and breaks an appointment without an adequate explanation." The so-called nonarbitrary equivalent situation was "Your date phones at the last minute and breaks an appointment because he (she) had suddenly become ill." Blame and aggression are therefore linked with perceptions of causal controllability.

In contrast to the linkage between controllability and anger, uncontrollable causes are associated with pity. (In this context, emotions such as compassion and sympathy often are not distinguished from pity, although they might indeed be discriminable.) Another's loss of a loved one because of an accident or illness (a cause external to the target of the pity, and uncontrollable by that person) and failure of another because of a physical handicap (internal to the target of pity and uncontrollable) are prevalent situations that elicit pity. Uncontrollability, however, is not likely to be a sufficient condition for the generation of pity. After all, we may not pity a child who is not tall enough to reach a toy on a high shelf. It appears that objects of pity must be suffering a severe distress, one that is perhaps central to their lives. In addition, the other person might have to be defined as "fundamentally different" to be the target of a full-blown pity reaction, whereas this may not be true for a reaction of sympathy.

Inasmuch as pity is associated with perceptions of uncontrollability and a fundamental (and adverse) difference, communicated pity could serve as a cue promoting the self-perception of difference, deficiency, and inadequacy (see Graham, 1984; Weiner, Graham, Stern, & Lawson, 1982).

For this reason, when the teacher of Helen Keller began her training, it is reported that she stated to the Keller family, "We do not want your pity!" Similarly, a contemporary author, Robertson Davies, wrote, "I will not expose myself to the pity of my inferiors," thus conveying that a target of pity is associated with some deficiency.

In one pertinent investigation conducted by Weiner, Graham, and Chandler (1982), college students were asked to describe instances in their lives in which they experienced pity or anger. After subjects recounted two experiences for each emotion, the concept of causal dimensions was introduced and defined. The subjects then rated the causes of the events in question, if applicable, on each of the three dimensions.

Concerning pity, 71% of the causes were rated as stable and uncontrollable, with equal apportionment between the internal and external alternatives. Two quite typical instances were as follows:

(1) A guy on campus is terribly deformed. I pity him because it would be so hard to look so different and have people stare at you.

(2) My great-grandmother lives in a rest home, and every time I go there I see these poor old half-senile men and women wandering aimlessly down the halls. . . . I feel pity every time I go down there. (Weiner, Graham, & Chandler, 1982, p. 228)

For the affect of anger, 86% of the situations involved an external and controllable cause, as Averill (1982) and others also have documented. Here are two typical anger-arousing situations:

(1) My roommate brought her dog into our no-pets apartment without asking me first. When I got home she wasn't there, but the barking dog was. . . . As well, the dog had relieved itself in the middle of the entry.

(2) I felt angry toward my boyfriend for lying to me about something he did. All he had to do was tell me the truth. (Weiner, Graham, & Chandler, 1982, p. 228)

Emotions and Motivation

A great deal of evidence supports the contention that beliefs about responsibility guide the emotional reactions of anger and pity (as well as the self-directed emotions of guilt and shame examined in Chapter 6). I will now document that causal attributions regarding responsibility, which is here considered to be closely related to the causal concept of personal controllability, and the linked emotions of anger and pity are central in determining a great diversity of social motivation. Among the topics examined are altruism, particularly as related to social stigmas such as persons

with AIDS and the poor; aggression; social rejection; achievement evaluation; and excuse giving (impression management). When engaging in this
vast array of social behaviors, individuals act as judges. They determine if
the other, or the self, is or is not responsible for a given behavior, state, or
condition. Then, based on this conclusion, emotional reactions of anger or
pity are evoked. These emotions, in turn, direct the decisions to punish, to
help, to neglect, to reject, what to communicate, and so on. A number of
important everyday social implications in relation to family dynamics,
reactions of teachers in the classroom, and of policymakers are amenable
to the same analysis. The argument being proposed is that thoughts (attributions) determine what one feels (e.g., anger or pity), and that feelings
guide what one does. This is a major metaphorical shift, from rationality
and the scientist to emotions as well as rationality and the judge.

The position advocated in the remainder of this chapter includes the
belief that motivation is moving from intrapsychic psychology (the machine, decision-maker, and scientist metaphors) to interpersonal concerns
(the judge metaphor). In addition, the field of motivation is increasingly
being tied to emotional life. The emotional reactions, however, are pro-
moted by specific attributional thoughts. Thus the judge metaphor supplements rather than supplants the rational connotations of expectancy-value
and attribution theories, adding an emotional component that remains
consistent with the overall Godlike metaphor.

Helping Behavior

A huge array of factors influence the decision to help or not to help
another person in need. Among the documented determinants of help
giving are the perceived cost and benefit to the help giver as well as to the
recipient of the aid, the number of people available to help (i.e., the amount
of responsibility that the potential help giver must take), the values and
norms of the culture, the behavior of models, and on and on. But most
important in the present context, it also has been documented that the
perceived cause of a need is one of the major determinants of the decision
to help or to neglect a person requiring aid.

The Effects of Perceived Causality on Helping

An often-cited investigation by Piliavin, Rodin, and Piliavin (1969)
demonstrated that the perceived reason help is needed influences the
decision to help or to neglect another. In the methodology employed by
these researchers, a person obviously drunk or obviously ill falls down
while riding a subway. Observations of the behavior of the passengers

revealed that help was more likely to be offered to the ill person than to the drunk person. Piliavin et al. reasoned that there are great potential costs when helping a drunk: The person might resist aid, be aggressive, and so on. These costs, in turn, were presumed to hinder the likelihood of helping.

A study published in the same year by Berkowitz (1969) was among the first to demonstrate explicitly an effect of causal ascriptions on help giving. Subjects in this experiment requested aid from another subject. The reason for the need was manipulated and was due to an experimenter error or to the subject "taking it easy." These were conceived as differing on the locus dimension of causality, with experimenter error being external to the subject whereas "taking it easy" is an internal ascription. The data clearly revealed that more aid was extended when the cause of the need was attributed to the experimenter rather than to the subject.

Helping from an Attributional Perspective

It was not until a decade later that Barnes, Ickes, and Kidd (1979) recognized that helping behavior is amenable to a more complete attributional analysis than the locus-only approach suggested by Berkowitz. In the Barnes et al. study, students were telephoned by an alleged classmate who asked to borrow their class notes. The classmate indicated that the reason for his need was either low ability (uncontrollable) or lack of effort (controllable). In addition, it was reported that this was either a stable or an unstable condition. Hence two dimensions of causality were independently varied to determine their influence on help giving. Inasmuch as ability and effort are internal ascriptions, the locus dimension was held constant. Barnes et al. found that more helping requests were granted when low ability rather than lack of effort was given as the cause of needing notes, and help was increased given a stable rather than an unstable causal ascription.

These data suggested a reinterpretation of the findings reported by Berkowitz (1969) and Piliavin et al. (1969). In the experiment by Berkowitz, two causes of a need were compared: the experimenter (external and not controllable by the subject) and lack of effort (internal and controllable by the subject). Berkowitz contended that aid giving was a function of the locus of the cause, with external causes generating more help giving than internal causes. But locus and control were inseparable and thereby confounded in his experiment. Thus the differential helping might have been due to the controllability rather than (or in addition to) the locus of the cause. The data reported by Barnes et al. (1979), which held the locus dimension constant by manipulating only the internal causes of ability and effort, strongly suggest that the disparate effects found by Berkowitz were due to differences in the perceived controllability of the cause of the need.

The controllability explanation first offered by Barnes et al. also may be applied to the data reported by Piliavin et al. (1969). Drinking is perceived as a controllable cause of a need—people typically are held responsible for their alcohol consumption. There is a wealth of data supporting this conclusion. For example, ratings of a variety of stigmatized groups, including the mentally ill, homosexuals, and the obese, revealed that alcoholics are often perceived as the group most responsible for their own plight. Beckman (1979) reported that female alcoholics are held responsible by others as well as by themselves for their drinking behavior. And the recent attacks by Mothers Against Drunk Driving (MADD) quite clearly hold drunk individuals responsible for any untoward events that happen when they are under the influence of alcohol. On the contrary, one usually is not held responsible or blamed for being ill (see Reisenzein, 1986; Weiner, 1980a), although one can create special situations in which this could be the case.

Because of the robustness of only the controllability explanation first suggested by Barnes et al., I continued with this line of thought (Weiner, 1980a). Helping situations were created in which students again were asked about their likelihood of lending another student their class notes. In this investigation, a more complete sampling of causes was employed, and three (rather than two) dimensions of causality were varied. This resulted in eight experimental conditions corresponding to the eight cells of a 2 (locus) × 2 (stability) × 2 (controllability) matrix. For example, it was indicated that the notes were needed because of low ability (internal, stable, uncontrollable), because the teacher was unable to give clear lectures (external, stable, uncontrollable), and so on. The effects of locus and controllability on judgments of help giving are shown in Table 7.1, which reveals that help was reported as unlikely only when the cause was internal to the subject and controllable (lack of effort); in all other conditions in which the person in need was described as unable to control the reason for the need, help was stated as likely to be offered. Hence the central prediction regarding the importance of perceived personal control was replicated.

Brophy and Rohrkemper (1981) subsequently applied attributional principles in another school-related context (see also Rohrkemper, 1985). They presented teachers with 12 vignettes portraying students with classroom problems. In some, the behavior of the students interfered with general classroom learning. These problems were labeled "teacher-owned" (this does not represent a locus attribution, but rather implicates who experiences the problem). Defiance and hyperactivity exemplified two such teacher-owned problems. Other vignettes portrayed pupils with "student-owned" problems; these difficulties blocked student performance but did not interfere with the learning of others. Shyness and perfectionism exemplify two maladaptive obstacles experienced by students.

Brophy and Rohrkemper (1981) found that teacher-owned problems were perceived by teachers as controllable by the pupils; defiant and hyperactive children were held responsible for their disruptive actions. On the other hand, pupil-owned problems such as shyness were perceived by teachers as not controllable. To cope with these two types of adversities, the

TABLE 7.1 Mean Likelihood of Helping as a Function of Locus and Control of the Cause

Locus	Controllable	Uncontrollable
Internal	3.13	6.74
External	7.35	6.98

Source: Weiner (1980b, p. 189).
Note: The higher the number, the greater the likelihood of help-giving.

teachers selected different strategies. Teacher-related (controllable) problems were treated with punishment and threatening actions. In contrast, given student-owned difficulties,

> teachers' responses . . . featured extensive talk designed to provide support, nurturance, and instruction. . . . The teachers frequently mentioned working on long term goals with these students . . . teaching them coping techniques that would allow them to succeed in situations in which they were now failing. (pp. 306-307)

That is, uncontrollable problems "apparently translated into teaching commitments to help these students" (Brophy & Rohrkemper, 1981, p. 306).

A rather evident conclusion emerges from the disparate investigations conducted by Piliavin et al. (1969), Berkowitz (1969), Barnes et al. (1979), Weiner (1980a), and Brophy and Rohrkemper (1981): Causes perceived as subject to personal control by the individual in need give rise to neglect, whereas causes perceived as uncontrollable by that person generate help. Hence there is an association between a dimension of causality (controllability) and a behavioral consequence (help versus neglect).

This linkage is quite prevalent in everyday affairs and even guides government actions with regard to financial aid. Consider the following analysis of former President Reagan's social policy:

> One cannot avoid the impression that the cuts in social spending the Reagan Administration is proposing are not simply the means toward the end of economic recovery, *they are the ends themselves*. What Reagan proposes to do, by his own admission, is to get the federal government out of the social welfare business.
>
> The Administration has attempted to soften this position by promising to retain the "social safety net of programs" that benefit the "truly needy." In his address to Congress, Reagan defines the "truly needy" as "those *who through no fault of their own* must depend on the rest of us." That definition implies a moral distinction between those whose poverty is unavoidable and those whose poverty is "their own fault." Thus presidential counselor Edwin Meese III has spoken in terms of the "deserving" and the "undeserving" poor. (*Los Angeles Times*, December 8, 1982)

It is evident from this quote that the government is offering to help those with uncontrollable causes of their problems (the "truly" needy) but not those with causes of need that the administration perceives as controllable.

The relation between perceived controllability and help giving is so pervasive that it also apparently has an influence on medical decisions. Brewin (1984b) gave a group of medical students a list of some stressful life events, such as divorce and illness, and ascertained how controllable these events were perceived to be. He then asked whether the students would be willing to prescribe tranquilizers or antidepressants to help someone cope with each of the events. Independent of the perceived severity of the event (the amount of readjustment required), medical students were more willing to prescribe tranquilizers for perceived uncontrollable than for perceived controllable stress.

The Focus on Process and Temporal Sequence

But why should we not want to aid those with needs that are contingent upon personal actions, and why should we want to help those whose needs are due to uncontrollable factors? Common sense dictates that individuals with needs due to controllable factors are responsible (able to respond) and thus must take personal blame, or be held accountable, for their plight. The prior discussion indicated that we do not feel sorry for those who fail and are in control of their own destiny. On the contrary, their failures tend to generate anger. But we do feel pity and sympathy for those who fail and are unable to help themselves. Thus the reason we neglect those with controllable needs may be that this causal perception elicits anger, which in turn evokes neglect. Conversely, we may help those with uncontrollable needs because this perception elicits pity (sympathy), which in turn evokes approach behavior and help. A large research literature has documented that empathic responses (sympathy) promote prosocial behavior (see Miller & Eisenberg, 1988). These motivational sequences can be depicted as follows:

personal control over the cause of need $\longrightarrow$ anger $\longrightarrow$ neglect

lack of personal control over cause of need $\longrightarrow$ sympathy $\longrightarrow$ help

A more general depiction of the sequences outlined above is

$$\text{causal controllability} \begin{cases} \text{anger} \longrightarrow \text{neglect} \\ \text{sympathy} \longrightarrow \text{help} \end{cases}$$

This, of course, is a subset of the even more general sequence:

causal attribution $\longrightarrow$ emotion $\longrightarrow$ action

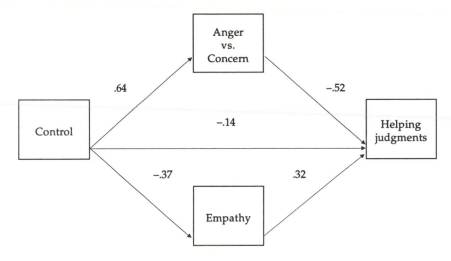

Figure 7.3. Simplified attributional model of helping behavior with results of path analysis. The variables are scored in the controllable, anger, empathy, and high likelihood of helping directions. (From Meyer & Mulherin, 1980, p. 209. Reprinted by permission.)

This sequence also was evident in the discussion of achievement strivings, where causal attributions were linked with pride, guilt, and shame, which were presumed to have motivational functions. However, in the discussion of achievement strivings it was noted that expectancy of success also had a central motivational role.

Before going on to consider the research examining this sequence, the reader has an opportunity to complete an experiment in which attributions, emotions, and actions are included. Please complete Experiment 7.1 before reading on.

Meyer and Mulherin (1980) were among the first to test the hypothesized attribution-emotion-helping sequence. They described hypothetical situations in which an acquaintance was portrayed as asking for financial aid. The reasons for the need of money were manipulated and fit within the eight classifications created by varying the three dimensions of causality. For example, financial aid was said to be required because the acquaintance never liked to work (internal, stable, controllable), because of conditions of high unemployment (external, unstable, uncontrollable), and so on. Subjects then rated the degree to which they would experience each of 25 affects in these situations, their beliefs about how much the person would require aid in the future, and their likelihood of offering financial assistance.

The affective ratings could be described by two distinct dimensions, labeled anger versus concern (a bipolar dimension) and empathy (sympathy). A path analysis was then constructed to account for the helping judgments (see Figure 7.3). Figure 7.3 indicates that perceived causal

Experiment 7.1

The following stories concern a student seeking to borrow your class notes. In each instance the story describes this event and indicates why he is seeking help. After each story, you will be asked to relate your thoughts and feelings about the person involved and what you might do.

At about 1:00 in the afternoon you are walking through campus and a student comes up to you. He says that you do not know him, but you are both enrolled in the same class and he has happened to notice you. He asks if you would lend him the class notes from the meetings last week. He indicates that he needs the notes because he skipped class to go to the beach and generally "take it easy."

Please answer the following questions about the incident.

(1) How much anger and annoyance do you feel toward the person?

a great deal   no anger and
of anger and ————————————————————— annoyance
annoyance

(2) How much sympathy do you have toward the person?

a great deal ————————————————————— no sympathy
of sympathy

(3) How likely is it that you would lend your class notes to this person?

definitely   definitely
would lend ————————————————————— *would not* lend
the notes   the notes

(4) How controllable is this reason? That is, is the reason that he does not have the notes subject to personal influence? One might think that one should be able to control the amount that one is influenced by external sources, or that such distractions are not under personal control.

under   not under
personal ————————————————————— personal
control   control

(Continued)

Experiment 7.1 (Continued)

The following stories concern a student seeking to borrow your class notes. In each instance the story describes this event and indicates why he is seeking help. After each story, you will be asked to relate your thoughts and feelings about the person involved and what you might do.

At about 1:00 in the afternoon you are walking through campus and a student comes up to you. He says that you do not know him,, but you are both enrolled in the same class and he happened to notice you. He asks if you would lend him the class notes from the meetings last week. He indicates that he needs the notes because he was having difficulty with his eyes, a change in glasses was required, and during the week he had difficulty seeing because of eye drops and other treatments.

Please answer the following questions about the incident.

(1) How much anger and annoyance do you feel toward the person?

a great deal
of anger and   _____   no anger and
annoyance   annoyance

(2) How much sympathy do you have toward the person?

a great deal   _____   no sympathy
of sympathy

(3) How likely is it that you would lend your class notes to this person?

definitely   definitely
would lend   _____   *would not* lend
the notes   the notes

(4) How controllable is this reason? That is, is the reason that he does not have the notes subject to personal influence? One might think that one should be able to control the amount that one is affected by this problem (for example, he could have brought a tape recorder) or that such a plight is not under personal control.

under   not under
personal   _____   personal
control   control

control relates positively to anger, negatively to empathy, and negatively with help. Anger, in turn, relates negatively to helping, whereas sympathy relates positively to helping judgments.

The final studies to be discussed in this section on the attributional determinants of helping were conducted by Reisenzein (1986). He differentiated five possible attributional models of helping and then used path-analytic techniques to test these disparate models. The five are as follows:

(1) eliciting stimuli →perceived controllability ⟨ anger ↗ ↘ help ↖ sympathy ↗

This is the model most explicitly tested in the prior investigations.

(2) eliciting stimuli →perceived controllability ⟨ anger ↘ → help ↖ sympathy ↗

In this model, there is a direct as well as an indirect path between controllability and help.

(3) eliciting stimuli → perceived controllability ⟨ anger ↘ ↕ help ↖ sympathy ↗

This model adds a path between anger and sympathy. It may be that these affects are mutually inhibitory or hedonically incompatible.

(4) eliciting stimuli → perceived controllability ⟨ anger ↘ → ↕ help ↖ sympathy ↗

Here the additional paths in Models 2 and 3 are combined.

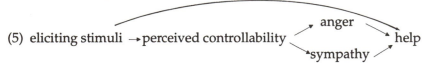

(5) eliciting stimuli →perceived controllability ⟨ anger ↘ help ↖ sympathy ↗

This final model includes a direct path from the eliciting stimuli to help giving. For example, it may be that falling down in a subway elicits more help than a request for class notes because less "cost" is involved, it is more dramatic, physical needs are associated with stronger cultural norms to help, and so forth.

To test these models of helping, Reisenzein (1986) again made use of a role-playing methodology. The two most prevalent situations examined in past attribution research—a person falling down in a subway and someone requesting class notes—again were presented in vignette form. The reasons for the need were varied in the usual manner (drunk versus ill, and went to the beach versus eye problems), and the subjects were queried regarding their perceptions of causal controllability, feelings of sympathy and anger, and likelihood of help giving.

The data in the subway scenario displayed the quite reliable drunk-controllable-anger-neglect and ill-uncontrollable-sympathy-help relations. Model 1 significantly fit these data; the added paths depicted in Models 2-4 did not enhance the effectiveness of the model. Thus a direct path between controllability and help was not supported, nor were the two affects mutually inhibitory. Model 5, however, which added a path between the situation and helping, did slightly improve the fit of the model to the data. This pattern of findings also characterized the class notes scenario, although the inclusion of the path between the eliciting situation and help added relatively little in accounting for the behavioral judgments (see also Betancourt, 1990; Schmidt & Weiner, 1988).

While it is not possible for the reader to test these models fully, it is possible to compare the responses in the uncontrollable (eye problems) and controllable (beach) conditions in Experiment 7.1. It should be found that anger is low in the eye condition, whereas pity and helping are rated highly relative to the situation in which the cause was "going to the beach." The latter reason should elicit much anger, little sympathy, and relatively little help.

Reactions to the Stigmatized:
Further Examinations of Help-Giving

Prior to reading further, the reader should now complete Experiment 7.2.

Now let us return to the topic of this section—social stigmas. Reactions to social stigmas also are amenable to the analyses suggested above—that is, an interpretation that includes responsibility and affective reactions as determinants of intended or actual behavior. Indeed, stigmas already have been introduced; in the investigation reviewed above, responsibility was manipulated by portraying a person as drunk or ill—two stigmas.

A great deal of research has revealed that both the stigmatized person and others search for the origin of a stigma and the possible presence of personal responsibility. As documented by Wright (1983), physically handicapped persons often ask themselves the existential attribution question, "Why me?" and frequently are confronted with the question, "How did this happen?" This search is not limited to physical abnormalities; one often hears such queries as "Why is he drinking so much?" or "What caused the nervous breakdown?" In many instances, however, the stigma itself implies a cause, thus negating the need for further information. For example, drug abuse may automatically be linked with "moral weakness" and AIDS with

Experiment 7.2

Assume that you are the head of a charity organization and are going to dispense $1,000 in funds that you have accumulated. The funds are to go to clinics that treat the following types of people:

(1) paraplegics (loss of limb movement)
(2) obese people
(3) alcoholics
(4) child abusers
(5) Alzheimer's disease sufferers
(6) heart disease patients

Distribute the funds so they total $1,000:

paraplegics	_____
obese people	_____
alcoholics	_____
child abusers	_____
Alzheimer's disease sufferers	_____
heart disease patients	_____

Total $1,000

Now, rank order the groups in terms of your likelihood of giving money, with Rank 1 most likely to receive money, down to Rank 6 being least likely:

paraplegics	_____
obese people	_____
alcoholics	_____
child abusers	_____
Alzheimer's disease sufferers	_____
heart disease patients	_____

---

promiscuous or aberrant sexual behavior. According to the previous analysis, judged responsibility for having the stigma should then guide affective reactions toward the stigmatized person and a variety of behavioral responses including, for example, the help-related actions of charitable donations and personal assistance.

A number of investigations have examined perceived responsibility for a stigma, or what is sometimes referred to as a "social mark" (Jones et al.,

TABLE 7.2 Mean Ratings of Stigmas on Responsibility, Affect, and Helping

Stigma	Responsibility	Blame	Like	Pity	Anger	Assistance	Charitable donations
Alzheimer's disease	0.8	0.5	6.5	7.9	1.4	8.0	6.9
Blindness	0.9	0.5	7.5	7.4	1.7	8.5	7.2
Cancer	1.6	1.3	7.6	8.0	1.6	8.4	8.1
Heart disease	2.5	1.6	7.5	7.4	1.6	8.0	7.5
Paraplegia	1.6	0.9	7.0	7.6	1.4	8.1	7.1
Vietnam War syndrome	1.7	1.5	5.7	7.1	2.1	7.0	6.2
AIDS	4.4	4.8	4.8	6.2	4.0	5.8	6.5
Child abuse	5.2	6.0	2.0	3.3	7.9	4.6	4.0
Drug abuse	6.5	6.7	3.0	4.0	6.4	5.3	5.0
Obesity	5.3	5.2	5.7	5.1	3.3	5.8	4.0

Source: Data from Weiner, Perry, and Magnusson (1988).

1984). As already indicated, Beckman (1979) asked both alcoholic and nonalcoholic respondents to rate a number of statements concerning the causes of excessive drinking. Among both groups, the drinking individual was held responsible for drunkenness. In a similar manner, there also have been many reports of connections between obesity and personal responsibility. For example, Mackenzie (1984) stated that fat and thin people share the opinion that fatness indicates a loss of personal control, which is "considered the ultimate moral failure in our culture."

Numerous investigations also have documented that disparate stigmas elicit differential liking and help giving and that those reactions are related to suppositions about personal responsibility for the stigma. For example, obese people often are least likely to be chosen in sociometric studies of friendship and are ranked low on liking when depicted in drawings (Richardson, Hastorf, Goodman, & Dornbusch, 1961; Staffieri, 1967). DeJong (1980) found, however, that when obesity was attributed to a thyroid condition, the overweight individual was relatively liked.

My colleagues and I directly examined the relations among stigma, perceived responsibility, affect, and intended action (Weiner, Perry, & Magnusson, 1988). In these investigations, 10 stigmas (AIDS, Alzheimer's disease, blindness, cancer, child abuse, drug addiction, heart disease, obesity, paraplegia, and Vietnam War syndrome) were rated on responsibility and blame for these conditions, affective reactions of liking, anger, and pity, and help-related actions of charitable donations and personal assistance. Ratings were made on 9-point scales anchored at the extremes with labels such as entirely responsible—not responsible at all and no anger—a great deal of anger.

The data from one representative study are given in Table 7.2, which shows that six of the stigmas were rated low on perceived personal responsibility and blame (Alzheimer's disease, blindness, cancer, heart disease, paraplegia, and Vietnam War syndrome), whereas the remaining four

(AIDS, child abuse, drug addiction, and obesity) were rated high on these variables. Hence stigmatized persons were generally not held responsible for physical problems, whereas stigmas for which individuals were held responsible were primarily behavioral/mental problems. Clearly, whether the "victim is blamed" (a phrase often accepted among psychologists) depends on the answer given to the question, Blamed for what? A more accurate statement is that we judge others, and some of them are blamed.

Table 7.2 also reveals that individuals not held responsible for their stigmas were rated high on liking, elicited pity but not anger, and generated high ratings on judgments of helping. Conversely, persons with stigmas for which they were held responsible were rated relatively low on liking, evoked little pity and relatively high anger, and elicited comparatively low help-giving responses.

It is also of interest that the degree of moral condemnation and the associated affects and behaviors can be altered by communicating further information. For example, when subjects are told that heart disease was caused by smoking and drinking and that AIDS was contracted through a blood transfusion, AIDS is perceived as uncontrollable and heart disease as controllable. This changes the affects and behavioral judgments toward individuals with these stigmas. However, not all stigmas are subject to attributional change; for example, we have not found any way to make a child abuser be perceived as not responsible.

In sum, reactions to the stigmatized are in part based on moral evaluations. Stigmatized people held responsible for their marks are construed as moral failures, which generates morality-related negative affects and correspondent negative thoughts and behaviors. On the other hand, stigmatized individuals not held responsible for their stigmas are considered "innocent victims" and elicit altruism-generating affects as well as positive actions.

Returning to Experiment 7.2, it is likely that the reader was more altruistic toward paraplegics and those with Alzheimer's or heart disease because these are perceived as uncontrollable stigmas; individuals with these problems are not held personally responsible. On the other hand, less charity was probably directed toward the obese, alcoholics, and child abusers, for these groups are held responsible for their problems. Others think they "should" not and "need not" drink, eat, and harm innocent others.

AIDS

There have been great shifts in the government's and the public's reactions toward persons with AIDS. The concept of perceived responsibility sheds light on this fluctuation. When AIDS was initially acknowledged as a serious problem, the response of the government and the population was primarily neglect. From the discussion in this chapter, such a reaction was to be expected, since the perceived cause of AIDS was homosexual activity (and, later, drug use). Table 7.2 shows that both AIDS and drug abuse are perceived as controllable and thus elicit relatively high anger, low pity, and few indications of desire to help (see Triplet & Sugarman, 1987). Subsequently, however, the known population of AIDS victims began to include recipients of blood transfusions, infants of mothers with AIDS, and heterosexuals. Hence AIDS also began to elicit perceptions of non-responsibility ("Public Is Polled," 1987). These perceptions evoke relatively high pity, low anger, and altruistic help (see Weiner et al., 1988). It now appears that AIDS contracted from transfusions has been greatly reduced because of blood testing, there are increased abortions of children of AIDS-infected mothers, and there is some suggestive evidence that the spread of AIDS among heterosexuals is less than anticipated. Thus altruistically motivated help will likely decrease (see Sheer, 1987). Of course, help might still be given, but motivated by fear or cost-benefit concerns, rather than generated by sympathy and caring.

Poverty

The search for causal explanation has been extended to a variety of contexts. In this book I have examined the causes of success and failure in achievement contexts, criminal behavior, AIDS, and a diversity of additional outcomes, events, states, and so forth. Another topic that has received a reasonable amount of attention has been perceptions of the causes of poverty. Investigators have attempted to identify laypersons' beliefs about why people are poor.

Feagin (1972), and subsequently Feather (1974), developed a list of causes of poverty, which were classified into three types: individualistic explanations, such as laziness, which place responsibility for poverty on the poor themselves; structural (social) explanations, such as no available jobs, which hold external economic and social factors responsible; and fatalistic explanations, which blame fate or bad luck. Great diversity in the endorsement of these causes of poverty was found, although American subjects tended to blame the individual more than did Australian subjects.

One possible explanation of the wide range of responses is that differences in causal ascriptions for poverty are influenced by ideological variation. A link between ideology and causal explanation has long been recognized. As stated by Lane (1962), "At the roots of every ideology there are premises about the nature of causation, the agents of causation, and appropriate ways for explaining complex events" (p. 318).

To explore this hypothesis, Zucker and Weiner (in press) first gave their subjects a conservatism scale to ascertain their political ideology on a dimension ranging from conservative to liberal. Then the participating subjects rated a number of causes of poverty representing individualistic, social, or fatalistic alternatives. In addition, the subjects indicated the controllability of the causes, the blame given that causal perception, anger

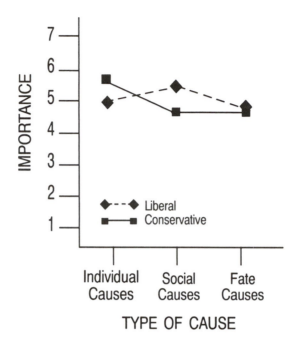

Figure 7.4. Causal importance as a function of political ideology. (From Zucker & Weiner, in press.)

and pity, and made judgments regarding two types of help giving: personal help and social welfare.

As shown in Figure 7.4, conservatives endorsed individualistic causes to a greater extent than did liberals, who in turn rated social causes as more important than did the conservatives. In addition, conservatives also expressed more blame and less pity for the poor and judged them to be less deserving of help than did liberals.

Further analyses are shown in Figure 7.5, which depicts the relations between the judgments. Figure 7.5 reveals that, as already indicated, conservatism relates negatively to perception of social causes and positively to perception of individual causes of poverty. These, in turn, relate to perceptions of responsibility (personal controllability). When the poor are judged as responsible, they are reacted to with anger and no pity. Affects, in turn, determine personal help—when the poor are pitied, personal help would be extended, but not when they are reacted to with anger. Welfare, however, is also directly determined by perceptions of responsibility and ideology, so that decisions about helping that do not involve personal intervention seem in part to be directly determined by thoughts as well as affect.

In sum, while all individuals act as judges of the impoverished, some persons are harsher in their evaluations than are others. In the case of poverty, one determinant of blame, responsibility, and the evoked affects

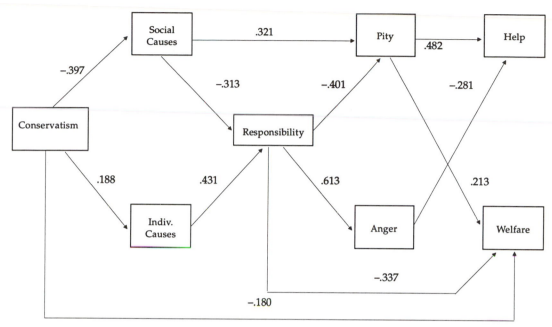

Figure 7.5. Path model relating perceived causes of poverty to helping. (Data from Zucker & Weiner, in press.)

of pity and anger is political ideology. Conservatives tend more to blame the person, and liberals tend more to blame society. These tendencies have far-reaching consequences, particularly regarding intentions to help.

Aggression

There is growing interest in what is known as the social-cognitive approach to the study of aggression. As explained by Dodge and Crick (1990):

> This theory of aggressive events considers the cognitive processes involved in an individual's response to a provocative social stimulus . . . [and] relies heavily on an understanding of how individuals perceive cues, make attributions and inferences about those cues, generate solutions to interpersonal cues and problems, and make behavioral decisions about how to respond to those problems (including decisions to aggress). . . . The social-cognitive theory maintains that an aggressive response is not inevitable but, rather, is contingent on specific thoughts and patterns of processing information. (p. 9)

This perspective has been supported by an array of empirical evidence. In this context, what is most pertinent is the relation between aggression and a tendency to make incorrect inferences about the intentions of others (Dodge & Coie, 1987). A number of studies report that aggressive children display a marked attributional bias to infer hostile intent following a peer-instigated negative event, such as being shoved while waiting in line. This bias is particularly evident when the cause of the event is ambiguous (see review in Dodge & Crick, 1990). Biased intentionality, in turn, has been postulated to lead to retaliatory behavior.

More generally, it is suggested here that even among nonaggressive populations, the person who believes that another acted with malicious intent feels justified in the endorsement of aggressive behavior. That is, the knowing judge recommends punishment for the wrongdoer. One dysfunctional mechanism concerning aggressive children, then, is that they more often inappropriately assume hostile peer intent in situations of attributional uncertainty than do nonaggressive children.

Guided by the judge metaphor of motivation, and the finding that helping behavior is mediated by the emotions of sympathy and pity, it has been suggested that aggressive behavior also is emotionally mediated, in this case by the affect of anger (see Berkowitz, 1983; Ferguson & Rule, 1983). Specifically, following an aggressive action, individuals search for the cause of that act. If the cause is perceived as intentional and/or the person could have volitionally controlled the act, then anger is experienced. Anger, in turn, leads to retaliation. On the other hand, if intention and control are not inferred, then anger is not experienced and the behavioral consequence of aggression is not displayed.

In one test of this application of attribution principles to aggression, Graham, Hudley, and Williams (in press) gave children labeled as aggressive or nonaggressive a set of scenarios describing negative outcomes initiated by a peer. For example, in one story a child dropped his homework and it was stepped on by that peer. The causes of the outcome were prosocial (the peer stepped on the paper so it would not blow away), accidental, ambiguous, or hostile (the peer laughs and says, "Tough luck!").

The subjects then made judgments about the intentions of the peer, their own feelings of anger, and the likelihood that they would behave aggressively toward the peer. It was found that aggressive adolescents perceived the peer's actions as more intentional than did the nonaggressive children, thus replicating prior findings. In addition, they reported greater anger and were more likely to endorse hostile behavioral options. Finally, in general there were systematic relations among perceptions of intent, anger, and aggressive judgments, with anger tending to mediate the relation between intent and retaliation (also see Betancourt & Blair, in press).

In sum, judges may help or they may punish, depending on the situational context. Altruism and aggression are theoretically complementary motivational domains, and in both evoked emotions organize and regulate adaptive behavior (see Thompson, 1990). From an attributional perspective, both domains can be represented with thinking-feeling-behaving sequences that include both rational and emotional components, or Godlike implications.

Interpersonal Relationships

Thus far, altruism and aggression have been examined. I now turn to more long-term social relationships and the determinants of acceptance and increased bonding versus rejection and withdrawal from the relationship. Three areas of research are briefly considered: peer acceptance and rejection, marital happiness and distress, and family approval and disapproval.

Peer Acceptance and Rejection

The area of peer relations has been an active research topic, and a great deal is known about children who are rejected by their peers (see Hymel & Rubin, 1985). Children who are not accepted tend to be aggressive, unattractive, and/or socially withdrawn. However, while children tend not to accept peers who display nonnormative characteristics, their reactions vary according to the type of deviance. Children who display aggressive, antisocial, or hyperactive behaviors are rated as least liked, whereas physically handicapped, mentally disabled, and socially withdrawn children tend to be more "preferred" among the deviant groups (see Sigelman & Begley, 1987).

These differential reactions can be understood from the judge perspective presented in this chapter. Aggressive and hyperactive children are held responsible and blamed most by their peers, whereas physically disabled and mentally impaired children are perceived as least responsible and are least blamed for their plights. Thus, consistent with the prior discussion, two proposed motivational sequences pertinent to peer rejection are as follows:

deviance
(aggressive & hyperactive) →controllable →blame →rejection

(physically handicapped) →uncontrollable →no blame →less rejection

To test these hypothesized relations, Juvonen (1991) had children rate their classmates on measures of social acceptance and rejection. The children also described three peers who were most "different" from others; how responsible these deviant classmates were for their states; affective reac-

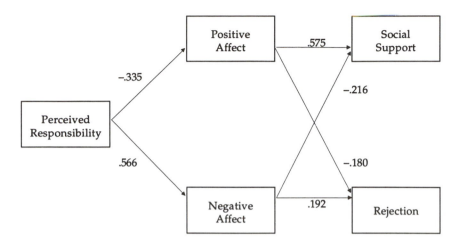

Figure 7.6. Causal model relating responsibility for deviance to social support and rejection. (From Juvonen, 1991, p. 679.)

tions of sympathy, liking, anger, and disliking toward those peers; and whether or not they would help these classmates if they were in need.

Figure 7.6 shows the analyses of these data. The figure reveals that perceived responsibility relates negatively to the positive affects and positively to the negative affects. For example, those who are aggressive are given least sympathy and evoke most anger. Positive affect, in turn, positively relates to support and negatively to rejection, while the reverse is true of anger and negative affect. Thus hyperactives, for example, are rejected, and this is mediated by attributions of personal responsibility and anger. In addition, emotions but not thoughts (attributions of responsibility) are proximally linked to behavior.

What is evident, then, is the same general motivational sequence depicted in the study of altruism and aggression. In this case, peer rejection and acceptance are part of the general evaluation process of considering others who are deviant as "good" or "bad," which in part determines their place in the social network.

Marital Happiness and Distress

Marital dissatisfaction is the most common reason people seek psychological help in the United States. While early research in this domain primarily monitored only the behavior of marital partners, more recent studies have addressed the cognitive and affective components of marital interaction. The most thoroughly researched topic in this emerging area concerns attributions that spouses make for events that occur in the marriage (see review in Bradbury & Fincham, 1990). One of the major findings

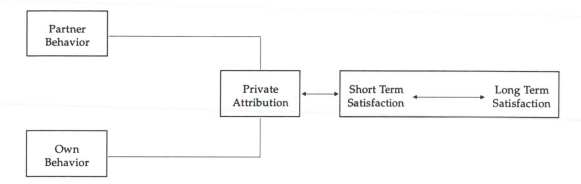

Figure 7.7. A framework relating attributions, behavior, and marital satisfaction.

in this research is that there exists an association between "marital dissatisfaction and the tendency to view positive partner behavior as less intentional . . . , motivated by selfish concerns, and less worthy of praise," as well as between marital dissatisfaction and a tendency to infer more intent and more negative intent for negative relationship events (Bradbury & Fincham, 1990, pp. 5, 14). Hence partners judge each other concerning why positive or negative events occurred. If the event is bad, for example, and if one spouse perceives that the other has done this act intentionally, then the marital bond is strained. This hypothesized sequence is depicted in Figure 7.7.

Of course, it also could be argued that if the marriage is under stress, then the partners tend to perceive that negative acts are intentionally caused. On the contrary, however, Bradbury and Fincham (1990) offer suggestive evidence that attributions actually precede the onset of marital distress. However, the causal role of causal cognitions remains an unresolved issue, and affective considerations remain to be incorporated into this analysis.

Family Approval and Disapproval

There are many situations in which there is disagreement about the perceived causes of a negative event or outcome. This disagreement may be between family members, and often includes issues of responsibility and blame.

One specific area of disagreement concerns the causes of depression. It has been documented that those interacting with depressives, including family members, often experience anger (Coates & Wortman, 1980) and perceive that those depressed are responsible for their own state (Sacco &

Dunn, 1990). That is, it is believed that depressed persons should be able to control and thereby change their affective state and maladaptive behaviors (see Hooley, Richters, Weintraub, & Neal, 1987; Sacco, Milana, & Dunn, 1985). However, it appears that depressives sometimes believe that their emotional valley is not subject to volitional control and change. Thus sympathy and concern are the "deserved" emotional supports. This incongruent emotional fit concerns the issue of whether the depressed person is sick and good or is committing a sin and is bad.

Attributions of responsibility for other negative states revolve around a similar set of issues. For example, as already indicated, hyperactive children are often perceived as responsible for their behavior, and they tend to elicit anger and no help from teachers as well as peers (Brophy & Rohrkemper, 1981). This is in contrast to shy and withdrawn pupils, who are perceived by both teachers and peers as not responsible for their plights and are offered sympathy and help.

Prescription of medication for hyperactivity, however, implies that the problem is one that the person cannot control without outside aid. Whalen and Henker (1976) point out that when hyperactivity is attributed to inborn, neurological factors, both the children and the parents are less likely to blame themselves or one another. New information, then, is used in a rational manner to alter judgments and negative evaluations.

Achievement Appraisal

I shall now turn back to the achievement domain. We will see that achievement evaluation is subject to the same analyses as those given for helping behavior, general reactions to the stigmatized, aggression, and rejection.

A voluminous literature exists regarding the determinants of the evaluation of individuals in achievement contexts (at school, in sporting competition, on the job). In some of this research, the perceived responsibility for success and failure has been varied, and the influence of this causal property on evaluation has been assessed. A series of investigations by Weiner and Kukla (1970) provided the prototypical evaluation method. Students were described as succeeding or failing on an exam. This outcome information was factorially combined with descriptions of each student's ability level and effort expenditure. Thus, for example, in one condition a student was described as high in ability, low in effort, and failing an exam, whereas in a contrasting condition another student was characterized as low in ability, high in effort, and succeeding. The subjects were asked to evaluate (provide feedback to) each of these students. The reader also can participate in this research, which is given in Experiment 7.3. Please do that now before reading on.

Experiment 7.3

Evaluate these eight hypothetical students using a 10-point scale, ranging from +5 for the highest reward to –5 for the maximum punishment.

Student	Ability	Effort	Outcome	Student Feedback (Evaluative Judgment)
1	high	high	success	_____
2	high	high	failure	_____
3	high	low	success	_____
4	high	low	failure	_____
5	low	high	success	_____
6	low	high	failure	_____
7	low	low	success	_____
8	low	low	failure	_____

Calculations for main effects:

    success (lines 1, 3, 5, 7)   =

    failure (lines 2, 4, 6, 8)   =

        difference   =

    high effort (lines 1, 2, 5, 6)   =

    low effort (lines 3, 4, 7, 8)   =

        difference   =

    low ability (lines 5, 6, 7, 8)   =

    high ability (lines 1, 2, 3, 4)   =

        difference   =

Magnitude of the main effects: (difference scores)

		Rank (1-3)
outcome	_____	_____
effort	_____	_____
ability	_____	_____

It is presumed here that students are perceived as responsible for their effort expenditure, in that effort is subject to volitional control and change. Lack of effort particularly activates thoughts of responsibility, since not trying is carried out "knowingly and recklessly" (Fincham & Jaspers, 1980). On the other hand, it also is presumed that students are not perceived as responsible for their level of ability, which in this research is intimated to be a fixed characteristic.

The data from one investigation reported by Weiner and Kukla (1970) are shown in Figure 7.8. The outcomes represented ranged from excellent (exc) through fair, borderline (border), moderate failure (mod fail), and clear failure (clear fail). Furthermore, evaluation ranged from maximum

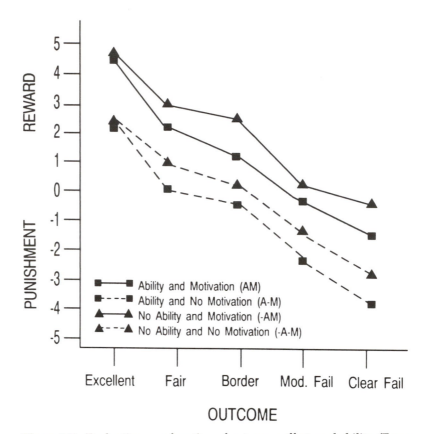

Figure 7.8. Evaluation as a function of outcome, effort, and ability. (From Weiner & Kukla, 1970, p. 3. Copyright 1970 by the American Psychological Association. Reprinted by permission of the publisher.)

reward (+5) to maximum punishment (–5). Figure 7.8 reveals, as one would expect, that positive outcomes were rewarded more (punished less) than were negative outcomes. Of greater importance in the present context, high effort or motivation (M) was rewarded more for success and punished less for failure than was lack of effort or motivation (–M). Lack of effort accompanied by high ability (A-M), which is the causal configuration in which the student is clearly responsible for failure, elicited the greatest punishment. These data suggest that it is most immoral not to utilize one's capacity. The general pattern of data shown in Figure 7.8 has been replicated in many cultures, including Brazil, England, Germany, India, and Iran. The findings have also been documented in actual classrooms, work environments, and athletic settings (see review in Weiner, 1986).

This pattern also should be evident in the reader's ratings, which should especially show that the combination of low ability, high effort, and success is maximally rewarded, whereas that of high ability, low effort, and failure is maximally punished. Thus achievement evaluation also is a moral evaluation. It is considered by others to be immoral not to perform to one's maximum capabilities.

The investigation by Weiner and Kukla (1970) and others guided by that paradigm have not collected affective data, so the mediating role of anger and sympathy cannot be determined. Nonetheless, there is an abundance of evidence that students who do not try evoke anger, whereas students who are low in ability elicit pity (see, for example, Weiner, Graham, Stern, & Lawson, 1982). In one investigation, Stahelski, Patch, and Enochson (1987) replicated the Weiner and Kukla procedure but also obtained affective ratings. They found that surprise was the dominant affective reaction by others given failure paired with both high ability and high effort; sympathy and pity dominated the ratings when there was failure paired with low ability and high effort; and anger and disgust were the most evident emotions given high ability, low effort, and failure. Although these data do not directly address the issue of affect as a mediating variable, they are consistent with the judge argument that has been put forth.

Impression Management Techniques

Excuse Giving

It is evident from the data presented thus far that there are advantages to not being considered personally responsible for needing aid, for having a particular stigma such as AIDS or poverty, for being aggressive or deviant, or for failing an exam. It would therefore be functional for the needy, the stigmatized, the aggressive and rejected, and the failing to manipulate perceptions regarding responsibility and in so doing control or alter affective reactions and their correlated consequences. For example, one might want to make potential lenders think one has tried when one needs class notes, to make potential friends think one's obesity is due to a glandular dysfunction rather to overeating, and to make teachers believe one's failure was due to temporary illness. One way this impression management might be accomplished is by consciously providing false public information or reasons for a need, stigma, outcome, or such. In this context, substituting a false cause for a true cause in a public setting will be called an excuse (*ex* = from, *cuse* = cause). Reducing responsibility, blame, and anger have been identified as among the main purposes of excuse giving (Weiner, Amirkhan, Folkes, & Verette, 1987; Weiner, Figueroa-Muñoz, & Kakihara, 1991).

The role of responsibility, blame, and anger in excuse giving can be readily illustrated in the breaking of a social contract—for example, not appearing for a social engagement or arriving late. This behavior typically elicits attributional search; the "wronged" person is likely to ask, "Why didn't you show up?" or "Why are you so late?" In addition, that person

TABLE 7.3 Excuse Classification as a Function of Experimental Condition

	Experimental Condition		
Excuse Classification	Bad Excuse	Good Excuse	Any Excuse
Not responsible	2	15	11
Accept responsibility	13	0	2

may display irritation or anger. The issue raised here is, What does the transgressor do to mitigate this anger?

To explore this question, my colleagues and I asked college students to recall recent occasions when social contracts had been broken and to provide the true and false reasons that were communicated, as well as any uncommunicated (withheld) reasons (Weiner et al., 1987). We also asked the participants how angry the recipients of the communication actually did feel when receiving the reasons and how they might have felt had the withheld reasons been known.

Analysis of the withheld (true) reasons revealed that they were ones for which the social transgressor would be held responsible. These reasons primarily were negligence (forgetting) and intentional actions (e.g., "Decided to go to another party instead"). On the other hand, the communicated false reasons (lies) absolved the wrongdoer of responsibility. The four main categories of excuses were transportation problems (e.g., "My car broke down"), work/school demands (e.g., "I had to do homework"), prior commitments (e.g., "I had to take my parents to the airport"), and illness. Other data also revealed that the recipient of the communication was rated higher on anger when it was assumed that the withheld (real) explanation was known, as opposed to the actual reaction when the false communication (the excuse) was given. Data confirming associations among responsibility for a social transgression, anger, and response withholding have been reported among children ages 5-12 (Weiner & Handel, 1985; Yirmaya & Weiner, 1986).

Laboratory investigations have confirmed these findings. In one pertinent study reported by Weiner et al. (1987), subjects were detained by the experimenter so that they would arrive late for an experiment in which another student was participating. In three experimental conditions, the instructions to the tardy subject were to (a) give an excuse that would make the waiting person angry, (b) give a "good" excuse, and (c) give any excuse. Classification of the excuses revealed that "bad" excuses conveyed that the transgressor was personally responsible for being late (see Table 7.3). The content of these excuses again primarily involved forgetting and intended actions. On the other hand, the "good" excuses communicated that the transgressor was not responsible for being tardy. These excuses primarily concerned transportation problems, other commitments, and so forth. Finally, when instructions were to give any excuse, "good" excuses were given. Other ratings gathered in the study revealed that those giving bad excuses (ones for which they were held responsible) elicited more unfavorable emotions, negative personality evaluations, and social rejection than persons giving a "good" excuse or "any" excuse.

In sum, there is a naive belief that anger is in part influenced by causal ascriptions concerning why a social contract has not been fulfilled. To ward off these negative consequences, people may withhold the truth (lie), substituting explanations they anticipate will lessen anger. These good or functional excuses relieve the transgressor of personal responsibility. That is, excuses for a broken social contract are given to foster the perception that the wrongdoer is a "moral person." This certainly increases the likelihood that the relationship will be maintained. Hence the motivational sequence apparently is as follows: behavior (social transgression) → perceived or actual personal responsibility → anticipated anger from other → excuse → offset of personal responsibility → offset of anger → increased likelihood of social bonding.

Confession

Excuse giving is but one method to reduce perceived responsibility and in so doing modify others' anger. Among the other possible "accounts" that are used, or techniques of impression management, are denial of wrongdoing, apology, and confession. In this context, confession is of special interest inasmuch as in a confession there is acceptance of responsibility and personal blame. This acknowledgment of sin also may be accompanied by reparation (restitution). Yet this admission of responsibility has the paradoxical effect of reducing responsibility and eliciting forgiveness.

It should not be surprising that there is a confession-forgiveness association, given that this relation is even found in aphorisms, as in the saying "A fault confessed is half forgiven." Writings in the Scriptures also point to a relation between confession and forgiveness. It is clearly stated that confession is the *conditio sine qua non* for Divine pardon. In the Saint John affirmation of the Divine, it is written: "If we confess our sins, He is faithful and righteous to forgive us" (I John 1:9a). Prayers also are based on this belief; witness the supplication, "I have sinned, O Lord; forgive me." Hence confession to fellow humans demonstrates implicit acceptance of the belief that others also can be Godlike, and will forgive.

Why might confession give rise to forgiveness? That is, what theoretical tools and mediating processes are available to account for this hypothesized relation? To answer this question, we turn to correspondent inference theory as espoused by Jones and Davis (1965) and to some tenets of attribution theory.

It has been contended that a confession signals recognition of the basic rule that has been violated and reaffirms that the transgressor values that rule (Darby & Schlenker, 1982). Hence accepting personal responsibility may alter inferences about the person who violated expectations and social norms and restore perceptions of that person's moral character. As Blumstein et al. (1974) cogently write:

> An offender may also return to a proper moral position by a display of penitence. By showing respect for the rule he broke, the offender lays claim to the right to reenter the moral graces of the offended party who, by demanding an account, becomes the momentary guardian of responsibility (Goffman, 1971, p. 107). Showing penitence, like claiming reduced responsibility, splits the identity of the offender. He asserts his own guilt for the act and accepts the momentary blow to his moral character, while at the same time reaffirms his overriding righteousness (awareness of the rules) and acknowledges the offended's rights to demand an account (Gusfield, 1967, p. 179; Sykes & Matza, 1957, p. 666). (p. 552)

According to the prior analysis, the linkage between the negative act and the correspondent inference of unfavorable personality characteristics of the actor is lessened by the carrying out of a confession. That is, the behavior and the intention that produced it are less likely to be perceived as corresponding to some underlying dispositional property of the person. When viewed from a correspondent inference perspective, confession is then presumed to have the same severing effect on act-to-disposition correspondence as does information that all others have engaged in the same action, the existence of situational constraints that did not allow the confessor choice in his or her behavior, and the presence of mitigating circumstances (Kremer & Stephens, 1983). These factors also reduce perceived personal responsibility and trait inferences.

Confession is anticipated to have other consequences in addition to altering perceptions of responsibility and moral character. Guided by the prior discussion of correspondent inference, confession is expected to result in attributions that are both more external and more uncontrollable by the confessor. The specific effects revealed in the prior pages—decreased anger, increased sympathy, and reduced negative repercussions of the untoward act—also should then be displayed.

In a series of experiments examining the effects of confession, Weiner, Graham, Peter, and Zmuidinas (1991) had subjects respond to vignettes of political figures who were accused of a financial misdeed. The politicians either denied the deed or gave a full confession. In a variety of situations and conditions, it was found that confession invariably resulted in a more positive impression of the doer of the misdeed, as well as reduced anger, level of recommended punishment, and so on.

In sum, there are ways to sway the actions of a judge. One can give an excuse and thereby disclaim responsibility, or confess and assume responsibility for the act while claiming one is a responsible person. What is evident, then, is that we know that others are judging us, and techniques have developed to influence those judgments. These influence attempts primarily relate to perceptions of responsibility.

SUMMARY

In this chapter the "person is a judge" metaphor has been introduced. The judge metaphor became prevalent because (a) the "person is a scientist" metaphor and the associated implication of complete human rationality was increasingly called into question; (b) emotions began to play an increasingly important role in the psychology of motivation, with specific affects, based entirely on cognitive appraisals, given specific directional functions; and (c) the psychology of motivation turned from intrapsychic phenomena to interpersonal concerns.

The "person is a judge" metaphor is directly linked with attribution theory, inasmuch as attribution theorists contend that causal controllability (and the associated concept of personal intentionality) gives rise to the other-directed affects of pity and anger. These emotions, in turn, mediate a variety of actions, including altruism and help giving to those with stigmas such as AIDS and poverty, aggression, rejection, and achievement evaluation. In these disparate social domains, individuals construe whether or not others are responsible for needs, stigmatized states, aggressive acts, deviance, or failures. If the persons are judged responsible, then lack of help, aggressive retaliation, rejection, and punishment are likely, mediated by the affective reaction of anger. On the other hand, if they are judged not to be responsible, then pity and sympathy are the affective reactions and they are helped, are not aggressed against, are relatively accepted by the social group, and are not punished for failure.

Because of the anticipated punitive responses directed toward individuals who are perceived to be responsible for negative acts, failures, social transgressions, and the like, strategies are used by "wrongdoers" to alter the impressions others have of them and to convince others that they "could not have done otherwise." Excuse giving, in which an uncontrollable cause is communicated to replace a controllable cause, is one effective strategy. In addition, at times admitting responsibility and confessing has the ultimate function of reducing the belief that the offender is a "bad" person, thereby increasing forgiveness.

In considering this set of problems, attribution theorists have addressed one of the most basic philosophical and psychological issues—the existence of free will. It is evident that the naive person believes that others do have free will, or the ability to act or not act, and bases social judgments and interpersonal behaviors on this belief. In addition, it also is accepted that some actions and states are determined; that is, the person is not free to act otherwise. The Godlike evaluator takes note of this, for one of the basic dimensions along which the world is construed is that of controllable-uncontrollable. Furthermore, the world also is construed along an evaluative dimension, so that external objects as well as the self are considered to be "good" or "bad." These two levels of interpretation and evaluation now play an important part in the study of human motivation. Hence, just as Christian theology was in part responsible for Cartesian dualism, the separation of humans from infrahumans, and the metaphors of the person as Godlike and the person as a machine, it also is in the background for the disparate Godlike metaphors and the dominance of judgments and behaviors guided by the perceived worth of others.

Review, Theoretical Comparisons, and Final Comments

In this book I have attempted to place the major theories of motivation within a broad historical framework and within a metaphorical context. The shortcoming of this endeavor is that the metaphors are not entirely appropriate, generating the fear that they do not adequately represent the foundations for the theories that have been discussed. For example, it was argued that (a) Freud adopted a machine metaphor, although he dealt with mental processes, including the unconscious; (b) Lewin adopted a machine metaphor, although he was a phenomenologist, believing that behavior depends on the subjective interpretation of the world; (c) expectancy-value theorists adopted a Godlike metaphor, although God is not conceived as calculating probabilities and selecting the most hedonic goal; (d) attribution theorists adopted a Godlike metaphor, although God also is not conceived as searching for causality; and so on.

On the other hand, every metaphor is limited in this way—contending that a person is a shark might fly in the face of knowledge that this person cannot even swim! Thus it must be understood that only certain aspects of the comparison object "fit" and are illuminating. Furthermore, acceptance of a metaphor, even when flawed, may lead one in unexpected directions. For example, avowal of the Godlike metaphor may have resulted in an examination of the centrality of evaluation in everyday life and realization of the importance of judgments of others as good or bad. Recognizing the broader context of evaluative judgments and using the "judge" submetaphor also produced the somewhat surprising insight that, for example, rejection of a deviant peer and giving an excuse or a confession can be encompassed within the same theoretical network, which is based on the concept of perceived responsibility.

In the initial chapter of this book, I indicated that many metaphors may exist side by side without contradicting one another. For example, use of the machine metaphor and the associated implication that behavior is regulated by energy distribution and employment of a Godlike metaphor suggesting that people are totally knowledgeable about potential goals are not mutually exclusive. Evidence that deprivation of a need and nonattainment of a goal increase the likelihood of approaching alternate and perhaps similar goals, suggested by a hydraulic metaphor as used by ethologists and Lewin, does not disprove that behavior is guided by rationality.

On the contrary, the existence of multiple metaphors calls attention to the multifaceted nature of human motivation. There are many determinants of human action, some derived from a machine metaphor, others derived from a Godlike metaphor, and still others awaiting to be uncovered by as yet unspecified metaphors. As stated earlier, one of the reasons that drive theory died in the psychology of motivation is that it was appraised as "wrong"; humans are not machines, it was ruled. But in some respects we may be considered to be like machines, just as in other respects we may be considered to be unlike machines but to be like scientists or judges. Acceptance of these metaphors allows one to recognize the complexity and the mosaic nature of human motivation.

Diverse influences on specific phenomena and behavior were addressed in the prior chapters, although they were not highlighted and are likely to have been overlooked by the reader. In a textbook organized according to issues rather than theories, multidetermination of action is often the focus of discussion. In a chapter on aggression, for example, the effects of temperature, social class, and family dynamics all might be presented. Conversely, in a book organized around the theme of theories, it is more likely to be the case that a few determinants of aggression are mentioned in each chapter, but the factors that are discussed also would be shown to influence other facets of human behavior, thus documenting the generality of the principles being presented.

In the next section of this concluding chapter, I examine a few motivational topics and briefly review discussions in the prior chapters revealing the manner in which the metaphors and the theories to which they gave rise distinctly address these phenomena. This will call attention to the multifaceted and intricate nature of human motivation.

Altruism and Help Giving

Prosocial behaviors, which include altruistic acts and help giving, are prevalent phenomena in everyday life and therefore are central concerns in the understanding of human motivation. Three of the theories examined in this book directly address altruism: sociobiology, ethology, and attribution theory.

Recall that, according to sociobiology, genes are selfish and the ultimate goal of human behavior is the perpetuation of one's genetic pool. At times, this can be best accomplished by sacrificing oneself or reducing one's "fitness" in order to help others, that is, to increase their likelihood of survival. These others may share one's genetic pool (as do parents and offspring), they may be potential breeders to reproduce one's genes, or they may have "agreed" to help in return if there is a need ("reciprocal altruism"). In Experiment 2.1 it was documented, for example, that most persons would save their 5-year-old rather than their 1-year-old child, and their 20-rather than 40-year-old son or daughter. This was considered support for the sociobiological position in that those selected for help are more likely to reproduce and thus enhance one's own genetic pool. In addition, it was documented that physical features associated with infants, such as a large forehead and a small chin, promote help giving. Clearly, it is in service of one's genetic pool to be motivated to help offspring, thus aiding in their survival.

Ethologists also have addressed infant care and altruism. They have isolated some of the immediate determinants of caregiving, particularly the hormonal readiness that accompanies the birth process. Thus they have identified the proximal and immediate causes of action, as opposed to the distal and ultimate determinants of behavior that have guided the interpretations of evolutionary biology and sociobiologists.

Finally, attribution theorists contend that help giving is mediated by the perception that those in need are not responsible for their plight. This gives rise to sympathy (pity), an emotion having a "go toward" directive function. This position was supported in Experiment 7.1, which documented that the reader was more likely to lend class notes to another student with "eye problems" (an uncontrollable cause of need) than to one who "went to the beach" (a controllable cause).

The machine metaphor, which guides the biological conceptions, has been valuable in identifying some of the determinants of helping that are not in conscious awareness, that "demand" or automatically evoke action with little cognitive intervention. These are among the associated implications of a machine. On the other hand, attribution theorists, directed by the Godlike metaphor that the person is a judge, point out that others are evaluated as good or bad, or as deserving or undeserving, and this determines whether help is offered or withheld.

Which of these explanations is "correct"? Obviously, all are (or none is). The varied interpretations of altruistic behavior, and their metaphorical underpinnings, can all exist with relatively little conflict or exclusiveness. Motivated behavior is complex, and there are advantages and richness that accompany the holding of many metaphors and multiple theories.

Aggression

Inasmuch as antisocial behavior (aggression) and prosocial behavior (altruism) appear to be opposite sides of a coin, it might be anticipated that the theories addressing altruism would also consider aggression, perhaps using the same concepts to deal with these contrasting behavioral patterns. However, this is not entirely true inasmuch as some theories have incorporated aggression but have not been concerned with altruism.

Evolutionary theories, including sociobiology, account for aggression by noting that those most aggressive have an increased likelihood of getting food and mating. Hence the aggressive survive and aggressive genes get passed on to succeeding generations. That is, inasmuch as aggression is a strategy that "works" to perpetuate the genetic pool, it is part of the behavioral repertoire of organisms.

Ethologists have examined the proximal as well as the ultimate determinants of aggression, such as the red belly of the stickleback fish. They presume that one function of aggression is to drive away competitors and hence to spread the species to geographical areas where there is less competition for food. Some ethologists also have suggested that aggression is a basic instinct or drive, striving for expression but blocked until an appropriate stimulus (e.g., the color red) releases an inhibiting mechanism, thus permitting aggressive expression. If this response is not released, it has been argued, then the aggressive energy accumulates and a weaker stimulus can serve as a releaser.

The notion of aggressive instinct also was part of Freudian theory, associated with survival of the self and survival of the species. It was specified to be cyclical in nature and had the properties of aim and intensity, as well as a source and a good object. As ethologists also specified, aggression was believed to be reducible by means of alternative or substitute goal activity. For Freud, this included fantasies or hallucinations that had the identical function as "real" goal attainment, with the consequence of freeing psychological energy. Fantasy behavior was believed to be engaged in if a desired goal was not available or if the higher (ego) structures prevented goal attainment because it might lead to more pain than pleasure.

Like Freud, Hull and drive theorists also addressed aggressive actions but not prosocial behavior. Perhaps this is because, being functionalists, they could not deduce what function or survival value might be associated with altruism (a puzzle that sociobiologists claim to have solved). Here I somewhat shortchanged drive theory, noting only that aggressive drives might be displaced if the avoidance tendency exceeded the approach tendency toward the object of aggressive desires. That is, I examined the selection of objects to aggress against, rather than the origin of aggression.

It is interesting to note that aggression has been more thoroughly considered by mechanistic theorists than by those adhering to a Godlike metaphor, perhaps because aggression is considered an irrational and implosive response. Among the cognitive theories reviewed here, only the attributional conception, and its linkage with the judge metaphor, directly deals with aggression. Attributionists note that if an aversive act toward the self is perceived as having been controllable or intended, then anger is elicited. Anger is a cue to "eliminate" the aversive object, and gives rise to aggressive retaliation or at least a tendency toward overt aggression. Thus aggression is mediated by beliefs about the causes of an act and the elicited emotion of anger.

In sum, the determinants of aggression—its instinctive origin; regulation by principles of energy, conservation of energy, hydraulic spreading of energy, and interplay of structures; its function and goals; and its automatic evocation and unconscious representation—are all consistent with the associated implications of a machine. But there is no doubt that perceptions of causation and judgments of good and bad also determine human aggressive actions. Thus again there is overdetermination of motivated behavior, and the contributions of multiple metaphors and theories are evident.

Achievement Strivings and Expectancy of Success

As might be anticipated, none of the theories guided by the machine metaphor seriously have attempted to account for achievement strivings. However, this motivational domain has been at the center of the Godlike metaphor, and has been the focus of both the expectancy-value (the person is a rational decision maker) and the attribution (the person is a scientist; the person is a judge) conceptions.

According to resultant valence theory as formulated by Lewin and his colleagues, as well as Atkinson's version of expectancy-value theory, individuals know all the alternative achievement-related choices and calculate the expected utility for each, ultimately selecting the most hedonic of the options. Expected utility, in turn, is determined by individual differences in resultant achievement needs, as well as by the expectancy and the incentive value of success and failure. Expectancy is typically influenced by information regarding the difficulty of the task, while incentive value is presumed to be the anticipated pride or shame that accompanies success or failure, respectively. Hence affective anticipations, in conjunction with expectancy of success, pull the organism toward or away from the goal.

In Rotter's variation of expectancy-value theory, achievement strivings are in part determined by the perceived skill versus chance characteristic of the task. This perception influences expectancy of success (as demonstrated in Experiment 5.2), as does prior behavior in the specific task situation, prior behavior in similar situations, and individual differences in locus of control.

Attribution theorists departed from the expectancy-value tradition in the explanation of achievement-related behavior. In the attributional formulation, achievement strivings are based on causal interpretations of past outcomes—that is, whether prior success and failure were due to internal or external causes, stable or unstable causes, and controllable or uncontrollable causes. Expectancy of success is linked with causal stability, and causes have affective consequences. Achievement striving is then determined by expectancy of success and affects tied to causal perceptions that push or goad the organism toward or away from the goal.

The judge metaphor associated with attribution theory also has been applied in achievement contexts, but in the evaluation of the actions of others rather than in the direct determination of behavior. Those who do not try and fail are punished, for they are considered to be responsible for their failure. This is not the case when failure is ascribed to internal, uncontrollable causes such as lack of ability, or to causes external to the person. This was documented in Experiment 7.3.

In sum, although achievement strivings have been examined only by theorists accepting the Godlike metaphor, even here many different behavioral determinants have been identified, and different aspects of achievement-related actions have been examined using the rational and the judge-associated implications of God. The behavioral determinants of achievement-related behavior include individual differences in the need for achievement and locus of control; disparate determinants of expectancy of success, including information about task difficulty, prior performance, and attributions for that past performance; and emotions that push and/or pull the person. And, as might be anticipated, many other factors that influence achievement behavior have been identified by theorists not represented in this book.

Affective Antecedents and Consequences

Emotion has not yet been given adequate attention by motivational psychologists. Its importance has been tacitly acknowledged by virtually all of the theorists who have been discussed, but lip service rather than systematic thinking and research has been the rule. In this section of the chapter, I review how the various theories and their metaphors describe and account for the antecedents and the consequences of affect, and which emotions they consider.

In Freudian theory, anticipated pleasure and pain, or the pleasure-pain principle, is the basic spring of action. These emotions are experienced when desired goals are attained or not which, respectively, frees energy or leaves it bound (cathected). Freud did examine specific affects, including guilt and grief, but these were less integrated into his machine metaphor and were not examined in this book.

Hull and drive theorists also contended that pleasure and pain, again determined by attainment or nonattainment of a goal and subsequent need offset or maintenance, are central in directing action. These affects "stamp in" and perhaps "stamp out" the association between a stimulus and an instrumental response, thus producing learning. This conception has been called a "hedonism of the past" and, as revealed earlier, contrasts with Freud's "hedonism of the future." That is, for Hull affects influence learning (habit strength) and therefore the subsequent direction of behavior, whereas for Freud anticipated emotions influence immediate behavior.

Other drive theorists, including Spence, Miller, and Mowrer, also considered the specific affects of fear and anxiety. These emotional states were believed to be instigated by an aversive stimulus such as shock, or by the pairing of an originally neutral stimulus with an aversive stimulus. These affects were conceptualized as drives or energizers, activating the organism to take action to reduce this drive state.

Sociobiologists, in contrast to the other mechanistic theorists, speculated about the connections between emotions and social control, and the relation between emotions and the effects of an event on one's genetic pool. They contended that certain emotions have arisen to maintain the social order and a balanced social state. Pity, guilt, and gratitude all tend to result in an exchange that benefits the recipient of these affects, whereas anger is a signal that the other should cease engaging in a behavior that is not mutually beneficial. Thus emotions have both behavioral control and communicative functions. In addition, sociobiologists have considered the emotion of grief and its elicitation in situations where an organism's genetic pool has been depleted (see Experiment 2.1).

In sum, hedonism as a motivational goal and determinant of learning and homeostasis as a mechanism are among the emotion-related concepts incorporated by many (but not all) of the mechanists. In addition, some specific affects, including fear, anxiety, guilt, and grief, have been addressed. In discussion of these emotions, there is minimal recognition of cognitive work or appraisal among the emotional antecedents. Rather, emotions typically are responses to an aversive stimulus, nonattainment of a goal, lessening of one's genetic pool, and so on, and primarily (but not exclusively) "crank up" the machine.

In contrast to the environmentally located antecedent stimuli and the restricted range of emotions addressed by the mechanists, theories directed by the Godlike metaphor have expanded the antecedents of emotion to include numerous cognitive variables, and have broadened the range of emotions that have been examined. As already indicated, Atkinson included both pride and shame within his conception, linking these affects to the perceived difficulty of the attempted task. G. Kelly addressed a different subset of emotions, which he related to cognitive structure. For Kelly, anxiety and threat indicate a deficient construct system about to undergo change because of failure to confirm predictions. Attribution theorists have associated the dimensions of causal perceptions to affects including pride, shame, guilt, anger, and pity (see Experiment 7.1). For them, pride, shame, and guilt require a self-attribution for success and failure; anger presumes that others are responsible for a self-related negative action, whereas guilt requires self-responsibility; and pity follows when a negative state or act was not controllable by the other, just as shame seems to require an act not controllable by the self. These emotions then provide messages or information to the actor to go toward or away from, to help or to neglect, to make amends or withdraw, and so on.

In sum, theories guided by the Godlike metaphor have searched for the cognitive antecedents of emotions, assuming that affective reactions depend on the appraisal or meaning given to a situation. The feelings therefore are "logical" or "rational," and one can be "talked out of" or "talked into" particular emotional states. Again it should be emphasized that mechanistic and Godlike approaches are not antithetical—they have pointed out a different set of emotional antecedents, address different emotions, and consider disparate emotional functions.

Behavioral Change

It will come as no surprise to the reader that the different theories that have been examined make quite different recommendations regarding methods of behavioral change. After all, the major schools of psychotherapy, which include psychoanalytic, behavioral, and cognitive approaches, are in part derived from the thinking of Freud, Hull, Rotter, G. Kelly, and others considered in the prior pages. Indeed, Freud, Rotter, and Kelly are among the theorists represented in this book who also were clinical practitioners.

In this section, I will ever so briefly highlight some of the specific intervention techniques suggested earlier in the book as ways to alter maladaptive behavior. Obviously, I will not be reviewing psychoanalytic therapy, principles of behavior modification, and the like; rather, I merely am calling attention to some possible change procedures that vary as a function of the motivational metaphors and theories that have been introduced.

Psychoanalytic theory and ethology both regard instincts as "building up" as a function of the time since the last discharge of instinctive energy. This can result in maladaptive behaviors and expressions toward inappropriate goals, as evidenced, for example, in vacuum behavior. Hence both of these biological conceptions suggest that the "draining" of energy, via sports, artistic expression, fantasy activity, and the like, can be functional and can produce positive behavioral consequences. In contrast, rather than focusing on energy constructs, drive theorists have centered on habits, or learning, when considering methods of behavioral change. Problems can be ameliorated by "stamping in" appropriate responding and "stamping out" inappropriate responding by means of rewards (drive reducers) or punishments (drive inducers). In sum, for the mechanists, change is accomplished by actions that do not involve volitional control or even awareness of the change process by the individual undergoing "treatment."

The cognitive approach to behavioral change, as suggested in the Godlike metaphors, varies across different theories. In Rotter's expectancy-value formulation, maladaptive behavior is viewed as particularly likely given a low expectancy for a highly valued goal. Expectancies can be altered by means of skill training, information that the expectancy is not being "correctly" gauged, and so on. In addition, behavioral change can be reached by emphasizing the value of alternative goals, given that the most highly valued goal is unattainable.

Within G. Kelly's system, behavioral change is directly related to changing one's construct system. This can be produced by means of a variety of methods, including role playing and conscious testing of alternative hypotheses. These should result in a better match between predictions and actual occurrences. Finally, attribution theorists bring about change by altering causal constructions. For example, failure ascribed to low ability may be changed to lack of effort through the use of a model verbalizing that ascription, feedback from the change-producing agent that one's failure is due to lack of effort, and so on. This theoretically results in higher expectancies of success, more guilt, and less shame, all of which should produce motivational increments. In sum, metaphors including the associated implications that the person is rational and a scientist offer a number of avenues for positive behavioral change.

I do feel somewhat embarrassed about discussing major issues in psychotherapy in about one book page. The reader will recognize that injustice has been done and, I hope, will accept this confession while acknowledging that some of the basic principles of psychotherapy can be traced back to metaphysical views about what the person "is."

Theoretical Comparisons

It is evident from the just-completed discussion that the theories of motivation often address similar issues and phenomena, such as altruism, aggression, and achievement strivings, but offer disparate (albeit not necessarily contradictory) accounts. But it is not unusual for each theory to consider some unique behaviors, such as humor by the Freudians or task recall by the Lewinians. In addition to this heterogeneity, the theories presented in the book are unlike one another in some of their fundamental assumptions and beliefs. I will next consider some of these underlying theoretical characteristics, describing the theories as I go along. The overall classification scheme is shown in Table 8.1. The first and main distinguishing feature, which has been the focal point of this book, is whether the theory is guided by a machine or a Godlike metaphor. This is indicated in the first row of Table 8.1, and nothing further need be said about this.

TABLE 8.1 Distinguishing Characteristics of Theories of Motivation

	Biological					Expectancy-Value		
	Psycho-analytic	Ethology	Socio-biology	˙Drive	Gestalt	Atkin-sonian	Rotter	Attribu-tion
Metaphor	machine	machine	machine	machine	machine	Godlike	Godlike	Godlike
Genetic versus culture/ learning	genetic	genetic	genetic	culture/ learning	culture/ learning	culture/ learning	culture/ learning	culture/ learning
Homeo-stasis	yes	yes	no	yes	yes	no	no	no
Hedonism versus mastery	hedonism	neither	neither	hedonism	hedonism	hedonism	hedonism	mastery
Math model	no	no	no	yes	yes	yes	yes	no
Focus and range	sex and aggression; conflict; neurosis; catharsis	repro-duction; aggression	altruism; repro-duction; gender advantages	food and water deprivation; anxiety; conflict; fear; frustration	task recall and re-sumption; conflict; substitution	task choice	expectancy; skill versus chance task	achieve-ment behavior; affect; helping

Genetic Versus Cultural/Learning Determinants

The biologically based theories (psychoanalytic, ethological, and socio-biological) accept that behavior is greatly determined by genetic givens and evolutionary history, as opposed to the culture in which the person is living and learning history. As shown in Table 8.1, all the genetic theories adopt a machine metaphor, but not all the machine metaphor theories also accept the dominance of genetic determinants (e.g., Hullian theory, with its emphasis on reinforcement). In addition, as would be anticipated, the expectancy-value and attributional theories presume that behavior is more a function of culture and learning than it is fixed by inborn factors.

Homeostasis

Four of the five mechanistic theories postulate that organisms are governed by the principle of homeostasis—the tendency to seek a balanced state, where forces are in equilibrium and there are no extant needs. This does not characterize any of the Godlike theories, which are not based on viscerogenic or sexual needs, and sociobiologists do not consider this issue.

Hedonism Versus Mastery as the Basis of Action

The single principle on which most theories of motivation agree is that persons seek to maximize pleasure and to minimize pain, with motivation derived from this fundamental law. But, as shown in Table 8.1, ethologists and sociobiologists seem not to have been concerned with hedonism, instead focusing on survival tendencies without attaching affective inferences. Further, attribution theorists (as well as G. Kelly) presume that mastery or understanding, the work of a scientist, is of greater importance than hedonism in promoting action.

Math Model

Another theoretical characteristic cutting across the mechanical and the Godlike metaphors is the development of simple mathematical statements to describe motivated behavior. Regardless of the guiding metaphor, the most dominant theories of motivation have attempted to isolate the determinants of behavior and to specify their mathematical relations (see Experiment 3.1). The theories and their terms—$D \times H \times K$ (drive theory); Va_g/e (Lewinian theory); $M_s \times P_s \times I_s$ (Atkinson's theory); and E & RV (Rotter's conception)—are very much alike. Each specifies a person variable (a temporary need state or trait), an environmental variable (incentive or reinforcement value), and a component to capture learning (habit strength or expectancy) as the determinants of behavior. The biologically based theories are not involved in this type of motivational endeavor, nor is attribution theory, although sociobiologists and attribution theorists certainly have made important use of mathematical derivations. It is evident that this approach is most closely adhered to by expectancy-value theory, which was derived from decision theory.

Empirical Focus and Range

Perhaps what most distinguishes the theories from one another is their empirical focus, or what the theory has most strived to predict, and their range, or what other facets of motivated behavior are amenable to explanation from this point of view. As shown in Table 8.1, Freudian theory arguably has as its focus and range sexual and aggressive behavior, conflict, neurosis, and catharsis; like Freud, the ethologists closely examined repro-ductive-relevant actions and other behaviors relevant for survival of the self or the species, such as aggression; sociobiologists have concentrated their attention on altruism and reproduction-related behaviors such as courtship and sexual advantages of each gender; drive theorists primarily have considered the energizing effects of hunger and thirst, but they also examined conflict, fear, anxiety, and frustration; and finally, among the machine-guided theorists, Lewin was concerned with the recall and re-sumption of interrupted tasks, substitution, and conflict. Thus it is perhaps surprising to note that conflict and seeking alternate goals are basic themes addressed by those accepting a machine metaphor, not typical implications of a machine. In addition, sexual and reproductive behaviors, and satisfac-tion of needs related to survival of the self and the species, have elicited most inspection by mechanists.

The theories based on Godlike metaphors have been especially con-cerned with achievement strivings. Within this domain, Atkinson was primarily interested in choice among tasks of varying difficulty, Rotter examined expectancy shifts given skill versus chance tasks, and attribution theorists included affective reactions and help giving among their central topics of study.

There may be a principle pertaining to motivational theories that could incorporate much of Table 8.1, but that is unclear to me. It is evident, however, that there is some (but not a perfect) correlation among a few of the characteristics (such as acceptance of genetics as a determinant of behavior and adherence to a machine metaphor). Once a metaphor is established, it brings with it other motivational assumptions.

Barriers to the Formulation of a General Theory of Motivation

Now that the various theories of motivation have been described, both regarding their theoretical structure and empirical base, it might be specu-lated that it is possible to develop a more general theory, one that incorpo-rates the varied motivationally relevant observations examined in this book. I believe that will be a difficult, or more likely impossible, task at this point in time. This book has championed the position that the field is so complex that multiple metaphors not only do exist, but should and must, to account for the diversity of pertinent phenomena. Thus plurality and incommensurability, rather than an all-encompassing theory, will describe the field of motivation for many years to come. What are, then, some of these contrasting phenomena that create empirical barriers to the formula-tion of a general motivational theory?

Homeostatic Versus Nonhomeostatic Phenomena

From the origins of the scientific study of motivation around 1920 until perhaps 1955, psychoanalytic (Freudian) and drive (Hullian) theories dominated the field. Both conceptions are grounded in the notion that individuals strive to reduce internal tension; their fundamental motivational principle is that any deviation from equilibrium produces a motivational force to return to the prior state of internal balance. The prototypical observation from which this tenet may be derived is that of the behavior of a newborn infant. When all biological needs are satisfied—that is, when internal equilibrium is attained and no tension from biological deficits exists—the infant rests. There is a state of sleep or quiescence. The onset of hunger or thirst, which signals biological needs that if unsatisfied may cause tissue damage, gives rise to activity such as reflexive sucking, which may reduce the need state. If the instrumental activity results in goal attainment, then there is an offset of the need and a return to the quiet state. But this tranquility is only temporary; because of the cyclical nature of needs, the behavior is reinitiated. Hence disequilibrium cannot be avoided, and behavior fluctuates from rest to activity and again back to inactivity.

An array of clinical and empirical evidence supports the intuitively appealing homeostatic principle. There can be little doubt that, given a biological deficit, behaviors typically are instigated to reduce that deficit. After all, we generally eat when hungry (if food is available), drink when thirsty, and attempt to flee from pain. Furthermore, some psychogenic (as opposed to viscerogenic) need states can also be conceptualized according to homeostatic principles. For example, conflicting cognitions create a state of "mental disequilibrium"—for instance, I smoke and smoking causes cancer; I like Jane and the president, whereas Jane dislikes the president. The individual then may bring the system back into balance by, for example, discounting the evidence that smoking causes cancer or devaluing his opinion of Jane.

Given the seeming robustness of the homeostatic principle, why should it not provide the foundation for a general theory of human motivation? The major difficulty with this rule of conduct is that the greater part of human behavior cannot be subsumed within the concept of homeostasis. Humans often strive to induce states of disequilibrium: We ride roller coasters, read scary mystery stories, seek new and exciting forms of entertainment, and quit comfortable jobs and even comfortable marriages for more challenge. Furthermore, the prominent psychogenic motivations, such as the desire to attain success, win friends, gain power, and help others, fall beyond the range of homeostatic explanations. Such motivational concerns as hunger and thirst may even be overlooked by a person striving for achievement success, affiliative goals, or spiritual growth.

An additional, although somewhat less central, point is that not all bodily needs instigate behavior. Theorists who posit automatic connections between internal disequilibrium and instigation to action have difficulty dealing with this fact.

To summarize, homeostatic mechanisms often govern viscerogenic or bodily needs and goal-oriented instrumental behavior. Some psychogenic needs may be guided by the same principle. Hence the concept of homeostasis is an important component in a theory of motivation. But homeostasis cannot account for the variety of human actions and most everyday behaviors. It is difficult for a motivational theory to incorporate both the viscerogenic needs governed by homeostatic rules and the vast array of human behaviors that fall beyond the range of this principle.

Hedonic Versus Nonhedonic Actions

An axiom of virtually all the theories of motivation is that organisms strive to increase pleasure and to decrease pain. The unassailable acceptance of hedonism, or what is known as the pleasure-pain principle, characterizes both psychoanalytic and drive theories, as well as the cognitive theories of motivation proposed by Lewin, Atkinson, and Rotter. To repeat a quote used earlier from Freud (1920/1955): "The impressions that underlie the hypothesis of the pleasure principle are so obvious that they cannot be overlooked" (p. 1). In addition to these "impressions," hundreds of experiments document that reward (pleasure) increases the probability of repeating a response, whereas punishment (pain) decreases the probability of the response preceding the negative outcome. Homeostatic theories, derived from biology, and hedonism, derived from philosophy, are closely linked, for hedonic theorists assume that a return to a state of equilibrium produces pleasure.

There can be no doubt that the pleasure-pain principle guides human (and infrahuman) conduct; prior theories have not been remiss in having this principle as their foundation. But reward (pleasure) does not inevitably increase the likelihood of a response, nor does punishment (pain) assuredly decrease the probability of the reoccurrence of the punished behavior. For example, expectation of a reward for the performance of an intrinsically interesting activity can, under some circumstances, reduce the interest in that activity. For example, if one tells children they will get candy for playing a game they like, the children may engage in the game less when this reward is withdrawn because they have come to believe that "playing" is for the purpose of collecting the external reward (Deci, 1975). In addition, success is considered rewarding, but if a task is too easy, goal attainment reduces motivation and produces boredom. And praise for success at an easy task provides information to the individual that he or she is perceived as low in ability, which reduces motivation (see Graham, 1990), whereas punishment reveals that he or she failed because of lack of effort, an attribution that tends to increase motivation.

In addition to the behaviors that are decreased by reward and increased by punishment, Freud pointed out that some of life's activities, including traumatic dreams, games of disappearance (peekaboo), and aspects of transference (reenacting significant conflicts with one's parents through the therapist), apparently do not increase pleasure. The pleasure-pain principle also cannot account for the focus of thoughts on, for example, past or present wrongs that others are perceived as having perpetrated (paranoia), goods that one does not possess but others do (envy), or the success of rivals (jealousy). One might contend that such deployment of attention has instrumental value in that it promotes goal attainment. That is, the unpleasant thoughts or behaviors serve the pleasure principle. Quite often, however, this is clearly not the case. What instrumental value is there in being obsessed over one's neighbors' more beautiful homes or their more considerate children?

If humans do not always act as hedonic maximizers, then other motivational principles are needed. As motivational psychologists progressed from the study of infrahuman to the study of human actions, nonhedonic aspects of thinking and acting became increasingly evident. One of the most important of these other "motive forces" is the desire to understand the environment and oneself, or what might be called cognitive mastery. Cognitive mastery has been thought to instigate behaviors ranging from the acquisition of language to the selection of actions that can reveal information about one's capacities.

Motivational goals are often interrelated and complexly intertwined. For example, cognitive mastery or knowledge aids in goal attainment, which increases pleasure. Thus it might be contended that mastery is subsumed under hedonic motivation. However, some knowledge has no apparent value for reaching end states. A different reason to believe that mastery is incorporated within the pleasure principle is that information search is influenced by the hedonic desire to increase self-esteem and to protect oneself from anxiety. For example, cancer patients tend to compare themselves with other, more seriously ill victims. This promotes the conclusion that life could be worse, a reassuring thought for the sick as well as the healthy (Taylor, 1983). Here again, mastery or knowledge seems to be in the service of hedonic goals. On the other hand, it is also the case that truth is sought even though the information might cause great displeasure. I am sure that the reader can remember being asked a question preceded by the phrase, "Now, tell me the truth . . . ," although the questioner knew full well that the answer might "hurt." Hence cognitive mastery cannot merely be encompassed within the pleasure-pain principle. It is difficult for a motivational theory to incorporate both hedonic-guided and mastery-guided behaviors.

Rational and Conscious Versus
Irrational and Unconscious Behaviors

Many motivated actions are quite conscious and rational: Strategies are consciously selected to help control stress and anxiety (consider the current number of joggers), goal expectancies are calculated, information is sought and processed, and so forth. On the other hand, many aspects of our behavior are quite irrational and/or unconscious: Plans that could control stress and smoking are abandoned, expectancies are biased, information is improperly utilized, and there is great personal delusion. Psychoanalytic theory has best explained some of the apparent unreasonableness in our lives, whereas the cognitive conceptions and decision theories are more adept at dealing with the sensibility of action, although these latter theories are increasingly pointing out the boundaries of rationality.

A general theory of motivation will have to account for the conscious as well as the unconscious determinants of action, and the rational as well as the irrational. I doubt that this can be accomplished with needed empirical precision and theoretical parsimony.

Principles for the Construction of a General Theory of Motivation

A warning was just given that it is unlikely that a general theory of motivation—one that encompasses homeostatic and nonhomeostatic behaviors, actions in service of hedonism and mastery, and behaviors that are based on conscious and rational as well as unconscious and irrational forces—will soon be formulated. There are, nevertheless, some rules that I believe should be followed in the pursuit of a general motivational theory. Some of these are revealed below.

- **A theory of motivation must be built upon reliable (replicable) empirical relations.**

An adequate theory of motivation provides the opportunity for the creation of a laboratory course or some other setting where a variety of derivations from the theory can be demonstrated *with certainty*. This is true in the natural sciences and should apply to psychology as well. One of the reasons for the acceptance and popularity of Skinnerian psychology is the demonstration that the frequency of a response increases when an organism is rewarded for a particular behavior. Watching pigeons play Ping-Pong seems to be a sufficient antecedent for conversion to radical behaviorism.

Most (but not all) of the theories reviewed in this book are associated with a particular "reference experiment" that does always "work"; other empirical studies as well as theoretical growth are then derived from this experiment. For the Hullians, it was known that a variety of indicators of motivation increase with hunger deprivation and with the number of reinforced trials, or habit strength (see Experiment 3.1). The greater time taken to resolve avoidance-avoidance than approach-approach conflicts is among the replicable findings linked with Lewinian theory (see Experiment 4.1). In addition, Rotter's expectancy-value theory in part grew from the replicable findings that typical shifts are greater given performance at skill than at chance tasks (see Experiment 5.2). And attribution theory has among its reference experiments the findings that expectancy shifts are greater given stable than unstable attributions (Experiment 6.2), greater helping is given for uncontrollable than for controllable needs (Experiment 7.1), and there is increased reward and punishment when achievement failure is ascribed to effort, as opposed to ability (Experiment 7.3). I believe that the impact of theories is greatly enhanced when such reference experiments are available to provide a foundation for other research endeavors.

On the other hand, motivational theories also have been deficient in regard to the reliability of their empirical foundations. As indicated earlier, Freudian theory cannot be grounded to a particular, reliable finding. Furthermore, Lewin believed that "all later experimental investigations were built upon this [the greater recall of incomplete than completed tasks]" (p. 240). However, the differential recall observed by Lewin is not a reliable finding. In a similar manner, Atkinson (1964) contended that individuals classified as high versus low in achievement needs exhibit opposing risk preferences when given tasks differing in perceived difficulty. This central prediction from Atkinson's conception is not reliably found, and one suspects this is partially responsible for the lessening influence of his conceptions. Further, differences in expectancy shifts between people labeled internal versus external in their perceptions of control cannot reliably be demonstrated, although this is a fundamental prediction of Rotter's (1966) social learning theory.

One cannot build a theory on a weak reference experiment. Motivational theories must have reference experiments with results as certain as the outcome of mixing two parts hydrogen and one part oxygen, or of giving a hungry rat food when it engages in a particular behavior.

- **A theory of motivation must be based on general laws rather than individual differences.**

Atkinson (1964) has been especially visible and persuasive among the motivational psychologists who argue that individual differences play a central role in the study of motivational processes. As already indicated, in Atkinson's theory of achievement strivings, persons labeled high in achievement needs are predicted to exhibit different risk-taking behavior than persons low in achievement needs. Disparities among individuals are therefore central to the testing of this conception. Atkinson's theory then falls prey to all the complex issues and obstacles faced by trait psychologists. For example, persons are not equally motivated to achieve in all situations; in other words, there is discriminativeness in behavior. Individuals may be highly motivated to achieve in tennis, but not in the classroom, or perhaps not even at other sports. Atkinson's theoretical formulation does not recognize this possibility—individuals are classified merely as high or low in achievement needs. It is not surprising that tests of this theory that occur in many disparate situational contexts often prove unsatisfactory.

In a similar manner, Rotter's current conception of social learning is linked with an individual difference labeled *locus of control*. However, individuals are not equally motivated to have or to relinquish control in all settings, and they might perceive control of reinforcement as possible in some situations but not in others. For example, perceptions of success as due to internal (personal) factors are uncorrelated with perceptions of failure as internally caused. Specificity is not well integrated into the theory, and hypotheses using perception of control as a predictor variable are often disconfirmed.

Given the difficulties of personality measurement and the situational specificity of behavior, it will be more fruitful to search first for general laws rather than to explore person × situation interactions. This can then be followed, if necessary, by the inclusion of individual differences to refine the generalizations that have been made or to uncover more complex associations that might have been overlooked.

An identical position has been expressed by many psychologists. For example, Festinger (1980) poetically stated:

> The philosophical ideas that explain [the ignoring of individual differences] are easy to locate. They are perhaps best expressed in the paper by Lewin on Aristotelian and Galilean conceptions of science. Too much concern with individual differences could create a mask that hid the underlying dynamic processes. These underlying processes had to be discovered. The kind of analogy that existed in our minds was something like the following. It would be hopeless to have tried to discover the laws concerning free-falling objects by concentrating on measuring the different rates of descent of stones, feathers, pieces of paper, and the like. It is only after the basic dynamic laws are known that one can make sense of the individual differences.
>
> The way I have always thought about it is that if the empirical world looks complicated, if people seem to react in bewildering different ways to similar forces, and if I cannot see the operation of universal underlying dynamics—then it is my fault. I have asked the wrong questions; I have, at the theoretical level, sliced the world up incorrectly. The underlying dynamics are there, and I have to find the theoretical apparatus that will enable me to reveal these uniformities. (p. 246)

Although operating from a quite different theoretical perspective, Berlyne (1968) reached the same conclusion. To repeat a quote, he stated:

It is perfectly obvious that human beings are different from one another in some respects but alike in other respects. The question is whether we should first look for statements that apply to all of them or whether we should first try to describe and explain their differences. The behavior theorist feels that research for common principles of human and animal behavior must take precedence. This, he would point out, is how scientific inquiry must proceed. . . . Until we can see what individuals of a class or species have in common, we cannot hope to understand how their dissimilarities have come about or even to find the most fruitful way to describe and classify these dissimilarities. (p. 640)

- **A theory of motivation must include the self.**

There are numerous indications that the self plays a fundamental role in human motivation: Many actions serve to sustain or enhance self-esteem; one's self-concept frequently determines one's thoughts and behaviors; individuals tend to maintain self-consistency in their actions; and self-perception provides one thread to the stability of personality and behavior over time. The concept of the self has been relatively neglected in the study of motivation. It surely did not fit into behavioristic conceptions, which used lower organisms as their main source of experimental evidence. In addition, the cognitive theories of motivation focused on the more manageable concept of subjective expectancy, perhaps preferring to postpone a consideration of the subtle and vague role played by concern with the self. However, the self lies at the very core of human experience and must be part of any theoretical formulation in the field of human motivation.

- **A theory of motivation must include the full range of cognitive processes.**

A broad array of mental processes, including information search and retrieval, short- and long-term memory, categorization, judgment, and decision making, play essential roles in determining behavior. Just as behavior often is functional, aiding in goal attainment, cognitions also serve adaptive functions for reaching desired end states. Cognitive functionalism must play as central a part in a theory of motivation as behavioral functionalism.

Earlier cognitive conceptions of motivation, such as those formulated by Atkinson, Lewin, and Rotter, focused on the expectancy of goal attainment as a major determinant of action. They unfortunately neglected a multitude of other mental structures and processes that influence behavior. This restriction greatly limits the capacity of these theories to account for human conduct.

- **A theory of motivation must include the full range of emotions.**

In reviewing the conceptions of motivation, it was revealed that pleasure and pain are incorporated into virtually all of the theories. In addition,

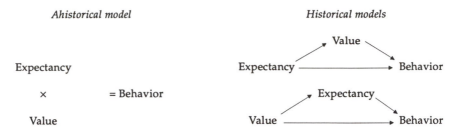

Figure 8.1. Ahistorical and historical approaches to motivation.

a vast array of emotions, including fear, anxiety, anger, threat, sympathy, pride, guilt, and shame, have been addressed at some time by some of the theories. Furthermore, the role of emotion in motivational processes is increasingly being recognized. A general theory of motivation surely will have to include a great diversity of emotions, and give emotion a central role in determining action.

- **A theory of motivation must include sequential (historical) causal relations.**

The prominent theories of motivation, with the exception of the psychoanalytic approach, are ahistorical. These theories attempt to identify the immediate determinants of action, such as drive and habit, or expectancy and value, and specify the manner in which they influence behavior at a given moment in time. Knowledge of the antecedent historical conditions, or why an individual perceives the present situation as he or she does, is not necessary to predict behavior. What is essential is the specification of the present determinants of action.

One of the shortcomings of an ahistorical approach is that the influence of the components of the theory on one another have to be ignored. In expectancy-value theories, for example, if value is biased upward by high expectancy (one likes what one can get), or if high value biases expectancy upward (one expects to get what one likes), then a temporal sequence is implicated. In these instances, the magnitudes of the components in the theory cannot be determined simultaneously; respectively, value cannot be ascertained prior to expectancy, or expectancy prior to value. This is illustrated in Figure 8.1, along with the ahistorical expectancy-value approach.

The ahistorical analysis of motivational processes was enhanced by the growth of parametric statistics, particularly the analysis of variance. This technique enables investigators to determine which factors are affecting the dependent variable at a moment in time, and allows the mathematical relations among the independent variables to be specified. A newer approach in statistical analysis is causal modeling, including path analysis. This methodology helps in uncovering the causal chain of influencing factors. Acceptance of a historical sequence suggests that one should search for the causal relations between the determinants of action.

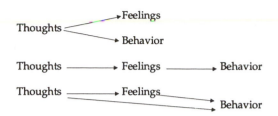

Figure 8.2. Some possible relations among thoughts, feelings, and actions.

One of the essential sequences examined in this book concerns the relations among thinking, feeling, and acting. I have already contended that a theory of motivation should include the full range of both thoughts and feelings. But how do these influence behavior? Many possibilities arise. It might be that (a) thoughts produce both feelings and behavior, or that (b) thoughts antedate feelings, whereas feelings give rise to action, or that (c) thoughts generate feelings, and thoughts and feelings together produce behavior. These possible permutations are shown in Figure 8.2. A historical position permits exploration of these different possibilities.

- **A theory of motivation must be able to account for achievement strivings and affiliative goals.**

A theory has a focus and a range of convenience—observations that can be best explained, and observations to which the theory can be generalized. The focus of convenience of a theory of human motivation should be those activities that are most prevalent in everyday life. It would be unwise to base a general theory of human motivation on very uncommon behaviors. Hence psychoanalytic theory, which is grounded in sexual and aggressive relations among family members, and Hullian theory, which examined the behavior of hungry and thirsty rats, developed conceptual frameworks inadequate to account for the modal activities of humans.

In our culture, two sources of motivation are most dominant: achievement strivings and social bonding. Freud recognized these with the more general terms of *Arbeit und Liebe* (work and love). Most preadults at a given moment are in school, doing schoolwork, engaged in some other achievement-related activity such as sports or a hobby, or with their friends of the same or the opposite sex. Adults typically are working in their selected occupation or are engaged in social activities with their friends or family. Of course, there are many other motivational pursuits: aggression, altruism, curiosity, lust, and power, to name just a few. But the most prevalent concerns are achievement success and social acceptance. Self-esteem has been documented to be determined by experiences of competence and incompetence in the achievement domain, and by acceptance and rejection in the interpersonal arena (O'Brien & Epstein, 1974). These topics therefore should be at the focus of a theory of human motivation.

• **A theory of motivation must consider some additional commonsense concepts.**

As additional metaphors are introduced and explored, surely a number of new insights about human motivation will be attained. Furthermore, with the new metaphors will come previously unknown concepts and novel empirical studies.

Even at this point, however, there are a number of expressions that appear to have motivational significance, yet have not been systematically considered by motivational theorists. Among these terms is *value*. It can often be heard, for example, that an individual "values" achievement success or "values" an object, and therefore that person is motivated to attain a particular goal or object. But how is this translated into the scientific language of motivation? The expectancy-value theorists have not at all come to grips with this problem. Indeed, for Atkinson, value is entirely linked with probability of success and does not make contact with our commonsense notion of "value."

Another of the commonsense terms that must have motivational significance is *interest*. One might say, "I am interested in this type of problem." We know, then, that presentation of this problem will engage motivational processes and result in persistence and working with intensity. But how should this be incorporated into motivational theories? *Importance* is yet another such label that surely has motivational impact. The person on the street might exclaim, "It is important for me to do this!" and the listener can then infer that motivation will be high. Is importance merely another word, a synonym, for motivation, or will it also require incorporation into the systematic study of motivation, along with value, interest, desire, want, and a host of other phrases that permeate everyday language and connect with motivational issues? I believe that these matters should be pursued and these concepts incorporated into the search for general motivational laws.

A CONCLUDING NOTE

Tracing the history of the field of motivation, and examining the major theories and their supporting empirical base, has revealed great vigor and movement. In just about 60 years since the insights of Freud and Hull, there have been major upheavals in the field, metaphors replaced, theories and concepts introduced, and novel research directions taken. As indicated, there are yet many barriers to face in the search for scientific laws, and great complexity in this area. Shortcomings must be admitted, but there can be no doubt that progress has been and is being made.

References

Abelson, R. P., & Rosenberg, M. J. (1958). Symbolic psycho-logic: A model of attitude cognition. *Behavioral Science, 3*, 1-13.

Abramson, L. Y., Metalsky, G. I., & Alloy, L. B. (1989). Hopelessness depression: A theory-based subtype of depression. *Psychological Review, 96*, 358-372.

Abramson, L. Y., Seligman, M. E. P., & Teasdale, J. (1978). Learned helplessness in humans: Critique and reformulation. *Journal of Abnormal Psychology, 87*, 49-74.

Adler, D. L., & Kounin, J. S. (1939). Some factors operating at the moment of resumption of interrupted tasks. *Journal of Psychology, 7*, 255-267.

Allport, F. H. (1955). *Theories of perception and the concept of structure.* New York: John Wiley.

Amsel, A. (1967). Partial reinforcement. In K. W. Spence & J. A. Taylor (Eds.), *The psychology of learning and motivation* (Vol. 1). New York: Academic Press.

Amsel, A. (1990). Arousal, suppression, and persistence: Frustration theory, attention, and its disorders. *Cognition and Emotion, 4*, 239-268.

Amsel, A., & Roussel, J. (1952). Motivational properties of frustration: I. Effect on a running response of the addition of frustration to the motivational complex. *Journal of Experimental Psychology, 43*, 363-368.

Amsel, A., & Ward, J. S. (1954). Motivational properties of frustration: II. Frustration drive stimulus and frustration reduction in selective learning. *Journal of Experimental Psychology, 48*, 37-47.

Amsel, A., & Ward, J. S. (1965). Frustration and persistence: Resistance to discrimination following prior experience with the discriminanda. *Psychological Monographs, 79*(4, Whole No. 597).

Anderson, C. A., & Jennings, D. L. (1980). When experiences of failure promote expectations of success: The impact of attributing failure to ineffective strategies. *Journal of Personality, 48*, 393-407.

Arkin, R. M., & Baumgardner, A. H. (1985). Self-handicapping. In J. H. Harvey & G. Weary (Eds.), *Attribution: Basic issues and applications* (pp. 169-202). New York: Academic.

Arkoff, A. (1957). Resolution of approach-approach and avoidance-avoidance conflicts. *Journal of Abnormal and Social Psychology, 55*, 402-404.

Aronson, E., & Carlsmith, J. M. (1963). Effects of severity of threat on the deviation of forbidden behavior. *Journal of Abnormal and Social Psychology, 66*, 584-588.

Aronson, E., & Mills, J. (1959). The effect of severity of initiation on liking for a group. *Journal of Abnormal and Social Psychology, 59*, 177-181.

Atkinson, J. W. (1953). The achievement motive and recall of interrupted and completed tasks. *Journal of Experimental Psychology, 46*, 381-390.

Atkinson, J. W. (1957). Motivational determinants of risk-taking behavior. *Psychological Review, 64*, 359-372.

Atkinson, J. W. (Ed.). (1958). *Motives in fantasy, action, and society.* Princeton, NJ: Van Nostrand.

Atkinson, J. W. (1964). *An introduction to motivation.* Princeton, NJ: Van Nostrand.

Atkinson, J. W., & Feather, N. T. (Eds.). (1966). *A theory of achievement motivation.* New York: John Wiley.

Atkinson, J. W., & Litwin, G. (1960). Achievement motive and test anxiety conceived as motive to approach success and motive to avoid failure. *Journal of Abnormal and Social Psychology, 60*, 52-63.

Averill, J. R. (1982). *Anger and aggression: An essay on emotion.* New York: Springer-Verlag.

Averill, J. R. (1983). Studies on anger and aggression. *American Psychologist, 38*, 1145-1160.

Bakan, P. (1960). Response tendencies in attempts to generate random binary series. *American Journal of Psychology, 73*, 127-131.

Bandura, A. (1986). *Social foundations of thought and action: A social cognitive theory.* Englewood Cliffs, NJ: Prentice-Hall.

Bannister, D., & Fransella, F. (1971). *Inquiring man.* Baltimore: Penguin.

Barker, R. G., Dembo, T., & Lewin, K. (1943). Frustration and regression. In R. G. Barker, J. S. Kounin, & H. F. Wright (Eds.), *Child behavior and development.* New York: McGraw-Hill.

Barlow, G. W. (1989). Has sociobiology killed ethology or revitalized it? In P. P. G. Bateson & P. H. Klopfer (Eds.), *Perspectives in ethology* (Vol. 8, pp. 1-45). New York: Plenum.

Barnes, R. D., Ickes, W. J., & Kidd, R. (1979). Effects of perceived intentionality and stability of another's dependency on helping behavior. *Personality and Social Psychology Bulletin, 5*, 367-372.

Battle, E., & Rotter, J. B. (1963). Children's feelings of personal control as related to social class and ethnic groups. *Journal of Personality, 31*, 482-490.

Beach, F. (1955). The descent of instinct. *Psychological Review, 62*, 401-410.

Beach, F. A. (1978). Animal models for human sexuality. Sex, hormones, and behavior. *Ciba Foundation Symposium, 62*, 113-143.

Beckman, L. (1970). Effects of students' performance on teachers' and observers' attributions of causality. *Journal of Educational Psychology, 61*, 76-82.

Beckman, L. J. (1979). Beliefs about the causes of alcohol-related problems among alcoholic and non-alcoholic women. *Journal of Clinical Psychology, 35*, 663-670.

Bentham, J. (1948). *An introduction to the principles of morals and legislation.* Oxford: Basil Blackwell. (Original work published 1779)

Berglas, S. (1989). Self-handicapping behavior and the self-defeating personality disorder: Toward a refined clinical perspective. In R. Curtis (Ed.), *Self-defeating behaviors: Experimental research, clinical impressions, and practical implications* (pp. 261-288). New York: Plenum.

Berkowitz, L. (1969). Resistance to improper dependency relationships. *Journal of Experimental Social Psychology, 5*, 283-294.

Berkowitz, L. (1983). The experience of anger as a parallel process in the display of impulsive, "angry" aggression. In R. Geen & E. Donnerstein (Eds.), *Aggression: Theoretical and empirical reviews: Vol. 1. Theoretical and methodological issues* (pp. 103-133). New York: Academic Press.

Berlyne, D. (1968). Behavior theory as personality theory. In E. F. Borgatta & W. W. Lambert (Eds.), *Handbook of personality theory and research.* Chicago: Rand McNally.

Bernard, L. L. (1924). *Instinct: A study of social psychology.* New York: Holt.

Berry, D. S., & McArthur, L. Z. (1986). Perceiving character in faces: The impact of age-related craniofacial changes in social perception. *Psychological Bulletin, 100*, 3-18.

Betancourt, H. (1990). An attribution-empathy model of helping behavior: Behavioral intentions and judgments of help-giving. *Personality and Social Psychology Bulletin, 16,* 573-591.

Betancourt, H., & Blair, I. (in press). A cognition (attribution)-emotion model of reactions to violence in conflict situations. *Personality and Social Psychology Bulletin.*

Bindra, D. (1969). The interrelated mechanisms of reinforcement and motivation, and the nature of their influence on response. In W. J. Arnold & D. Levine (Eds.), *Nebraska Symposium on Motivation.* Lincoln: University of Nebraska Press.

Birney, R. C. (1959). The reliability of the achievement motive. *Journal of Abnormal and Social Psychology, 58,* 266-267.

Blank, T. O., Staff, I., & Shaver, P. (1976). Social facilitation of word associations: Further questions. *Journal of Personality and Social Psychology, 34,* 725-733.

Blodgett, H. C. (1929). The effect of the introduction of reward upon maze performance of rats. *University of California Publication in Psychology, 4*(8), 113-134.

Blumstein, P. W., Carasow, K. G., Hall, J., Hawkins, B., Hoffman, R., Ishem, E., Maurer, C. P., Spens, D., Taylor, J., & Zimmerman, D. L. (1974). The honoring of accounts. *American Sociological Review, 39,* 551-566.

Bolles, R. C. (1967). *Theory of motivation.* New York: Harper & Row.

Bolles, R. C. (1975). *Theory of motivation* (2nd ed.). New York: Harper & Row.

Boring, E. G. (1950). *A history of experimental psychology* (2nd ed.). New York: Appleton-Century-Crofts.

Bradbury, T. N., & Fincham, F. D. (1990). Attributions in marriage: Review and critique. *Psychological Bulletin, 107,* 3-33.

Bradley, G. W. (1978). Self-serving biases in the attribution process: A reexamination of the fact or fiction question. *Journal of Personality and Social Psychology, 36,* 56-71.

Brehm, J. W. (1962). Motivation effects of cognitive dissonance. In M. R. Jones (Ed.), *Nebraska Symposium on Motivation.* Lincoln: University of Nebraska Press.

Brehm, J. W. (Ed.). (1966). *A theory of psychological reactance.* New York: Academic Press.

Brewin, C. R. (1984a). Attributions for industrial accidents: Their relationship to rehabilitation outcome. *Journal of Social and Clinical Psychology, 2,* 156-164.

Brewin, C. R. (1984b). Perceived controllability of life-events and willingness to prescribe psychotropic drugs. *British Journal of Social Psychology, 23,* 285-287.

Brophy, J. E., & Rohrkemper, M. M. (1981). The influence of problem ownership on teachers' perceptions of strategies for coping with problem students. *Journal of Educational Psychology, 73,* 295-311.

Brown, J. S. (1948). Gradients of approach and avoidance responses and their relation to level of motivation. *Journal of Comparative and Physiological Psychology, 41,* 450-465.

Brown, J. S. (1961). *The motivation of behavior.* New York: McGraw-Hill.

Brown, J. S., & Farber, I. E. (1951). Emotions conceptualized as intervening variables: With suggestions toward a theory of frustration. *Psychological Bulletin, 48,* 465-495.

Brown, J. S., & Weiner, B. (1984). Affective consequences of ability versus effort ascriptions: Controversies, resolutions, and quandaries. *Journal of Educational Psychology, 76,* 146-158.

Brown, M., Jennings, J., & Vanik, V. (1974). The motive to avoid success: A further examination. *Journal of Research in Personality, 8,* 172-176.

Bruner, J. S. (1956). A cognitive theory of personality. *Contemporary Psychology, 1,* 355-357.

Buss, D. M., & Barnes, M. (1986). Preferences in human mate selection. *Journal of Personality and Social Psychology, 50,* 559-570.

Carlsmith, J. M., & Gross, A. E. (1969). Some effects of guilt on compliance. *Journal of Personality and Social Psychology, 11,* 232-239.

Carroll, J. S. (1978). Causal attributions in expert parole decisions. *Journal of Personality and Social Psychology, 36,* 1501-1511.

Carroll, J. S., & Payne, J. W. (1976). The psychology of the parole decision process: A joint application of attribution theory and information processing psychology. In J. S.

Carroll & J. W. Payne (Eds.), *Cognition and social behavior*. Hillsdale, NJ: Lawrence Erlbaum.

Carroll, J. S., & Payne, J. W. (1977). Judgments about crime and the criminal: A model and method for investigating parole decisions. In B. D. Sales (Ed.), *Perspectives in law and psychology: Vol. 1. The criminal justice system*. New York: Plenum.

Cartwright, D., & Harary, D. (1956). Structural balance: A generalization of Heider's theory. *Psychological Review, 63*, 277-293.

Chapman, L. J., & Chapman, J. P. (1969). Illusory correlation as an obstacle to the use of valid psychodiagnostic signs. *Journal of Abnormal Psychology, 74*, 271-280.

Chwalisz, K., Diener, E., & Gallagher, D. (1988). Autonomic arousal feedback and emotional experience: Evidence from the spinal cord injured. *Journal of Personality and Social Psychology, 54*, 820-828.

Clore, G. L., Ortony, A., & Foss, M. A. (1987). The psychological foundations of the affective lexicon. *Journal of Personality and Social Psychology, 53*, 751-766.

Coates, D., & Wortman, C. B. (1980). Depression maintenance and interpersonal control. In A. Baum & J. E. Singer (Eds.), *Advances in environmental psychology: Vol. 2. Applications of personal control* (pp. 149-182). Hillsdale, NJ: Lawrence Erlbaum.

Cofer, C. N., & Appley, M. H. (1964). *Motivation: Theory and research*. New York: John Wiley.

Cohen, J., & Hansel, C. E. M. (1956). *Risk and gambling*. London: Longmans Green.

Cottrell, N. B. (1972). Social facilitation. In C. G. McClintock (Ed.), *Experimental social psychology*. New York: Holt, Rinehart & Winston.

Cottrell, N. B., Wack, D. L., Sekarak, G. J., & Rittle, R. (1968). Social facilitation of dominant responses by the presence of an audience and the mere presence of others. *Journal of Personality and Social Psychology, 9*, 245-250.

Covington, M. V., & Omelich, C. L. (1984). An empirical examination of Weiner's critique of attribution research. *Journal of Educational Psychology, 76*, 1199-1213.

Crandall, V. J. (1955). An investigation of the specificity of reinforcement of induced frustration. *Journal of Social Psychology, 41*, 311-318.

Crawford, C., Smith, M., & Krebs, D. (Eds.). (1987). *Sociobiology and psychology: Ideas, issues and applications*. Hillsdale, NJ: Lawrence Erlbaum.

Crespi, L. P. (1942). Quantitative variation of incentive and performance in the white rat. *American Journal of Psychology, 55*, 467-517.

Crocker, J., & Major, B. (1989). Social stigma and self-esteem: The self-protective properties of stigma. *Psychological Review, 96*, 608-630.

Crocker, J., Voelkl, K., Testa, M., & Major, B. (1991). Social stigma: The affective consequences of attributional ambiguity. *Journal of Personality and Social Psychology, 60*, 218-228.

Cunningham, J. D., & Kelley, H. H. (1975). Causal attributions for interpersonal events of varying magnitude. *Journal of Personality, 43*, 74-93.

Darby, B. W., & Schlenker, B. R. (1982). Children's reactions to apologies. *Journal of Personality and Social Psychology, 43*, 742-753.

Darwin, C. (1936). *The origin of species*. New York: Modern Library. (Original work published 1859)

Davitz, J. R. (1969). *The language of emotion*. New York: Academic Press.

Dawes, R. M. (1988). *Rational choice in an uncertain world*. San Diego, CA: Harcourt Brace Jovanovich.

Dawkins, R. (1976). *The selfish gene*. London: Oxford University Press.

de Charms, R. (1968). *Personal causation*. New York: Academic Press.

de Charms, R. (1972). Personal causation training in the schools. *Journal of Applied Social Psychology, 2*, 95-113.

de Charms, R., & Moeller, G. H. (1962). Values expressed in American children's readers: 1800-1950. *Journal of Abnormal and Social Psychology, 64*, 136-142.

Deci, E. L. (1975). *Intrinsic motivation*. New York: Plenum.

DeJong, W. (1980). The stigma of obesity: The consequences of naive assumptions concerning the causes of physical deviance. *Journal of Health and Social Behavior, 21*, 75-87.

Dember, W. N. (1956). Response by the rat to environmental change. *Journal of Comparative and Physiological Psychology, 49,* 93-95.

Dember, W. N. (1960). *The psychology of perception.* New York: Holt.

Dember, W. N., & Earl, R. W. (1957). Analysis of exploratory, manipulatory, and curiosity behavior. *Psychological Review, 64,* 91-96.

Descartes, R. (1911). *Passions of the soul.* In E. S. Haldane & G. R. T. Ross (Eds.), *The philosophical works of Descartes.* Cambridge, MA: Harvard University Press. (Original work published 1649)

Dodge, K. A., & Coie, J. D. (1987). Social information processing factors in reactive and proactive aggression in children's peer groups. *Journal of Personality and Social Psychology, 53,* 1146-1158.

Dodge, K. A., & Crick, N. R. (1990). Social information-processing bases of aggressive behavior in children. *Personality and Social Psychology Bulletin, 16,* 8-22.

Dunlap, W. (1919). Are there any instincts? *Journal of Abnormal Psychology, 14,* 35-50.

Duval, S., & Wicklund, R. A. (1973). Effects of objective self-awareness on attribution of causality. *Journal of Experimental Social Psychology, 9,* 17-31.

Escalona, S. K. (1940). The effect of success and failure upon the level of aspiration and behavior in manic-depressive psychoses. *Studies in Child Welfare, 16,* 199-302.

Feagin, J. (1972). Poverty: We still believe that God helps them who help themselves. *Psychology Today, 6,* 101-129.

Feather, N. T. (1961). The relationship of persistence at a task to expectation of success and achievement-related motives. *Journal of Abnormal and Social Psychology, 63,* 552-561.

Feather, N. T. (1965). The relationship of expectation of success to n Achievement and test anxiety. *Journal of Personality and Social Psychology, 1,* 118-126.

Feather, N. T. (1967). Valence of outcome and expectation of success in relation to task difficulty and perceived locus of control. *Journal of Personality and Social Psychology, 7,* 372-386.

Feather, N. T. (1974). Explanations of poverty in Australian and American samples: The person, society, or fate? *Australian Journal of Psychology, 26,* 199-216.

Feld, S. (1967). Longitudinal study of the origins of achievement strivings. *Journal of Personality and Social Psychology, 7,* 408-414.

Ferguson, T., & Rule, B. (1983). An attributional perspective on anger and aggression. In R. Geen & E. Donnerstein (Eds.), *Aggression: Theoretical and empirical reviews: Vol. 1. Theoretical and methodological issues* (pp. 41-74). New York: Academic Press.

Feshbach, S. (1964). The function of aggression and the regulation of aggressive drive. *Psychological Review, 71,* 257-272.

Feshbach, S., & Weiner, B. (1991). *Personality.* Lexington, MA: D. C. Heath.

Festinger, L. (1942). A theoretical interpretation of shifts in level of aspiration. *Psychological Review, 49,* 235-250.

Festinger, L. (1957). *A theory of cognitive dissonance.* Stanford, CA: Stanford University Press.

Festinger, L. (1961). The psychology of insufficient rewards. *American Psychologist, 16,* 1-11.

Festinger, L. (1980). Looking back. In L. Festinger (Ed.), *Retrospections on social psychology* (pp. 236-254). New York: Holt, Rinehart & Winston.

Festinger, L., & Carlsmith, J. M. (1959). Cognitive consequences of forced compliance. *Journal of Abnormal and Social Psychology, 58,* 203-210.

Festinger, L., Riecken, H. W., & Schachter, S. (1956). *When prophecy fails.* Minneapolis: University of Minnesota Press.

Fincham, F. D., & Jaspers, J. M. (1980). Attribution of responsibility: From man the scientist to man as lawyer. In L. Berkowitz (Ed.), *Advances in experimental social psychology* (Vol. 13, pp. 82-139). New York: Academic Press.

Fiske, S. T., & Taylor, S. E. (1984). *Social cognition.* New York: Random House.

Folkes, V. S. (1982). Communicating the causes of social rejection. *Journal of Experimental Social Psychology, 18,* 235-252.

Folkes, V. S. (1984). Consumer reactions to product failure: An attributional approach. *Journal of Consumer Research, 11,* 398-409.

Försterling, F. (1985). Attributional training: A review. *Psychological Bulletin, 98,* 495-512.

Försterling, F. (1988). *Attribution theory in clinical psychology.* New York: John Wiley.

Försterling, F. (1989). Models of covariation and attribution: How do they relate to the analogy of analysis of variance? *Journal of Personality and Social Psychology, 57,* 615-625.

Frank, J. D. (1935). Individual differences in certain aspects of the level of aspiration. *American Journal of Psychology, 47,* 119-128.

Freud, S. (1934). *A general introduction to psychoanalysis.* New York: Washington Square. (Original work published 1915)

Freud, S. (1936). *The problem of anxiety.* New York: W. W. Norton. (Original work published 1926)

Freud, S. (1938). The interpretation of dreams. In A. A. Brill (Ed.), *The basic writings of Sigmund Freud.* New York: Modern Library. (Original work published 1900)

Freud, S. (1955). *Beyond the pleasure principle: The standard edition* (Vol. 18). London: Hogarth. (Original work published 1920)

Freud, S., & Breuer, J. (1959). On the theory of hysterical attacks. In S. Freud, *Collected papers* (Vol. 5). New York: Basic Books. (Original work published 1892)

Frijda, N. (1986). *The emotions.* Cambridge: Cambridge University Press.

Geen, R. G. (1991). Social motivation. *Annual Review of Psychology, 42,* 377-399.

Gilovich, T. (1983). Biased evaluation and persistence in gambling. *Journal of Personality and Social Psychology, 44,* 1110-1126.

Glanzer, M. (1953). The role of stimulus satiation in spontaneous alternation. *Journal of Experimental Psychology, 45,* 387-393.

Glixman, A. F. (1949). Recall of completed and incompleted activities under varying degrees of stress. *Journal of Experimental Psychology, 39,* 281-295.

Goffman, E. (1971). *Relations in public.* New York: Harper Colophon.

Graham, S. (1984). Communicated sympathy and anger to black and white children: The cognitive (attributional) consequences of affective cues. *Journal of Personality and Social Psychology, 47,* 40-54.

Graham, S. (1990). On communicating low ability in the classroom: Bad things good teachers sometimes do. In S. Graham & V. S. Folkes (Eds.), *Attribution theory: Applications to achievement, mental health, and interpersonal conflict* (pp. 17-36). Hillsdale, NJ: Lawrence Erlbaum.

Graham, S., Hudley, C., & Williams, E. (in press). Attributional and emotional determinants of aggression among African-American and Latino young adolescents. *Developmental Psychology.*

Green, D. R. (1963). Volunteering and the recall of interrupted tasks. *Journal of Abnormal and Social Psychology, 66,* 397-401.

Grinker, J. (1967). *The control of classical conditioning by cognitive manipulation.* Unpublished doctoral dissertation, New York University.

Guerin, B. (1986). Mere presence effects in humans: A review. *Journal of Experimental Social Psychology, 22,* 38-77.

Gusfield, J. R. (1967). Moral passage: The symbolic process in public designations of deviance. *Social Problems, 15,* 175-188.

Hall, C. S., & Lindzey, G. (1957). *Theories of personality.* New York: John Wiley.

Hamilton, V. L. (1980). Intuitive psychologist or intuitive lawyer? Alternative models of the attribution process. *Journal of Personality and Social Psychology, 39,* 767-772.

Haner, C. F., & Brown, J. S. (1955). Clarification of the instigation to action concept in the frustration-aggression hypothesis. *Journal of Abnormal and Social Psychology, 51,* 204-206.

Heider, F. (1958). *The psychology of interpersonal relations.* New York: John Wiley.

Heider, F. (1960). The Gestalt theory of motivation. In M. R. Jones (Ed.), *Nebraska Symposium on Motivation* (Vol. 8, pp. 145-171). Lincoln: University of Nebraska Press.

Heider, F., & Simmel, M. (1944). An experimental study of apparent behavior. *American Journal of Psychology, 57,* 243-259.

Henle, M. (1944). The influence of valence on substitution. *Journal of Psychology, 17,* 11-19.

Hewstone, M., & Jaspers, J. (1987). Covariation and causal attribution: A logical model of the intuitive analysis of variance. *Journal of Personality and Social Psychology, 53*, 663-672.

Higgins, E., Strauman, T., & Klein, R. (1986). Standards and the process of self-evaluation. In R. M. Sorrentino & E. T. Higgins (Eds.), *Handbook of motivation and cognition* (pp. 23-63). New York: Guilford.

Hilton, D. J., & Slugoski, B. R. (1986). Knowledge based causal attribution: The abnormal conditions focus model. *Psychological Review, 93*, 75-88.

Hinde, R. A. (1960). Energy models of motivation. *Symposium of the Society of Experimental Biology, 14*, 199-213.

Hiroto, D. S., & Seligman, M. E. P. (1975). Generality of learned helplessness in man. *Journal of Personality and Social Psychology, 31*, 311-327.

Hoffman, M. L. (1975). Developmental synthesis of affect and cognition and its implications for altruistic motivation. *Developmental Psychology, 11*, 607-622.

Hoffman, M. L. (1982). Development of prosocial motivation: Empathy and guilt. In N. Eisenberg-Borg (Ed.), *Development of prosocial behavior* (pp. 281-313). New York: Academic Press.

Hokanson, J. E., & Burgess, M. (1962). The effects of three types of aggression on vascular processes. *Journal of Abnormal and Social Psychology, 64*, 446-449.

Holt, E. B. (1931). *Animal drive and the learning process: An essay toward radical empiricism* (Vol. 1). New York: Holt.

Hooley, J. M., Richters, J. E., Weintraub, S., & Neal, J. M. (1987). Psychopathology of marital distress: The positive side of positive symptoms. *Journal of Abnormal Psychology, 96*, 27-33.

Hoppe, F. (1930). Untersuchungen zur Handlungs—und affekt—psychologie. IX. Erfolg und Misserfolg. *Psychologische Forschung, 14*, 1-63.

Horner, M. S. (1968). *Sex differences in achievement motivation and performance in competitive and non-competitive situations.* Unpublished doctoral dissertation, University of Michigan.

Hull, C. L. (1943). *Principles of behavior.* New York: Appleton-Century-Crofts.

Hull, C. L. (1951). *Essentials of behavior.* New Haven, CT: Yale University Press.

Hull, C. L. (1962). Psychology of the scientist: IV. Passages from the "Idea Books" of Clark L. Hull (R. Hays, Ed.). *Perceptual and Motor Skills, 15*, 807-882.

Hume, D. (1888). *A treatise of human nature.* London: Clarendon. (Original work published 1739)

Hymel, S., & Rubin, K. H. (1985). Children with peer relationship and social skills problems: Conceptual, methodological, and developmental issues. In G. J. Whitehurst (Ed.), *Annals of child development* (Vol. 2, pp. 251-297). Greenwich, CT: JAI.

Insko, C. A. (1984). Balance theory, the Jordan paradigm, and the Wiest tetrahedron. In L. Berkowitz (Ed.), *Advances in social psychology* (Vol. 18, pp. 89-141). New York: Academic.

Izard, C. E. (1977). *Human emotions.* New York: Plenum.

James, W. (1890). *Principles of psychology.* New York: Henry Holt.

Janoff-Bulman, R. (1979). Characterological versus behavioral self-blame: Inquiries into depression and rape. *Journal of Personality and Social Psychology, 37*, 1798-1809.

Jenkins, H. M., & Ward, W. C. (1965). Judgment of contingency between responses and outcome. *Psychological Monographs, 79*(1, Whole No. 594).

Jessor, R., Carman, R. S., & Grossman, P. H. (1968). Expectations of need satisfaction and drinking patterns of college students. *Quarterly Journal of Studies in Alcohol, 29*, 101-116.

Jessor, R., Graves, T. D., Hanson, R. C., & Jessor, S. L. (1968). *Society, personality, and deviant behavior.* New York: Holt, Rinehart & Winston.

Johnson, T. J., Feigenbaum, R., & Weiby, M. (1964). Some determinants and consequences of the teacher's perception of causation. *Journal of Educational Psychology, 55*, 237-246.

Jones, E. (1953-1957). *The life and work of Sigmund Freud* (Vols. 1-3). New York: Basic Books.

Jones, E. E., & Berglas, S. (1978). Control of attributions about the self through self-handicapping strategies: The appeal of alcohol and the role of underachievement. *Personality and Social Psychology Bulletin, 4,* 200-206.

Jones, E. E., & Davis, K. E. (1965). From acts to dispositions: The attribution process in person perception. In L. Berkowitz (Ed.), *Advances in experimental social psychology* (Vol. 2, pp. 219-266). New York: Academic Press.

Jones, E. E., Farino, A., Hastorf, A. H., Markus, H., Miller, D. T., & Scott, R. A. (1984). *Social stigma.* New York: Freeman.

Jones, E. E., Kanouse, D. E., Kelley, H. H., Nisbett, R. E., Valins, S., & Weiner, B. (Eds.). (1972). *Attribution: Perceiving the causes of behavior.* Morristown, NJ: General Learning.

Jones, E. E., & Nisbett, R. E. (1972). The actor and the observer: Divergent perceptions of the causes of behavior. In E. E. Jones, D. E. Kanouse, H. H. Kelley, R. E. Nisbett, S. Valins, & B. Weiner (Eds.), *Attribution: Perceiving the causes of behavior.* Morristown, NJ: General Learning.

Jones, M. R. (1955). Introduction. In M. R. Jones (Ed.), *Nebraska Symposium on Motivation* (pp. vii-x). Lincoln: University of Nebraska Press.

Jordan, N. (1953). Behavioral forces that are a function of attitude and cognitive organization. *Human Relations, 6,* 273-287.

Juvonen, J. (1991). Deviance, perceived responsibility, and negative peer reactions. *Developmental Psychology, 27,* 672-681.

Kagan, J., & Moss, H. A. (1959). Stability and validity of achievement fantasy. *Journal of Abnormal and Social Psychology, 58,* 357-364.

Kant, I. (1952). *The critique of pure reason.* In R. M. Hutchins (Ed.), *Great books of the Western world* (Vol. 42). Chicago: Encyclopedia Britannica. (Original work published 1781)

Kaplan, R. (1975). The cathartic value of self-expression: Testing catharsis, dissonance and interference explanations. *Journal of Social Psychology, 97,* 195-208.

Katkovsky, W. (1968). Social learning theory and maladjustment. In L. Gorlow & W. Katkovsky (Eds.), *Readings in the psychology of adjustment* (2nd ed.). New York: McGraw-Hill.

Kelley, H. H. (1967). Attribution theory in social psychology. In D. Levine (Ed.), *Nebraska Symposium on Motivation.* Lincoln: University of Nebraska Press.

Kelley, H. H. (1972). Causal schemata and the attribution process. In E. E. Jones, D. E. Kanouse, H. H. Kelley, R. E. Nisbett, S. Valins, & B. Weiner (Eds.), *Attribution: Perceiving the causes of behavior.* Morristown, NJ: General Learning.

Kelly, G. A. (1955). *The psychology of personal constructs.* New York: W. W. Norton.

Kelly, G. A. (1958). Man's construction of his alternatives. In G. Lindzey (Ed.), *Assessment of human motives.* New York: Grove.

Kelly, G. A. (1962). Europe's matrix of decision. In M. R. Jones (Ed.), *Nebraska Symposium on Motivation.* Lincoln: University of Nebraska Press.

Kelly, G. A. (1970). A summary statement of a cognitive-oriented comprehensive theory of behavior. In J. C. Mancuso (Ed.), *Readings for a cognitive theory of personality.* New York: Holt, Rinehart & Winston. (Original work published 1966)

Kingdon, J. W. (1967). Politicians' beliefs about voters. *American Political Science Review, 14,* 137-145.

Koffka, K. (1935). *Principles of Gestalt psychology.* New York: Harcourt.

Köhler, W. (1925). *The mentality of apes.* New York: Harcourt & Brace.

Kolb, D. (1965). Achievement motivation training for underachieving high-school boys. *Journal of Personality and Social Psychology, 2,* 783-792.

Konecni, V. J. (1975). Annoyance, type and duration of postannoyance activity, and aggression: The "cathartic effect." *Journal of Experimental Psychology: General, 104,* 76-102.

Korman, A. (1974). *The psychology of motivation.* Englewood Cliffs, NJ: Prentice-Hall.

Kremer, J. E., & Stephens, L. (1983). Attributions and arousal as mediators of mitigation's effect on retaliation. *Journal of Personality and Social Psychology, 45,* 335-343.

Kukla, A. (1972). Foundations of an attributional theory of performance. *Psychological Review, 79,* 454-470.

Kun, A., & Weiner, B. (1973). Necessary versus sufficient causal schemata for success and failure. *Journal of Research in Personality, 7*, 197-207.

Kuo, Z. Y. (1924). A psychology without heredity. *Psychological Review, 31*, 427-451.

Lakoff, G. (1987). *Women, fire, and dangerous things.* Chicago: University of Chicago Press.

Lakoff, G., & Johnson, M. (1980). *Metaphors we live by.* Chicago: University of Chicago Press.

Lane, R. (1962). *Political ideology: Why the American common man believes what he does.* New York: Macmillan.

Langer, E. J. (1975). The illusion of control. *Journal of Personality and Social Psychology, 32*, 311-328.

Lawrence, D. H., & Festinger, L. (1962). *Deterrents and reinforcement.* Stanford, CA: Stanford University Press.

Lawson, R. (1965). *Frustration: The development of a scientific concept.* New York: Macmillan.

Lazarus, R. S., & Smith, C. A. (1988). Knowledge and appraisal in the cognition-emotion relationship. *Cognition and Emotion, 2*, 281-300.

Leary, D. E. (Ed.). (1990). *Metaphors in the history of psychology.* Cambridge: Cambridge University Press.

Lecky, P. (1945). *Self-consistency: A theory of personality.* New York: Island.

Lefcourt, H. M. (1973). The function of illusions of control and freedom. *American Psychologist, 28*, 417-425.

Lefcourt, H. M. (1976). *Locus of control.* Hillsdale, NJ: Lawrence Erlbaum.

Lehrman, D. S. (1953). A critique of Konrad Lorenz's theory of instinctive behavior. *Quarterly Review of Biology, 28*, 337-363.

Lepper, M. R., Greene, D., & Nisbett, R. E. (1973). Undermining children's intrinsic interest with extrinsic reward: A test of the overjustification hypothesis. *Journal of Personality and Social Psychology, 28*, 129-137.

Levis, D. J. (1976). Learned helplessness: A reply and an alternative S-R interpretation. *Journal of Experimental Psychology: General, 105*, 47-65.

Lewin, K. (1935). *A dynamic theory of personality.* New York: McGraw-Hill.

Lewin, K. (1936). *Principles of topological psychology.* New York: McGraw-Hill.

Lewin, K. (1938). *The conceptual representation and the measurement of psychological forces.* Durham, NC: Duke University Press.

Lewin, K. (1946). Behavior and development as a function of the total situation. In L. Carmichael (Ed.), *Manual of child psychology.* New York: John Wiley.

Lewin, K. (1951). *Field theory in social science.* New York: Harper.

Lewin, K., Dembo, T., Festinger, L., & Sears, P. S. (1944). Level of aspiration. In J. M. Hunt (Ed.), *Personality and the behavioral disorders* (Vol. 1). New York: Ronald.

Lewis, O. (1961). *Children of Sanchez.* New York: Random House.

Lissner, K. (1933). Die Entspannung von Bedürfnissen durch Ersatzhandlungen. *Psychologische Forschung, 18*, 218-250.

Littlefield, C. H., & Rushton, J. P. (1986). When a child dies: The sociobiology of bereavement. *Journal of Personality and Social Psychology, 51*, 797-802.

Litwin, G. H. (1966). Motives and expectancies as determinants of preference for degrees of risk. In J. W. Atkinson & N. T. Feather (Eds.), *A theory of achievement motivation.* New York: John Wiley. (Original work published 1958)

Lorenz, K. (1952). The past twelve years in the comparative study of behavior. In C. H. Chiller (Ed.), *Instinctive behavior: The development of a modern concept.* New York: International Universities Press.

Lorenz, K. (1966). *On aggression.* New York: Harcourt, Brace & World.

Mackenzie, M. (1984). *Fear of fat.* New York: Columbia University Press.

Mahler, V. (1933). Ersatzhandlungen verschiedenen Realitätsgrades. *Psychologische Forschung, 18*, 26-89.

Mahone, C. H. (1960). Fear of failure and unrealistic vocational aspiration. *Journal of Abnormal and Social Psychology, 60*, 253-261.

Mahrer, A. R. (1956). The role of expectancy in delayed reinforcement. *Journal of Experimental Psychology, 52*, 101-105.

Major, B., Carrington, P. I., & Carnevale, P. (1984). Physical attractiveness and self-esteem: Attributions for praise from an other-sex evaluator. *Personality and Social Psychology Bulletin, 10*, 43-50.

Major, B., Mueller, P., & Hildebrandt, K. (1985). Attributions, expectations, and coping with abortion. *Journal of Personality and Social Psychology, 48*, 585-599.

Mallick, S. K., & McCandless, B. R. (1966). A study of catharsis aggression. *Journal of Personality and Social Psychology, 4*, 591-596.

Mandler, G., & Sarason, S. B. (1952). A study of anxiety and learning. *Journal of Abnormal and Social Psychology, 47*, 166-173.

Manning, S. A., & Taylor, D. A. (1975). Effects of viewed violence and aggression: Stimulation and catharsis. *Journal of Personality and Social Psychology, 31*, 180-188.

Marrow, A. J. (1938). Goal tensions and recall: I. *Journal of General Psychology, 19*, 3-35.

Marshall, G. D., & Zimbardo, P. G. (1979). Affective consequences of inadequately explained physiological arousal. *Journal of Personality and Social Psychology, 37*, 970-988.

Marzocco, F. N. (1951). *Frustration effect as a function of drive level, habit strength and distribution of trials during extinction.* Unpublished doctoral dissertation, State University of Iowa.

Maslach, C. (1979). Negative emotional biasing of unexplained arousal. *Journal of Personality and Social Psychology, 37*, 953-969.

Matlin, M. W., & Zajonc, R. B. (1968). Social facilitation of word associations. *Journal of Personality and Social Psychology, 10*, 455-460.

Mayer, H. H., Walker, W. B., & Litwin, G. H. (1961). Motive patterns and risk preference associated with entrepreneurship. *Journal of Abnormal and Social Psychology, 63*, 570-574.

McClelland, D. C. (1955). Some social consequences of achievement motivation. In M. M. Jones (Ed.), *Nebraska Symposium on Motivation* (Vol. 3). Lincoln: University of Nebraska Press.

McClelland, D. C. (1957). Freud and Hull: Pioneers of scientific psychology. *American Scientist, 45*, 101-113.

McClelland, D. C. (1958). Methods of measuring human motivation. In J. W. Atkinson (Ed.), *Motives in fantasy, action, and society.* Princeton, NJ: Van Nostrand.

McClelland, D. C. (1961). *The achieving society.* Princeton, NJ: Van Nostrand.

McClelland, D. C. (1965). Toward a theory of motive acquisition. *American Psychologist, 20*, 321-333.

McClelland, D. C., Atkinson, J. W., Clark, R. W., & Lowell, E. L. (1953). *The achievement motive.* New York: Appleton-Century-Crofts.

McClelland, D. C., & Winter, D. G. (1969). *Motivating economic achievement.* New York: Free Press.

McDougall, W. (1923). *Outline of psychology.* New York: Scribner.

McGuire, W. J. (1966). The current status of cognitive consistency theories. In S. Feldman (Ed.), *Cognitive consistency.* New York: Academic Press.

Meehl, P. E. (1990). Appraising and amending theories: The strategy of Lakatosian defense and two principles that warrant it. *Psychological Inquiry, 1*, 108-141.

Merton, R. K. (1957). *Social theory and social structure.* Glencoe, IL: Free Press.

Meryman, J. J. (1952). *Magnitude of startle response as a function of hunger and fear.* Unpublished master's thesis, University of Iowa.

Meyer, J. P., & Mulherin, A. (1980). From attribution to helping: An analysis of the mediating effects of affect on expectancy. *Journal of Personality and Social Psychology, 39*, 201-210.

Meyer, W. U., Folkes, V. S., & Weiner, B. (1976). The perceived informational value and affective consequences of choice behavior and intermediate difficulty task selection. *Journal of Research in Personality, 10*, 410-423.

Michotte, A. (1963). *The perception of causality.* New York: Basic Books. (Original work published 1946)

Mikulincer, M., Bizman, A., & Aizenberg, R. (1989). An attributional analysis of social comparison jealousy. *Motivation and Emotion, 13*, 235-258.

Miller, D. T., & Ross, M. (1975). Self-serving biases in the attribution of causality: Fact or fiction? *Psychological Bulletin, 82*, 213-225.

Miller, N. E. (1944). Experimental studies of conflict. In J. M. Hunt (Ed.), *Personality and the behavioral disorders* (Vol. 1). New York: Ronald.

Miller, N. E. (1948). Studies of fear as an acquirable drive: I. Fear as motivation and fear-reduction as reinforcement in the learning of new responses. *Journal of Experimental Psychology, 38*, 89-101.

Miller, N. E. (1951). Learnable drives and rewards. In S. S. Stevens (Ed.), *Handbook of experimental psychology*. New York: John Wiley.

Miller, N. E. (1959). Liberalization of basic S-R concepts: Extensions to conflict behavior, motivation, and social learning. In S. Koch (Ed.), *Psychology: A study of a science* (Vol. 2). New York: McGraw-Hill.

Miller, P., & Eisenberg, N. (1988). The relation of empathy to aggressive and externalizing/anti-social behavior. *Psychological Bulletin, 103*, 324-344.

Mischel, W. (1961). Delay of gratification, need for achievement, and acquiescence in another culture. *Journal of Abnormal and Social Psychology, 62*, 543-552.

Monson, T. C., & Snyder, M. (1977). Actors, observers, and the attribution process: Toward a reconceptualization. *Journal of Experimental Social Psychology, 13*, 89-111.

Montanelli, D. S., & Hill, K. T. (1969). Children's achievement expectations and performance as a function of two consecutive reinforcement experiences, sex of subject, and sex of experimenter. *Journal of Personality and Social Psychology, 13*, 115-128.

Montgomery, K. C. (1952). A test of two explanations of spontaneous alternation. *Journal of Comparative and Physiological Psychology, 45*, 287-293.

Mook, D. G. (1987). *Motivation*. New York: W. W. Norton.

Morgan, C. L. (1896). *An introduction to comparative psychology*. London: Walter Scott.

Morris, J. L. (1966). Propensity for risk taking as a determinant of vocational choice: An extension of the theory of achievement motivation. *Journal of Personality and Social Psychology, 3*, 328-335.

Mosher, D. L. (1968). The influence of Adler on Rotter's social learning theory of personality. *Journal of Individual Psychology, 24*, 33-45.

Moss, F. A. (1924). Study of animal drives. *Journal of Experimental Psychology, 7*, 165-185.

Moss, H. A., & Kagan, J. (1961). Stability of achievement and recognition seeking behaviors from early childhood through adulthood. *Journal of Abnormal and Social Psychology, 62*, 504-513.

Moulton, R. W. (1965). Effects of success and failure on level of aspiration as related to achievement motives. *Journal of Personality and Social Psychology, 1*, 399-406.

Mowrer, O. H. (1960). *Learning theory and behavior*. New York: John Wiley.

Mowrer, O. H., & Viek, P. (1948). An experimental analogue of fear from a sense of helplessness. *Journal of Abnormal and Social Psychology, 43*, 193-200.

Mukherjee, B. N., & Sinha, R. (1970). Achievement values and self-ideal discrepancies in college students. *Personality: An International Journal, 1*, 275-301.

Mullen, B., & Riordan, C. A. (1988). Self-serving attributions for performance in naturalistic settings: A meta-analytic review. *Journal of Applied Social Psychology, 18*, 3-22.

Murray, H. A. (1938). *Explorations in personality*. New York: Oxford University Press.

Murray, H. A. (1959). Preparation for the scaffold of a comprehensive system. In S. Koch (Ed.), *Psychology: A study of a science* (Vol. 3). New York: McGraw-Hill.

Newcomb, T. M. (1953). An approach to the study of communicative acts. *Psychological Review, 60*, 393-404.

Newman, J. R. (1955). *Stimulus generalization of an instrumental response as a function of drive strength*. Unpublished doctoral dissertation, University of Illinois.

Nisbett, R. E., & Schachter, S. (1966). Cognitive manipulation of pain. *Journal of Experimental Social Psychology, 2*, 227-236.

O'Brien, E. J., & Epstein, S. (1974). *Naturally occurring changes in self-esteem*. Paper presented at the 82nd Annual Convention of the American Psychological Association, Montreal.

Orne, M. T. (1962). On the social psychology of the psychological experiment. *American Psychologist, 17*, 776-783.

Ortony, A. (Ed.). (1979). *Metaphor and thought*. Cambridge: Cambridge University Press.

Osgood, C. E. (1953). *Method and theory in experimental psychology*. New York: Oxford University Press.

Osgood, C. E., & Tannenbaum, P. H. (1955). The principle of congruity in the prediction of attitude change. *Psychological Review, 62*, 42-55.

Osgood, C. E., Tannenbaum, P. H., & Suci, G. I. (1957). *The measurement of meaning*. Urbana: University of Illinois Press.

Ovsiankina, M. (1928). Die Wiederaufnahme unterbrochener Handlungen. *Psychologische Forschung, 11*, 302-379.

Pastore, N. (1952). The role of arbitrariness in the frustration-aggression hypothesis. *Journal of Abnormal and Social Psychology, 47*, 728-732.

Peak, H. (1958). Psychological structure and psychological activity. *Psychological Review, 65*, 325-347.

Perin, C. T. (1942). Behavior potentiality as a joint function of the amount of training and the degree of hunger at the time of extinction. *Journal of Experimental Psychology, 30*, 93-113.

Phares, E. J. (1957). Expectancy changes in skill and chance situations. *Journal of Abnormal and Social Psychology, 54*, 339-342.

Phares, E. J. (1976). *Locus of control in personality*. Morristown, NJ: General Learning.

Piliavin, I. M., Rodin, J., & Piliavin, J. A. (1969). Good Samaritanism: An underground phenomenon? *Journal of Personality and Social Psychology, 13*, 289-299.

Platt, C. W. (1988). Effects of causal attributions for success on first-term college performance: A covariance structure model. *Journal of Educational Psychology, 80*, 569-578.

Power, H. W. (1975). Mountain bluebirds: Experimental evidence against altruism. *Science, 189*, 242-243.

Public is polled on AIDS. (1987, August 30). *New York Times*, pt. 1, p. 12.

Rajecki, D. W., Kidd, R. F., Wilder, D. A., & Jaeger, J. (1975). Social factors in the facilitation of breeding in chickens: Effects of imitation, arousal, or disinhibition? *Journal of Personality and Social Psychology, 32*, 510-518.

Rapaport, D. (1959). The structure of psychoanalytic theory: A systematizing attempt. In S. Koch (Ed.), *Psychology: A study of a science* (Vol. 3, pp. 55-183). New York: McGraw-Hill.

Rapaport, D. (1960). On the psychoanalytic theory of motivation. In M. R. Jones (Ed.), *Nebraska Symposium on Motivation* (Vol. 8, pp. 173-247). Lincoln: University of Nebraska Press.

Raynor, J. O. (1970). Relationships between achievement-related motives, future orientation, and academic performance. *Journal of Personality and Social Psychology, 15*, 28-33.

Reisenzein, R. (1983). The Schachter theory of emotion: Two decades later. *Psychological Bulletin, 94*, 239-264.

Reisenzein, R. (1986). A structural equation analysis of Weiner's attribution-affect model of helping behavior. *Journal of Personality and Social Psychology, 50*, 1123-1133.

Richardson, S. A., Hastorf, A. H., Goodman, N., & Dornbusch, S. M. (1961). Cultural uniformity in reaction to physical disabilities. *American Sociological Review, 26*, 241-247.

Richter, C. P. (1927). Animal behavior and internal drives. *Quarterly Review of Biology, 2*, 307-343.

Richter, C. P. (1958). The phenomenon of unexplained sudden death in animals and man. In W. H. Gant (Ed.), *Physiological basis of psychiatry*. Springfield, IL: Charles C Thomas.

Rogers, C. R. (1951). *Client-centered therapy*. Boston: Houghton Mifflin.

Rohrkemper, M. (1985). Individual differences in students' perceptions of routine classroom events. *Journal of Educational Psychology, 77*, 29-44.

Roseman, I. J. (1984). Cognitive determinants of emotion: A structural theory. In P. Shaver (Ed.), *Review of personality and social psychology* (Vol. 5, pp. 11-36). Beverly Hills, CA: Sage.

Rosenstein, A. (1952). *The specificity of the achievement motive and the motivational effects of picture cues*. Unpublished doctoral dissertation, University of Michigan.

Rosenzweig, S. (1943). An experimental study of "repression" with special reference to need-persistive and ego-defensive reactions to frustration. *Journal of Experimental Psychology, 32,* 64-74.

Ross, L., & Nisbett, R. E. (1991). *The person and the situation.* New York: McGraw-Hill.

Rotter, J. B. (1954). *Social learning and clinical psychology.* Englewood Cliffs, NJ: Prentice-Hall.

Rotter, J. B. (1966). Generalized expectancies for internal versus external control of reinforcement. *Psychological Monograph, 80*(1, Whole No. 609).

Rotter, J. B. (1975). Some problems and misconceptions related to the construct of internal vs. external control of reinforcement. *Journal of Consulting and Clinical Psychology, 43,* 55-67.

Rotter, J. B., Chance, J. E., & Phares, E. J. (1972). An introduction to social learning theory. In J. B. Rotter, J. E. Chance, & E. J. Phares (Eds.), *Applications of a social learning theory of personality.* New York: Holt, Rinehart & Winston.

Rotter, J. B., & Hochreich, D. J. (1975). *Personality.* Glenview, IL: Scott, Foresman.

Rotter, J. B., Seeman, M., & Liverant, S. (1962). Internal versus external control of reinforcement: A major variable in behavior theory. In N. F. Washburne (Ed.), *Decisions, values, and groups* (Vol. 2). London: Pergamon.

Rowell, C. H. F. (1961). Displacement grooming in the chaffinch. *Animal Behavior, 9,* 38-63.

Rule, B. G., & Neasdale, A. K. (1976). Emotional arousal and aggressive behavior. *Psychological Bulletin, 83,* 851-863.

Rychlak, J. F. (1968). *A philosophy of science for personality theory.* Boston: Houghton Mifflin.

Ryle, G. (1949). *The concept of mind.* New York: Barnes & Noble.

Sacco, W. P., & Dunn, V. K. (1990). Effect of actor depression on observer attributions: Existence and impact of negative attributions toward the depressed. *Journal of Personality and Social Psychology, 59,* 517-524.

Sacco, W. P., Milana, S., & Dunn, V. K. (1985). Effect of depression level and length of acquaintance on reactions of others to a request for help. *Journal of Personality and Social Psychology, 49,* 1728-1737.

Saulnier, K., & Pearlman, D. (1981). The actor-observer bias is alive and well in prison: A sequel to Wells. *Personality and Social Psychology Bulletin, 7,* 559-564.

Schachter, S. (1964). The interaction of cognitive and physiological determinants of emotional state. In L. Berkowitz (Ed.), Advances in experimental social psychology (Vol. 1). New York: Academic Press.

Schachter, S., & Singer, J. E. (1962). Cognitive, social, and physiological determinants of emotional state. *Psychological Review, 69,* 379-399.

Schlosberg, H. (1954). Three dimensions of emotion. *Psychological Review, 61,* 81-88.

Schmidt, G., & Weiner, B. (1988). An attribution-affect-action theory of motivated behavior: Replications examining judgments of help-giving. *Personality and Social Psychology Bulletin, 14,* 610-621.

Sears, R. R. (1942). *Success and failure: A study of motility.* New York: McGraw-Hill.

Sears, R. R., & Sears, P. S. (1940). Minor studies of aggression: V. Strength of frustration-reaction as a function of strength of drive. *Journal of Psychology, 9,* 297-300.

Seligman, M. E. P. (1975). *Helplessness: On depression, development, and death.* San Francisco: Freeman.

Seligman, M. E. P., & Maier, S. F. (1967). Failure to escape traumatic shock. *Journal of Experimental Psychology, 74,* 1-9.

Shakow, D., & Rapaport, D. (1964). The influence of Freud on American psychology. *Psychological Issues, 13.*

Sheer, R. (1987, August 14). AIDS: Is widespread threat an exaggeration? *Los Angeles Times,* pt. 1, pp. 1, 18.

Sigelman, C. K., & Begley, N. L. (1987). The early development of reactions of peers with controllable and uncontrollable problems. *Journal of Pediatric Psychology, 12,* 99-115.

Simon, H. A. (1957). *Models of man: Social and national.* New York: John Wiley.

Slovic, P. (1972). From Shakespeare to Simon: Speculations and some evidence about man's ability to process information. *Research Bulletin of the Oregon Research Institute, 12*(2).

Smedslund, J. (1963). The concept of correlation in adults. *Scandinavian Journal of Psychology, 4,* 165-173.

Smith, C. A. (1987). Patterns of appraisal and emotion related to taking an exam. *Journal of Personality and Social Psychology, 52,* 475-488.

Smith, C. A., & Ellsworth, P. C. (1987). Patterns of appraisal and emotion related to taking an exam. *Journal of Personality and Social Psychology, 52,* 475-488.

Snyder, M. L., Stephan, W. G., & Rosenfield, D. (1976). Egotism and attribution. *Journal of Personality and Social Psychology, 33,* 435-441.

Solomon, R. L. (1964). Punishment. *American Psychologist, 19,* 239-253.

Spence, K. W. (1956). *Behavior theory and conditioning.* New Haven, CT: Yale University Press.

Spence, K. W. (1958a). Behavior theory and selective learning. In M. R. Jones (Ed.), *Nebraska Symposium on Motivation.* Lincoln: University of Nebraska Press.

Spence, K. W. (1958b). A theory of emotionally based drive (D) and its relation to performance in simple learning situations. *American Psychologist, 13,* 131-141.

Spence, K. W., Farber, I. E., & McFann, H. H. (1956). The relation of anxiety (drive) level of performance in competitional and non-competitional paired-associates learning. *Journal of Experimental Psychology, 52,* 296-305.

Spence, K. W., & Taylor, J. A. (1951). Anxiety and strength of the US as a determinant of the amount of eyelid conditioning. *Journal of Experimental Psychology, 42,* 183-188.

Spence, K. W., Taylor, J. A., & Ketchel, R. (1956). Anxiety (drive) level and degree of competition in paired-associates learning. *Journal of Experimental Psychology, 52,* 306-310.

Staffieri, J. R. (1967). A study of social stereotype and body image in children. *Journal of Personality and Social Psychology, 7,* 101-104.

Stahelski, A. J., Patch, M. E., & Enochson, D. E. (1987). *Differential effects of ascribed ability and effort on helping, emotion, and behavior.* Unpublished manuscript, Portland State University, Portland, OR.

Steiner, I. D. (1970). Perceived freedom. In L. Berkowitz (Ed.), *Advances in experimental social psychology* (Vol. 5). New York: Academic Press.

Stevenson, H. W., & Zigler, E. (1957). Discrimination learning and rigidity in normal and feeble-minded individuals. *Journal of Personality, 25,* 699-711.

Stipek, D. J. (1983). A developmental analysis of pride and shame. *Human Development, 26,* 42-54.

Strickland, L. H. (1958). Surveillance and trust. *Journal of Personality, 26,* 200-215.

Strodtbeck, P. L., McDonald, M. R., & Rosen, B. (1957). Evaluations of occupations: A reflection of Jewish and Italian mobility differences. *American Sociological Review, 22,* 546-553.

Swann, W. B., Jr. (1987). Identity negotiation: Where two roads meet. *Journal of Personality and Social Psychology, 53,* 1038-1051.

Swann, W. B., Jr., Pelham, B. W., & Krull, D. S. (1989). Agreeable fancy or disagreeable truth? How people reconcile their self-enhancement and self-verification needs. *Journal of Personality and Social Psychology, 57,* 672-680.

Sykes, G. M., & Matza, D. (1957). Techniques of neutralization: A theory of delinquency. *American Sociological Review, 22,* 664-670.

Tavris, C. (1984). On the wisdom of counting to ten: Personal and social dangers of anger expression. In P. Shaver (Ed.), *Review of personality and social psychology* (Vol. 5). Beverly Hills, CA: Sage.

Taylor, J. A. (1953). A personality scale of manifest anxiety. *Journal of Abnormal and Social Psychology, 48,* 285-290.

Taylor, J. A., & Chapman, J. P. (1955). Anxiety and the learning of paired-associates. *American Journal of Psychology, 68,* 671.

Taylor, S. E. (1983). Adjustment to threatening events. *American Psychologist, 38,* 1161-1173.

Tetlock, P. E., & Levi, A. (1982). Attribution bias: On the inconclusiveness of the cognition-motivation debate. *Journal of Experimental Social Psychology, 18,* 68-88.

Thibaut, J. W., & Kelley, H. H. (1959). *The social psychology of groups.* New York: John Wiley.

Thilly, F. (1957). *History of philosophy* (3rd ed.). New York: Holt, Rinehart & Winston.

Thompson, R. (1990). Emotion and self-regulation. In R. Thompson (Ed.), *Nebraska Symposium on Motivation* (Vol. 36, pp. 367-468). Lincoln: University of Nebraska Press.

Thorndike, E. L. (1911). *Animal intelligence.* New York: Macmillan.

Tinbergen, N. D. (1951). *The study of instinct.* Oxford: Oxford University Press.

Tinbergen, N. D. (1952). Derived activities: Their causation, biological significance, and origin and emancipation during evolution. *Quarterly Review of Biology, 27,* 1-32.

Tinbergen, N. D., & van Iersel, J. J. (1947). Displacement reactions in the three-spined stickleback. *Behaviour, 1,* 56-63.

Tolman, E. C. (1932). *Purposive behavior in animals and men.* New York: Appleton-Century-Crofts.

Tomkins, S. (1970). Affect as the primary motivational system. In M. B. Arnold (Ed.), *Feelings and emotions* (pp. 101-110). New York: Academic Press.

Tresemer, D. (1974). Fear of success: Popular, but unproven. *Psychology Today, 7,* 82-85.

Triplet, R. G., & Sugarman, D. B. (1987). Reactions to AIDS victims: Ambiguity breeds contempt. *Personality and Social Psychology Bulletin, 13,* 265-274.

Triplett, N. (1897). The dynamogenic factors in pacemaking and competition. *American Journal of Psychology, 9,* 507-533.

Trivers, R. L. (1971). The evolution of reciprocal altruisms. *Quarterly Review of Biology, 46,* 35-57.

Trope, Y. (1975). Seeking information about one's own ability as a determinant of choice among tasks. *Journal of Personality and Social Psychology, 32,* 1004-1013.

Trope, Y., & Brickman, P. (1975). Difficulty and diagnosticity as determinants of choice among tasks. *Journal of Personality and Social Psychology, 31,* 918-926.

Tversky, A., & Kahneman, D. (1974). Judgments under uncertainty: Heuristics and biases. *Science, 185,* 1124-1131.

Valins, S. (1966). Cognitive effects of false heart-rate feedback. *Journal of Personality and Social Psychology, 4,* 400-408.

Valle, F. P. (1975). *Motivation: Theories and issues.* Monterey, CA: Brooks/Cole.

Webb, W. B. (1949). The motivational aspect of an irrelevant drive in the behavior of the white rat. *Journal of Experimental Psychology, 39,* 1-14.

Weber, M. (1958). *The Protestant ethic and the spirit of capitalism.* New York: Scribner's Sons. (Original work published 1904)

Weiner, B. (1966). Effects of motivation on the availability and retrieval of memory traces. *Psychological Bulletin, 65,* 24-37.

Weiner, B. (1970). New conceptions in the study of achievement motivation. In B. A. Maher (Ed.), *Progress in experimental personality research* (Vol. 5). New York: Academic Press.

Weiner, B. (1972). *Theories of motivation: From mechanism to cognition.* Chicago: Rand McNally.

Weiner, B. (1979). A theory of motivation for some classroom experiences. *Journal of Educational Psychology, 71,* 3-25.

Weiner, B. (1980a). A cognitive (attributional)-emotion-action model of motivated behavior: An analysis of judgments of help-giving. *Journal of Personality and Social Psychology, 39,* 186-200.

Weiner, B. (1980b). *Human motivation.* New York: Holt, Rinehart & Winston.

Weiner, B. (1985). An attribution theory of achievement motivation and emotion. *Psychological Review, 92,* 548-573.

Weiner, B. (1986). *An attributional theory of motivation and emotion.* New York: Springer-Verlag.

Weiner, B., Amirkhan, J., Folkes, V. S., & Verette, J. A. (1987). An attributional analysis of excuse giving: Studies of a naive theory of emotion. *Journal of Personality and Social Psychology, 52,* 316-324.

Weiner, B., Figueroa-Muñoz, A., & Kakihara, C. (1991). The goals of excuses and communication strategies related to causal perceptions. *Personality and Social Psychology Bulletin, 17,* 4-13.

Weiner, B., Frieze, I. H., Kukla, A., Reed, L., Rest, S., & Rosenbaum, R. M. (1971). *Perceiving the causes of success and failure.* Morristown, NJ: General Learning.

Weiner, B., Graham, S., & Chandler, C. C. (1982). Pity, anger, and guilt: An attributional analysis. *Personality and Social Psychology Bulletin, 8,* 226-232.

Weiner, B., Graham, S., Peter, O., & Zmuidinas, M. (1991). Public confession and forgiveness. *Journal of Personality, 59*, 281-312.

Weiner, B., Graham, S., Stern, P., & Lawson, M. E. (1982). Using affective cues to infer causal thoughts. *Developmental Psychology, 18*, 278-286.

Weiner, B., & Handel, S. (1985). Anticipated emotional consequences of causal communications and reported communication strategy. *Developmental Psychology, 21*, 102-107.

Weiner, B., & Kukla, A. (1970). An attributional analysis of achievement motivation. *Journal of Personality and Social Psychology, 15*, 1-20.

Weiner, B., Perry, R. P., & Magnusson, J. (1988). An attributional analysis of reactions to stigmas. *Journal of Personality and Social Psychology, 55*, 738-748.

Weiner, B., & Rosenbaum, R. M. (1965). Determinants of choice between achievement and nonachievement-related activities. *Journal of Experimental Research in Personality, 1*, 114-122.

Weiner, B., Russell, D., & Lerman, D. (1978). Affective consequences of causal ascriptions. In J. H. Harvey, W. J. Ickes, & R. F. Kidd (Eds.), *New directions in attribution research* (Vol. 2, pp. 59-88). Hillsdale, NJ: Lawrence Erlbaum.

Weiner, B., Russell, D., & Lerman, D. (1979). The cognition-emotion process in achievement-related contexts. *Journal of Personality and Social Psychology, 37*, 1211-1220.

Weiss, R. F., & Miller, F. G. (1971). The drive theory of social facilitation. *Psychological Review, 78*, 44-57.

Wertheimer, M. (1912). Über das Denken des Naturvolker. *Zeitschrift Psychologie, 60*, 321-378.

Whalen, C., & Henker, B. (1976). Psychostimulants and children: A review and analysis. *Psychological Bulletin, 83*, 1113-1130.

Wicker, F. W., Payne, G. C., & Morgan, R. D. (1983). Participant descriptions of guilt and shame. *Motivation and Emotion, 7*, 25-39.

Wicklund, R. A., & Brehm, J. (1976). *Perspectives on cognitive dissonance.* Hillsdale, NJ: Lawrence Erlbaum.

Williams, S. B. (1938). Resistance to extinction as a function of the number of reinforcements. *Journal of Experimental Psychology, 23*, 506-522.

Wilson, E. O. (1975). *Sociobiology: The new synthesis.* Cambridge, MA: Harvard University Press.

Wilson, T. D., & Linville, P. W. (1982). Improving the academic performance of college freshmen: Attribution theory revisited. *Journal of Personality and Social Psychology, 42*, 367-376.

Wilson, T. D., & Linville, P. W. (1985). Improving the performance of college freshmen with attributional techniques. *Journal of Personality and Social Psychology, 49*, 287-293.

Wilson, T. D., & Schooler, J. W. (1991). Thinking too much: Introspection can reduce the quality of preferences and decisions. *Journal of Personality and Social Psychology, 60*, 181-192.

Woodworth, R. S. (1918). *Dynamic psychology.* New York: Columbia University Press.

Wright, B. A. (1983). *Physical disability: A psychological approach* (2nd ed.). New York: Harper.

Yates, A. B. (1962). *Frustration and conflict.* London: Methuen.

Yirmaya, N., & Weiner, B. (1986). Perceptions of controllability and anticipated anger. *Cognitive Development, 1*, 273-280.

Young, P. T. (1943). *Emotion in man and animal.* New York: John Wiley.

Young, P. T. (1961). *Motivation and emotion: A survey of the determinants of human and animal activity.* New York: John Wiley.

Zajonc, R. B. (1965). Social facilitation. *Science, 149*, 269-274.

Zajonc, R. B. (1968). Cognitive theories in social psychology. In G. Lindzey & E. Aronson (Eds.), *The handbook of social psychology* (Vol. 1). Reading, MA: Addison-Wesley.

Zajonc, R. B., & Brickman, P. (1969). Expectancy and feedback as independent factors in task performance. *Journal of Personality and Social Psychology, 11*, 143-156.

Zajonc, R. B., & Sales, S. M. (1966). Social facilitation of dominant and subordinate responses. *Journal of Experimental Social Psychology, 2*, 160-168.

Zanna, M. P., & Cooper, J. (1976). Dissonance and the attribution process. In J. H. Harvey, W. J. Ickes, & R. F. Kidd (Eds.), *New directions in attribution research* (Vol. 1). Hillsdale, NJ: Lawrence Erlbaum.

Zeigarnik, B. (1927). Uber das Behalten von erledigten und unerledigten Handlungen. *Psychologische Forschung, 9*, 1-85.

Zeigler, H. P. (1964). Displacement activity and motivational theory: A case study in the history of ethology. *Psychological Bulletin, 61*, 362-376.

Zigler, E. (1962). Rigidity in the feebleminded. In E. P. Trapp & P. Himmelstein (Eds.), *Readings in the exceptional child*. New York: Appleton-Century-Crofts.

Zillmann, D. (1978). Attribution and misattribution of excitatory reactions. In J. H. Harvey, W. J. Ickes, & R. F. Kidd (Eds.), *New directions in attribution research* (Vol. 2). Hillsdale, NJ: Lawrence Erlbaum.

Zimbardo, P. G. (1969). *The cognitive control of motivation*. Glenview, IL: Scott, Foresman.

Zucker, G., & Weiner, B. (in press). Conservatism and perceptions of poverty: An attributional analysis. *Personality and Social Psychology Bulletin*.

Zuckerman, M. (1979). Attribution of success and failure revisited, or: The motivational bias is alive and well in attribution theory. *Journal of Personality, 47*, 245-287.

Author Index

Subject Index

About the Author

Bernard Weiner completed his undergraduate training at the University of Chicago and received his Ph.D. from the University of Michigan in 1963. After being an Assistant Professor at the University of Minnesota, he moved to the University of California, Los Angeles, where he has remained since 1965. He is now Professor of Psychology. He has written, coauthored, or edited 13 books, including *Theories of Motivation* (1972) and *Human Motivation* (1980). He is a leading contributor to the field of attribution theory, and was one of the coauthors of the seminal book, *Attribution: Perceiving the Causes of Behavior.* In addition to book writing, he has published more than 125 journal articles and book chapters. For these accomplishments, he has received a Guggenheim Fellowship, was designated the recipient of the Donald Campbell Distinguished Research Award from the Division of Personality and Social Psychology of the American Psychological Association, and has received an honorary doctorate from the University of Bielefeld, Germany.